Virtute · et · Opera

FIFE LOOKS AHEAD

Mott, Hay, & Anderson, Civil Engineers

Drawn by F. A. Evans

THE NEW FORTH ROAD BRIDGE

FIFE LOOKS AHEAD

A REGIONAL SURVEY
OF THE COUNTY

The Report of the Fife County Council
Planning Advisory Committee

with Appendices on Initial Surveys and Public Meetings

Published by
C. J. COUSLAND & SONS LTD.
30 Queen Street, Edinburgh 2
and printed at the Press of the Publishers
1946

Printed 1946

CONTENTS

LIST OF MAPS

LIST OF ILLUSTRATIONS

INTRODUCTION

THE County Council of Fife as a Planning Authority has always been alive to its responsibilities for the proper planning of the County, and when the suggestion was made, in the beginning of 1944, that the time had now come when consideration should be given to seeking public opinion regarding the future development of the County, no hesitation was manifested by the Council in adopting this suggestion. On 25th January, 1944, the County Council made the following remit :—

" Having regard to the history, traditions, and past development in the County, to examine the resources of the County in minerals, agriculture, and others ; to consult with all interested bodies and persons ; and to make recommendations to the Planning Committee of the County Council with respect to the future development of that part of the County coming within the planning jurisdiction of the County Council."

A Committee, composed of the Chairman of the County Council along with non-County Councillors, was appointed as an Advisory Committee to the Planning Committee of the County Council. This Advisory Committee was very carefully selected in order that its views might be quite unaffected by any considerations of purely local interest or of party which might have been reflected in reference to the best planning of the whole County. Consultation took place with bodies representing industry, nominations were received of several individuals for each appointment, advertisement was made for independent representatives, and from the nominations thus received the County Council, on the advice of their Planning Committee, appointed the following Committee as Planning Advisory Committee :—

Brig.-General J.D. Crosbie, C.M.G., D.S.O., D.L. (Chairman), Muircambus House, Kilconquhar.

Mr. John Whiteford, Castle Farm, Leuchars (Agricultural Employers)

Mr. R. L. Christie, Durie, Leven (Land Owners)

Principal Sir James Irvine, F.R.S., the University, St. Andrews

Mr. C. Augustus Carlow, D.L., The Fife Coal Company, Ltd., Leven (Miners Employers)

Mr. Peter M'Arthur, 182 Foulford Road, Cowdenbeath (Miners-Employees)

Captain Michael Wemyss, Red House, Wemyss Castle, East Wemyss (Independent)

Mrs. R. Officer, 24 Kinloss Crescent, Cupar (Independent)

Mr. R. S. Douglas, District Goods and Passenger Manager, L.N.E. Railway Company, Dundee (Railway-Employers)

Mr. George Prentice, Rowanlea, Kingskettle (Railway-Employees)

Mr. J. Black, F.C.I.S., Tullis, Russell & Co., Ltd., Markinch (Industry-Employers)

Mr. R. R. Taylor, 13 Queen's Crescent, Markinch (Industry-Employees)

Mr. J. B. Rae, A.C.I.S., Tullis, Russell & Co. Ltd., was appointed to fill the vacancy caused by the death of Mr. Black, and Mr. J. Lorimer, M.B.E., was appointed to fill the vacancy caused by the retirement of Mr. R. S. Douglas.

The Committee has been assisted in making its inquiries by Sir F. C. Mears, P.R.S.A., and by the County Council's Planning Officer, Mr. M. E. Taylor, M.T.P.I., and his assistant, Mr. A. W. Landau, A.M.T.P.I.

The Advisory Committee has held many meetings. The first meeting took place on 15th September, 1944, when arrangements were made regarding holding of regular meetings and a general discussion took place upon the means by which the remit to them from the County Council should be discharged. The Advisory Committee has been consulted by the County Council from time to time on one or two problems which have arisen regarding planning development, but, in the main, its whole attention has been devoted to the principal purpose for which it was appointed.

Conferences have been held as follows :—

On 17th November, 1944, attended by representatives of the Advisory Committee, of the Scottish Council of Social Service, of the Scottish Country Industries Development Trust, of the Department of Agriculture, of the East Fife Agricultural Executive Committee, and of the County Council's Planning Committee. The purpose of this conference was to discuss rural development and particularly the setting up of light industries and the provision of recreational facilities and other amenities to attract people back to the land.

On 9th July, 1945, attended by representatives of the Advisory Committee, of Industry (Mr. W. B. Robertson, D.L., of Messrs. Hay and Robertson, Ltd., Dunfermline ; Mr. John Balmain, of Messrs. Henry Balfour & Co., Ltd., Durie Foundry, Leven ; Mr. J. B. Rae, of Messrs. Tullis, Russell & Co., Ltd., Markinch ; Provost Anderson, Leslie, of Messrs. Smith, Anderson & Co., Ltd., Leslie); and of the Scottish Development Council (Lord Elgin, Chairman ; and Mr. W. C. Kirkwood, Secretary). The purpose of the conference was to get into touch with industrialists in the County, in order to find out at first-hand what was desired in regard to trade and industry, and how far the Committee could assist them in their plans for the future.

On 16th July, 1945, attended by representatives of the Advisory Committee and Agriculturists (Mr. A. Dryburgh, Methilhill Farm, Methil ; Mr. J. Whiteford, Castle Farm, Leuchars ; Mr. James Paton, Kirkness, Glencraig ; Mr. F. W. Roger, Kenly Green, by St. Andrews ; Mr. D. L. Buttercase, Broomholme, Leuchars ; Mr. P. T. Sutherland, Factor, Charleton Estate Office, Colinsburgh ; Mr. Alexander Fair, Duniface Farm, by Windygates ; Mr. G. R. M'Garva, Factor, Balcarres Estate Office, Colinsburgh ; Mr. J. C. M'Intyre, of East Fife Agricultural Executive Committee ; Mr. A. J. Cuthill, Easter Kincaple, St. Andrews ; Mr. G. T. Clark, Pitlochie, Gateside ; and Mr. J. Melville, Carskerdo, Ceres). The purpose of the conference was to consult with skilled agriculturists first of all to see if they could guide the Committee on questions such as housing of agricultural workers, maintenance of farm buildings, and the question of the depopulation of the rural areas.

On 16th February, 1945, the Advisory Committee reviewed the stage they had then reached in regard to the examination of the resources of the County, and decided that the time had now come for consultation with interested bodies and persons, and for the preparation of their draft Report. They accordingly decided as follows :—

(1) That an Editorial Sub-Committee, consisting of Mr. C. Augustus Carlow (Chairman), Sir James Irvine, and Mr. Christie, should undertake the drafting of the Report.

(2) That this Sub-Committee should visit each Burgh in the County and confer with the Provosts, Local County Councillors, District Councillors, Agricultural Executive Committees, Youth Organisations, W.R.I., W.V.S., Rotary Clubs and Co-operative Women's Guilds, and that the local member of the Advisory Committee should in each case be invited to the conferences ; that the conferences called should be intimated by public advertisement so that any member of the public interested could attend the meetings.

On 30th April, 1945, the Committee instructed the issue of a questionnaire designed to provide the industrialists in the County with an opportunity of expressing their views.

The procedure normally adopted by the Sub-Committee was first of all to confer with the Provost and Local Councillors of each Burgh, secondly to call a public meeting in the Burgh, and thirdly to call a further public meeting at which all interested were asked to give their considered observations on what had taken place at the previous public meeting. In all, the Sub-Committee held 38 meetings of this nature, visiting districts in all parts of the County.

Notes of the discussions at the conferences held appear in Appendix I. to this Report, Appendix II. deals with Initial Surveys and Public Meetings, and a summary of the points raised at the various meetings appears in Appendix III.

It was perhaps a somewhat novel method of procedure for the County Council to entrust this important work to a Committee whose members had no official connection with the Council, but on broadly democratic grounds it was amply justified. In the course of its work the Sub-Committee held meetings in every part of the County. It interviewed the Provost and Council in each of the 23 Small Burghs and everywhere met with a cordial reception.

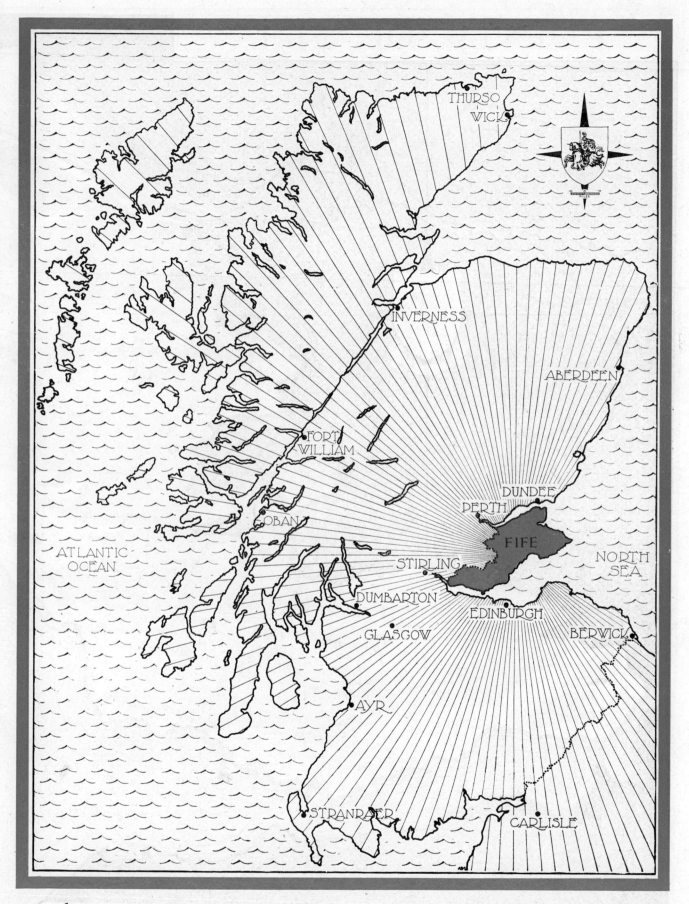

THURSO
WICK
INVERNESS
ABERDEEN
FORT
WILLIAM
DUNDEE
PERTH
OBAN
FIFE
ATLANTIC
OCEAN
STIRLING
NORTH
SEA
DUMBARTON
EDINBURGH
GLASGOW
BERWICK
AYR
STRANRAER
CARLISLE

b 1

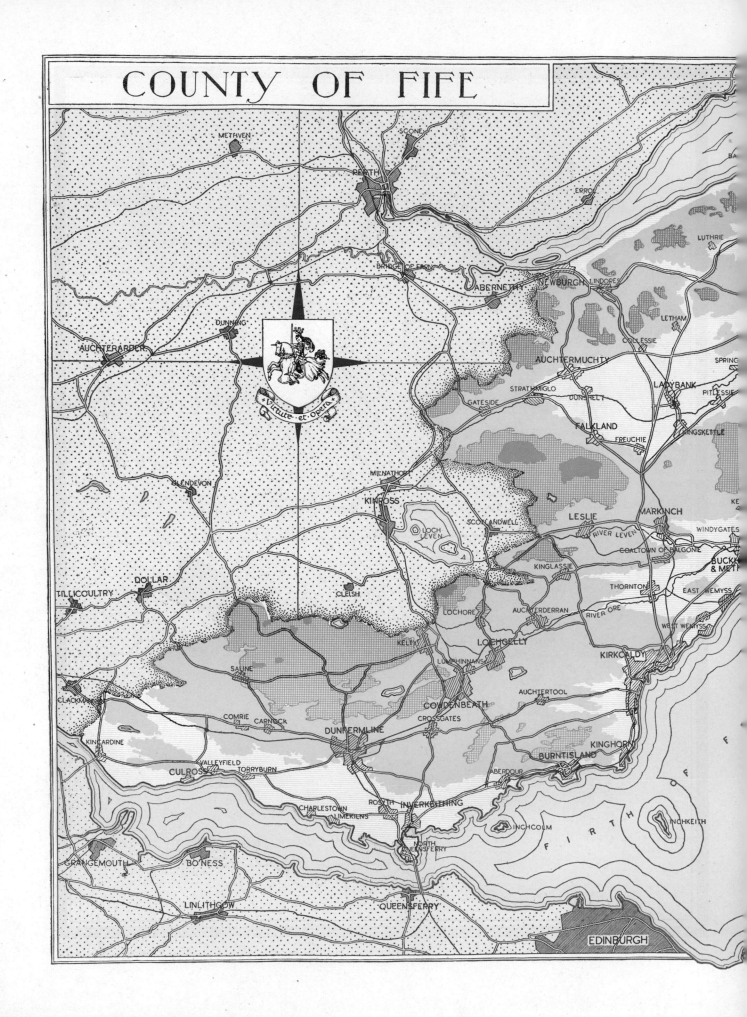

COUNTY OF FIFE

CONTOUR MAP

THE County is characterised by broad stretches of fertile plain in the valleys of its three main rivers, the Eden, the Leven and the Ore. From these flat plains the bounding hills seem to rise abruptly.

In the north-west the land rises sharply from the valley of the Tay into local eminences, the highest of which is about **900** feet, then falls again into the broad acres of the Howe of Fife. The Lomond Hills, a short range running from east to west, form the south boundary of this plain, rising into the two characteristic terminal peaks known as the East and West Lomonds, fourteen and seventeen hundred feet high respectively. Eastwards, the rocky promontory of Fife Ness stands up from the sea, with a broad, gently rising land, stretching back up from the coast. Local prominences like Largo Law, Kellie Law, etc., rise up abruptly to dominate this plain. The south-western part of the County, containing the outriders of the Cleish Hills, is more elevated than the remainder, the highest hills being Benarty (**1167** feet), Knock Hill (**1189** feet) and Saline Hill (**1178** feet).

PLANNING LEGISLATION AND PROCEDURE

THREE Acts and a considerable number of Orders and Regulations constitute the existing law on the subject of planning in Scotland. The Act of 1932 still remains the main source of planning control, the Acts of 1943 and 1945 tending mainly to extend and rectify the provisions of the earlier Act.

Let it be said without equivocation that we are of the opinion that the detailed and cumbersome steps of procedure in the framing of a planning scheme are obsolete and out of keeping entirely with present-day tendencies. Simplicity and resiliency should be the keynote of planning, and we unhesitatingly record our opinion that the provisions of the Acts, Orders and Regulations should be modified with this aim in view.

All land in Fife is under planning control. Resolutions covering the whole County took effect in May, 1939, and this committed the County Council to the preparation and adoption of planning schemes for its area. We record, too, in passing that certain Small Burghs did seek to obtain planning powers from the Department of Health, but that, with the exception of St. Andrews, they were not successful. The County Council therefore has had for some years planning jurisdiction over the whole area of the County with the exception of the three Royal Burghs of Dunfermline, Kirkcaldy and St. Andrews.

When the Resolutions to prepare its planning schemes for the County took effect, the County Council immediately assumed responsibility as Interim Development Authority for the general oversight of all development in the County, pending the adoption of complete planning schemes. This interim period presents difficulties, as many cases arise which may affect the future plan for an area, and decisions have to be taken without full knowledge of all the facts, such as would be available had a scheme been prepared. It is of importance that the interim development period should be as short as possible and the scheme for an area adopted. We accordingly advocate the adoption of planning schemes covering the whole of the County as soon as this can be done, but we suggest that in preparing schemes there should be kept clearly to the fore the necessity for ensuring flexibility and avoiding a multiplicity of detail so rigid in character as to be a future impediment to real progress.

We note that a planning scheme, *where adopted*, has the full force and effect of an Act of Parliament. We note, too, that the County Council has been put under obligation by law to prepare planning schemes for their area.

In the words of Section 1 of the 1932 Town and Country Planning Act, a planning scheme is to be prepared with the general object of :—

(*a*) controlling development of land ;

(*b*) securing proper sanitary conditions, amenity and convenience ;

(*c*) preserving existing buildings or other objects of architectural, historic or artistic interest and places of natural interest and beauty ; and (*d*) generally protecting existing amenities whether in rural or urban portions of the area.

In framing our recommendations in the succeeding chapters, we have endeavoured to keep these objects in view, but we think it worthy of mention that, Fife being pre-eminently a County rich in historical associations, there may arise occasions, before schemes can be prepared, when recourse may require to be had to the powers contained in the Acts to prevent demolition, alteration or extension of buildings in the County which possess historical or architectural value.

We note that the powers now available to Interim Development Authorities under the 1943 Planning Act extend to enforcing, under pain of penalties, compliance with the wishes of the Local Planning Authority. It appears, however, that nothing much may be done to the individual who ignores the necessity for making application but whose development, by good fortune, coincides with the intentions of the authority. In our view, in order to control development properly, application for consent should be made in every case, and power, to be used with discretion, should be conferred on local authorities for dealing with offenders.

We commend the powers given to the County Council to reach agreements with proprietors in regard to the development of their lands, and, in general, we endorse the principle of negotiation and adjustment in preference to the arbitrary determination of future development without full consultation.

In reaching our various recommendations, we have not kept in the forefront the provisions of the Acts relative to compensation and betterment, but we have generally assumed that economic considerations will be kept carefully before the County Council in preparing its planning schemes.

We realise that staffing and other considerations do not permit of one scheme being prepared for the whole County at the one time, even were this desirable. We therefore recommend that there should be several planning schemes, and, in our view, these schemes should be prepared having regard to the areas of the County likely to be most affected by early development. In this connection, we call attention to the need for concentrating as soon as possible upon the areas surrounding Kennoway, Markinch and Woodside, Cardenden, Lochgelly and Lochore, and Comrie.

It would be a serious omission in this Report not to refer to the position of the Small Burghs in the County Council's Planning Area. In their contacts with us, all, without exception, have shown a keen interest in, and have manifested a ready sympathy with, the subject of planning. We are aware of the necessity laid down by statute for consulting them in the course of the preparation of schemes, and we also realise that in the schemes themselves it is possible for the Burghs to be entrusted with considerable powers. Having in view our strong preference for planning in its broader sense, and our convictions in favour of flexibility and elasticity, we desire to record our opinion in favour of planning control being administered by a body, such as the County Council, having the oversight of an area considerably greater than that of any of the Small Burghs.

CROWN

Falkland Palace, a royal dwelling of the Stuart kings

CHURCH

The Abbey Church of Dunfermline, the "resting-place" of Bruce

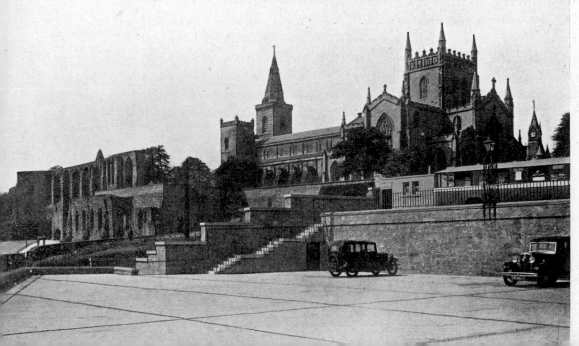

THE GEOLOGICAL, GEOGRAPHICAL AND HISTORICAL BACKGROUND TO THE PROBLEM

THE " Kingdom of Fife " is more than a romantic name ; the description can be The
" Kingdom
of Fife." justified, for, from the distant ages when Scotland was shaped by geological forces and fashioned as a geographical entity, Fife has been a region set apart. Projecting far into the sea on the east, separated from the north and from the south by great rivers opening into tidal estuaries, this section of Scotland was placed by Nature in a position of detachment. Inevitably, this geographical factor laid its imprint on the County's long history, and it remains a fundamental consideration in planning for immediate needs and for the future.

In the chapters which follow, it will be evident that the Planning Advisory The Layout Committee has kept this in mind, and, in consequence, the geological, geographical and historical background of the planning problem need be given here only in outline. It will be generally agreed that the essence of successful planning lies in utilising natural resources to the best advantage, and in adapting them to the promotion of human well-being and happiness. Equally it is evident that, in undertaking this duty, we are limited by the fact that Nature has already prepared the raw material and that we have to make the best of what we have. Originally, geological evolution dictated geographical configuration, and this, in turn, has affected profoundly the art of living throughout the ages. This is clearly illustrated in the history of Fife, for, in a geological sense, the peninsula may be divided approximately into a northern half, where the Old Red Sandstone stretches from the Tay to the Eden Valley, and a southern half, which is essentially Carboniferous in origin. But this clean-cut division, based on solid geology, is largely obscured by the fact that the surface deposits have been glacially transported from the west, with the result that light loamy soils, naturally fertile, line the valleys and the coastal fringes. In the interior, the higher ground of the Carboniferous area retained many stretches of cold, retentive clay, and these have been rendered productive only by generations of hard work and fertilisation. Here we have the scientific explanation underlying King James's description of Fife as " a beggar's mantle fringed with gold," and we are given a clear lead to utilise the resources of the soil by the preservation and development of a vigorous agricultural industry. But the geological evolution of Fife provided more than areas of fertile land. A considerable variety of minerals is found scattered throughout the County, and although, for the most part, these occur only in small uneconomic amount, the extent and richness of the Fife coal measures have for long stabilised coal-mining as a major industry.

It is evident, then, that geological and geographical factors, working in unison, The Social
Evolution. have sharply focussed the activities of the County on agriculture, mining and fishing, but more is involved in the planning of Fife than the safeguarding and expansion of these essential industries. There remain human problems—many of which originated in prehistoric times. After our distant forefathers found a foothold on the coastal fringes, they gradually worked their way up the fertile valleys, winning their livelihood from the land or from the sea and forming settlements or primitive villages. In the course of time they developed a form of community life, highly diversified but nevertheless showing marked common characteristics. This vigorous tradition is reflected in the relatively large number of ancient burghs in Fife—many of them Royal Burghs—and to these must be added the numerous villages, such as Ceres, which are old " Burghs of Barony." To this day these population centres retain a distinctive individuality, as shown by their churches and tolbooths, their wynds and their ancient houses.

Church and University.

In the creation of this communal structure the Church played an all-important part, for the north-east and south-west corners of Fife were two focal points in the spread of Christianity in Scotland. The great Abbey Church of Dunfermline and the Cathedral City of St. Andrews were early foundations and became ecclesiastical and educational centres of first importance. Their influence radiated over Fife, from Fife over broad Scotland, and from Scotland far beyond. Even though most of their buildings now lie in ruins, that influence still persists. The ancient University of St. Andrews, the oldest in Scotland and in order of foundation the third in Britain, was established by the Church, and for more than five centuries has nourished the sons—and now the daughters also—of Fife. Small wonder that Fife has exercised a remarkable power of arousing the affections and loyalties of all who dwell there, and that a sound educational system has always been cherished in this unique corner of the country.

A Royal County.

Fife is no longer a " beggar's mantle," and, although at times it may seem whimsical to speak of Fife as a " Kingdom," it is pre-eminently the *royal* county of Scotland. Dunfermline was our first capital and still retains the memorials of a city of kings. It was there that Malcolm Canmore and Margaret, the Queen-Saint of Scotland, made their abode, and the venerable Abbey is the shrine of Scotland's greatest national hero, Robert the Bruce. Nearby stand the ruins of the palace where Charles Stuart began the tragic life's journey which led to the scaffold in Whitehall. In Falkland, almost in the centre of the County, stands the most attractive of the royal palaces, a place intimately linked with the tragedy and the romance of the Stuarts. Memories of Queen Mary cling about St. Andrews, and the thorn-tree she planted still flowers in the quadrangle of St. Mary's College. On her journeys to and from St. Andrews, it was her custom to halt at Wemyss Castle, prolonging in this way the fleeting periods when happiness came to her, and it was in the courtyard of the castle that she first saw Henry Darnley with whom her fate was to be so intimately linked. There is hardly a spot in the County which is not associated in one way or another with the fate and fortune of the Royal line. The planning of Fife is no simple problem if we are to plan for progress while preserving, as we must, so much that is valuable in our inheritance.

Photo—Valentine, Dundee

St. Mary's College, St. Andrews

Photo—Valentine, Dundee

Leonard's School and Lawn, St. Andrews

Wemyss Castle

A 1

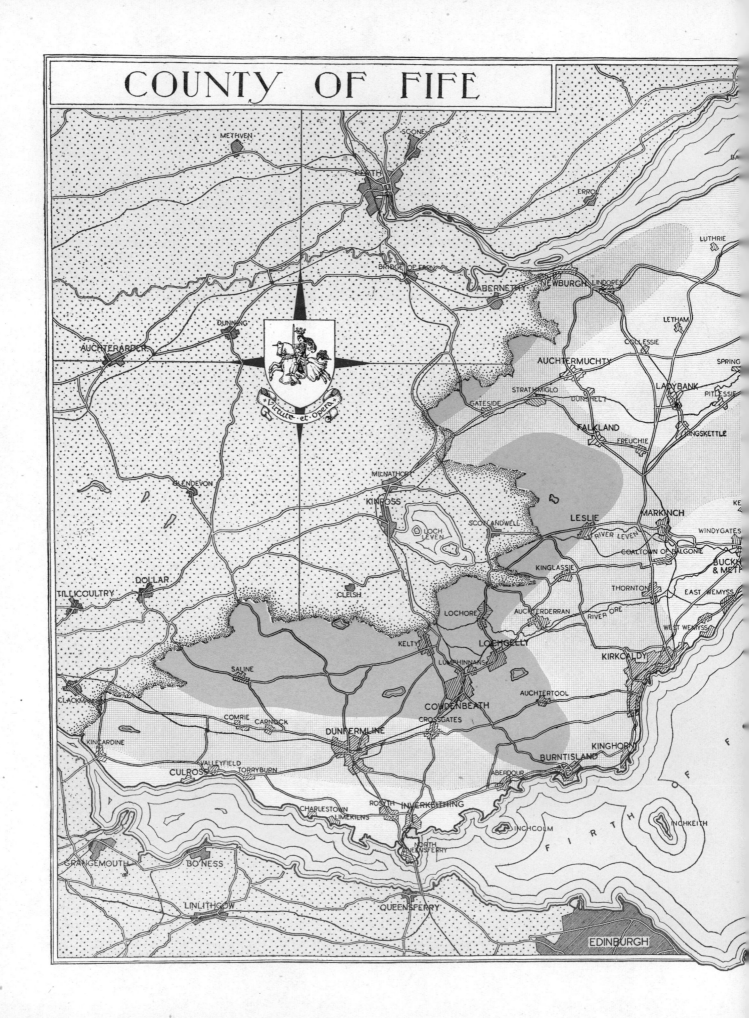

COUNTY OF FIFE

Virtute et Opera

METHVEN
SCONE
PERTH
ERROL
BAR
BRIDGE OF EARN
ABERNETHY
NEWBURGH
LINDORES
LUTHRIE
DUNNING
LETHAM
COLLESSIE
AUCHTERARDER
AUCHTERMUCHTY
SPRING
STRATHMIGLO
LADYBANK
GATESIDE
DUNSHELT
PITLESSIE
FALKLAND
FREUCHIE
KINGSKETTLE
GLENDEVON
MILNATHORT
KINROSS
SCOTLANDWELL
LESLIE
MARKINCH
KE
LOCH LEVEN
RIVER LEVEN
WINDYGATES
COALTOWN OF BALGONIE
BUCK & METH
KINGLASSIE
DOLLAR
CLEISH
THORNTON
EAST WEMYSS
TILLICOULTRY
LOCHORE
AUCHTERDERRAN
RIVER ORE
WEST WEMYSS
KELTY
LOCHGELLY
SALINE
LUMPHINNANS
KIRKCALDY
CLACKMANNAN
AUCHTERTOOL
COMRIE CARNOCK
COWDENBEATH
KINCARDINE
CROSSGATES
DUNFERMLINE
KINGHORN
VALLEYFIELD
BURNTISLAND
CULROSS TORRYBURN
ABERDOUR
CHARLESTOWN
ROSYTH INVERKEITHING
LIMEKILNS
INCHCOLM
INCHKEITH
GRANGEMOUTH
NORTH QUEENSFERRY
FIRTH
BO'NESS
LINLITHGOW
QUEENSFERRY
F
EDINBURGH

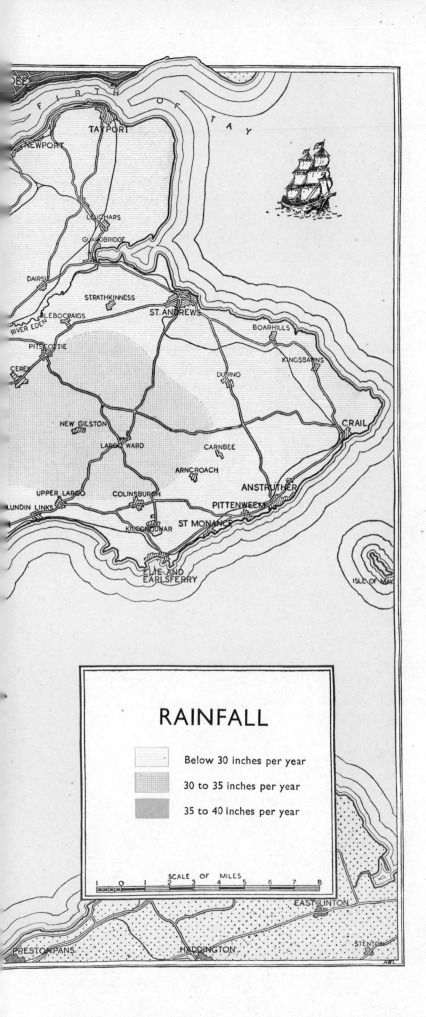

RAINFALL

	Below 30 inches per year
	30 to 35 inches per year
	35 to 40 inches per year

SCALE OF MILES

RAINFALL MAP

THIS map shows the average rainfall throughout the County. Precipitation is greater in the hilly country to the west, while the agricultural and recreational areas in the east have a relatively drier climate.

AGRICULTURE

I.
Population
engaged.

ACCORDING to the census statistics in 1931, there were 8,685 people directly engaged in agriculture in the County. Although this represents only 3 per cent. of the population, the ancillary occupations, *e.g.*, engineering, milling, agricultural merchants, tradesmen of all trades, indirectly and directly dependent upon agriculture, would, if they could be included, make the figure much greater.

II.
Previous
surveys.

The last comprehensive survey seems to have been that undertaken in the year 1800, when the Rev. John Thomson, D.D., minister of Markinch, produced his *General View of the Agriculture of the County of Fife, with observations on the Means of its Improvement*; *drawn up for the consideration of the Board of Agriculture and Internal Improvement* (Edinburgh, 1800).

A later survey was published in the *Transactions of the Highland and Agricultural Society of Scotland* in 1876, and, although not so comprehensive, it is of value as showing the state of agriculture at that date.

III.
Modern
comprehen-
sive survey
required.

There are ample reasons for stating that a modern detailed survey would prove to be of value.

IV.
Principal
crops and
figures for
stock, p. 7.

The total area of the County is 323,012 acres, of which 35,121 acres are mountain and heath land used for grazing and 225,004 acres are under crops and grass. The principal crops, according to the Department of Agriculture returns for various years from 1856, are shown in the table on page 7. To complete the picture, figures for stock are also given.

V.
Holdings.

At present there are 1,970 holdings in the County, classified as follows :—

1- 5 acres	....	....	....	....	....	311 ⎫ 889
5- 50 acres	....	....	....	....	....	578 ⎭
50-100 acres	....	....	....	....	....	246 ⎫ 1081
Above 100 acres	....	....	....	....	....	835 ⎭

1,970

For purposes of comparison, figures of holdings in 1875 are given :—

1- 5 acres	....	....	....	....	....	565 ⎫ 1209
5- 50 acres	....	....	....	....	....	644 ⎭
50-100 acres	....	....	....	....	....	224 ⎫ 1032
Above 100 acres	....	....	....	....	....	808 ⎭

2,241

TABLE SHOWING RETURNS OF CROPS AND STOCK

		1856	1869	1875	1881	1890	1903	1910	1918	1923	1931	1938	1944
In Acres	Wheat	34,099	21,433	16,748	13,142	11,321	9,043	11,228	15,113	12,821	10,898	17,266	22,318
	Barley	22,856	25,935	30,037	30,024	23,265	21,299	19,578	12,532	14,070	8,552	8,374	16,849
	Oats	42,328	39,274	37,646	39,111	39,330	39,814	39,496	54,422	44,177	37,714	35,699	38,715
	Sown-grasses	68,898	51,394	56,430	62,147	68,342	64,748	63,052	54,034	58,319	58,368	51,204	44,960
	Potatoes	17,269	18,566	17,746	19,155	15,188	15,319	15,393	18,358	15,901	14,959	15,946	25,411
	Turnips	29,739	28,375	28,514	27,547	26,334	24,046	23,166	20,543	21,719	18,611	15,312	16,472
In Head	Cattle	40,611	36,986	39,540	39,076	48,004	51,678	45,589	46,544	42,495	46,139	51,761	54,094
	Sheep	57,306	61,135	69,609	69,275	105,093	110,599	107,075	107,003	96,773	161,919	149,043	89,934
	Horses	12,258	10,495	9,699	10,166	9,481	9,811	10,624	10,636	10,675	7,442	7,083	5,646
	Pigs	8,734	5,931	6,050	5,366	6,669	5,407	5,943	6,712	9,803	8,639	13,264	9,963

It will be noted that there are 271 fewer holdings in 1945 than there were in 1875, and that the loss is almost entirely in holdings under 50 acres.

VI.
Fertility.

Fife is a peculiarly fertile county, with a long tradition of good farming, and justly proud of its husbandry. Much of its best land under skilful management can and does produce yields per acre equal to, if not better than the yield from the same quality of land in any part of Europe. As will be seen from the map on pp. 12, 13, this rich land (coloured dark brown) forms a fringe round the southern and northern shores, and in pockets throughout the river valleys.

VII.
Steadings.

On this rich land are to be found the massive steadings of hewn sandstone or of whin that are a feature of the County. These steadings, built to suit the conditions existing a hundred years ago or more, when labour was plentiful and cheap, are, in the main, inadequate for present-day requirements and inconvenient and expensive to work. A Committee has been appointed by the Department of Agriculture to consider the question, and, while it would be outwith our province to make recommendations as to types and the size of buildings to suit the varied conditions existing throughout the County, attention must be drawn to certain difficulties which face owners and farmers in adapting these massive old steadings to modern requirements, especially in dairying. But in most cases intelligent adaptation of existing steadings to modern conditions will be found practical and economical.

VIII.
Secondary
land.

Next to the rich fertile stretches referred to above comes a large area of secondary land that has not, owing to years of depression, been tended or developed as it otherwise would have been. It is in need of drainage, of roads, of fertilisers and of steadings. But the exigencies of war have brought some of this land back into a high state of cultivation and demonstrated the possibilities of a long-term policy of development.

IX.
Undeveloped
land.

There remain certain areas of land that have gone out of cultivation altogether, areas which, in living memory, carried good crops. The area involved is impossible to assess but would be found to be considerable. Some of these areas have gone out of cultivation because of the breakdown in the old road system. (See Photographs pp. 9, 11).

X.
Notable
tendencies.

A noticeable feature in agricultural development is the change to dairying. In 1800, according to Thomson in his *General View*, referred to previously : " There are but few instances where it (dairying) is considered as a leading object, or where the farmer counts much upon its produce."

In 1875, " The total number of cows and heifers in milk or in calf is 8,494 (or about 1,000 less than in 1856—EDs.), the 8,494 cows being made up chiefly by small lots which must necessarily be kept at every farm to supply the residents with milk." [To-day the figure is 18,303.]

(James Macdonald. *Trans. of H. and A. Soc. of Scot.*, p. 47, 1876.)

In 1895, " Fife is a good County for live stock. Little dairying is carried on."

(A. H. Millar. *Fife—Pictorial and Historical*, p. 40.)

There has been a very definite development of dairying in the last half-century, and indications point to a further development. In part of Fife, at least, the future of agriculture will be found to be bound up with the development of more dairies, attached to arable farms ; and with the breeding of high-class stock.

XI.
Distribution
of dairies.

The map (pp. 20, 21) shows distribution of registered dairies, of which there are 310.

8

OLD ROADS IN FIFE

(See Map on page 17)

Cause and Effect

Looking West

From same point as 1, looking East.

Old road taken over and " classified " in road system maintained by County. 1

2 The continuation of the same road as shown in 1. Road abandoned. This abandoned road, in many places 60 feet wide, once served the great area shown in 3.

3   4

Great area once served by road shown in 2, but now without access.

Inevitable result. Abandoned house, abandoned steading, steady deterioration of area.

B

Dairying is somewhat complicated as there are no less than four recognised grades of milk. *Ordinary*, where buildings and equipment require to conform to specified standards (marked in black on the map on pp. 20, 21); *Standard*, where in addition the milk produced must conform to a specified standard of bacteriological purity (marked in orange on the map); *Tuberculin Tested*, where a higher bacteriological standard and better equipment are required and the herd is certified to be free from tuberculosis (marked in blue on the map); and *Certified*, where a still higher standard of purity is required, in addition to up-to-date equipment, a tubercle-free herd and the cooling and bottling of milk on the premises (marked red on the map).

A strenuous campaign is being carried on by propaganda and frequent inspections and issuing of licences to raise the whole standard of milk production. This should be encouraged in every way and pursued unflinchingly until Fife is declared a clean area into which only tuberculin-tested animals are admitted.

Certain difficulties must be stressed. One is that already referred to—the massive nature of the old steadings, leading to high and often prohibitive costs of alteration. The second is the lack of enough good, clean, high-class, young dairy stock. Many animals on sale at public auction are bound to be animals rejected because of defects or disease, and if a number of breeding farms could be established on the eminently suitable and, at present, semi-derelict ground referred to in para. VIII (secondary land), a sufficient supply of sound Fife stock might be developed to permit of sterner methods being applied in the case of diseased stock than can, at present, be contemplated. It is understood that in Australia cows proved positive to the tuberculin test are branded so that they can never be sold in open market for anything but what they really are.

Opinions as to the value of artificial insemination differ widely, but this method, whereby calves could be sired by bulls of outstanding merit, may be found of value in the breeding farms referred to.

XII.
Economic pressure leading to extinction of small farms.

In para. V it is noted that there are 271 fewer farms in 1945 than there were in 1875. This is of serious import to agriculture; and a brief analysis of the causes and of some of the results that inevitably accrue, is necessary.

1. Towns have grown rapidly and many farms have been extinguished.
2. Mechanisation has made it possible to work larger units.
3. Economic pressure is forcing owners of estates to unite farms in order to avoid crippling maintenance costs.

In our investigations, we have been particularly impressed by the evidence obtained on this matter. For a number of years, this tendency has been noticeable and is increasing. Small farms are often the first to go; and small farms are the main " breeding ground " of future farmers. But larger farms also are being made into bigger units; and there is a very real dearth of farms to meet demand. The matter is of such importance to the agriculture of Fife that some space must be given to make the matter clear. It constitutes a crisis that is the result of causes originating prior to 1875. It is a crisis clearly recognised by the Department of Agriculture but one for which no solution has yet been found; and although nothing but a major and long-term Government policy can alter the present trends fundamentally, no survey of agriculture to-day would be complete or present a true picture without reference to the pressing need for a solution.

splendid stretch that only needs a road

Old main road Kennoway to Cupar.   This steading is now 800 yards from the present main road

Example of solidly built old steading modernised at great cost

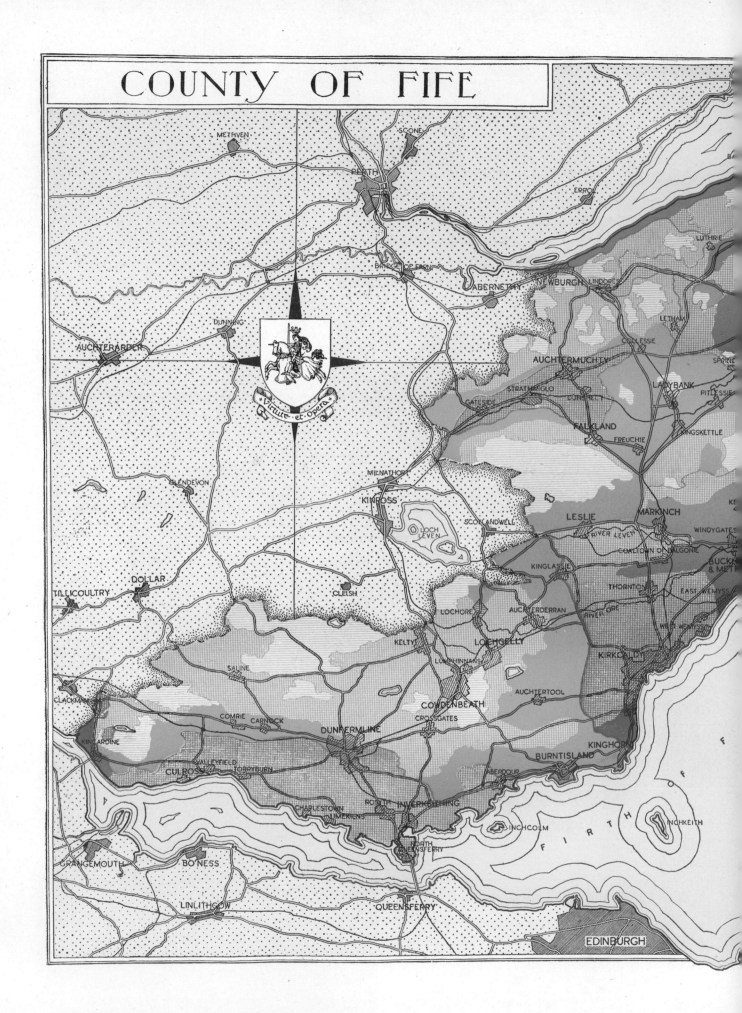

COUNTY OF FIFE

Virtute et Opera

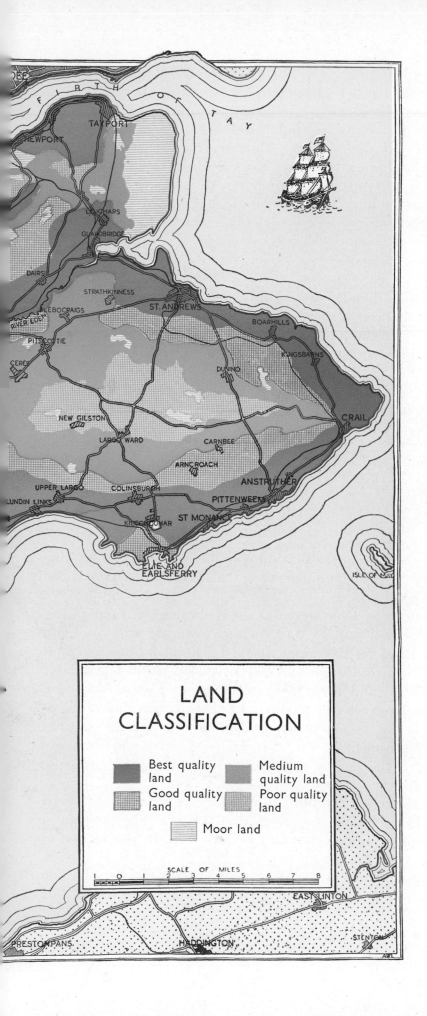

LAND CLASSIFICATION

THIS map gives a picture of the fertility of the soil in the County. Surface deposits have been glacially transported from the west with the result that light loamy soils, naturally fertile, line the valleys and the coastal fringes.

Fife is a peculiarly fertile County with a long tradition of good farming and justly proud of its husbandry. Much of its best land under skilful management can produce yields per acre equal to, if not better than, any other land in Europe. As may be seen from this map, this rich land forms a fringe round the southern and northern shores and in pockets throughout the river valleys.

Next to these rich fertile stretches comes a large area of secondary land that has not, owing to the years of depression, been tended or developed as it otherwise would have been. A vigorous policy directed to the repair of the old road system that once served these areas of secondary land would have far-reaching results for future developments in Fife.

LAND CLASSIFICATION

- ■ Best quality land
- ▨ Good quality land
- ▦ Medium quality land
- ▨ Poor quality land
- ▨ Moor land

SCALE OF MILES

1 0 1 2 3 4 5 6 7 8

Nevertheless, it is possible that a far-sighted planning policy by the County Council might do something to counteract a tendency that is in great measure bad.

One of the greatest of British historians has fully analysed the situation in his *English Social History*, pp. 552-555. He there says : " But the greatest single event of the seventies, fraught with immeasurable consequences for the future, was the sudden collapse of English agriculture. From 1875 the catastrophe set in." (G. M. Trevelyan.)

Rents to-day are the same as, or less than, they were in 1800. Costs of maintenance, of repairs and of wages are anything from 200 to 400 per cent. higher. As a result, and as one method of easing the burden of rising costs, small steadings are being dropped— in many cases larger steadings also—and farms united, for the upkeep of one steading is much less than the upkeep of two.

During the last seventy-five years " Landlords' Capital " (buildings, drains, etc.) has wasted, and " Tenants' Capital " also. From a survey report issued at the end of August, 1945, the following sample figures are taken :—

Holdings lacking adequate buildings—East Fife—15%. (The figure for Scotland as a whole is 37%.)

Production retarded by reason of lack of Tenants' Capital, negligence or incapacity, lack of labour, inaccessibility or poor layout—West Fife and Kinross—69%. (The figure for Scotland as a whole is 47%.)

Land requiring drainage :—

East Fife—8,533 acres.

West Fife and Kinross—12,604 acres.

Land requiring fertilisers :—

East Fife—44,610 acres.

West Fife and Kinross—41,167 acres.

It is the considered opinion of the Committee that dung is the basis of good farming and it is essential, if soil fertility is to be maintained, that the total animal population is kept at the highest possible figure.

The actual result of the tendencies here outlined is a great shortage of small farms, and only a small percentage of men who want to start on their own are able to obtain farms. Great stretches of suitable land for development exist ; numbers of men want farms and there are no steadings. Now that water and electricity can be made available the land referred to can be developed and roads and steadings built.

XIII. Continuous migration from the land. Since 1875, as a result of the collapse referred to, there has been a continuous migration from the land till the situation has become serious. During the war the gap has been filled by the W.L.A. and by prisoners of war, first Italians and later Germans ; but it has been calculated that when this help is withdrawn there will be a shortage of approximately 900 men.

XIV. Rural housing. Put bluntly, agriculture, in its depressed condition, has failed to offer wages at a level to induce men to stay on the land, or housing conditions that satisfy. The problem of the housing of rural workers is of grave importance and is dealt with in the section of this Report dealing with housing.

XV. Rural education. There is an aspect of the housing problem that is closely linked with the question of education. A start has already been made in Fife with the experiment of building

14

houses for farm workers, to be occupied by families working on farms, but away from the farm, in village centres. We have been impressed by the divergence of views on the question. A very careful estimate contained in a report submitted for the consideration of the Committee suggests that out of 99 workers employed on 17 farms within the area covered by the report referred to, 35 workers could be housed in village centres or in one village centre without detriment to the work of the farms. It has, however, become clear in assessing the views of a cross-section of rural workers (owners, farmers, grieves, byremen, in various areas of Fife) that the majority of the farming community, which we have been able to contact, are of the opinion that children brought up away from the farms are unlikely to take up work on farms as they grow up. Those who hold this view stress the outstanding advantage of the " farm environment " during early years for those who may later become farmers. We have to report, therefore, that the majority opinion is in favour of farm cottages *on* the farms.

It has also to be noted that opinion has been widely met with in favour, wherever possible, of avoiding over-centralisation of schools and stressing the value of rural schools. It has been calculated that over 80% of the people of Britain are now town-dwellers, and the point of view that town children might, as facilities can be made available, be taken out of towns to rural schools is one that should not be too lightly disregarded.

It is felt that consideration should be given to the suggestion for the provision of residential training schools for future farmers. Great stress is being laid upon the necessity for vocational training. Every opportunity should be taken to provide a thorough training in farming for boys and girls who choose to make farming their career in life. The scientific advance in agriculture has been so rapid, the need for well-trained recruits is so great, that the obvious difficulties in this suggestion should not be permitted to debar the Planning Committee from its most careful consideration. Control, staffing, and cost, offer problems of inherent difficulty. It is felt, however, that these are capable of solution. On the question of residential training, however, it must be stated that several members of the Committee strongly disagree.

XVI. Training farms.

Reference was made in para. IX to certain areas which have gone out of cultivation because of the breakdown in the old road system. Almost invariably, steadings were sited close to the then existing main roads. The revolution in road transport which followed the system of road-building by Macadam, and the tremendous road developments necessitated by the introduction of motoring and motor haulage, forced a concentration of attention upon the main highways and many of the older roads had to be left untended. In spite of the efforts of the neighbouring owners and tenants to keep these roads in passable condition, large stretches have now become quite impassable and many more are actually breaking down and will soon be unusable. Built or " bottomed " to carry farm carts with the usual one-ton load, these roads are now called upon to carry lorries with loads of eight, ten or twelve tons.

XVII. Transport and roads.

A survey of a sample area has shown that, in addition to some 6,000 yards of farm roads, which are genuinely interior roads linking farms to the main road system of the County, there are more than 13,000 yards of old public roads that have fallen, or are falling, into a condition of total disrepair. A considerable proportion of these 13,000 yards consists of roads essential to the continuance of the steadings which are served by them. It is thought that the time has come when the County should make a detailed survey of the older road system and determine which of the roads can and should be regenerated.

The accompanying map (p. 17) shows the sample area referred to.

Reference has been made to the possible provision of a training farm or training farms.

XVIII.
Experimental farms.

There is also the question of an experimental farm. Valuable work is being done for horticulture sponsored by the Department of Agriculture, but there is room for an experimental farm in the County to try out the best variety of seeds, the best methods of manuring and of feeding, and the best type of machinery, and to give the benefit of their tests to the farming community. Linked to such an experimental farm, there might be a research station dealing with animal diseases.

The losses due to disease among animals amount to a very considerable sum annually, and progress with scientific research into animal diseases does not appear to have kept pace with other research activities. Progress has been made with diseases affecting sheep but very little progress has been made with diseases affecting cattle. The losses in dairy herds due to mastitis, Johnes disease, contagious abortion and infertility are enormous, and practically no progress in finding the causes and cures has been made. Research stations should be supported by the farming community, and it might accelerate results if there was more co-operation between the practical farmer and the scientific departments. In connection, however, with an experimental farm and research stations, it is thought by some that this work need not be carried out on a County basis, but should be located so as to take advantage of the greatest skill wherever such is available.

XIX.
Advisory service on agriculture.

For some time an advisory service has been in existence for every county in Great Britain, but until the outbreak of war agriculturists did not make sufficient use of the service. With the appointment of Agricultural Executive Committees and the closer contacts between farmers and executive officers, the agricultural community gradually began to make better use of the service which undertook soil analysis, advice on manuring, grass seed mixtures, etc., with the result that during the past five years there has been a very considerable advance in the knowledge of soil requirements to produce maximum crops. Hitherto, it must be admitted that that knowledge was generally of a superficial nature and that agriculturists were sceptical of the expert. The ultimate object in any undertaking is to achieve the maximum output at the minimum cost, and in agriculture loss of fertility must be taken into account in arriving at the minimum cost. Maintenance of fertility must always be the guiding principle in agriculture and no risk should be taken of jeopardising the fertility of soil.

XX.
Soil survey.

It is suggested that the first step in any scheme for the benefit of agriculture would be to have a survey made of the County and an analysis made of the soil with a view to ascertaining its deficiencies of lime, phosphates and potash. Unless the deficiencies are made good the maximum output cannot be obtained, and it must be remembered that it is yield per acre which always makes the difference between profit and loss. Up to a certain yield a loss is sustained, but every hundredweight in excess of that figure is

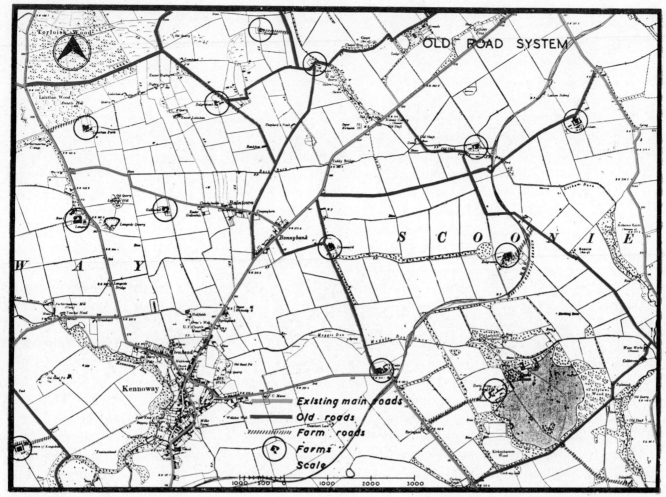

A sample area showing the old road system

C

17

more or less profit, as the following example taken from Walston & Seligman's Farm Costings for 1939/41 will show :—

Cost of production .... £8 13 11 per acre.
Loss on yield of 2 qrs. per acre .... 4 7 0 per acre.
Loss on yield of 3 qrs. per acre .... 2 7 11 per acre.
Loss on yield of 4 qrs. per acre .... 0 5 11 per acre.
Profit on yield of 5 qrs. per acre .... 1 16 1 per acre.
Profit on yield of 6 qrs. per acre .... 3 18 1 per acre.

This cannot be too strongly impressed upon everyone engaged in agriculture, and it is suggested that much could be done in the future to keep farmers in touch with the most up-to-date methods and discoveries.

XXI. Drainage. The question of drainage requires attention. Many field drains have ceased to function owing to outlets being choked and water-courses having become silted up, while large areas are ripe for redraining. All this involves the provision of drain tiles and of skilled labour, and there are openings for the establishment of tile-works and openings for contractors who could undertake draining, ditching, hedging, fencing and other such work which the average agricultural worker could not be expected to undertake efficiently.

There are certain areas throughout the County where combined drainage schemes are indicated, areas affecting several farms and too great as drainage schemes to be faced by any one owner or farmer. An Advisory Committee should be in a position to survey such areas, make recommendations either to the County direct or to the Department of Agriculture, and the County or the Department should possess powers to have such combined schemes carried through.

XXII. Link with Research Institutes. It is hoped that whatever organisation replaces the war-time Agricultural Executive Committee will be in touch with Animal Diseases Research Institutes, Experimental Farms, Colleges of Agriculture, Scottish Society for Research on Plant Breeding, and all other institutions connected with agriculture, so that it can keep those interested in agriculture informed of the results of all experiments and discoveries. Short courses of instruction conducted by experts might be instituted throughout the County, but these should be so conducted as to stimulate interest and discussion rather than take the form of an elementary lecture.

XXIII. Fruit-farming and market-gardening. Throughout the County there are areas where fruit-farming has proved successful. Approximately 140 acres are presently farmed in this way. Raspberries and black-currants are the main fruits grown, with some strawberries. Apples, it is found, are too unreliable as a profitable crop. There is, however, a great opening for skilled market-gardening. Excellent markets exist in the populated coastal districts. Little has been done in the way of market-gardening in the past, although small and thriving undertakings do exist, showing what is possible. There are areas particularly well adapted for the purpose, and an Advisory Committee would be in a position to tell intending market-gardeners where the ground is suitable and the markets good.

XXIV. Country joiners. The County is well served by country joiners, and it would be difficult to overrate the value of this particular trade to agriculture ; but this also is a trade where there are openings, and which could be encouraged in the future.

18

Evidence for the need of more smiddies has been prominent in the process of gathering information by the members of the Advisory Committee. Excellent work is being done by the Scottish Country Industries Development Trust in helping to keep this ancient and indispensable trade in existence. Nevertheless, there are disquieting indications that shoeing and repair of farm implements is a dying industry. The inadequacy of the older apprentice system is possibly one cause for the noticeable decline in the number of smiddies. Another is the evidently much greater attraction held by motor engineering, but smiddies will be required as long as agriculture survives, and it is suggested that part of the curriculum in any training farms of the future should be devoted to a complete and up-to-date course in smith's work, along with a thorough training in repair work to all agricultural machinery and all makes of tractors.

XXV.
Smiddies.

Part of what has been said about smiddies applies to the saddling trade. The saddler is an indispensable tradesman in agriculture, and the old apprenticeship system seems unlikely to supply the recruits necessary for the future needs. Again, it can be seen that some form of vocational training will have to be given if the old system should prove inadequate.

XXVI.
Saddlery.

Fife has been a beautifully wooded County. The fashion of planting which prevailed about 1760 to 1780 resulted then, and in a lesser measure ever since, in the production of shelter belts, strips and woods of a more ambitious acreage, which resulted in a complete transformation of the County. At the time of Dr. Johnson it is said that there was no tree visible to him on his journey from Edinburgh to St. Andrews, and it was only when he arrived at St. Andrews that he was shown, with much pride, two trees of very secondary value.

XXVII.
Woodlands.

Much of the timber in Fife, however, was planted about that time and, in consequence, has come to maturity at the same time, and there is a very real dearth of good young hardwood plantations at the present day. Such plantations do exist but are negligible so far as replacement needs are concerned. The whole question of woodlands requires careful analysis and treatment. Costs of planting are high, being in the neighbourhood of £20 to £30 per acre. With grants in the neighbourhood of only £7 the cost is too great for most owners, and once trees are felled woods too often remain unplanted. Owing to the need for timber during the war considerable areas have been felled, and many more are still scheduled for felling. From a purely forestry point of view the felling was probably an excellent thing—the timber was ripe, the trees were becoming brittle, and storms were taking an ever-increasing toll—but from an amenity point of view the wide clearings are a matter for regret and replanting is much to be desired.

One thing that stands in the way of replanting is the small acreage of many woodland areas controlled by one owner, too small to permit of the existence of even one forester with the time, the knowledge and the skill to supervise the necessary work.

One possible solution would be a co-operative approach on the part of small owners and the division of the County into areas under a forester and active staff, not only responsible to individual owners for the planting and management of woodlands, but, in addition, responsible for the supply of a team of men able to carry out fencing, hedging, ditching and draining.

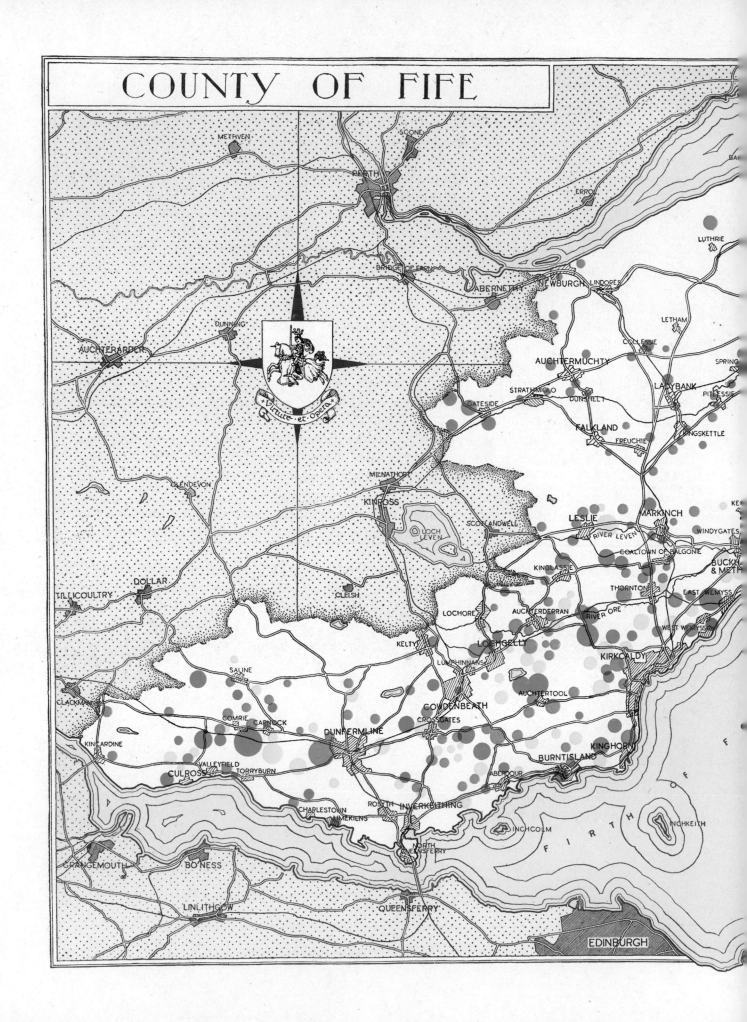

COUNTY OF FIFE

Virtute et Opera

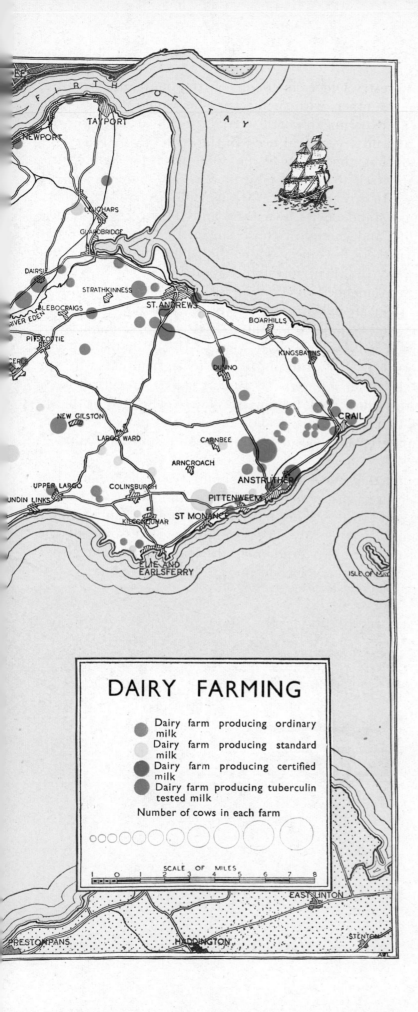

DAIRY FARMING

"THE future of agriculture in the County is bound up with the development of dairies attached to arable farms and the breeding of high-class stock. The map shows a general picture of the distribution of registered dairies in the County of which there are some 310. It also shows the four recognised grades of milk: (a) 'Ordinary'; (b) 'Standard,' where byres and buildings have been brought up to specified requirement; (c) 'Tuberculin Tested' which necessitates the specified standard of buildings and also close control of herds for the eradication of bovine tuberculosis; and (d) 'Certified,' where the buildings are standard, the herd is tuberculin tested and the milk cooled and bottled on the premises.

A continual 'grading up' is taking place, and even since this map was printed a number of dairies then registered as 'Ordinary' or 'Standard' now produce Tuberculin Tested milk."

The appointment of a County Forestry Officer in touch, on the one hand, with the County Planning Committee, and on the other, with such owners as would unite to take advantage of his services, might be an experiment worth a trial. Such an officer could plan areas and organise local staffs and fill a very real need in the economy of Fife.

XXVIII.
Conclusion.

In conclusion, it must be said that there can be no blue-print for agriculture. Agriculture is organic and must adapt itself to the needs of man as age succeeds age. It cannot fail or humanity would cease. In any given area, at one time or another, it may need support, but ultimately it must stand on its own legs, and its success or failure must depend mainly upon the ability and energy of those engaged. It is a fact that during the whole period of depression there have been some, and more than is generally believed, engaged in agriculture who, by their foresight, ability and energy, never failed to earn a profit while others were inclined to clamour for Government assistance.

Agriculture is something more than an industry; it is the foundation upon which the whole superstructure of industry and commerce is built. This has to be emphasised because of the inevitable criticism that will be levelled at some of the recommendations that the Advisory Committee put forward. "If a training school for agriculture, why not a training school for this, that, or the other industry?" But as G. M. Trevelyan says, "Political economy does not cover the whole field of human welfare. The men of theory in the past have failed to perceive that agriculture is not merely one industry among many, but a way of life, unique and irreplaceable in its human and spiritual values" (*English Social History*, pp. 554).

In the aggregate, it may be found that the Planning Committee of the County can accomplish comparatively little to ensure a prosperous agriculture, and that the creation of a policy that will ensure stability and prosperity lies more at a National than a County level. Nevertheless, it is the opinion of the Advisory Committee that some of the recommendations which are put forward are of a fundamental nature and might go far to counteract the tendency, so long in evidence, for good men to leave the land.

A corner of Pitlessie Village, near Ladybank

THE FISHING INDUSTRY

The Present Position.

THE fishing industry is centred in Anstruther and the neighbouring communities of Crail, St. Monance and Pittenweem. Of these Crail specialises in inshore fishing for lobsters and crabs, which command a ready market in London. About ten boats are employed, and a suitable train service permits of fish despatched from Crail in the afternoon reaching the London market early the following morning. Crail, for its prosperity, relies largely on its attractions as a summer resort, but in the others fishing is the main industry.

Anstruther is particularly well adapted as a fishing centre. The harbour is safe in all weathers and efficiently equipped. It is also one of the principal ports in Britain for the winter herring fishing. The difficulties and uncertainties, never absent from the fishing industry, have been rendered more difficult still by the war, and present serious problems that must cause anxiety but which are by no means incapable of solution.

What is Needed.

Before the war Anstruther had a fleet of 46 steam drifters. These have all been sold while on service and few are returning. At the present time two drifters and ten Diesel vessels are operating from the port. When the young fishermen return from war service there is nothing for them to do unless more boats can be procured. The younger men cannot find the necessary money, and the older fishermen, who may be presumed to have some capital on hand from the sale of their drifters and abnormal earnings during the war period, may hesitate to invest their money unless some guarantee for a steady market and better economic return is forthcoming.

Type of Boat Required.

The steam drifter is no longer the most suitable or the most economical type of vessel. The newer Diesel-driven type, 50 to 57 feet overall and requiring 6 or 7 men to work it, is much more useful. As it is not restricted to one type of fishing but can be used for herring, great line or whitefish seining, it can be at work for the greater part of the year, and being much more economical in running expenses it is obviously the kind of vessel to be employed.

Cost of Boats.

The cost per boat would run from £3,500 to £5,000, with nets and gear extra. Under the Herring Fisheries Act a fisherman who deposits 10% of the price can apply for a grant of one-third of the cost of the boat provided his financial position justifies this, and a loan for the balance could be obtained at $4\frac{1}{4}\%$ to $4\frac{1}{2}\%$ repayable over 20 years. On, say, a 52 feet boat costing £4,200 the fisherman would deposit £420, could claim a grant of £1,400 and raise the rest by loan. If one assumes a cost of £4,500 a complete equipment of nets and ropes would involve the following expenditure:—

Diesel-driven boat	£4,500
Herring drift nets and ropes	650
Ring nets	400
Seine nets and ropes	220
	£5,770

These boats could be built and serviced locally at St. Monance and Anstruther.

Launching a Modern Herring Vessel

A Modern Herring Drifter

FISHING

The fishing fleet finds good harbourage around the Fife coast

A Steam Drifter hurrying to Port

Photo—Jenkins

A Modern
Steam
Trawler

D

Can anything be done to relieve fishing, particularly herring fishing, of the difficulties which have hitherto seemed to be inseparable from it ? The " gluts " from which the industry has suffered can probably be avoided now through the use of freezing plants and the installation of dehydration systems. A good deal of research work has been done at the Torry Research Station, Aberdeen, and new methods of processing fish are now fairly well established. A freezing plant, if set up at Anstruther as the natural centre, would be invaluable, as it would enable heavy catches to be dealt with economically. Whitefish as well as herring could be stored. A freezing and storage plant suitable for the purpose would cost £5,000 approximately. This would include delivery to the site, complete erection and putting the plant in operation. If this could be worked co-operatively by the fishermen concerned it would go far to solve some of their difficulties. The fishing season with the new type of boat would be somewhat as follows :—

January to March—Winter herring fishing at Anstruther.

March to June—Whitefish seining.

June to September—Summer herring fishing.

October to November—East Anglian herring fishing.

This extended season, made possible by the use of Diesel vessels and backed by the use of freezing and storage plants, should make the industry more attractive, providing a decent wage for the men and a good percentage return on the boats.

TAY SALMON NETTING INDUSTRY

The Tay, which marks the northern boundary of Fife, is the most important salmon river in Britain. Tay salmon have a well-deserved reputation, and the salmon netting industry shared between Fife, Perth and Angus employs upwards of 300 net fishermen. A considerable proportion of these are recruited locally, the remainder coming from Skye and the Outer Hebrides. Apart from the men employed directly in netting the salmon, substantial employment is given to workers in ancillary occupations such as boat-building, net and rope-making, box-making and the making of boots and fishing gear. Local women are also required for braiding the nets. The netting season commences on 5th February and terminates on 20th August, the annual value of the fishing exceeding £20,000.

The industry is wholly dependent on the preservation of the spawning grounds in the upper reaches of the Tay and its headwaters and tributaries. The salmon breed in these waters and the young fish when two years old migrate to the ocean, where they grow rapidly and in due course return to their native river. It is obviously of great importance that the river and its tributaries should be kept free from pollution, hence the need for adequate arrangements for the disposal of sewage. Obviously, also, any interference with the volume of water in the main stream and its tributaries may have an adverse effect on breeding. The Hydro Electric Scheme, at present under consideration, is a matter of great concern in connection with the salmon netting industry. Any serious diversion of water or drying up of tributary streams will destroy the breeding of fish. It is therefore necessary to watch carefully all such schemes as well as all arrangements for setting up factories and new housing schemes that would involve exploitation of the water resources. It is to be hoped that all these considerations are being kept in mind in the interest of this valuable industry.

ting Herring for Export

Herring being Loaded for the Curer's Yard

FISHING

All of the work is not done at sea. Many hands have work to do before the harvest of the sea reaches the table

Fisher Girls Gutting Herring

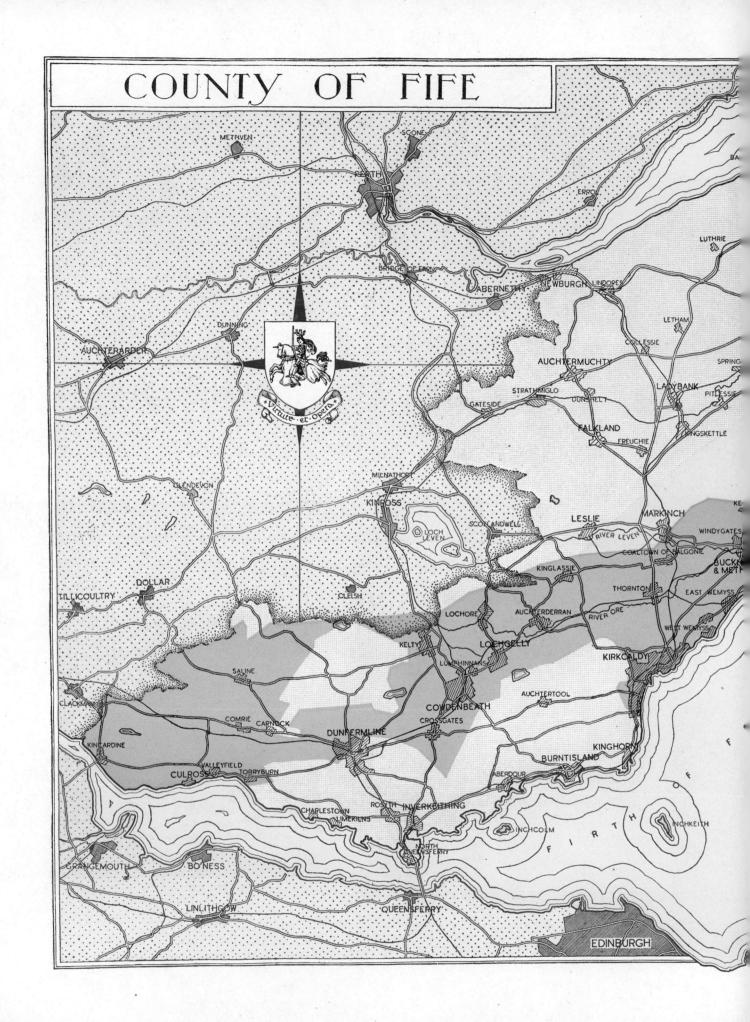

COUNTY OF FIFE

Virtute et Opera

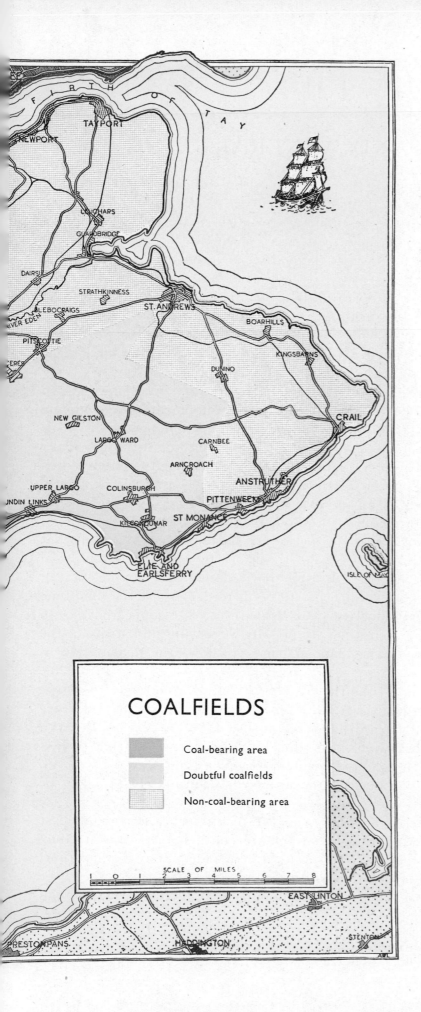

COALFIELDS

CONSIDERABLE thought has been given to the question of the preparation of a map which would show the safe areas for building purposes within the County. This map shows the coal-bearing areas, and within these areas it is advisable to obtain expert advice on the question of the safety of the ground before building operations are commenced. Within the light green and yellow areas it is considered perfectly safe for building purposes, although within the yellow area there are old workings and coal beneath the surface, but whether or not the remaining coal will ever be worked is doubtful.

COALFIELDS

Coal-bearing area

Doubtful coalfields

Non-coal-bearing area

SCALE OF MILES
1 0 1   2   3   4   5   6   7   8

MINES AND MINERALS

Historical. **A**PART from agriculture, coalmining is the most important industry in the County. Coal has been worked in Fife for more than seven centuries. We have documentary evidence of mining leases as early as the beginning of the 13th century. The monks of Dunfermline were mining coal in 1291, and there was evidently a coastal trade with England and probably also with France, even at that early time. The trade with London is of long standing. It was on a Fife coal-boat that the Earl of Mar escaped from London in disguise, landing at Elie on his way northwards to begin the Jacobite Rebellion of 1715. It is worthy of note that Scottish and English coalfields had been worked for centuries before coal was worked in other parts of the world. To the British export in coal Fife has all along made a valuable contribution, and its contribution for the future promises to be still more valuable.

Increased Importance of the Fife Coalfield. As a result of the continuing serious decline in the output of certain mining areas in Central and West Scotland there must be a considerable development of the mining resources of Fife if the Scottish average pre-war production of 30 million tons is to be maintained. The Fife and Clackmannan coalfield is the richest in quantity of coal per acre, both actually and potentially, in Scotland, and the developments contemplated there will necessitate the opening of new pits with the consequent provision of new houses and ancillary services. This will entail an increase of the population and presents us with what is probably the most difficult problem in our planning programme.

The Coal Reserves. The valuable workable seams of coal occur in two strata, the upper found in what is known as the " Productive Coal Measures " and the lower in the " Limestone Coal Group." These two are separated by the " Millstone Grit " (non-coal-bearing strata), in some places of considerable thickness, which has to be pierced to reach the limestone group below. In some places the Productive Coal Measures have disappeared due to denudation, folding or faulting, but where they are present we usually find strata of the Limestone Coal Group underneath. The map on page 31 shows the distribution of the reserves.

The richest coalfield in the County, the richest in Scotland as a matter of fact, lies on the coast, between Seafield and a point east of Leven. It extends inland for a distance of three to four miles and seawards for a distance not hitherto determined. The depth under the sea-bed is quite unknown, but the coalfield probably extends right across to the Lothian shore. It has been followed for a mile and a half seaward, but no approximate estimate is possible and much of the reserve may ultimately prove to be out of human reach.

Small Scattered Deposits. Small disconnected and scattered deposits occur at many points north and east of the main coalfield, *e.g.* at Balcormo, St. Monance, Largoward, Kilmux, Lochty, etc. Many old workings exist and they may have served local needs adequately in their time, but under modern conditions these detached deposits are unlikely to compete successfully with better equipped and richer mines. Their economic importance is therefore very limited.

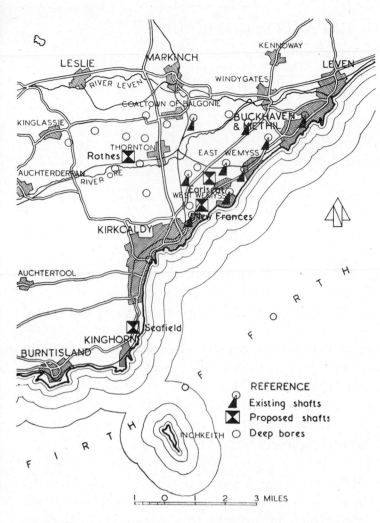

The Scottish Coalfields Report Total Reserves. gives the total reserves in Scotland as just under 8,000 million tons. This estimate is based on seams more than two feet thick. The inclusion of thinner seams would increase the figure but the thinner seams are less valuable economically. On whatever basis the figures are computed the Fife and Clackmannan field possesses more than half the reserves. The diagram on this page makes the position clear and brings out the striking advantage our coalfield enjoys.

The Coalfields Committee estimate Anticipated Increase in Output. that it should be possible to make a substantial increase over the figures for the year 1939 by anything from $3\frac{1}{2}$ to 5 million tons annually, though this increase could only be approached gradually. The lesser figure might be attainable in twenty years and the higher in thirty years. An important consideration here is that the increased output will be determined not merely by the proved capacity of the collieries individually, but by the number of miners that can be recruited and by the availability of houses. Prior to 1938 the output of coal was controlled not by the capacity of the pits but by the number of workers' houses. How much of this increase may Fife hope to contribute?

The answer to this question is to be found in the Report of the Scottish Coalfields Committee, pages 84 and 100, from which it appears that Fife output is estimated to rise to 10,460,000 tons per annum, as against 30,000,000 tons annually for the whole of Scotland. This would result in Fife providing 35% of the Scottish output as compared with about 23% in pre-war times.

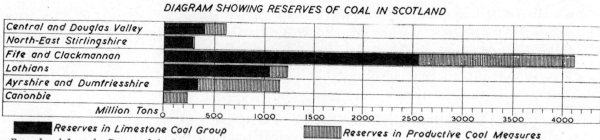

DIAGRAM SHOWING RESERVES OF COAL IN SCOTLAND

Reproduced from the Report of the Scottish Coalfields Committee with the permission of the Controller of H.M. Stationery Office

FOUR NEW LARGE CAPACITY COLLIERIES

The Fife Coal Company, Limited.

In addition to expansion at existing pits and the development of new fittings of lesser importance, the programme of this Company includes the sinking and equipment of large new collieries at :— Rothes—three miles north of Kirkcaldy.

New Frances—near Dysart.

Seafield—south of Kirkcaldy.

Each of these collieries will be fitted for an annual output of from 1,250,000 to 1,500,000 tons.

The completed plans for the first—Rothes Colliery—have been submitted to, and approved by, the Ministry of Fuel and Power.

The reserves of coal are fully adequate. The field has been proved by Bores in the landward area, the sites of Bores being indicated on the map on pp. 36, 37.

Rothes Colliery would be below the Millstone Grit and work the lower seams down to the Dunfermline Splint.

Frances Colliery would be above the Millstone Grit and work the Dysart Main and seams above.

Seafield Colliery would be below the Millstone Grit and level cross-cut mines would be driven seawards, cutting the Dunfermline Splint seam first, and continuing eastwards through the lower seams, then through the Millstone Grit and forward to the Dysart Main series, and ultimately all the upper seams if desired.

When these developments are completed, further sites for additional collieries will be considered, but these have not yet been completely surveyed.

The Wemyss Coal Company, Limited.

The coal seams in the True Coal Measures have been extensively worked in the Wemyss area, and the time has come when it is necessary to consider the working of the seams in the Carboniferous limestone series which lie intact.

Certain bores have proved these lower seams, but towards the River Leven, although the seams are known to exist, their positions are less certain. It is the intention of the Wemyss Coal Company to work these lower seams by a new deep shaft somewhere in the Lochhead-Duncan Pit-Earlseat area, but before deciding the exact location of this new shaft it is proposed to drive dipping mines from the Michael Colliery Pit Bottom for the purpose of proving the depth and strike of the lower seams in that region. After further data have been gained it is probable that a second shaft will be sunk to the east of Earlseat. It may be found that the best place to sink the first new shaft is near the existing Lochhead Colliery. The new colliery would work in conjunction with the existing Michael Colliery and would require extensive surface works. For this reason it is necessary to reserve a wide strip of ground from Duncan Pit through Lochhead Colliery to East Wemyss parallel with the existing railway.

It is important to bear in mind that the developments recorded above had been planned before nationalisation was decided upon.

MEASURES NECESSARY FOR DEVELOPMENT

Reservation of Sites for for New Collieries.

With modern requirements in view, it is probable that an area of at least 200 acres will be needed for each new site. There is usually only one suitable site for each development and the necessary ground must be reserved. When the ground is in private ownership reservation presents difficulties. Some statutory direction, therefore, would appear to be necessary where a site has been selected and approved by the Scottish Coal Board. A difficulty would arise in connection with the proposed new colliery at Seafield, for example. Here the minerals are all under the sea and the lease makes no provision for the occupation of the ground necessary for establishing a colliery.

It is obvious that successful planning for future development depends upon the provision of adequate housing. The responsibility for making such provision falls on the local authorities as a part of the general duty placed on them by the Housing (Scotland) Acts to provide housing for the working classes. After full investigation the Scottish Coalfields' Committee state the number required for Fife as follows :— Houses Required for Mining Communities.

Houses required to replace unsuitable houses	....	....	....	....	1,600
Houses required to secure additional output from existing pits				....	1,760
Houses required in connection with new collieries		....	....	....	4,400
		Total	....	....	 7,760

When we take into account the additional houses required for the non-mining population who provide the necessary communal services, it is obvious that the above estimate is much too low.

Under the Mining Industry Act of 1920 a Miners' Welfare Fund was instituted. This was reconstituted in 1939 and makes provision for recreation, social well-being, education and conditions of living generally. The Fund is made up of an output levy of 1d. on every ton of saleable coal, and since 1926 there has also been a levy of 1/- in the £ on coal-mining royalties. The total revenue up to 1941 had exceeded £21,000,000, and of this sum more than three-quarters of a million has been expended on pithead baths. The war has prevented a further advance, but even as it is pithead baths are available for distinctly more than half the mining population, and in this respect Fife has had its due share. The provision of pithead baths is an important consideration in connection with housing schemes. One can well understand the discomfort in the miner's home when pithead baths are not available. No one suffers more than the housewife. It is to be presumed that a further provision of baths will be made now that the war is over, particularly at collieries that have a long life before them. Welfare— Pithead Baths.

In connection with the mining industry many problems for research present themselves. The coalowners of Great Britain have provided a very large sum for the purpose of research into the various problems confronting the industry, including the better utilisation of coal. This is a matter of marked importance in Fife since the County is one of the major coalfields of the future. The field of research is one in which the University of St. Andrews might quite well be glad to co-operate. Research.

The unsightly coal-bings are a blot on the landscape, but hitherto no effective means of dealing with them has been found. It has to be remembered also that they tend Disposal of Refuse— the Coal Bings.

to grow larger than ever on account of the more general washing and cleaning of coal. The mass production by machinery conduces to more dirt. This would seem to indicate that there is need for a certain alteration in mining technique. A quantity of the refuse can be used for brick-making, but this affects only a small proportion. In some cases unsightly heaps have been improved by spreading soil over them and introducing certain hardy plants, but here again the number that can be so treated is relatively small. Some of the bings are subject to spontaneous combustion and emit unpleasant and unhealthy odours. For this no successful remedy has been found and further research is called for in the interests of health.

Where collieries have direct access to the foreshore the refuse may, in certain circumstances, be dumped in the sea or used for such purposes as land reclamation. Certain coal seams permit of part of the refuse being returned underground, thereby also assisting the prevention of subsidence. The problem is common to every coalfield and no practical remedy has yet been discovered, but in the interests of health and amenity further attempts should be made to solve it. Money spent in such research would be fully justified.

MINERALS OTHER THAN COAL

Fortunate in its reserves of coal, Fife is not particularly rich as regards other minerals. Limestone, whinstone, clay and ironstone are the only ones that count.

Limestone.
The limestone works already existing have more than a local clientele. Reserves would seem to be considerable, and it is particularly important, in the interests of agriculture and other industries, that they should be developed. The Cults works are probably the most suitable for further development, but housing accommodation there is inadequate, and the provision of the necessary housing in the district is of first importance if this valuable industry is to be extended.

Brick and Tile Clay.
There is a plentiful supply of clay but the bricks made from it cannot compete seriously with those made from colliery blaes. As regards drain tiles, the present supply comes mainly from outside the County. The fuel required for the kilns represents a large item in the expenditure, and it is only works situated near a colliery that can compete, as the added expense of transport puts up the cost.

Ironstone.
As regards ironstone, workable deposits are numerous, and many of these were worked fifty or sixty years ago, but the quality is not of the best and the richer ores imported from abroad make competition impossible.

Building Stone.
Sandstone is in plentiful supply, but the quality is not really good and its development is unlikely.

Whinstone.
An extensive trade in whinstone exists and could be extended, both at Newburgh and Inverkeithing, where there is a considerable export business. At Newburgh further dredging of the Tay is needed and also improved facilities in the way of piers. At Inverkeithing something similar is required. This would permit the use of a larger type of boat of 750/850 tons. It has been suggested that the County Council might arrange for the

use of a dredger which could be profitably employed in the various small harbours round the coast. Apart from the limestone and whinstone quarries, which are presently active and could be further developed, there does not seem to be much prospect of advance as regards other minerals.

Peat also exists in the County and may be developed in the future. Peat.

In the case of all the minor industries housing accommodation is the principal Housing necessity. There is a definite shortage almost everywhere, and if these industries are to and Transport. be expanded housing and road transport must be provided.

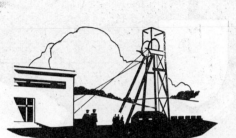

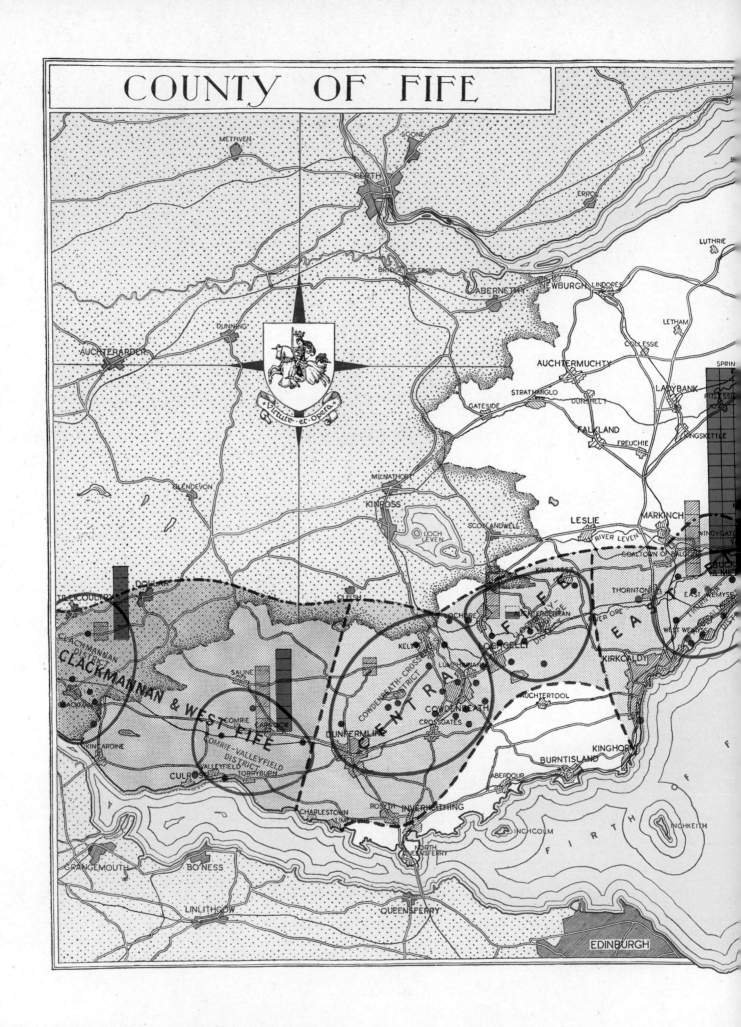

COUNTY OF FIFE

Virtute et Opera

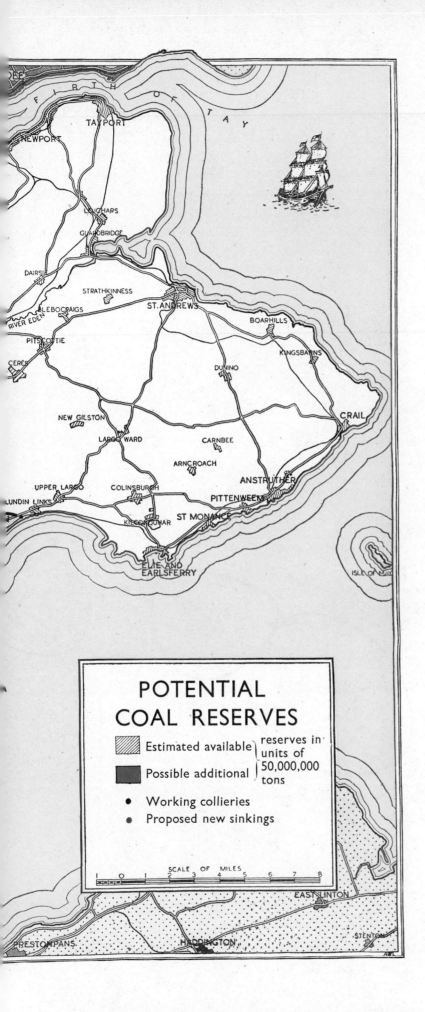

POTENTIAL COAL RESERVES

THE conservative basis adopted by the Scottish Coalfields Committee for estimating the coal reserves of Scotland yielded a figure of slightly under 8,000 million tons, of which fully one-half was allotted to the Fife and Clackmannan coalfields.

The Coalfields Committee further predict that the annual output in future years to be produced from Fife collieries will considerably exceed any figures achieved in the past.

The fulfilment of this forecast depends upon the securing of the necessary additional miners, and this in turn is contingent upon the provision of the necessary housing accommodation.

In all future planning the reservation of the necessary sites for new collieries is naturally a matter of greatest importance.

INDUSTRIES AND MANUFACTURES

I.
Fife
Industries.
WHILE mining and agriculture are undoubtedly the main industries in the County, Fife is fortunate in possessing a wide variety of industrial activities, some of minor but many of them of considerable importance. Certain of these industries were established long ago, and are intimately associated with the history and development of the County, others are of more recent date, but all of them bear witness to the enterprise and adaptability of the working population. The present position of these industries has been carefully surveyed, and is reported on in the notes appended.

Questionnaires issued to the various firms have been returned and the information thus provided is embodied in the following summary. The firms were asked to express their views on the housing shortage, the adequacy or otherwise of water, gas and electricity supplies, and the facilities for recreation and transport. In addition, they were invited to comment on the proposed road bridges over the Forth and the Tay, and to refer to any major development they had in contemplation. The industries may be classified as follows :—

Group I.   *Industries serving other Trades or Industries.*

       Aluminium Manufacture
       Paper-making
       Plastics Manufacture
       Engineering and Foundries
       Glass-lined Tanks Manufacture
       Bleaching and Spinning of Yarn
       Bottle Manufacture
       Bobbin and Shuttle-making
       Beet Sugar Manufacture
       Brick-making
       Preparation of Road-making Materials
       Lime Quarrying

Group II.   *Industries whose Products are Completed for Marketing.*

       Linoleum Manufacture
       Ship and Boat-building
       Linen Manufacture
       Blanket-making
       Bedding and Carpet Manufacture
       Furniture-making
       Oilskin Manufacture
       Whisky Distilling and Bottling
       Beet Sugar Manufacture
       Malt Manufacture
       Weighing Machine Manufacture

Golf-club Making
Rope-making
Salt Manufacture
Flour and Meal Milling

Generally speaking, industry in Fife is confined to a triangular area bounded by the coast-line between Inverkeithing and Leven and by lines drawn from Inverkeithing and Leven to the apex at Leslie. Outside this industrial area a few important industries and manufactures are carried on, but, in the main, the rest of the County is agricultural. _{II. Situation of industry.}

In the chief industrial area communications by rail and road are good, but it is clear that the industrialists do expect improvements to be made. _{III. Communications serving industry.}

While there is a feeling on the part of some that the provision of the Forth and Tay Road Bridges will not be an economic undertaking, the overwhelming majority of industrialists are in favour of the speedy erection of these bridges. It is feared by those not in favour of the bridges that the resultant transfer of traffic from rail to road will necessitate increased rail charges on the traffic which must be borne by rail. On the other hand it is contended that if Fife industrialists are to compete with manufacturers elsewhere, then they must be in a position to give speedy, efficient and cheap delivery, and it is claimed that in many cases this can best be effected by road transport.

From the east of Fife there is a fairly general complaint that the rail facilities on the coast-line connecting to Thornton Junction are capable of improvement, and it is suggested that some means be adopted to eliminate the delay at Thornton. While there is a general desire for the erection of the road bridge over the Forth, at the same time there are complaints that the roads from the industrial area of Fife to the Kincardine Bridge (which is the connecting link for the Port of Glasgow, and markets in the west and south of England) are inadequate. Strong representations to have these roads improved are put forward.

From industrialists situated at Leven, Buckhaven and Methil it is suggested that road transport facilities be provided at Methil Docks. Further suggestions made in connection with Methil Docks are that facilities be offered there for the handling of coastal shipping and for the development of the import trade at that point. Suggestions were made that the facilities at Methil Docks should be modernised and electrified. There is also a claim that improved facilities for loading and discharging should be offered at Burntisland.

The general opinion in connection with the new roads proposed throughout the County is that these will be very satisfactory, though it is felt in some quarters that the proposed coastal arterial road from Largo to Crail and St. Andrews is at present unnecessary.

In the mining districts situated in the industrial area it appears to be the general opinion that there is a surplus of female labour. While this labour during the war has been absorbed, it is feared that when war conditions no longer apply there will be unemployment among women workers. It is feared also that the surplus female labour will be greatly increased when the new mining developments in the County are completed. For these reasons there appears to be a general desire for the establishment of _{IV. Labour.}

light industries into which women workers could be absorbed. In fact, there is a general desire throughout the County for the establishment of light industries. In the mining areas there is a general fear of the hazard of having only one main industry, while in the rural areas, in order to stop the drift to the towns, the desire appears to be to have a more balanced economy and that light industries suitable for agriculture should be induced to settle there.

In connection with light industries the following suggestions have been made :—

(a) That there is room in Fife for the establishment of an agricultural engineering industry.

(b) That the banks of the River Leven in the vicinity of Methil should be zoned for light industrial development.

(c) That canning factories should be encouraged to settle in the agricultural areas.

In connection with the beet-sugar industry, it is pointed out that the co-operation from the Scottish farmer is not good, and there seems to be a general disinclination to grow sugar-beet. Before the war the Government decreed that 10,000 acres would be required to serve the beet-sugar factory, and while this has been suspended during the war it is possible that it may be reimposed. If this acreage is not forthcoming then it is stated that there is a possibility of the present beet-sugar factory being transferred. It would appear to be important that steps be taken to ensure this factory of supplies in future years.

V.
Housing.

There is no great need to comment on housing. The position is well known, and every industrialist who replied to the questionnaire agreed on the grave shortage of housing for workers. In Leven the need seems to be very acute, and in fact it is stated that if sufficient houses are not provided then major developments contemplated may be transferred elsewhere. It is not possible to say from the replies to the questionnaires whether industrialists are in favour of having employees housed near the factory or away from the factory. In some cases it is urged that the workers should be near the factory in order to save travelling time, while others consider it unfair to the worker and to the factory owners to have housing situated close to the factories.

VI.
Services.

(a) *Water*.—In general, water supplies for industry seem to be satisfactory, but at Guardbridge and Inverkeithing the lack of a good public supply, both for industrial and domestic use, is holding up major developments. In the Wemyss area and Leven, while there does not appear to be a shortage, it is pointed out that the pressure is too low, and in the case of fire this might be very dangerous. There is a shortage of domestic water at Balmullo and a potential shortage of industrial water at Burntisland.

(b) *Gas*.—Complaints are made that gas for industrial purposes in certain districts is much too costly. Increased supplies are required at Leven and in Dunfermline area.

(c) *Electricity*.—While only one or two industrialists have suggested that supplies of electricity are not adequate, there is a surprising number who state that the cost of electricity for industrial purposes in this County is much too high. Statements are made that compared with other parts of the country the rates charged, both for light and power, are excessive.

This was not touched on seriously in the reports except from the Dunfermline area, where it was felt that facilities for technical education ought to be improved. VII. Technical education.

While this is strictly not an industrial matter, nevertheless it has a distinct bearing on the contentment of workers employed in industry, and from various directions there are recommendations that recreational facilities be provided. These recommendations come from industrialists at Freuchie, Falkland, Gateside, Newton of Falkland, Leven, Inverkeithing, Wemyss, Burntisland, Auchtermuchty, East Wemyss and Anstruther. VIII. Recreational facilities.

NOTES ON THE INDUSTRIES OF FIFE

THE first thing that strikes a stranger is the great variety of industrial pursuits to be met with in Fife. Some of these industries are of long standing and are in the hands of firms whose origin dates back for more than two hundred years. The diversity of the trades and callings represented and the high technical skill they demand bespeak an adaptable and highly efficient working population and offer a guarantee to intending industrialists that they may confidently count on a body of capable and willing workers able to assure the success of any enterprise. Some of the firms enjoy a world-wide reputation. Thus the name of Kirkcaldy stands for linoleum the world over, Dunfermline linen is no less famous, and Haig's whisky is even more widely known. Many of the Fife firms are working at considerable disadvantage through the scarcity of materials, and they are hampered even more by the difficulty of housing their workers, but these drawbacks are not peculiar to Fife, and the prospects of industry are in general very bright.

LINOLEUM

Apart from agriculture and mining the manufacture of linoleum is one of the most significant and important of Fife industries. Kirkcaldy, its centre, has established a world reputation. Linoleum is also made at two other centres in the County—Falkland and Newburgh.

During the war period the industry was very much restricted, almost 80% of its activity being devoted to the production of war material. With the end of the war prospects are bright. There is still considerable difficulty in securing raw material, but the man-power situation is improving every day. For six years the home market has been starved and there is also an extensive export trade available. The various uses to which linoleum may now be put are too numerous to mention, but the Fife firms, with their up-to-date equipment and their expert staffs, are well placed to take advantage of the expected boom.

PAPERMAKING

Papermaking, established in Fife at the beginning of last century, is now one of the principal industries. It is carried on in six large and well-equipped modern mills situated at Guardbridge, Inverkeithing, Leslie, Leven and Markinch. Certain of the mills specialise in fine esparto printings and writings and in technical papers for plastics, electrical and other industries; others are concerned mainly with wrappings and bag and sack papers for commercial purposes. More than 3,000 persons are directly engaged in the industry, and the mills have a combined annual production of 75,000 tons of paper. The esparto grass and other raw materials are imported at Burntisland, Methil and Tayport. Woodpulp and wastepaper are imported also at Dundee and Leith. A feature of the industry in Fife has been its steady expansion. The prospects are very favourable.

SHIPBUILDING AT BURNTISLAND

INDUSTRIES

The County of Fife has a diversity of industries which many counties envy. This helps to assist in procuring balanced communities and thereby avoiding trade depressions

PAPER-MAKING, LEVEN VALLEY

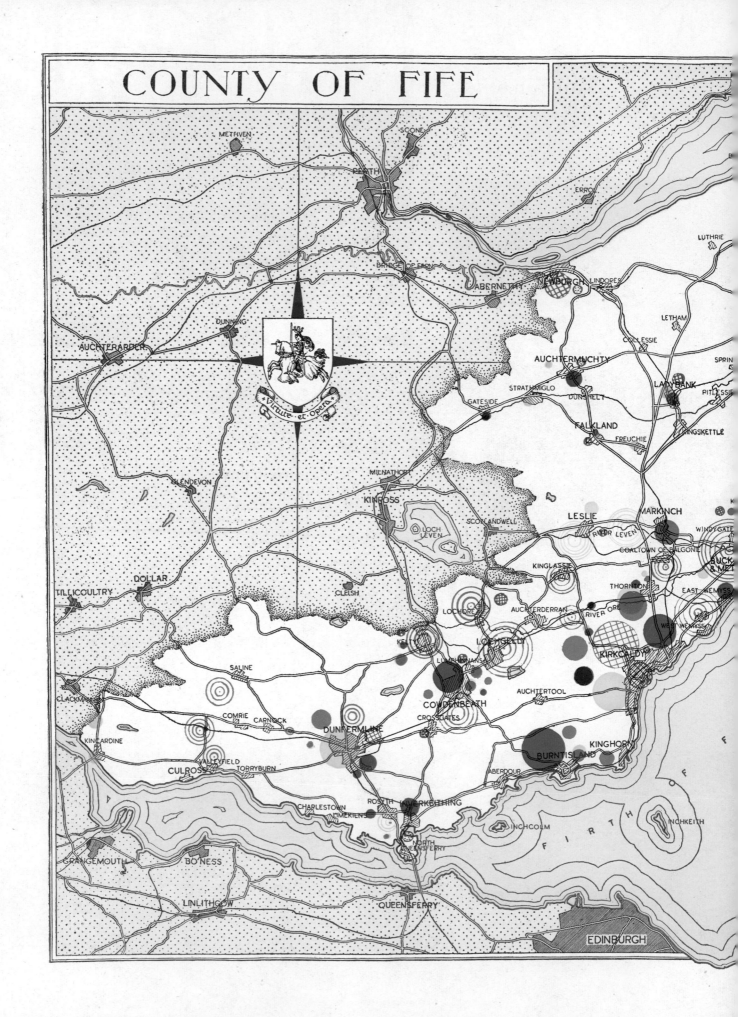

COUNTY OF FIFE

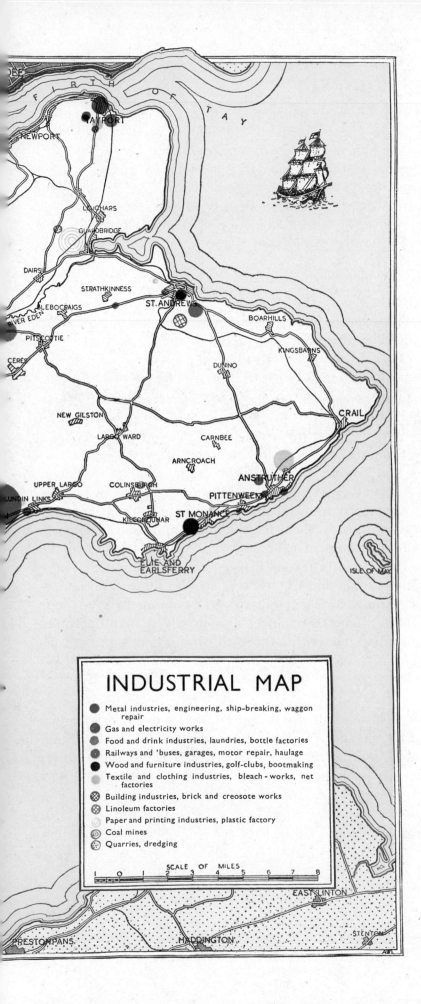

INDUSTRIAL MAP

WHILE mining and agriculture are undoubtedly the main industries in the County, Fife, as seen from this map, is fortunate in possessing a wide variety of industrial activities, some of minor, but many of them of major importance. Certain of these industries were established many generations ago, and are intimately associated with the history and development of the County ; others are of more recent date, but all of them bear witness to the enterprise and adaptability of the people of the County.

Generally speaking, industries in Fife other than agriculture are mainly confined to a triangular area bounded by the coast-line between Inverkeithing and Leven, and by lines drawn from Inverkeithing and Leven to the apex at Leslie. Outside this industrial area a few important industries and manufactures are carried out, but in the main the remainder of the County is agricultural.

WHISKY

At Markinch are the headquarters of John Haig & Co. Ltd., the oldest Scotch whisky distillers in the world. The products of various distilleries are brought to Markinch to be blended and bottled there and then despatched to all parts of the world. In normal times there is a staff of 500, many of them men with a life-long experience in the art of blending whisky. From the economic point of view the industry is of outstanding importance because of the substantial contribution it makes to the Exchequer in the form of excise duty. Scotch whisky is also the largest single export to the United States, and it is, therefore, a highly important source of dollars.

MALTING

The malting of cereals is an old industry, learned from the monks in all probability. It is carried on in Kirkcaldy, Sinclairtown, Newton of Falkland, Pitlessie, Ladybank, Windygates and Auchtertool, and provides steady employment for more than 500 men. Fife grows excellent barley, but also makes use of additional supplies from Angus, Perth and the Lothians. The industry is naturally sensitive to the fiscal policy of the Government as it affects brewing and distilling.

THE TEXTILE TRADE

The textile trade in Fife dates from the 15th century. It was at first confined to flax, producing sheets, pillow-cases and towels. Later came damask, first woven on hand looms and then on power. Of recent years the industry was extended to include cotton, and within the last 25 years rayon and artificial silk. All manner of textile goods for household purposes have been woven, most of them for the home market, but exports have also figured largely. At the present moment every effort is being made to revive foreign markets. The future of the textile industry in Fife is a promising one. There are looms within the County that can make the most attractive articles for general household use, and already buyers from various foreign countries are coming to study our local products. The industry never had a better chance, and provided manufacturers plan wisely and workers are quick to grasp modern methods of production, a prosperous future is assured.

THE FLAX INDUSTRY

Fife has always been famous for its flax productions and Dunfermline linen is known the world over. There are fewer firms engaged in the industry now, but the spinning, weaving and bleaching of linen goods is still an important industry. There are factories at Dunfermline, Kirkcaldy, Leven, Cupar, Falkland, Freuchie and Strathmiglo. The products are chiefly light linens of a domestic nature, damasks, sheeting, towels, etc. The bleaching of linen yarns and linen cloths has always been of the highest standard. Owing to the shortage of flax during the war all manufacturers converted a large number of their looms to the weaving of cotton goods, so urgently required by the forces. Flax is still in short supply, and the trade, while still using considerable quantities of cotton, is also producing a variety of rayon materials.

MALTING

Fife has a reputation for preparing and finishing malt. Here are two views of a malting-house

Malt on the germinating floor

Finished malt being weighed and put into bags for dispatch

DISTILLING

For the distilling and blending of whisky Fife is world-famous

Bottling whisky at a famous distillery in the county

The finished product—labelled, sealed and ready for dispatch

SILK

The imposition of the McKenna duties in 1925 accounts for the introduction of the silk industry into Fife. The decline of the linen damask industry also contributed, since factories and skilled textile workers then became available. The present state of the industry is rather low, but manufacturers have been able to keep the factories going by the production of nylon fabrics and a small quantity of silk fabrics for export.

BLANKET-MAKING

There is only one firm in the County making wool blankets. It is an old firm established 140 years ago, and specialises in medium and better quality blankets. Materials are still in short supply but the prospects for the future are very good.

BOBBINS AND SHUTTLES

These are manufactured at Gateside. The firm was established a century ago, for the purpose of serving the linen factories of Fife and the jute mills of Dundee. The mill was entirely rebuilt in 1939 and possesses the most up-to-date machinery. Bobbins and shuttles are produced not only for the linen and jute mills but for the cotton, wool and silk factories as well. The bulk of the orders are for export to the United States, South America, India, Australia, and Palestine. The present demands are greater than the firm can supply and prospects for the post-war period are bright.

HYGIENIC BEDDING

A bedding factory at Dysart was established 46 years ago. It was founded in order to meet the increasing demand for manufactured bedding to replace the older method of filling loose cases with straw or feathers. Production is hampered in the meantime by various restrictions, but the prospects are good. The firm also provides rugs, carpets, upholstery and all bedding accessories.

ENGINEERING AND FOUNDRIES

The activities included under this heading are so numerous that probably the best way to indicate their scope would be to describe briefly the work undertaken by one of the leading firms. This firm has a world-wide reputation. They are in the forefront as gas engineers and at the present moment are developing gas plants reckoned to be the most advanced in the world. They are the world originators of glass-lined equipment, have a vast export business in enamelled metal products and specialise in alloy equipment in stainless steel, aluminium, monel, inconel, copper, etc. They have one of the most efficient "Unionmelt" welding installations in Britain, and their X-ray laboratories, chemical and physical laboratories are amply equipped and staffed to carry out all the necessary research and testing. Their iron-foundries are on the point of being thoroughly overhauled and brought up to date so as to meet present-day demands. A considerable part of their activity is devoted to chemical engineering in all its branches. Among plants in which they specialise are the following :—evaporating plants, drying plants, extraction plants, oil-hardening, fat-splitting, milk products plant, caustic plant, soda recovery plant, ammonia plant, etc. This part of their

Weaving

LINEN
MANUFACTURE

The Calendar Machine

work involves the use of extensive laboratories and testing stations, and the services of a highly qualified scientific staff. Along with their associated companies they thus cover a very wide field. Their export trade alone brings in several million pounds, and the outlook for the future is very bright, provided the necessary housing accommodation for skilled workers can be provided.

ALUMINIUM

The aluminium works at Burntisland were erected in 1914 and have been extended several times since. The particular process carried out at Burntisland consists in refining the ore and providing a pure aluminium oxide with related products. Apart from the production of aluminium the oxide is used for a variety of purposes in the making of paper and pottery, in the refractory and abrasive trades and in the manufacture of sparking plugs. The site at Burntisland is a very suitable one with its excellent dock accommodation and abundant supplies of coal. About 600 people, chiefly men, are employed, and together with the shipbuilding industry it constitutes the main source of the prosperity of the burgh.

SALT MANUFACTURE

This is one of the earliest of our manufactures and has been carried on in certain small coast towns for centuries. The salt is made from a solution of rock salt in sea-water which is evaporated in open pans over slow furnaces. The rock salt has to be imported from England and Northern Ireland where the natural deposits are situated. Supplies were cheap at one time, but rising costs both of material and of freight have damaged the industry. Scottish salt sells at a higher price than English salt, being preferred by bakers, but English methods of manufacture have improved and the competition is now so keen that local prospects are no longer very bright.

GLASS MANUFACTURE

The only glass manufacturing concern in the County is situated at Pettycur, Kinghorn, where abundance of wind-blown sand, coupled with convenient supplies of lime and coal led to the establishment of a small glass factory more than forty years ago. Conditions have changed since then and the factory is no longer as dependent on local material. Manufacture is restricted to amber bottles and jars for the whisky, brewing and kindred trades. Bottles were at first mouth-blown, but the production is now fully automatic. Prospects for the future are good.

PRE-CAST CONCRETE

In Fife the manufacture of pre-cast concrete began after the last war. It is important in that it provides a cheap substitute for natural stone, a matter of consequence to-day with a heavy housing programme before us. It is still done only on a modest scale, but it should have a useful future.

PLASTICS

The plastic industry at Leslie is the largest of its kind in Scotland, its rapid growth being due to the war. Before the war the factory made pens, pencils, etc. At present the plant is being changed over to provide mouldings and a wide variety of domestic goods for export markets. There is still some difficulty about the raw materials, but although competition is likely to be keen the industry has a promising future. The personnel at present averages 650.

OATMEAL AND FLOUR

The milling of corn dates back to the beginning of recorded time. In Fife, as in most parts of Scotland, there gradually developed many small meal mills, situated wherever the weight of water was sufficient to drive the millstones. The natural tendency in later years has been to concentrate the work in a few large mills, and this is always the case in the milling of flour. Millstones are used in the making of oatmeal and wheaten meal; in the making of flour only roller mills are employed, the actual crushing being effected by rollers made of chilled steel. In Fife there are only two flour mills, both in Kirkcaldy. As a milling county Fife is favourably situated. Grain of the finest quality is grown, and the greatly extended use of oatmeal during the war period forecasts a better market than in previous years.

SUGAR BEET

The factory at Cupar is the only one in Scotland. It is run by the British Sugar Corporation Limited and is under Government control. During the war farmers were compelled to grow a certain amount of beet, and some 13,000 acres became available for supply. The farmers are doubtful about sugar beet, but the prospects may improve The tops and crowns are useful for feeding and the crop fertilises the soil. The money paid to the farmers in 1945 was approximately £470,000. The factory employs about 500 people. It handles 1,600 tons a day and uses each season a quarter of a million jute bags and large quantities of filter-cloth. The industry involves the use of 19,000 railway waggon loads and 13,000 lorry loads a year. Bridges over the Forth and Tay would probably lead to more beet being grown in the Lothians and Angus. This would help to secure the retention of the factory in Scotland. Unfortunately housing for the workers is a serious difficulty.

ROAD HAULAGE

Motor haulage sprang into importance after the Great War when army vehicles became available and many ex-Service men saw the possibilities of entering the carrying trade. The General Strike of 1926 led to a further advance, and now Fife is supplied with an extensive and well-organised system. Lorries from 30 cwts. to 15 tons are available, also special types of vehicles to meet the needs of farmers and heavy industry. In the meantime, until the Government's plans become clear, the prospects can only be guessed.

GOLF-CLUB-MAKING

With St. Andrews as its centre this industry is well established in Fife. It suffered partial eclipse during the war, but club-makers are now coming back from the Forces. Material is still in short supply but the position is improving. There is naturally much

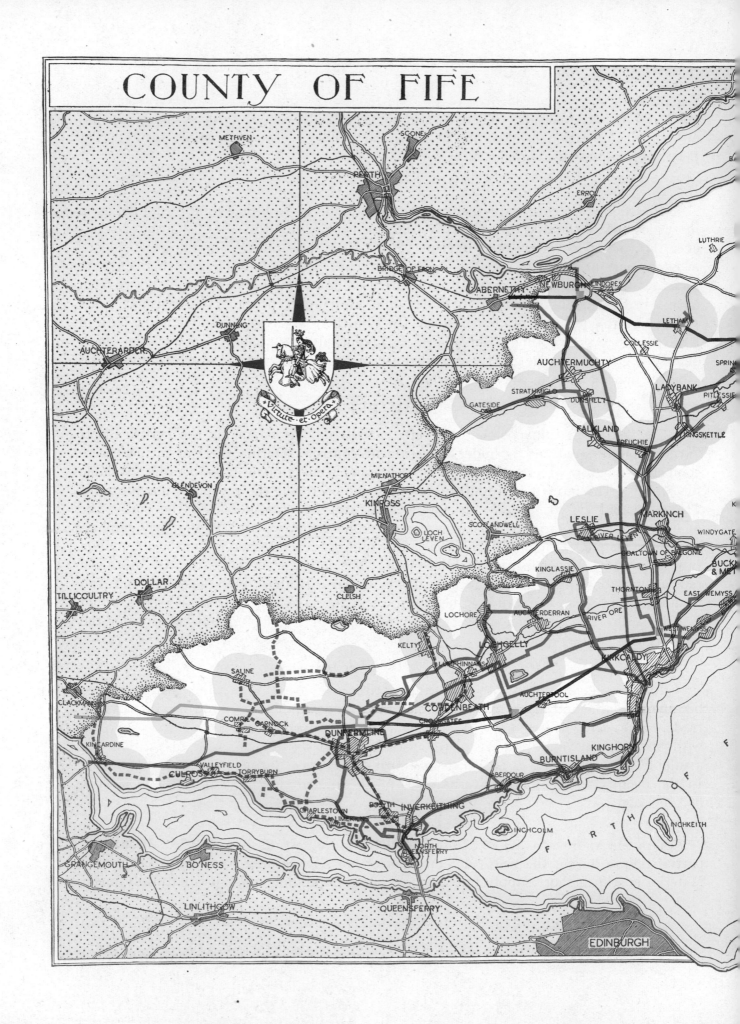

COUNTY OF FIFE

Virtute et Opera

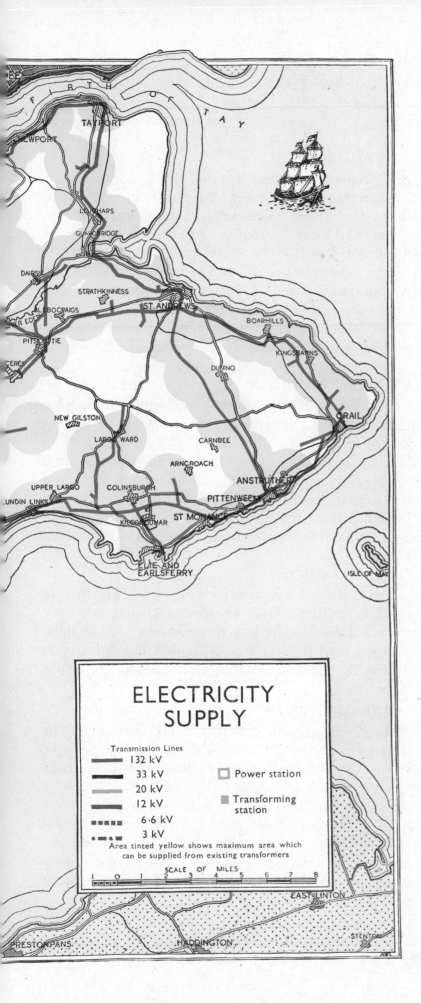

ELECTRICITY SUPPLY

THIS map shows the grid of high-tension lines through the County, with points where this high tension is transformed into electric power for domestic use. Land within a radius of one mile around these transformers can be supplied with electricity for domestic purposes. It will be seen that most of the County can be supplied in this way, and all industrialists consulted agree that supplies are adequate.

The Fife Electric Power Company operating these lines has in mind several new lines which will be considered for construction in the near future. The Committee is anxious to see the whole of the County, including the remotest parts of the agricultural area, adequately supplied with electricity.

ELECTRICITY SUPPLY

Transmission Lines
132 kV
33 kV
20 kV
12 kV
6·6 kV
3 kV

Power station

Transforming station

Area tinted yellow shows maximum area which can be supplied from existing transformers

SCALE OF MILES
1 0 1 2 3 4 5 6 7 8

leeway to make up. So many golfers have been denied the game during the war years that the trade may reasonably look forward to a bright future. There is every prospect of a good home market, with the probability of an even greater demand from America and the Dominions.

SHIPBUILDING

The building of small wooden fishing vessels has been a long-established industry on the coast of Fife. St. Monance and Anstruther are the chief centres. For work of this sort there should be a steady demand in the future. Vessels of a larger kind are constructed at Burntisland. In recent years the local Company has greatly extended its activities in the building of steam and motor ships for the coast trade, deep-sea carriers for grain and coal and short-sea cargo and passenger liners. It has important orders on hand at present for various foreign countries as well as for British owners. If the larger type of vessel is to be built the entrance to the West Dock would need to be widened. The Company is also experiencing some difficulty in housing their workers, some of whom, in the meantime, are obliged to travel daily from places as far away as Leith and Edinburgh.

ROPE AND TWINE-MAKING

The manufacturing of cordage is associated with the fishing and shipping industries. It has been developed mainly in Kirkcaldy and Dunfermline. The heavy cordage is used for shipping, fishing and agriculture, and the smaller twines and cords for warehouse and general use. During the war the industry was kept busy with demands from the Admiralty and the Ministry of Supply. Trade is good at present though there is a serious shortage of manila hemp, the principal rope-making fibre. For heavy ropes sisal hemp is being used instead. Demands from the fishing industry are now on the increase and there is also a heavy export demand for cordage. In spite of the difficulties of supply the prospects generally are good.

FURNITURE

The making of furniture on any large scale is a comparatively new industry in Fife It is carried on both in Kirkcaldy and in Dunfermline. In the past many country joiners made furniture which commanded a ready sale, but there is less of that now. Scottish furniture, like Scottish linen, has a high reputation. Although the industry is not indigenous in Fife as it is in Ayrshire, the present demand for houses and furniture should warrant a period of prosperous trade.

WEIGHING MACHINES

Weighing machines are made at Auchtermuchty. The firm established here can trace back its activities for more than two centuries. Beam scales were made as early as the time of the first Jacobite Rebellion. The machines provided to-day have a world reputation.

THE OILSKIN INDUSTRY

It was natural that this industry should have developed in a fishing centre like Cellardyke. In earlier days the fishermen had no wheel-house on deck and the steersman had to brave the weather and take all that was coming to him. The advent, therefore, of the oilproofed cotton garment was a blessing much appreciated. Nothing better

54

SUGAR BEET

The only beet sugar factory in Scotland is situated in Cupar, Fife

Sugar beet growers and officials discussing problems in the field

busy scene in the factory yard

or cheaper has been found to replace it, although some new form of " plastic " garment may come into competition. In the meantime the industry is holding its place. It is the main employment for women in Anstruther.

FERTILISERS AND FEEDING-STUFFS

A limited company specialising in the manufacture of fertilisers and feeding-stuffs has developed from an Agricultural Co-operative Society established in West Fife more than twenty years ago. In its early days the Society acted as commission agents only, but its operations have been greatly extended in recent years, and in its works the company has installed the most up-to-date plant for the preparation of manures and feeding-stuffs. Pioneering work has been undertaken in the granulating of compound fertilisers, and a new Porteous seed grain dressing plant has been installed recently. Some further extension of building accommodation is also in view. From a modest beginning in the interest of local farmers the Society has made striking progress, and it now has an annual turnover of more than £300,000. There are good prospects for the development of this agricultural co-operative movement. Many other similar organisations exist throughout the County.

BRICK-MAKING

Fife bricks are of composite material made of blaes from the coal heaps. Such pockets of clay as exist have been used for making tiles rather than bricks. Considerable improvements have been effected in recent years in the machinery that is used for grinding and pressing. All our unsightly " bings " cannot be used in this way, but where the material is suitable and the necessary trouble is taken in grading and processing we have thus a very valuable addition to our resources for house-building.

MISCELLANEOUS

It is difficult to give an account of all the Fife industries. In addition to those mentioned reference might be made to the making of boots and shoes. There is also the curing of herrings carried on at Anstruther and the neighbouring towns.

FIFE INDUSTRIAL COUNCIL

We have been impressed by the need for obtaining centrally particulars which would be necessary to enable a prospective industrialist to consider what the county of Fife has to offer in the way of sites, labour, etc. for new industries, and such inquiries should be addressed to the County Clerk. We have also felt that there is need in the County for co-operation between the County Council and industrialists in relation to questions such as water supply, drainage and general amenities, and it is our view that to enable these purposes to be accomplished there should be set up a Fife Industrial Council on which the County Council and industrialists should be equally represented. We feel further that the claims to special consideration of the case of the River Leven, which is one of the most highly industrialised rivers in the country, justify a proposal that a special section of the proposed Industrial Council should concentrate principally upon the particular problem presented by the River Leven with a view to reconciling the difference between the claims of public health and amenities and those of water power and industry. The River Eden also should receive similar attention.

PUBLIC HEALTH

WITH the spread of industry and the consequent growth of population, the major streams in Fife, as is common in industrial areas, have become increasingly polluted. The River Leven, for example, traverses the greater part of the Fife coalfield, and in its course receives the domestic sewage and trade waste of this populous and busy area. Apart from the domestic sewage (which is often in a crude state) the river carries the effluents of eight collieries, five paper works, one wool mill and one distillery. This state of affairs presents a problem of a type common enough in industrial districts, but one which, in the interests of public health, calls for efficient control, towards which end the services of a river inspector would be invaluable. Under the terms of the Fife County Council Order Confirmation Act, 1940, the local authority now have powers to lay an intercepting sewer along the river from the village of Prinlaws to the sea, with branches along the Lochty Burn and the River Ore, the two principal tributaries of the Leven.

The River Eden is also contaminated by domestic sewage and industrial waste, but not to the same extent as the River Leven. Nevertheless, the County Council will be obliged in the near future to obtain powers for the purification of this river also. We strongly recommend that the County Council should obtain statutory powers to enable it to undertake adequate inspection and secure supervision of the principal rivers and waterways of the County, to prevent pollution, to preserve the banks so as to avoid flooding of valuable agricultural land and in some cases the flooding of dwelling-houses, and to take all such steps as are necessary to ensure a clear and free-flowing river ; but in cases where subsidence can be shown to result in surface flooding and consequent blocking of streams and watercourses, the cost of clearance should be levied against the Ministry of Fuel and Power and not upon the surface owners. In many cases the preservation of rivers is no one's concern, and fallen trees are permitted to lie across waterways and obstruct the normal course of the flow of the river. If the County Council is given statutory powers to deal with such matters they should also be given power to charge the costs of clearing the rivers against the adjoining proprietors in proportion to the extent of frontage, or on some other basis. Both the Leven and the Eden have their channels obstructed from time to time by silt and debris. Similar circumstances affect the smaller streams, which suffer also from contamination in their passage through agricultural areas. Some of them feed reservoirs which are the sources of water supply for populous communities. This condition of affairs, with its attendant risks to health, engages the constant attention of the Health Department, but here again we advise that the County Council seek additional powers.

Linked up with the problem of sewage disposal is the problem of land drainage. In addition to the 25 separate burghal drainage authorities there are 45 landward special drainage districts. There is no common policy governing the situation, and any open or closed watercourse, no matter how unsuitable, is liable to be used as a means of disposal of noxious effluent because it is readily available. The situation is becoming exacerbated by the rapid development of housing and necessitates provision of a drainage service on a regional basis.

Industrial Waste.

Apart from the pollution of streams by domestic and industrial waste a special problem exists in Fife in the presence of numerous colliery refuse heaps, both large and small. These present a distressing picture and tend to degrade the landscape. Are they an avoidable adjunct to the mining industry? An everyday reminder of industrial activity, they bear testimony to the destructive and transient lives of collieries, but they can no longer be accepted as inevitable, and the time has come when a remedy must be sought and found. It may be that certain coal-bings will remain in perpetuity, but these should be camouflaged with plants and grasses. As regards the others, and especially the new bings, some better means of disposal of refuse should be adopted. Means must be found to avoid the accumulation of material liable to produce noxious fumes.

Scavenging.

There are forty-three special scavenging districts in the landward part of the County, and each of the twenty-three Small Burghs has its own separate scavenging arrangement. In recent years considerable improvement has taken place in methods of refuse disposal. Controlled tipping is now practised in the majority of local dumps and rat infestation is now less marked than it was at one time. While there are several excellent examples of modern tipping, involving land reclamation, in the County, there are still one or two old dumps which do not readily lend themselves to control by modern methods of refuse disposal.

Although the Committee have noticed this evidence of progress they are of opinion that the number of refuse tips in the County is greater than need be. It is understood that the County Council is considering a scheme for the amalgamation of special scavenging districts, but a further step would appear to be desirable, namely, co-operation between the County and the Burghal areas. The Committee would stress the value of controlled tipping, not merely on grounds of health: it can be made to facilitate important schemes of land reclamation. This matter is further discussed in the report on Amenities.

Water Supply.

As far as the western half of the County is concerned the water supply is generally sufficient, but the position in East Fife is much less satisfactory. The reports of the County Public Health Committee again and again refer to the unsatisfactory conditions there. In this part of the County there are twenty-three different water supply undertakings, all of them reserved for the use of thirteen Small Burghs and a few of the larger villages. Every Small Burgh has the right to secure and maintain its own source of supply, but it is unsatisfactory to have such a multiplicity of authorities, each catering for its own needs without reference to its neighbours.

The western part of the County receives copious supplies of good water from reservoirs in the Ochil Hills and from two smaller reservoirs on the south-eastern slopes of the Lomond Hills. In East Fife the number of reservoirs is sufficient, but the storage capacity is quite inadequate to meet the demands, especially during the summer months, and there is a pressing need for a linking up of existing systems and a supplementary supply being obtained from the County Council's regional supply. Under the Fife County Council's Order Confirmation Act, 1940, the local authority obtained powers to construct a regional water main for the purpose of linking up the eastern portion of the County with the reservoirs which supply the western division of Fife. This linking up will enable almost all the small villages and hamlets in the rural area of the County to obtain a gravitation water supply, and every Small Burgh willing to participate would secure a water supply amply sufficient for present needs and future development.

The arrangement of hospital and health services available for the County may be set out as follows :— Hospital and Health Services.

There are seven *infectious diseases hospitals* to which County patients are admitted.

For *Tuberculous subjects* the Sanatorium at Glenlomond, near Kinross, is available.

Cases of *General Sickness* are sent to the Royal Infirmaries at Edinburgh, Dundee and Perth, as well as to the general hospitals at Kirkcaldy and Dunfermline and the Cottage Hospitals at Cupar, St. Andrews and Buckhaven. Apart from a relatively small percentage of cases treated in Dundee and Perth the bulk of the cases are dealt with in the County or in the Edinburgh Royal Infirmary.

Maternity Cases are provided for in the Maternity Hospitals of Kirkcaldy, Dunfermline and Edinburgh. Cases are also admitted to the Cottage Hospital at St. Andrews, and in the meantime a few are treated in Stirlingshire and Perthshire. The Maternity Services Scheme is in operation throughout the County.

Orthopaedic cases go to Fairmilehead Hospital, Edinburgh.

Clinics, both ordinary and special, are held in connection with School Medical Inspection and under the Maternity and Child Welfare Schemes.

The facilities enumerated above lack co-ordination. There are too many infectious diseases hospitals, there is an unnecessary duplication of services, and there is inadequate provision for certain types of patients (cancer and rheumatism) and also for ailing babies.

The County Council has had the whole matter under consideration and has adopted a policy for the integration of hospital services. This would provide for the concentration of infectious diseases in two large hospitals ; would increase hospital accommodation for maternity cases and the diseases of women ; provide a hospital for the treatment of ailing babies ; arrange accommodation for cases of general sickness for the sick poor, for the aged and infirm, and also for the mentally defective ; provide for the treatment and rehabilitation of crippled persons both juvenile and adult, and in addition make arrangement for such clinics and outpatient departments as are deemed necessary. For highly specialised forms of investigation and treatment links with neighbouring medical schools and large hospitals are envisaged. Geographically and economically the County lends itself to development as a unit for purposes of curative and preventive medical services, and while we acknowledge the advantages of co-ordination with neighbouring central hospitals, we consider that the County should not further lose its identity in medical arrangements.

It has been brought to the notice of the Committee that in pre-war days there were 37 slaughterhouses of various standards in the County. Soon after the outbreak of Abbatoirs.

COUNTY OF FIFE

Virtute et Opera

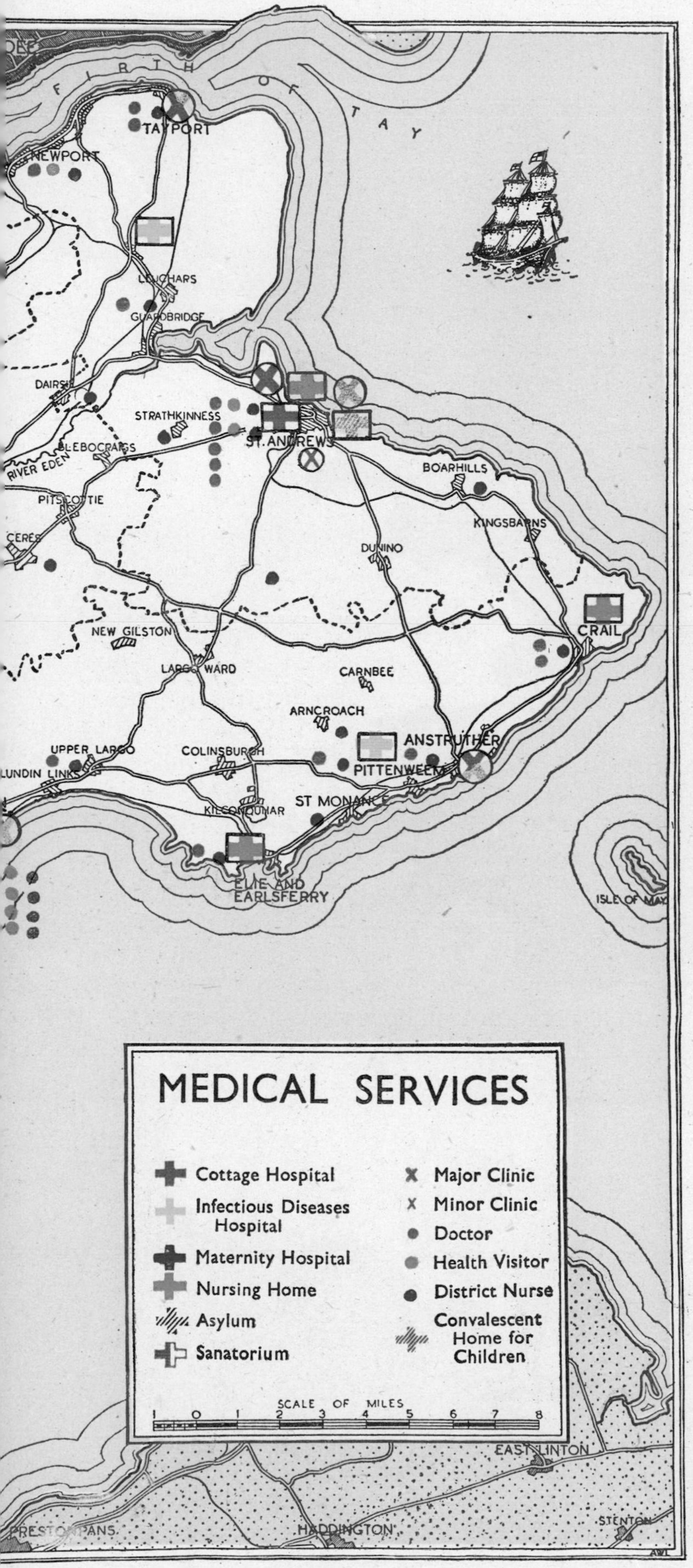

MEDICAL SERVICES

THE distribution of hospitals clinics, medical practitioners and nursing services is shown herewith. For the most part, general, medical and surgical cases are admitted to the Infirmaries in Edinburgh, Dundee and Perth, and to the hospitals in Dunfermline and Kirkcaldy. Maternity cases are also accommodated in hospitals outwith the County. With the object of creating a self-contained service, the County Council have decided upon an extensive programme of hospital reconstruction.

Map labels

FIRTH OF TAY

TAYPORT
NEWPORT
LEUCHARS
GUARDBRIDGE
DAIRSIE
STRATHKINNESS
BLEBOCRAIGS
RIVER EDEN
PITSCOTTIE
CERES
ST. ANDREWS
BOARHILLS
KINGSBARNS
DUNINO
NEW GILSTON
CRAIL
LARGOWARD
CARNBEE
ARNCROACH
UPPER LARGO
COLINSBURGH
ANSTRUTHER
LUNDIN LINKS
PITTENWEEM
KILCONQUHAR
ST MONANCE
ELIE AND EARLSFERRY
ISLE OF MAY
EAST LINTON
PRESTONPANS
HADDINGTON
STENTON

Legend

MEDICAL SERVICES

- ✚ Cottage Hospital
- ✚ Infectious Diseases Hospital
- ✚ Maternity Hospital
- ✚ Nursing Home
- Asylum
- ✚ Sanatorium
- ✕ Major Clinic
- ✕ Minor Clinic
- ● Doctor
- ● Health Visitor
- ● District Nurse
- Convalescent Home for Children

SCALE OF MILES
1 0 1 2 3 4 5 6 7 8

hostilities the Ministry of Food brought about the closure of all the small slaughter-houses and slaughtering became centralised at slaughterhouses in the following places :—

1. Cupar.
2. Anstruther.
3. St. Andrews.
4. Buckhaven.
5. Leven.
6. Cowdenbeath.
7. Markinch.
8. Lochgelly.
9. Springfield.

We are of the opinion that slaughtering should not take place in small slaughter-houses. We feel that slaughtering should continue to be centralised and that slaughterhouses should be of sufficient size to maintain a supervising staff. In addition, the structure of the slaughterhouse should be such that animals are slaughtered and carcases are cooled under the best hygienic conditions.

We do not feel that it is within our remit to say where the post-war slaughterhouses should be situated, but we desire to bring to the County Council's notice this important question so that this problem should be considered at an early date.

Camping Grounds. Throughout the summer months, and especially during the trades holiday periods and at week-ends, large numbers of people camp out in the country, particularly along the shores of the Firth of Forth between Aberdour and Kirkcaldy. In years immediately prior to the war the number and variety of tents and other structures, movable and fixed, in use as summer quarters greatly increased, and it was clear that this form of outdoor life was appealing to an increasing number of people. Complaints arising from lack of proper sanitary arrangements, and from promiscuous scattering of litter and refuse, were numerous, and the noisy and offensive conduct of the campers on occasion the subject of local protests. The situation was frequently worsened through lack of a wholesome water supply.

Camping, if properly controlled, need not detract from the amenity and beauty of the surroundings. In the interest of campers as well as of those who dwell in their neighbourhood the County Council should exercise powers conferred upon them by the Fife Order Confirmation Act, 1940, and frame bye-laws regulating camping.

There are areas of the County which are admirable for camping purposes, but interests of agriculture and of landowners have to be considered. Since, however, it is very advisable that camping should be encouraged as a form of holidaying on account of its health-giving benefits, the County Council should explore these areas with a view to those which are suitable and available being serviced and designated as camping grounds.

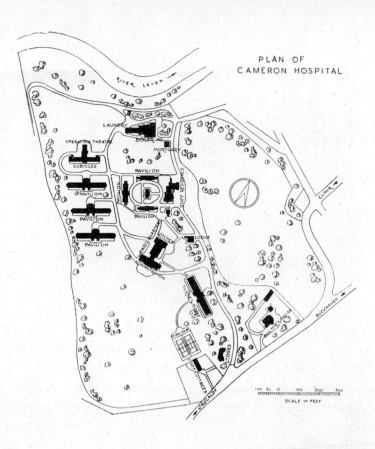

PLAN OF
CAMERON HOSPITAL

Aerial View of Cameron Hospital

POPULATION, ZONING AND HOUSING

Distribution of Population.

THE attached table, based on census returns, will show the changes in population during the last ninety years.

It will be noticed that the population has doubled in the course of the century. As was to be expected, the increase is most marked in the mining areas of Dunfermline, Wemyss and Beath, particularly the latter. There is also marked increase in the case of the Small Burghs. In the East Fife area there is a decline, most marked since the end of the 1914-18 war, associated with the decline in agriculture, but due in part to unsatisfactory housing conditions, increased mechanisation, and the attractions of life in populous communities. The fall in the Kirkcaldy landward area is more apparent than real, and is explained by the fact that Kirkcaldy has on several occasions during the century extended its Burgh boundaries to include certain populous areas in the vicinity.

Anticipated Increase in Population.

A considerable increase in the population of the mining areas is anticipated as the rich coal reserves are developed, but there does not seem to be much prospect of an increase in the rural areas, and the County is thus faced with the prospect of a considerable increase of population, but very unevenly distributed over the County area. We have here a problem that calls for serious consideration. As regards the Small Burghs no marked increase is anticipated. There light industries may be established and there is also the continued drift towards them from rural areas. There may also be for some of them a further extension of their holiday attractions, but on the whole the population of the Small Burghs is not likely to show any great increase.

Zoning.

It is obvious that, owing to underground workings, the prospects of future mining, or the lack of public services, certain land should not be built upon. In addition it will be noticed from the chapter on Agriculture that this County can boast some of the finest and most productive land in Scotland, and therefore this land should not be squandered in haphazard development. A Land Utilisation Map is provided, showing the predominant use of land as it exists at present, and it is the opinion of the Committee that suggested changes in such uses must be dealt with as they arise. After very careful consideration the Committee feels that no absolute zoning proposals are at the moment possible.

To our mind the best method of securing that development will take place on land which is most suited for the particular purpose in view is to prepare " character " zoning plans, so that the best use may be made of the lands of Fife.

Some idea, therefore, will be available not only to inquirers but to the County authorities and public service undertakings, so that it will be possible to concentrate public services at the minimum of cost to the ratepayers.

Owing to the geographical and geological features in the County, the predominating zones have already been defined. The coal industry is situated in the Wemyss area between Kirkcaldy and Buckhaven, the Central Fife area around Cowdenbeath and Lochgelly, and in the Valleyfield-Comrie area to the west. Industry other than mining

DISTRIBUTION OF POPULATION

Changes in the Population of Fife (Excluding Kirkcaldy and Dunfermline)

	1841	1851	1861	1871	1881	1891	1901	1911	1921	1931	Change in 90 years.	
											Nos.	%
Administrative County	140,140	153,546	154,770	160,735	171,931	187,346	218,837	267,733	292,925	276,368	+136,228	+97.20
Small Burghs	27,224	32,012	42,462	48,763	54,343	60,942	69,981	91,506	98,779	94,348	+67,124	+246.56
Landward	125,194	137,820	138,925	136,437	125,695	134,703	155,946	195,832	208,837	197,436	+72,242	+57.70
Wemyss Area	10,283	11,019	11,272	10,281	12,597	16,106	22,878	32,299	34,286	36,281	+25,998	+252.82
Kirkcaldy ,,	26,272	29,133	30,113	32,430	19,975	21,350	20,813	21,920	24,734	23,805	−2,467	−9.39
Lochgelly ,,	3,504	4,964	5,459	6,081	6,689	9,832	14,260	28,705	31,708	29,445	+25,941	+740.32
Beath ,,	973	1,252	2,390	3,534	5,442	8,298	15,812	24,351	24,912	21,523	+20,550	+2,112.02
Dunfermline Area	11,825	25,391	25,116	17,017	15,021	15,559	19,521	24,822	28,031	25,585	+13,760	+116.36
East Fife Area	62,347	66,061	64,575	66,094	65,971	63,558	62,668	63,735	65,166	60,797	−1,550	−2.48

I

is predominant in the Leven Valley and around the larger populated centres of Kirkcaldy and Dunfermline.

The residential areas of the County have naturally been determined by the employment of labour, the larger concentration being therefore in the above areas.

Agriculture is predominant in the east of the County, particularly within the "Golden Fringe." The residential areas of this section of the County are therefore mainly the villages and market towns, although round the south-east coast fishing and holiday resorts predominate.

We are of the opinion that the zoning proposals should bear these existing uses in mind and safeguards therefore be provided for their continuance. In the agricultural zone, however, we think that all other uses of this valuable land should be under the control of the Planning Committee.

We are of the opinion that the preliminary zoning proposals should define in broad outline the following areas:—(1) Agricultural, (2) Industrial and Commercial, (3) Residential, (4) Holiday Area and (5) the larger reservations such as the Lomonds and Tentsmuir.

Re-organisation and Development of Burghs.

As regards housing schemes it would be well if there were some general understanding between the County Council and the Small Burghs. Certain villages adjacent to the Small Burghs might have their housing needs met in the Burghs, and where the County Council has to develop new villages a mutual understanding with the nearest Small Burgh would obviously be an advantage. There are twenty-three Small Burghs in Fife, with populations ranging from 500 to 18,000. It would be worth consideration whether Local Government might not be co-ordinated in areas where there are several highly populated "islands." If such an area were worked as a single urban rural district, questions of water supply, housing, etc. could be treated in common.

The number of separate Local Government Authorities creates difficulty in administration in regard to the provision as well as the letting of houses. In Fife there are 26 separate Housing Authorities all competing with one another for labour and materials and all anxious to provide at the earliest possible date houses which are so much required at the present time. Prospective tenants in their desperation apply to one or two different authorities, and this results in several authorities having the same applicant on their lists. It is worthy of consideration whether a County Housing Association should be constituted comprising representatives from the Large and Small Burghs and from the County Council. It might also include representatives of the Department of Health in respect of the Government's interests, and the Association might be given power to co-opt such others as may be deemed necessary.

A County Housing Association would—

(a) Co-ordinate the demands for housing throughout the County ;

(b) Build or purchase house property throughout the County and control and manage the same ;

(c) Prepare an annual statement showing the financial results of its operations and the share to be contributed by the Exchequer and by local rates.

Size of Communities.

It is difficult to estimate what would be the most desirable size of population in an area partly rural, partly industrial. For industrial communities populations of 50,000 to 70,000 are probably best. Such a population is self-sufficient as regards all local services

KENNOWAY

PERSPECTIVE OF A NEW FIFE TOWN

THIS perspective view shows the lay-out of one of the new residential towns planned by the Fife County Council in order to relieve congestion in the Wemyss area. Construction is already under way and provision is designed for a population of about 10,000.

Note the shopping and business centre, the residential quarters, the schools, the recreation ground, the pleasant lines of trees and the by-pass road.

THE NEW

KENNOWAY

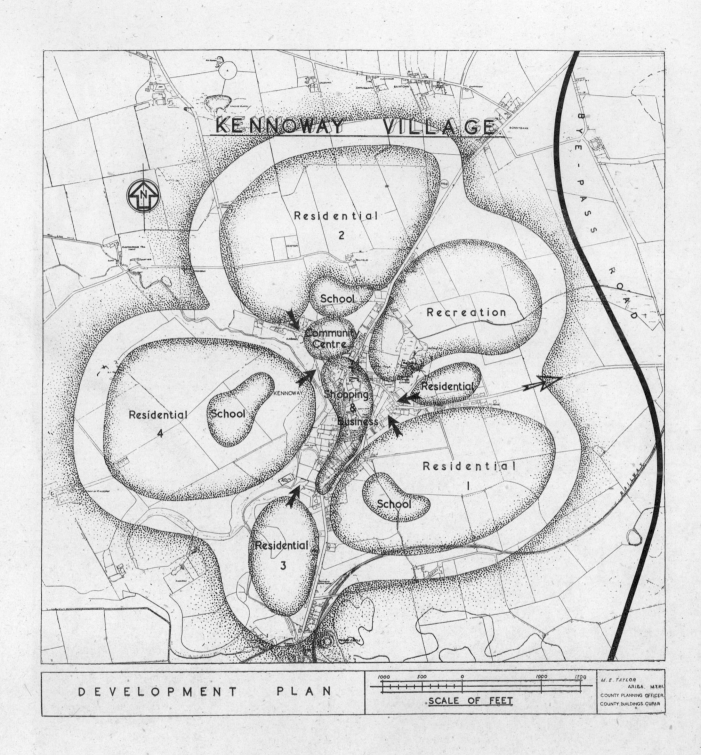

KENNOWAY VILLAGE

BYE - PASS ROAD

Residential 2

School

Recreation

Community Centre

Residential 4

School

KENNOWAY

Shopping & Business

Residential

Residential I

School

Residential 3

DEVELOPMENT PLAN

1000   500   0   1000   1500

SCALE OF FEET

M.E.TAYLOR
ARIBA. M.T.P.I.
COUNTY PLANNING OFFICER
COUNTY BUILDINGS. CUPAR

HOUSING

...gh examples of grouped development and of individual blocks

Three examples of pre-war County Housing Schemes

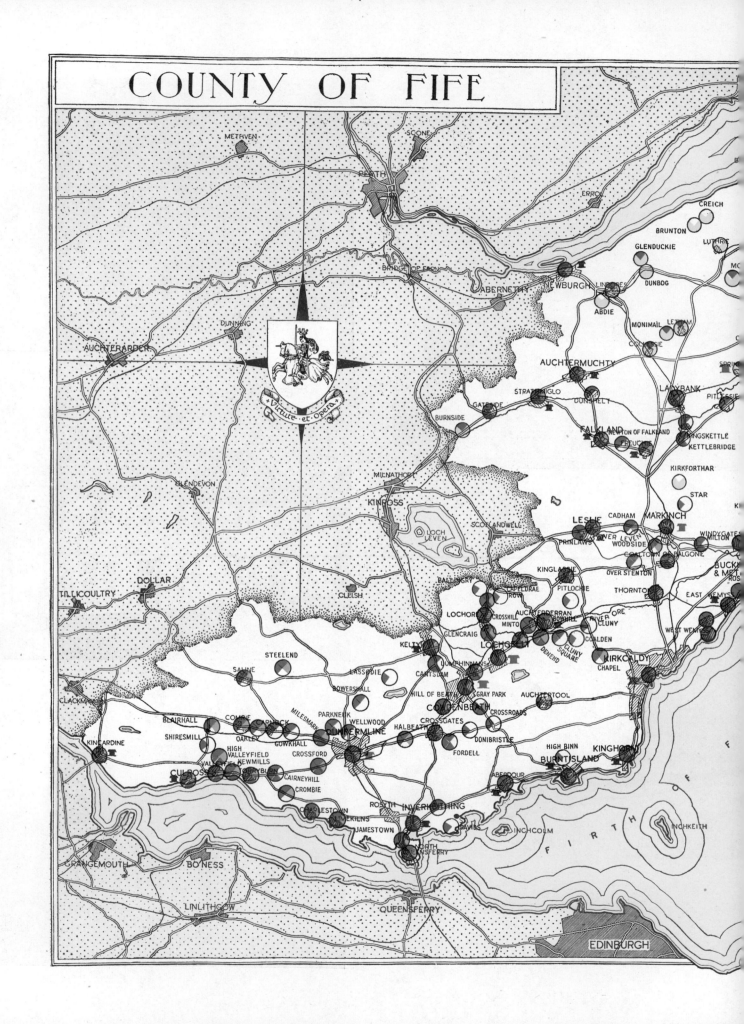

COUNTY OF FIFE

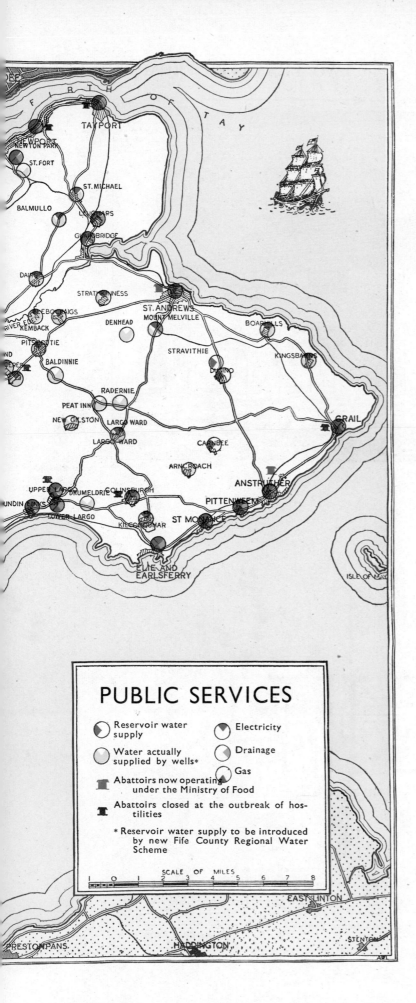

PUBLIC SERVICES

THIS map shows the distribution of public services throughout the County. As far as the western half of Fife is concerned the water supply is generally sufficient, but the position of East Fife is much less satisfactory. In this part of the County there are **23** different water supply undertakings, all of them reserved for the burghs and a few of the larger villages. There is therefore, a pressing need for an extended system of pipe-lines. There are also **43** Special Scavenging Districts in the landward part of the County, and each of the **23** Small Burghs has its own scavenging arrangements. It would obviously be to the advantage of the whole County if a voluntary system of amalgamation were instituted. Under the Fife County Council Order Confirmation Act, **1940**, the local authority received powers to construct a regional water-main which will enable almost all the small villages and hamlets in the rural area of the County, and every Small Burgh willing to participate, to secure a supply amply sufficient for present needs and future development.

Urban Cottage

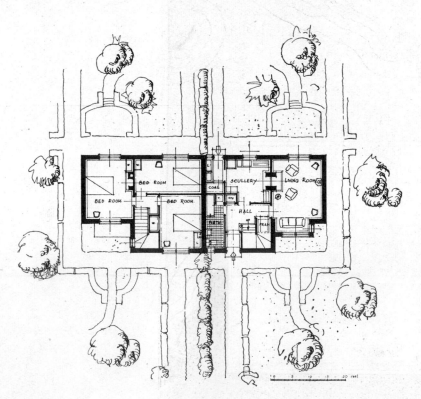

First floor plan   Urban Cottage Design   Ground floor plan

COUNCIL'S HOUSING DESIGNS

Rural Cottage

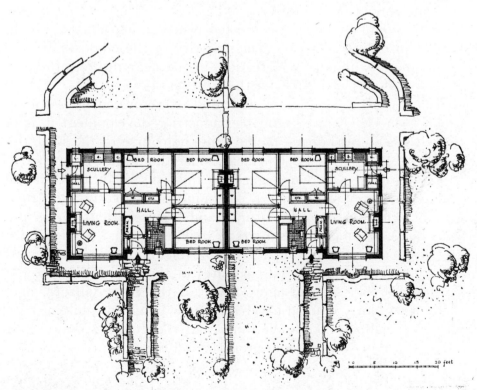

Rural Cottage Design

and is able to maintain communal institutions and places of recreation and amusement; but it is just here that rural areas are at a disadvantage, and for them one of the most urgent needs is the establishment of community centres to which the inhabitants of outlying hamlets and cottages could resort for the stimulation of their social and communal life. Adequate provision of motor transport is also essential.

Many of the Fife villages have pleasing architectural features, and where new housing is to be undertaken such features should be kept in view so as to secure a harmonious and agreeable setting. In this way the people retain a pride in their villages and local interests are encouraged. The County Council's building programme, especially in the mining areas, must continue to provide for the establishment of entirely new communities. This offers a magnificent opportunity for wise planning. These communities are likely to grow so that foresight is called for and a master-plan that will look ahead and provide for each section—houses, shops, schools, etc. as the need grows. The New Towns Act enables the Secretary of State to appoint corporations for the purpose of providing new townships. This novel Act may interfere with the functions of the County Council as Planning Authority and as Housing Authority, and it is hoped that the co-operation between the Secretary of State and the County Council will be a very close one so as to preserve the position of the County Council in carrying out its duties under the Statutes dealing with Town Planning and Housing. We think it is essential in a County such as Fife with so many Small Burghs that there should be the closest co-operation between the County Council and the Small Burghs in the provision of houses. Nor should it be forgotten that neighbouring counties have their planning problems. For example, the development of the coalfields in Clackmannan may compel consideration to be given to Fife County Council providing many more houses in the neighbourhood of the village of Kincardine than are necessary for local needs. Such a project will call for combined planning with a neighbouring authority.

Since 1919 the County Council has erected nearly 4,000 houses, 250 in rural areas and the remainder in industrial areas. The majority of these houses are of three apartments. The Council contemplates the erection, in the near future, of over 5,000 houses and is now in course of preparing sites for the erection of over 2,500. These are required to meet the needs of persons residing in unfit and overcrowded houses and for families residing in sublet rooms. To meet probable industrial development it is likely that at least three times the number will be required in the course of the next thirty years.

The traditional type of Scottish tenement house should not be erected in Fife. Any advantage they offer is greatly outweighed by their disadvantages. Preferable types are terraced houses in populous industrial communities and cottages in rural areas, due regard being paid to the use of agricultural land. More attention should be paid to external design and colouring to ensure that buildings blend aesthetically with their surroundings. The County Council in developing its building programme should keep in view the possibility of acquiring existing sites in the landward area, particularly in communities where derelict sites disfigure many of the rural villages, and these sites might be used by the County Council for erecting new houses or buildings architecturally in keeping with the neighbourhood. We think that the County Council should be given power to acquire, at a fair value, ruinous property and the sites upon which such property

Crail, a Fife holiday resort.

K

exists compulsorily, not only for the purpose of improving amenity, but for securing desirable sites on which new houses might be erected.

More attention also should be paid to the needs of the housewife, the person most concerned with house design. The design should be such that domestic work can be carried out with the least possible wasteful sacrifice on the part of the housewife, that meals can be easily prepared and served, that there is room for rest and refreshing sleep, and that there is room for children to play, room also where they may study in these days of an extended school age. The best size of family house is one of five rooms. While it is agreed that this is the desirable standard to be aimed at, it is essential that in all housing schemes provision should also be made for houses of less accommodation for newly married couples and older people.

The County Council in its house planning should keep in mind the environment by attention to lay-out, planting of trees and shrubs and the provision of open spaces. The householders should be encouraged to keep their gardens in good order. It is worthy of consideration whether the local authorities should not maintain a gardening adviser.

Recon-
struction
of Houses. The County Council has given grants under the " Housing Rural Workers Acts " Scheme towards reconstruction of more than 4,000 houses situated in rural and in industrial areas. There is no doubt of the great benefits under the scheme. A good standard of redesigning has been maintained and provision made for baths, hot-water supplies, washing facilities, good lighting and ventilation, etc. Farmers who have cottages reconditioned on modern lines are able to attract and keep a good type of worker. An excellent example of such renovations, showing also the preservation of typical Scottish architecture, may be seen in the village of Dunshelt. It is to be deplored that the " Housing Rural Workers Act " has been suspended.

Agri-
cultural
Housing. A problem for serious consideration is this. Should the County Council adopt a policy of providing accommodation for rural workers in villages rather than encourage building or reconstruction of houses at the farm itself ? Something might be said on both sides. It is important that the young potential rural workers of the future should be brought up in a rural atmosphere, that stock-men should be near the farm-steading and that shepherds should live near the grazing ground. If the workers' houses are in the village the cost of transport to the farm becomes an important item. There is also the problem of feeding workers at the dinner-hour. A further complication might arise if a farmer had to discharge a worker who occupied a village house. On the other hand, the education of the children would be easier if their homes were in the village. There would also be better opportunities for recreation, amusements and shopping.

The solution would seem to call for a compromise. It will probably always be necessary for certain workers to live on or near the farm, but if the others could be housed in the village this might tend to arrest the rural depopulation. We have here a difficult problem to solve.

AGRICULTURAL HOUSING

The Old, condemned

he New, built to take its place. Durie

Agricultural Cottages built during war years. Craigrothie

ld cottages renovated to meet modern standards. Woodside

Dunshelt

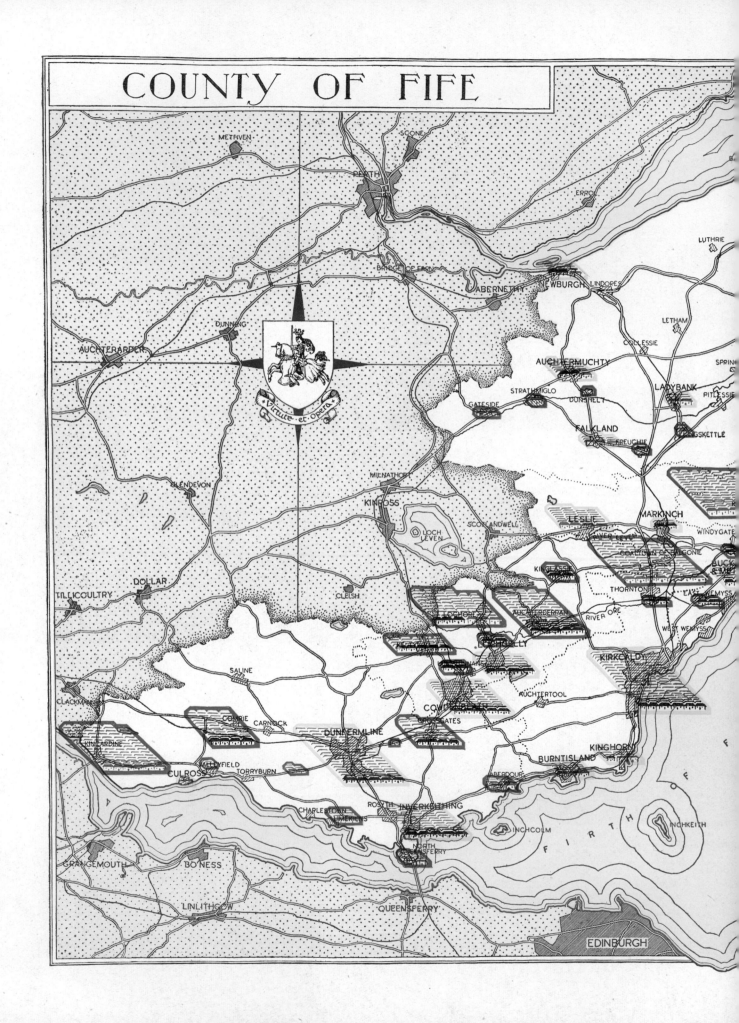

COUNTY OF FIFE

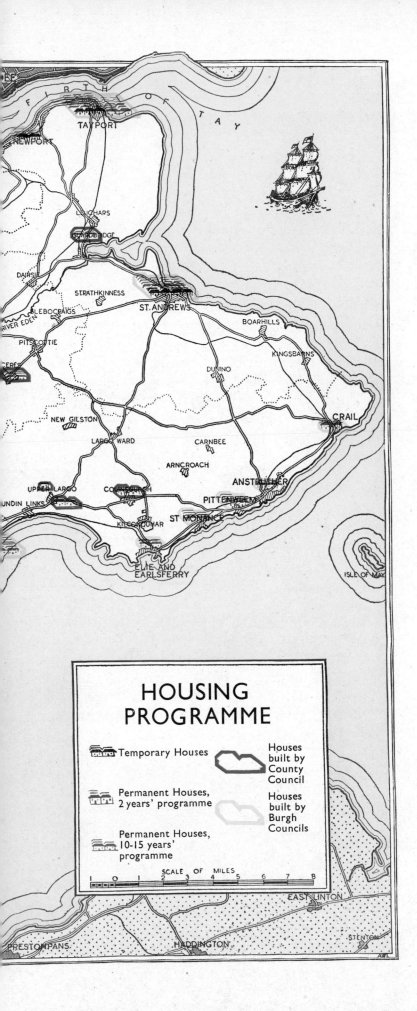

HOUSING PROGRAMME

THE map shows the extensive housing programme to be undertaken within the next fifteen years by the County Council and the Councils of the Large and Small Burghs.

HOUSING PROGRAMME

Temporary Houses

Permanent Houses, 2 years' programme

Permanent Houses, 10-15 years' programme

Houses built by County Council

Houses built by Burgh Councils

SCALE OF MILES
1 0 1 2 3 4 5 6 7 8

EDUCATION

Historical **T**HE educational tradition of Fife is a long and honourable one. To trace its story is to write the whole history of Scottish education. Amongst the very earliest of the written records of our country are the records of its schools. We know that there were schools in St. Andrews as early as A.D. 1120. Schools in Dunfermline are also referred to at about the same date. In both cases the mention is a casual one, offering no information about the founding of such schools : they may even at that early date have been centuries old. In those days St. Andrews and Dunfermline were the focal points of religion and learning. We must never forget the debt we owe to the Church, whether Celtic, Roman or Reformed. Through the long centuries its care for education has been unremitting. Learning and religion in Scotland have always gone hand in hand. To John Knox it seemed self-evident that a Christian should be an educated man. He would then be able to read and interpret for himself, and this Christian duty Knox tried to ensure by means of his system of parish schools, an arrangement that provided Scotland with a system of education well in advance of what was possible in most European countries at the time.

The
Universities The early Universities were also Church foundations. The fact that the first Scottish University was established in Fife bears witness to the important position the County held in national life in those days. Situated in a small provincial town St. Andrews University has preserved a character all its own. Its influence on our educational system has been profound and extends far beyond the limits of the County. Although its future is not directly linked up with the County plans the relations between the County and the University have always been of the friendliest.

Private
Schools Private schools in Scotland are relatively less numerous than in England, but those that we do have in Fife are well known and highly efficient. St. Leonard's School for Girls with its preparatory department St. Katherine's has probably no superior among the girls' schools of Britain, and amongst the boys' private schools, Lathallan, New Park and Craigflower maintain the good tradition. These too are outwith the control of the County Council.

Some
Famous
Names It would take a long time to enumerate the men and women educated in Fife schools who have made for themselves a national reputation. It should suffice to speak of Adam Smith, author of the *Wealth of Nations*, the Adam brothers, famous architects and decorators of the 18th century, James Wilson whose influence is writ large in the American Constitution. It is also worth recalling that at a time when, with political reform in view, it became imperative to raise the whole standard of education among the working population of Britain it was a St. Andrews man, Dr. Andrew Bell, whose Monitorial System, practised in what is now the West Infant School, St Andrews, provided just that impulse that was needed to raise the whole standard of literacy. Dr. Bell's money helped to establish three of our secondary schools besides endowing chairs of education in St

Andrews and Edinburgh, and he was just one of the many whose generous benefactions to education in the County are still bearing fruit to-day.

We have thus an honourable tradition to maintain, and with a view to assessing our present resources and our future needs we set out herewith a statement of the County system in order to show what is being done and what remains to do.

Knox's scheme of a school in every parish formed the basis of the school system until 1918. That it was successful there can be no doubt, as the Scottish dominie was renowned for his devotion to the education of the " lad o' pairts," who was sent to the University, and who so often found a place of honour in later life.

It became obvious that the controlling agency of the schools in the parish, the School Board, could not successfully organise the provision of secondary education for which there was an ever-growing demand. By the Education Act of 1918 *ad hoc* Education Authorities became responsible for the provision of all forms of education within the counties and the large cities.

In 1929, the functions of the Education Authority passed to the County and City Councils, which appointed Education Committees to which practically all matters relating to education were to be deferred. Certain local matters were referred to local committees called School Management Committees, of which there are seven in the County. Parents and teachers find a place on these School Management Committees.

The Education (Scotland) Act, 1945, does not disturb the general outline of the administration of education within the County, the County Council still remaining the Education Authority responsible for all educational administration. Prior to the establishment of the *ad hoc* Education Authority there were 65 School Boards in Fife controlling some 165 schools. Educational provision varied enormously from parish to parish. Some Boards took a pride in the educational standard while others functioned in the main to keep the education rate as low as possible. Premises, in many cases, were bad, and as there were no national scales for teachers, the quality of teacher varied according to the salary rate of the Board—in some cases it was not a far cry from Goldsmith's schoolmaster, " passing rich on £40 a year." It must be remembered, of course, that some Boards had a difficult task in raising finance to meet the increasing standard of education demanded by the Education Department. Secondary education was provided in fee-paying schools in the larger towns and was for those aiming at the professions. The influence of the dominie in the parish school was still a vital factor, but for many children education meant weary drudgery at the three " R's " until the welcome release from school at the age of 14.

The Fife Education Authority started out in 1919 with a broader vision than was possible in any School Board. In general, members standing for election were interested in education, and the experience of men from all parts of the County meeting together had an effect which was beneficial to all concerned. Finance was derived by a special Education rate common throughout the County and collected by the County Council. This system of dual rating was somewhat awkward, and in 1929 by the Local Government Act of that year the County Council became the Education Authority, but it can be said this transfer made no major alteration in the general educational policy throughout the County.

Nursery schools for children between the ages of 2 and 5 years were not part of the mandatory provision of educational facilities which was required for all children between the ages of 5 and 14 years. In the main, such schools were provided in large cities, but the Fife Authority, always keen to make more than the necessary provision, have nursery classes at Anstruther, Kirkcaldy, Buckhaven, Lumphinnans, Kelty, Leslie, and finance to a considerable extent a nursery school under voluntary auspices at Methil. Plans have been drawn up for classes in several other areas such as Cowdenbeath, Glencraig and Kirkcaldy.

In nursery schools the young children are trained in good physical and social habits, their diet is planned and a period for sleep is an essential part of the day's programme. Singing, games, exercise outdoors and indoors with special apparatus, and sense training form the major subjects of what can hardly be called the curriculum.

An essential part of the nursery school organisation is the Parents' Association. The parents have regular meetings and are given talks by the doctor, the psychologist and others on the development of the child's life. Under the New Education Act of 1945 the Authority will be required to make provision for nursery schools wherever there is a demand. Experience has shown that the demand invariably grows whenever a class is started in any area.

Primary education may be considered in two stages—the Infant Department for children 5 to 7 years of age and the Primary Department for children 7 to 12 years of age.

In the County there are 143 Primary Departments with 30,861 children in attendance. There has been in past years a gradual decrease in the school population in rural areas, and this has resulted not only in schools with considerable vacant accommodation but also in a certain number of schools being closed altogether. It is only with considerable reluctance that the Education Authority close any school in a rural area, as it is realised that many farm workers will not take up employment in an area where there is no school in the immediate neighbourhood. It is, however, both from an economic and educational point of view, a bad thing to have a handful of children in a small school.

Perhaps the greatest educational development since 1919 has been in the methods used in the Infant Department. Here it has been clearly realised that there are considerable individual differences among children, and while some may be able to quickly understand reading and arithmetic, the normal child approaches these subjects with some difficulty. Individual methods have completely changed the attitude and method of approach. Number is approached by the use of concrete materials, reading in a way which does not depend purely on phonetics, and the classrooms present a bright appearance, with children at small individual tables and chairs busily occupying themselves with problems at their own mental level and not worrying unduly as to how their neighbours are progressing.

In the Primary Department the foundations of higher education are laid. Methods here, however, have been altered due to advances in modern psychology, and an attempt is made to allow each child to develop at his own rate. When the child reaches the age of 12 years, there is a scheme whereby all possible means are taken to find out the secondary course for which the child is most suited. Not all pupils can benefit by an

SCHOOL BUILDINGS

—as they could be

As they are—

Temporary Huts 1919—still in use

EMERGENCY ACCOMMODATION

Prefabricated Hut, 1946

L

academic education provided in the High Schools, and the secondary courses are devised to cope with those pupils who will become normal citizens and who play an important part in the life of the community.

Secondary
Schools
These provide for the education of children beyond the age of 12 years. As has already been indicated, in the old parish school there was no special provision for an advanced education unless that of the academic type. In 1919, however, centres were set up throughout the County to provide a secondary education for all pupils beyond the age of 12 years. This meant centralising pupils in certain areas, a policy which withdrew rural children from primary schools. This policy has been questioned in many areas because the children of 12 years of age must travel some distance to the centralised secondary department. On the other hand the Authority have no doubt that the benefits of the secondary education outweigh the disadvantages.

(a) *Junior Secondary Schools.*

There are 49 such departments in the County. These provide three-year courses along practical lines. There is a wide variety of courses which, in the main, suit the area in which the school is situated. In the rural areas, for example, the course has a rural bias, whereas in the larger urban areas the course has a technical bias. The courses provide also a curriculum for all types of pupil from the dullest to the most highly endowed.

(b) *Senior Secondary School.*

There are eight senior secondary schools in the County—Dunfermline High School, Beath High School, Kirkcaldy High School, Buckhaven High School, Waid Academy (Anstruther), Madras College (St. Andrews), Bell-Baxter School (Cupar). The latter three schools were at one time under a Board of Governors but, owing to rise in costs, it was decided that they should become part of the County organisation. There is a central secondary school for Roman Catholic pupils at Cowdenbeath which acts as the secondary school for all Roman Catholic children in the County. These schools provide an academic education leading to the Leaving Certificate, and are intended, in the main, for pupils who tend to take up a professional career. In recent years, however, there has been a broadening of the Leaving Certificate curriculum, and subjects such as music, domestic science and art find a place. In some instances also courses are provided which give a training in technical subjects such as engineering, nursing, commerce and agriculture.

Classes for
Dull and
Backward
Children
In every community there is a proportion of children who are much less endowed than the normal child. Obviously these children cannot reach the same level of attainment and special courses must be arranged for them. For the very backward child who is mentally defective, special classes have been set up. There are schools of this nature in Dunfermline, Lochgelly, Cowdenbeath, Cupar and Buckhaven. In these schools children are given materials within their mental compass. There is no attempt to make them attain a high academic standard, but the objective is to make them fit to take their place in the life of the community. Such children by law must remain at school until they are 16 years of age. For the child who is not mentally defective but is very poorly endowed there have been set up in the County special classes in the normal schools so that an attempt can be made to make these children reach the maximum level of attainment corresponding to their mental ability. Such children at one time sat in the normal

class-room and sometimes became the butt of their fellows. To-day they are in classes with specially trained teachers who use all modern devices to make these children attain an added measure of self-respect.

In accordance with the Education (Scotland) Act, 1945, the local authority must Planning Ahead provide facilities for education from the nursery class stage to secondary courses leading to the University. Although the County Council is in no way responsible for University education, nevertheless it must assist financially pupils who have the ability to attend the University. Thus in many respects the system outlined by John Knox in his *First Book of Discipline* is being achieved.

The Planning Committee can materially assist the Education Committee in further- ing its plans. No longer should it be possible for a community to grow up and after- wards come to a decision that a school is necessary, resulting in a building being erected at a place unsuitable for a great number of the children of the community. In the future, the community should be planned as a whole and educational facilities should be considered along with housing.

This is particularly important in respect of nursery classes. Up to the present, nursery school facilities have been made available in schools where there is vacant accom- modation. Naturally in such places the school is not ideally situated for such young children, as the very fact that there is vacant accommodation in a particular school means that there is a dwindling population in the neighbourhood. Future housing sites should be planned so that it will be possible to erect nursery schools in a position ideal from the point of view of the children and ideal from the point of view of the school. Thus young children will be given an opportunity of growing up in a bright atmosphere and in pleasant surroundings.

The same general principle should apply to primary and secondary schools. In recent years there has been an alarming incidence of serious road accidents. It is almost impos- sible to train very young children to keep off the roads. As the majority of the primary schools are built on the main roads, freedom from accidents is exceedingly difficult to achieve. In the future, primary schools should be built on sites clear of main roads. and it is hoped that in this way one of the dreaded dangers of the modern community will be avoided.

As regards secondary schools, the main difficulty in the past has been that playing fields have been few in number. The future secondary school should be built in its own playing field so that facilities for sport, which plays such an important part in the school of to-day, will be readily accessible.

Again, it is important that the schools should fit in to the development of the community in which they are placed. For example, the Education Committee has decided to erect a new primary school in St. Andrews, and it would be a tragedy if the school were not worthy of the famous historical and educational background of St. Andrews.

Education in the past has been concerned, particularly in Scotland, with academic learning. New housing is in view, and attention must be paid to the social and physical recreation of the community. In the provision of playing fields and community centres the Planning Committee could play an important part. It is necessary, for example,

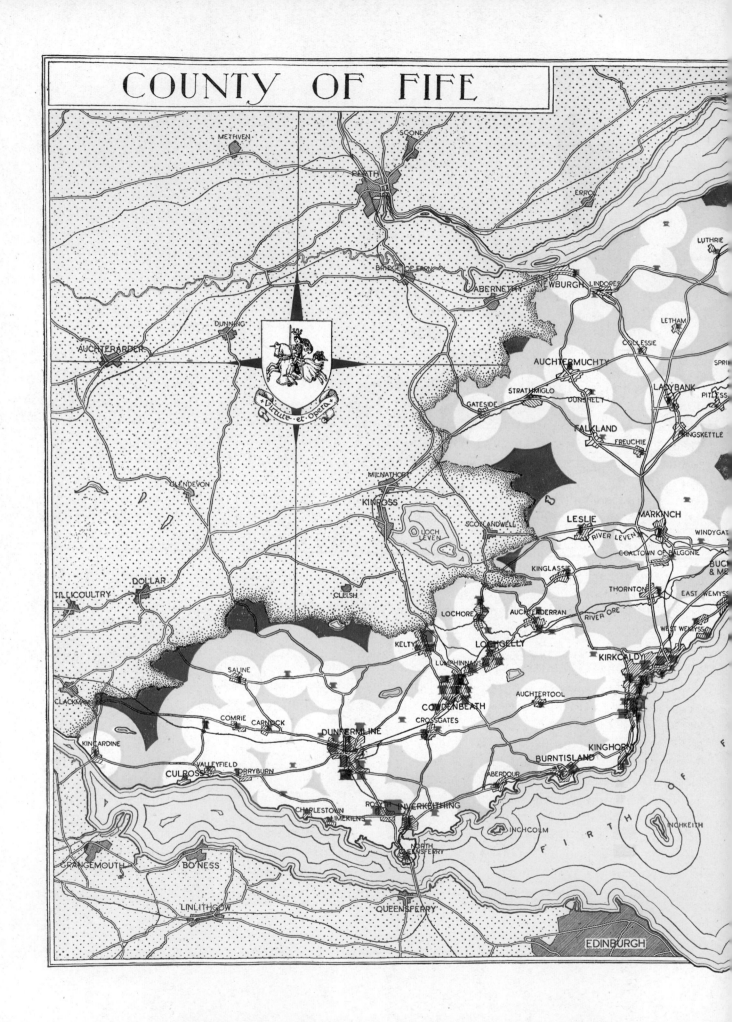

COUNTY OF FIFE

Virtute et Opera

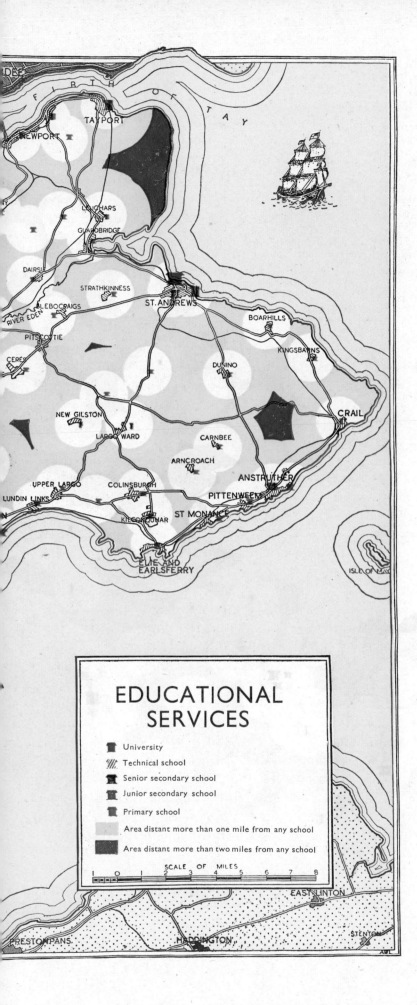

EDUCATIONAL SERVICES

IN the *First Book of Discipline*, John Knox outlined a scheme of education, from Primary School to University, for all children who had the necessary ability. To-day the County Council, as Education Authority, provides education from the Nursery School to the University.

The Nursery School educates children between the ages of two and five years, the Primary School thereafter carrying on instruction to the age of twelve. From the Primary School the child proceeds to the Secondary School, of which there are two types—the Junior Secondary School providing three years' courses (technical, commercial and rural), and the Senior Secondary School offering courses of five or six years' duration in preparation for the University and the higher ranks of industry and commerce. In addition, the County has four Technical Schools providing technical education for those beyond the legal age.

This provision is outlined pictorially in the above map.

that in any community there should not be overlapping. Various bodies may come forward wishing to erect village halls, and the Planning Committee provides a very useful service by co-ordinating the efforts of the various interested parties.

Technical
Education
In Scotland there has always been a certain measure of technical education, but it is hardly adequate now in the light of the striking advance in industry and industrial research that has characterised the last two or three decades. If we are to keep our place in the world of commerce and industry our schools and colleges must be second to none in their output of finely trained technicians and craftsmen.

Technical Schools.

Fife is particularly fortunate in the provision of technical schools. Three large technical schools were built in Kirkcaldy, Buckhaven and Cowdenbeath. These schools are equipped with very fine machinery and give a splendid opportunity for the most modern courses in technology.

At Dunfermline there is a technical school of a different nature. This is Lauder Technical School, specially equipped to meet the demands of the weaving industry which forms a large part of the industrial activities in the County. This school was provided through the good offices of Mr. George Lauder, thanks to a generous grant from Andrew Carnegie. Its very fine looms were the gift of the linen firms of Dunfermline.

The courses in these schools are of two types :—

(1) *Evening Courses.*

Here lads who are working during the day come in the evening and take courses leading to the National Certificate or the City and Guilds Certificate, courses which are provided only in the central institutions in other education areas. These Evening Courses have been termed '' The Artisans' University.''

In addition to the Evening Courses, several firms have been far-sighted and have released their apprentices during the day for special courses. At Fife Mining School also, day courses are run to meet the needs of those miners who are on the various shifts. The most recent developments are what have been termed Pre-Apprenticeship Courses. There are two for the engineering industry—one at Kirkcaldy, the other at Cowdenbeath ; and two for the building industry—one at Kirkcaldy and the other at Dunfermline. To these courses come specially selected boys who have had a complete three years' course at school and they receive training in the various branches of the respective industries. The authority actually pays these lads 12/- a day and provides their travelling expenses and a midday meal. This development is taking place in a great many industries. The mining industry in particular in the County has had a progressive outlook on this question, and the Fife authority has been running day classes to train the young miner prior to his going underground. With the new training order for the mining industries the authority will be responsible for the training of all lads who enter the mining industry, giving them a practical and theoretical training prior to their being taken on full-time in the respective coal-fields.

(2) *Evening Classes* are held in the various secondary schools according to the demand.

In Bell-Baxter School, Cupar, there has been running now for several years

TECHNICAL EDUCATION

A realistic approach in Technical Education

Engineering—
    Kirkcaldy Technical School

Weaving—
    Lauder Technical School, Dunfermline

a very successful Agricultural Course. Here the young farm workers come in the evening and receive an extensive training in the latest developments in agriculture.

Commercial Courses are extremely popular, and in the majority of large centres there is a relatively high attendance of students being trained in typewriting, book-keeping and other commercial subjects.

Adult Education Fife Education Authority has worked in connection with St. Andrews Regional Committee, the University and the Workers' Educational Association in providing courses of lectures on such subjects as Citizenship, Current Affairs, Economics, Psychology. The Committee has also been willing to pay part of the expense of students attending Adult Education Summer Schools. Under the new Education Act the Education Authority will still be responsible for the provision of adult education, and it is in this field that a considerable development must be made, as the approach in the past has been too academic. If there is to be further development, new methods will have to be studied and new procedures adopted.

During the war the Army Council did much to encourage adult education. Under regulations it was laid down that each unit should meet once a week for a talk and discussion on current affairs, and once a week for a talk and discussion on the problems of citizenship. This arrangement, followed at first with a certain amount of hesitation and even suspicion, tended latterly to become popular. It created an undoubted interest in the minds of many men and women in the services, an interest that is likely to bear fruit in civil life. The local Regional Committee of the University gave every assistance to the Service authorities, and now the Carnegie Trust has launched a scheme to still further encourage the movement. The Education Authority is thus presented with an excellent opportunity to develop this highly important aspect of education.

Education for Leisure and Recreation That the community has an obligation to provide for the social and recreational aspects of education is now generally accepted. Until recently the leisure time and recreational needs of youth were catered for almost entirely by voluntary bodies, whose provision varied greatly from one area to another. During the interwar years various features of our social life—the problem of juvenile delinquency, mass unemployment, disintegration of family life, the totalitarian challenge to democracy, the unhealthy mechanised amusements provided by our urbanised civilisation—made it obvious that much greater effort was essential to provide facilities for leisure and recreation and to educate youth to make better use of leisure time. One result was the development of the Youth Service.

In Fife the Youth Service expanded rapidly during the war years, working in close co-operation with various voluntary bodies. There are now in the County twenty full-time paid Youth leaders, who are responsible in all for 57 Clubs controlled by the authority or by non-statutory bodies, as follows :—

	Clubs	Leaders
1. Non-statutory bodies	9	7
2. Miners' Welfare Clubs	24	3
3. Appointed by authority	24	10

In running the clubs the full-time paid leaders co-operate with and supervise the work of the voluntary leaders. One of the clubs, the Kirkcaldy Y.W.C.A., approximates to a full community centre, and requires the services of three leaders in addition to thirty voluntary workers. The individual Miners' Welfare Clubs have voluntary leaders, while the work is co-ordinated by the supervisors. The following figures indicate the number of adolescents who are members of a club or youth organisation :—

Organisation	Age Group			Totals
	14-16	16-18	18+	
Clubs and non-uniformed	2150	1988	1382	5520
Uniformed	1153	462	200	1815
Pre-Service	1123	1371	453	2946
Totals	4426	3821	2035	10281

These figures show that approximately 55 per cent of the population in these age groups are associated with a youth organisation. Recently there has been a rapid falling-off in membership of pre-Service organisations, but a welcome increase in membership of clubs.

These clubs seek to provide education for leisure through a series of cultural, recreational and group activities which promote individual and social development in the fullest sense. In many of the clubs indirect education is given in a variety of subjects, often by way of projects such as Home Making Competitions.

The Scottish Education Act now lays on Education Authorities the obligation to provide " adequate facilities for recreation and social and physical training." In developing an organisation to carry out these duties the Education Authority " shall have regard to the expediency of co-operating with any voluntary societies or bodies whose objects include the provision of facilities for the organisation of activities of a similar character." These provisions make it plain that in the future education for leisure and recreation will become more closely linked with the general system of education. In carrying out its new powers and duties under the Act the Education Authority should exercise a co-ordinating and guiding influence over all the agencies and groups who are already engaged in the work of social and recreational education. A main feature of a democratic community is the variety of its groups, and in educating the community towards a wiser use of leisure and more cultural form of recreation there should be as many growing points as possible, provided growth is wisely directed.

According to the 1919 Education Act the school-leaving age in Scotland was to be raised to 15 on a date to be fixed by the Secretary of State. This date was ultimately fixed as 1st September, 1939, but owing to the outbreak of war the whole arrangements were deferred, and according to the new Act the age will be raised on 1st April 1947. The majority of children leave school at the age of 14 before secondary education has had an opportunity of developing their talents and creating good social habits. The manner in which the young people use their leisure time to-day is a clear indictment of the policy of sending children out from school before their education has been completed. Sir Richard Livingstone has declared that " to cease education at 14 is as unnatural as to die at 14—the one is physical death and the other is spiritual death." With this additional year it is hoped that all pupils will receive a three-years' course with a curriculum suited to their ability and with a bias towards the work of the community in which they are living.

Owing to difficult conditions existing as the result of the recent conflict, the additional accommodation for the purpose of the extension of the school-leaving age will be provided by temporary prefabricated huts. The importance of housing makes it clear that new school buildings cannot be erected until a later date, but it is hoped that the temporary accommodation provided at the end of the 1914 war and still standing in several school playgrounds will provide a warning that such accommodation must in no circumstances be allowed to become permanent.

The schools of the future must be well-planned. In some of the schools now being used there is a lack of playground space, classrooms are small, badly shaped sometimes and with steep galleries, lighting is poor and there is little or no deafening in the walls. One of the greatest drawbacks to efficient education is the provision of classrooms separated from each other by glass partitions, the only entry being through other rooms. It is hoped that the new schools will be situated on sites wherever possible adjoining a playing field, with halls where the school can meet as a unit for religious services and other social purposes, the furniture specially designed and the actual rooms decorated by carefully chosen and attractive schemes.

In the Authority's new plans provision has been made for the erection as soon as materials are available of two new senior secondary schools, one at Buckhaven and one at Kirkcaldy, junior secondary schools at Dunfermline and Cupar and a new primary school at St. Andrews. Although the Government's policy has been to put housing in the forefront of the reconstruction programme it must be recognised that as there is a compulsory education system, schools are the complement of houses and, therefore, where new housing schemes are being erected the Planning Authority must not only see that site provision for schools is made, but must also press for the erection of schools to meet the immediate need of the community.

The Education Authority must ensure that adequate playing facilities are provided for the school children. In the past this aspect of education has been neglected except in some instances for secondary school pupils, but it is hoped that in future, wherever possible, adequate playing fields will be adjacent to all secondary schools. Primary schools will also be catered for, and the youth who have left school will have continued opportunity of playing games.

School Meals

The School Meals Service was born during the war years, when it was essential that the last to suffer from the general want should be the children. On the other hand, the provision of a midday meal at school for many children was not merely a war-time necessity, and it has become clear that these meals are to be a feature of our post-war educational system. To quote a recent circular from the Scottish Education Department : " It should be recognised that the School Meals Service is part of the permanent educational provision." The average number of meals in the schools in the County at present is approximately 10,000, these meals being supplied at approximately 85 schools. Plans are at present in preparation for the provision of meals to be supplied at all schools in the County.

It is anticipated that 75% of the school population will dine in schools when free meals are provided under the Government Family Allowances Scheme. Preparations are, therefore, being made to have accommodation ready for that number in as many schools as possible. In the main, accommodation for dining must be governed by existing school accommodation, but it is hoped that every school of the future will have its own dining-hall and kitchen attached, where the pupils will sit down with members of the school staff and take a meal in ideal conditions. In this way the school meal will become part of the general educational system and will be used to inculcate good social habits.

Another development envisaged by the Education Authority is the provision of a scheme whereby pupils will receive guidance as to the type of job for which they are best suited. If the child has been under the Authority's jurisdiction from the age of 5 till the age of 15 by the time he is ready to leave school there must be a record indicating the child's ability, attainment and interests, and with modern psychological tests it will be possible to indicate the type of work in which the pupil is most likely to find success. In recent years several boys were extremely disappointed at not being able to complete their course leading to the Pilot's Certificate merely because it was later discovered that they were partially colour-blind. There seems no reason why such facts should not be found out prior to their leaving school. With this purpose in view a Fife Careers Advisory Council has been established in order to provide expert guidance for boys and girls in secondary schools as regards the jobs for which their education and ability have rendered them suited. The aims of the Careers Council are :— Careers Council

1. To ensure that advice as to their future careers is made available for boys and girls in secondary schools and to supply information regarding suitable positions.
2. To make contact with employers, professional bodies and the Ministry of Labour in order to ascertain the scope and prospects of employment and to make known to industry and the professional bodies the extent to which the Council can assist in filling vacancies on their staffs.
3. To compile and keep up to date, for the benefit of teachers, parents and pupils, an accurate register of information regarding suitable careers (conditions, prospects, modes of entry, methods of training, etc.).
4. To take such action as may further the aims and objects of the Council.

The Careers Council operates through seven Social Advisory Committees, one for each School Management Area, the local committee being charged with the responsibility of keeping in touch with the parents and of ensuring that the pupils enjoy the necessary vocational guidance.

HEALTH OF THE CHILD

The School Medical Service, since its introduction nearly forty years ago, has done much good work. No one who can recall the conditions prevailing in our schools before the passing of the Education Act of 1908 can fail to be impressed by the striking improvement in the health and physique of the school children of to-day. Under the new Education Act, the Education Authority will be responsible not only for the inspection of the children but must also guarantee that each child receives the necessary treatment. The School Medical Service will still remain part of the County Medical Service and will fit in to the State Medical Service which has been envisaged by the Government. This should result in children, while at school, being physically fit, for obviously where there is any physical defect or weakness the child cannot benefit by the educational provision, no matter how good. An extension of the dental service is also very desirable. The condition of the children's teeth in our schools is far from satisfactory and would seem to indicate that the number of dentists available is far below the needs of the community. Regular inspection and treatment every six months would seem to be the standard required, a standard which has already been reached in certain other countries. It would entail a considerable addition to the County Medical Service but in the interests of the health and education of the children it is a reform worth pressing.

The new Education Act lays down that an education system must be adapted to the age, ability and aptitude of the child. This is no new outlook ; it has been a determining factor in the whole educational system in the County, and any future development will be an extension and development of the existing system.

The war which has just ended has been fought for the cause of freedom, freedom to think for oneself and express one's thoughts no matter what they are. In a democratic community the citizens have to be more than individuals who put a cross on a ballot paper at local or national elections. They must be capable of giving independent judgment on important problems and see the community take a form and character shaped by their own wills. This can only be achieved by a sound system of education, for " upon the education of the people the fate of this country depends."

We consider it is imperative that the Education Authority should give very early attention to the remedying of insanitary conditions existing in certain schools in the County.

AMENITIES

IT must not be forgotten that under the Planning Acts the Council is responsible for preserving the amenities of the County and that it has statutory powers with this in view. Fife has a beauty and seemliness of its own, and the careful preservation of its attractions should be the concern of all its citizens. Unfortunately its natural beauty has often been marred. The rapid extension of industrial life may account for this, but, when we consider the fine heritage of building design and the graceful groups and lines of trees bequeathed to us from the 18th and early 19th centuries, it is difficult to resist the feeling that there has been a progressive decline in public taste since those days. Mansions and country houses erected then have an artistic appropriateness and a harmonious relation to their surroundings that we seem to miss in modern buildings, and those sturdy stone farm steadings, still extant, seem to grow out of the environment in a natural and pleasing way, even although they may no longer be entirely convenient for modern conditions. These are inheritances from a time when Scottish architecture was at its best : they should still serve for an inspiration.

Design in Buildings

To-day, in common with other industrial areas, we have too many ugly and aggressive buildings, entirely out of harmony with their environment, too many untidy and sprawling factories, too many villages, once attractive, but now disfigured by buildings inartistically planned. New buildings should show evidence of discrimination as regards design, colouring and choice of building material, and something should be done to get rid of those unseemly poster advertisements, most of them unnecessary.

Ribbon and Grouped Development

Towns and villages, up to the end of the 19th century, developed in a natural way, their growth being governed chiefly by transport facilities and public utility services. With the advent of motor transport ribbon development began along our main traffic arteries, such roads being already serviced with water, sewerage, gas and electricity mains. The result was a sprawl and intermingling of communications such as we find in central Fife, where, for example, a ribbon of houses connects Cowdenbeath with Lumphinnans and Lochgelly. A similar ribbon has formed along the road to the north through Glencraig, Crosshill and Lochore. Against the misuses of this kind of development a planned development must be introduced, based legally on the Planning Acts and on the Act for the Prevention of Ribbon Development. The natural propensity to build houses wherever an owner or a local authority thinks fit must be controlled by zoning and grouping in well-defined communities. It would greatly facilitate the work of the Planning Committee if owners of property, when preparing plans for new buildings and extensions, would consult the Committee. Without such friendly co-operation the Council cannot effectively discharge its obligations under the Planning Acts.

Our planning proposals are based generally on developments which may reasonably be expected in the course of the next fifty to sixty years. Admitting that the future cannot be foreseen with any accuracy over such a period or beyond it, we nevertheless think that tentative zoning proposals of a flexible nature should be drawn up for the whole County so that future developments may proceed on systematic lines.

Design of
Industrial
Premises

Factories, mines and other industrial premises are often sprawling and unattractive in design. There is surely now no justification for this, and, fortunately, we have some examples of the right kind of lay-out. A good example, for instance, is the new Comrie Pit. Another is represented by the pithead baths erected by the Miners' Welfare Committee. These buildings, as well as being pleasing to the eye, give an observer a feeling of efficiency. A pleasing architectural design in a factory is probably a better advertising agent than street placards of the goods produced.

Left over from the era of industrial expansion certain obsolete factories, of unpleasing design, are still in active use because they were solidly built and seem too good to be condemned. Keeping in view the rapid changes in industrial technique, there is no reason why a factory, because it is built of temporary material, should not be well designed.

We suggest that the Planning Committee give very careful consideration to the design of all plans submitted to them as interim development authority for industrial premises. The matter should be discussed with the firm concerned, particularly if the design appears to be out of keeping with the surroundings. We also urge that industrialists, when preparing plans for new buildings, should employ trained and qualified architects to work in collaboration with their engineers.

Bings and
Open-Cast
Coal
Workings

" God made the country and man made the towns." Man also made the colliery refuse heaps (bings), and while the country is clothed with mountain and forest, man has left the colliery bings naked and unashamed. Seldom, indeed, has any attempt been made to deal with these unsightly desecrations. As explained in the section on Mines and Minerals the County of Fife is to have several new pits. What about the new bings, and what is to be done with the existing bings? We understand that research has been undertaken in order to find a suitable means for their disposal, but so far without any marked success.

We advise that the Planning Committee approach the Ministry of Fuel and Power with a view to the encouragement of further research on this problem in consultation with the University authorities if need be. We feel that the question of disposal is an urgent one, whether the solution is to be found by dumping the material in the sea, using it for reclamation schemes, or stowing it underground. If any hardy plants can be induced to grow on these unsightly heaps, the conical shape of the bing might first be reduced to a more natural contour.

The open-cast coal workings, which ruin good agricultural land, are a result of war-time necessity. It will be generally agreed that they should be discontinued. All possible measures should be taken to see that the authorities concerned restore the sites of these workings to their previous condition.

Household
Refuse

Local communities often show lack of foresight by thoughtless dumping of household and other refuse in unsuitable places. The natural beauty of the countryside is often marred in this way. Such dumps are not only blots on the landscape : they constitute a danger to public health as well. Fortunately we have, in the case of some communities, examples of good sense and judgment. Tayport Burgh, for example, by " controlled tipping," has converted a derelict piece of the foreshore into a pleasant recreation park,

COAL AND AMENITIES

These two contrasting illustrations—the old and the new—show that there is no need for colliery workings to desecrate the landscape

Comrie New Colliery, Fife

A Fife pit as it once was, now very much improved.

Photo—Valentine, Dundee

Wellesley Pithead Baths— Miners' Welfare Commission

Architects: Messrs. J. A. Dempster and D. Jack

We recommend the use of this controlled tipping system. It is practised on a large scale, and with excellent effect, in the city of Bradford. We suggest also that, before any local authority choose a new site for a refuse dump, it consult the Planning Committee in order to discuss how far the site may ultimately be made available for playing fields or other recreational purposes. We also urge that consideration be given, where it is economically possible, to the introduction of modern plant for refuse disposal.

Railway Stations Railway stations are not always things of beauty. For the most part they are purely utilitarian structures, erected at spots conveniently situated for traffic; but their fences and walls are frequently plastered over with unsightly advertisements. Some station buildings, originally in rural surroundings, are now, on account of the spread of population, surrounded by built-up streets, and are out of keeping architecturally with their surroundings.

New station buildings should be constructed on a design appropriate as regards style and material, and the Planning Authority should be consulted beforehand. A uniform plan for railway buildings is, of course, neither necessary nor desirable.

As regards existing station buildings we think that the Company should be asked to suppress advertisements on buildings and fences which are visible from outside the station, and also that the Planning Committee should prepare reconstruction plans for the approaches to certain of the stations. Unfortunately the Advertisement Act does not apply to railway companies.

Ferries Ferries over the Tay and the Forth play an important role in the road traffic of Fife. Their importance may cease when the two road bridges are constructed, but in the meantime, and probably for a number of years to come, these ferries will be the entrance gates to the County. We think, therefore, that their surroundings should form an ensemble worthy of the County of Fife.

Both Ferryheads, in Newport and in Queensferry, present to-day an unattractive aspect, and we are of opinion that comprehensive plans should be drafted for their reconstruction. The question of appropriate road communications would have to be considered so as to enable a speedy clearance of vehicular traffic. For the convenience and comfort of passengers transferring to the 'buses, 'bus stations should be provided. The sites of the Ferryheads, when their present function ceases, might be acquired and laid out as attractive open spaces.

Overhead Wires If oil lamps in the rural areas are to be replaced by cheap electric power some disfiguration of the countryside by transmission lines is inevitable. As it would probably entail a considerable addition to the cost we can hardly ask that these lines be put underground, but, if they must be installed above-ground, careful consideration should be given to their siting. A ridge line is not the most desirable site for those high pylons. Here a question of amenity arises, and it is to be hoped that consideration of scenic beauty will not be sacrificed for mere convenience.

We hope therefore that, before any new line is laid across the countryside, the plan will be submitted to the Planning Committee, who should study it carefully from the amenity standpoint before approving. The transmission poles should be of pleasing design, but where possible underground cables are much to be preferred. The siting and design of transformer stations should also, we feel, be given more consideration, particularly in rural areas.

Coal Bings

This is a typical illustration of a colliery spoil heap. Are they to remain for all time naked? Are the new pits likewise to have these monuments?

Photo—Caithness

Kinglassie Coal Bing, Fife

Open Cast Coal Workings

These illustrations from Fife show what a war-time necessity has brought about. Is this upheaval of a peaceful country-side to remain, or will an enlightened peace ensure a full and proper return of the land to agriculture?

Photo—Caithness

Open Cast Coal Workings, Bogside, Fife

Photo—Caithness

Open Cast Coal Workings, Bogside, Fife

On approaching St. Andrews from Cupar one has a picturesque view of the town rising above the famous golf-course. Unfortunately, as one comes round a bend the view is ruined by a large hoarding. This, alas, is not an isolated case : many of our country roads are disfigured in a similar way by glaring advertisements. It is much to be regretted that in this way certain of the approaches to our beauty-spots should be ruined. In the opinion of the Planning Advisory Committee no advertisements should be allowed close to the margins of the roads. Where in the past these advertisement hoardings have played the part of traffic direction lights, warnings adaptable to day or night use should be erected by the Highway Authority.

We feel that the right place for advertisements is the daily and weekly newspaper, and we therefore suggest that the County Council, under its Bye-laws and the Town and Country Planning Acts, take every step to have its advertisement regulations strengthened.

As motor traffic increases the number of petrol-filling stations and garages is bound to increase also. Too many of the existing buildings are either untidy adaptations of buildings originally meant for a different purpose, or, where they have been specially erected, of poor design in themselves and out of harmony with their surroundings. There is scope for considerable variation in the design of filling stations, and the Committee has in mind successful attempts made by the Socony Company (Standard Oil Company of New York) in providing a variety of picturesque and effective designs, the erection of these buildings having already introduced a great improvement into the appearance of the highways of New England.

While appreciating that filling stations are necessary, we would urge the Committee, through their interim development powers and the powers conferred by the Petroleum Act, to see that new proposals are approved, only if their design is satisfactory and if advertisements are kept within reasonable bounds. A survey of existing garages might be made with a view to enlisting the help of the proprietors in preserving the amenities of the district.

If the saying " Once a common, always a common " is to remain a true saying, we suggest that the Planning Committee prepare a map showing throughout the County the commons that still remain and that they be recorded as public open spaces.

There is no need to emphasise the importance of golf in the County of Fife. Fife is essentially its home, and the prosperity of the County is associated with the game. Apart from their sporting value, golf-courses help to beautify the landscape, forming, at times, a part of the green belt round the built-up area.

We recommend that the Planning Committee approach the owners of the various golf-courses, with a view to impressing on them the desirability of preserving the courses in perpetuity if possible. An agreement might be entered into under the Planning Acts.

Fife, sharply cut off from the rest of Scotland by the estuaries of the Tay and the Forth, has a long coast-line, extending over 120 miles, and showing a marked variety of scenery—high cliffs, picturesque projecting rocks and golden sands. Here and there, however, the beauty of the coast is marred by man's handiwork—badly designed bungalows, unsightly shacks, etc.

GOLF

Fife is the home of golf. Every town has its course. These open lungs should be maintained

Photo—Cowie, St. Andrews

" The Road Hole." The Old Course and Royal and Ancient Clubhouse, St. Andrews

Fife has 120 miles of varying coastline, the natural character of which should be preserved

River Forth and Inchcolm

Photos—Valentine, Dundee

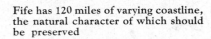

Photo—Valentine, Dundee

Rock and Spindle, St. Andrews

Silver Sands, Aberdour

N 1

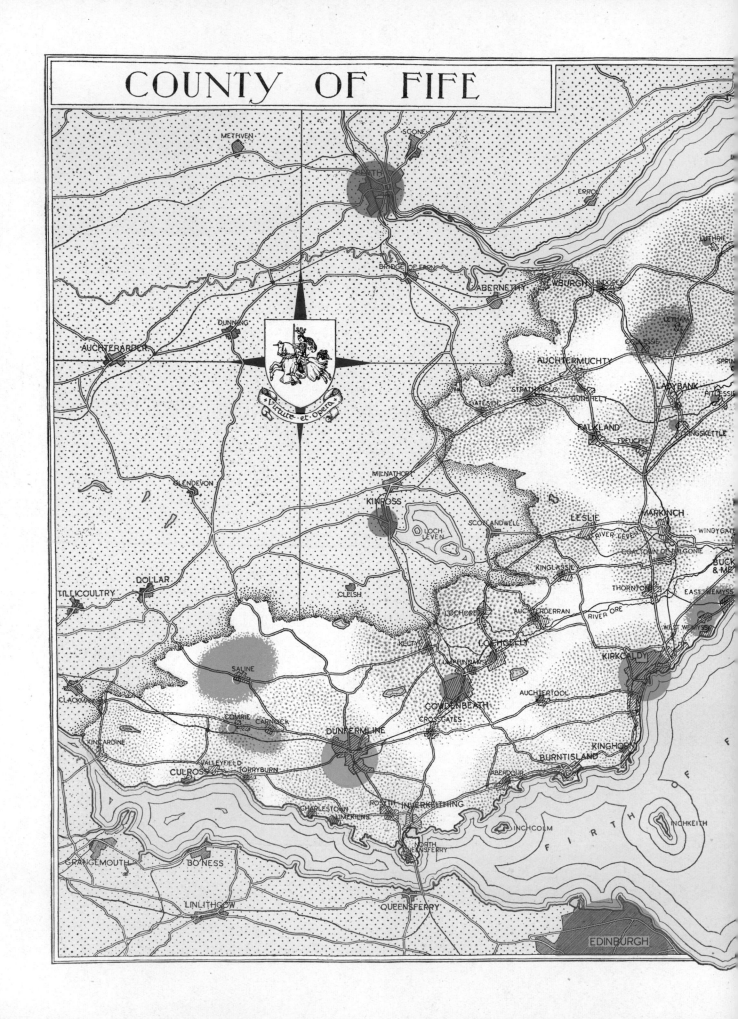

COUNTY OF FIFE

Virtute et Opera

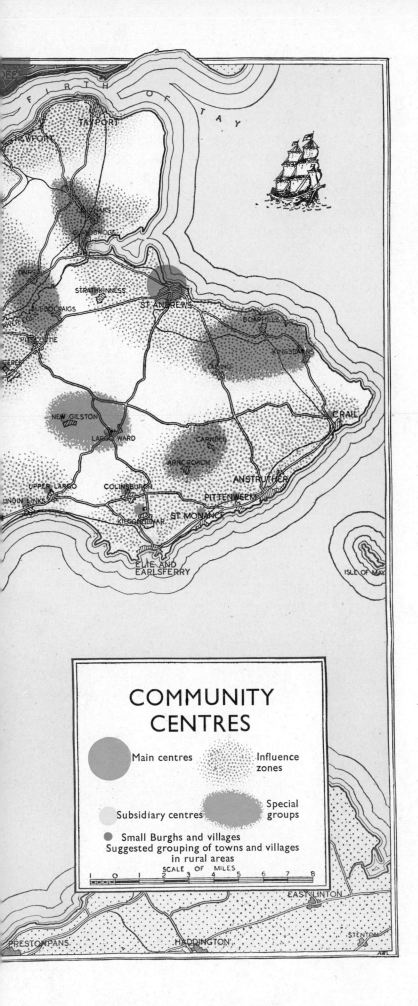

COMMUNITY CENTRES

COMMUNITY Centres are recreational and cultural institutions which may be run with the assistance of grants provided under the terms of certain Acts of Parliament.

In urban areas the siting of such centres presents little difficulty; but in rural areas, where no one village has a population large enough to justify a centre, some system of grouping becomes necessary. The obvious plan is to select the village whose situation marks it out as the natural centre.

The map shows a proposed grouping of the villages of Fife.

The Planning Committee should prepare at an early date a coastal survey and draw up a plan for the preservation of the coast. That would involve two things—(1) the reservation of certain carefully selected points for the grouping of planned future industrial and other developments, and (2) protecting against thoughtless interference the rest of the coast-line so that it might remain in its natural state.

Coastal Road

A good sea-front is the envy of every seaside resort. In Fife a coastal road runs at many parts parallel to the sea, affording a wealth of attractive views. Sometimes a strip of agricultural land intervenes between the road and the sea. It is important that this strip should not be built up, but that public footpaths should cross it here and there leading from the road to prominent views and beauty-spots. It is undesirable that the coastal road should become a main traffic artery. This would necessitate its being widened, would make it noisy and busy and would interfere seriously with its amenity.

Playing Fields and Recreation Areas

We wish to impress upon the Planning Committee the desirability of reserving land in suitable situations for playing fields and recreation areas, for the younger generation as well as for the adult populace. There is a natural tendency for a Burgh authority to keep its building programme strictly within the Burgh boundaries, and this is apt to result in their failure to reserve suitable accommodation within the boundaries for children's playing-fields. If these are not kept in view at the same time as the housing proposals the children are left with the streets as their only playground. We earnestly hope that this question of reserving land for open spaces will receive the early attention of the Planning Committee.

Open Areas Surrounding Towns

We have often been distressed at the appearance of many of the entrances and exits in our towns. Little attention seems to have been paid to the need for conserving an appearance of seemliness and dignity. While we appreciate that it may be desirable to reserve an area for industrial buildings, we see no reason why these should not be sited and laid out in such a manner that, while paying due attention to the provision of storage, transport and other necessities, the structure should be a pleasing feature rather than an eyesore. The entrance to a town should be made as attractive as possible.

It is our opinion, therefore, that in the preparation of the Planning Scheme, careful consideration should be devoted to the approaches to the towns and that the architectural features of the immediate surroundings should be kept in view.

Riverside Preservation

A river frontage in a town should not be looked on merely as an ideal site upon which to pack factories. A river and its banks can be made a thing of beauty, given the necessary thought and planning.

A survey of the rivers of Fife should be made and a plan be prepared for preserving the amenities along their banks, particularly where they run through built-up areas. A strip of land should be reserved and carefully laid out, and to this the public should have access. It is recognised that industrial development must from time to time take advantage of the proximity of a river or a sea-front, but it is nevertheless felt that under systematic planning there should remain always strips of land reserved and carefully laid out to which the public should have access.

Preservation of Trees and Woodlands

The scenery of Fife (and we have some reason to be proud of it) has been materially helped by its groups and belts of trees. They add charm and dignity to the land. Although heavily forested at one time the County lost the bulk of its trees in the 15th century in

RECREATION

Amenity and recreation go hand in hand

Paddling Pond, Cowdenbeath

Photo—Valentine, Dundee

ANCIENT MONUMENTS

Links with the past—large or small—should
be preserved in the natural settings

Photos—Valentine, Dundee
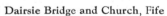
Leuchars Church, Fife

Dairsie Bridge and Church, Fife

order to build up the first Scottish Navy, and the woodlands that we have to-day are for the most part an inheritance from the 18th century when the Fife lairds did much to beautify their estates.

We think it specially important, in connection with the new housing estates, to keep in mind the value of trees and woods as a source of beauty in the landscape, and we recommend that a survey be made of the various belts and groups of trees throughout the County. It may be noted that continual vigilance will be necessary in the administration of the housing estates to secure that young growing trees are protected so that they will reach the maturity and beauty we have in mind. Owners should be encouraged to preserve these until such time as they are ready for felling. They should be encouraged also to undertake replanting and to embark on new planting of woodlands as well as of individual trees. The Committee desires to record its opinion that the present practice, largely dictated by the immediate economic results, of favouring conifers as opposed to hardwoods, is to be deplored, and in our opinion a mixed forestry plan is much to be preferred.

Rights of Way

The County is fortunate in possessing a number of attractive right-of-way paths, very delightful to traverse when the highroads are so thronged with motor traffic. These should be carefully preserved and sign-posted. Where the necessary stiles and gates are provided they can be enjoyed without creating a nuisance for the farmer, or interfering with industry.

Ancient Monuments and their Preservation

We are proud in this County of our ancient monuments, not only of such well-known examples as Falkland Palace, St. Andrews Cathedral, Dunfermline Abbey, but also of the less well-known country houses, ancient castles, bridges and ecclesiastical buildings. We have also many buildings which cannot be classed as ancient monuments, but which by their design and character add charm to their surroundings and constitute a link with the past.

We recommend that all ancient monuments be surveyed and scheduled under the Planning Acts, and that, in addition, buildings which by their design and character are worthy of preservation should be listed and every attempt made to preserve them. The attractions of ancient monuments are often enhanced by their surroundings, and we think, therefore, that in addition to listing them for preservation their surroundings should also be preserved.

Community Centres

Community Centres are recreational and cultural institutions which may be run with the assistance of grants provided under the terms of certain Acts of Parliament.

Under the Physical Training and Recreational Act of 1937 the Scottish Home Department has power to make grants towards the expenses incurred by public bodies or voluntary organisations in providing facilities for physical training and recreation. Assistance in respect of the capital cost of such projects may also be considered.

Under the Education (Scotland) Act, 1945, the Education Authority is charged with the responsibility of securing that there should be available to all people, young and old, in all parts of the authority's area, possibilities of meeting together to promote their communal life and to engage in such cultural and recreational activities as may seem appropriate.

These two Acts are of unusual significance and importance at the present time.

PRESERVATION OF TREES, WOODLANDS AND RIVERSIDE WALKS

A beautiful roadside scene sacrificed to the war effort

Melville Lodge, Fife

Photo—Valentine, Dundee

A sylvan scene within a burgh. Heritages such as this must be preserved for the community for all time

ade Braes, St. Andrews

Fhoto—Valentine, Dundee

Leven Woods, Markinch

Photo—Valentine, Dundee

The County abounds in stately trees. These must not be felled indiscriminately

Their objects can be best achieved by the institution of Community Centres, for the establishment of which the new housing schemes offer an excellent opportunity. We have all of us become more neighbourly and friendly as a result of the voluntary activities undertaken so willingly during the war. Home Guard parades, Red Cross working parties, Fire Watching parties, Report Centre duties, etc. have brought us all together on a more friendly and intimate footing, and the return of the young men and women from the Forces has but served to stimulate the feeling. That feeling can be best fostered by the establishment of Community Associations and Community Centres. Already institutions of this kind are taking shape in various parts of the country to the advantage and satisfaction of the communities concerned.

A Community Centre, however, can be a success only if the people concerned really want it and are prepared to run it. The general idea is to provide a place where the various members of the community, young and old, may meet together for social, recreational and cultural activities. The following list suggests the kind of equipment desirable :—

1. A hall, for concerts, lectures, films, plays, dances, etc.
2. A common room for conversation and friendly intercourse.
3. A canteen.
4. A reading room.
5. A games room.
6. A crafts room.
7. One or two rooms available for discussions and Adult Education Classes.
   Larger centres might ultimately be able to add a gymnasium, a swimming-bath, a clinic, etc.

When it is remembered that grants are available both for capital outlay and for running expenses, and when it is considered further that revenue may accrue from membership fees, letting of rooms, refreshments and sale of cigarettes, there is nothing that need hinder a vigorous community from undertaking such a venture. It would at once appeal to members of musical associations, chess clubs, photographic associations, debating societies, clubs and youth activities of every sort, and would provide what is so often wanting in our midst, a focal point where people could meet and realise that they are indeed members of a community. There is probably no county better circumstanced than Fife for the institution of such centres of communal life.

We have been impressed by the proposal put forward that in order to foster nature study and a liking for open-air life there should be set aside areas of the County, of which possible examples are Lomond Hills, Tentsmuir and Norman's Law, wherein free access to organised youth movements would be provided for the purpose of recreation, week-end camps, and practical study of forestry.

Inchcolm Abbey in the Firth of Forth

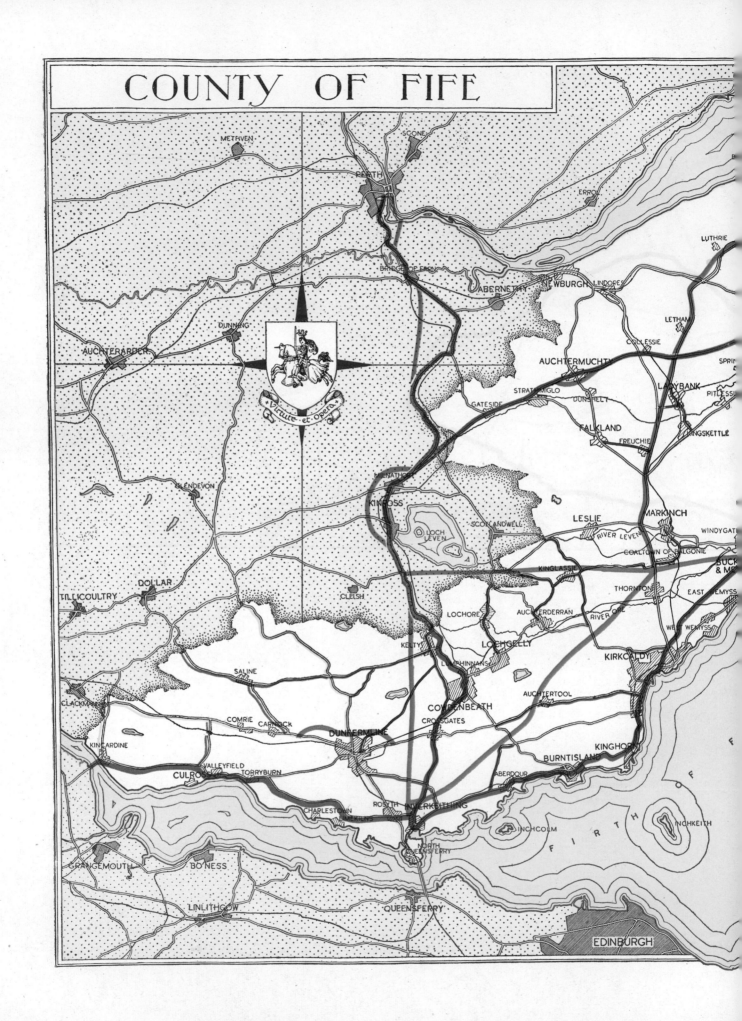

COUNTY OF FIFE

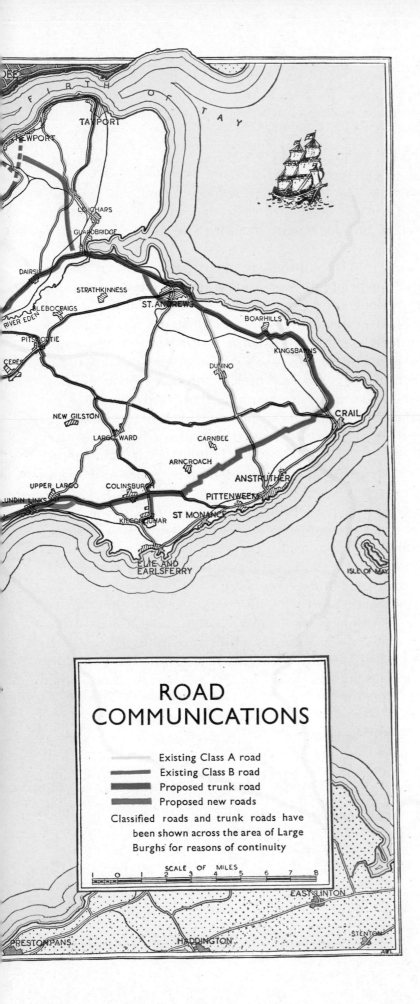

ROAD COMMUNICATIONS

THE system of roads shown on the map is the result of a gradual development during the eighteenth and nineteenth centuries, but with the great increase of motor traffic new roads have to be introduced to avoid existing villages. These roads should be carried out on independent tracks and built as trunk roads, as far away as possible from inhabited localities.

The map shows the existing system of classified roads with the proposed new roads and bypasses as suggested by the Committee.

ROAD COMMUNICATIONS

— Existing Class A road
— Existing Class B road
— Proposed trunk road
— Proposed new roads

Classified roads and trunk roads have been shown across the area of Large Burghs for reasons of continuity

SCALE OF MILES
1 0 1 2 3 4 5 6 7 8

COMMUNICATIONS

Road
System

THE system of roads as it exists to-day in Fife was developed during the 18th and 19th centuries. The main routes then laid down still exist, but with the advent and great increase of motor traffic they are no longer entirely adequate as regards surface and width of carriageway.

As will be seen from the map on pp. 108, 109, all these roads with their numerous links and connections were in excellent condition before the war, and, in spite of heavy war traffic, hey have deteriorated only slightly. So long as access to the County from south and north is effected by means of ferries this road system is reasonably adequate, although some of the routes are rather heavily burdened, and there is some confusion of traffic where important crossings occur in towns and built-up areas. Certain by-passes constructed in the last century to meet such difficulties have become useless through ribbon development, and it follows that care must be taken in future planning that by-passing does not create conditions that demand further by-passing. The busiest spots in the County as regards road traffic are the High Street of Kirkcaldy and the bridge over the estuary of the River Leven. This is borne out by inspection of the Traffic Density Map reproduced. Fortunately the topographical structure of the County does not offer any serious difficulty regarding the lay-out of new roads.

Special mention might be made of the road bridge at Kincardine, in the south-western corner of the County. This links the industrial areas of Fife and Clackmannan with Stirling and the Lothians. Completed in 1937 by the joint efforts of Fife, Clackmannan and Stirling, it has a carriageway of 30 feet, with two footpaths of 5 feet each, and there is also a central swing span to facilitate river navigation.

Modern
Tendencies
in Road
Lay-out

Modern tendencies have been summarised in the memoranda issued by the Ministry of Transport (Nos. 336, 483 and 575). Although the memoranda aim at the widest possible standardisation of road lay-out and construction, the Ministry admit that a mechanical rigidity is not always desirable, and that many cases should be treated individually, especially in relation to the surroundings of the road, and that consideration should be given to the preservation of the amenities.

It may be a commonplace to say that a road is primarily designed to facilitate traffic, but it is unfortunately too often used for many other purposes ; sometimes as a market-place, sometimes a parking place, often even as a playground for children. For each of these purposes special provision should be made independent of the traffic, which should alone be admitted to the road. Signal posts and instructions are useless unless proper space is provided for markets, and playgrounds for children, and unless shopping centres and residential areas are segregated from traffic roads. The provision of service roads alongside traffic roads is not a good solution even if " unclimbable " fences be provided between main road and service road. Otherwise the public cannot be prevented from crossing the strip between the road and the service road, thus making the service road useless. Neither is the growing of hedges, where it has been tried, a proper remedy, as the inhabitants tend to cross the road in its early days, and thus prevent the hedge developing as an effective barrier.

After all undesirable uses of the highways have been eliminated by provision of market places and of playing fields for children it still remains necessary to pay attention to road safety. Speed may be dangerous even if obstacles can be seen at such a distance that a fast car can be brought to a standstill in time. The tendency should be, first, to avoid obstacles, and second, where they are unavoidable, to secure that they can be seen at a distance ahead. Road crossings constitute one of the principal obstacles, and the policy should be to reduce the number of these as much as possible, by joining points of access together before they reach the main road. One point which demands special attention is provision of well-designed and well-constructed footpaths.

No less desirable is the provision of side-tracks for cyclists, and, as recommended under " Amenities," the erection of adequate warning and direction signs should be stressed. Equally necessary is the use of white lines on the roads.

The width of a traffic lane for quick-moving traffic has been established at 11 feet, and the whole width of the carriageway has therefore to be as many times 11 feet as there are traffic lanes in both directions. Where three or more traffic lanes are required the width may be ten feet. The division of the carriageway into two one-way parts is to be recommended where the traffic density reaches 400 vehicles during the peak hour. A road may also be considered to require a dual carriageway where there is a heavy vehicular traffic consisting of vehicles varying greatly in speed, and where the traffic is of about the same importance in both directions at most times of the day. In the case of very heavy traffic in one direction at certain times the construction of three carriageways may be necessary, the central carriageway being allocated by means of automatic signposts to one or other direction. Avoidance of accidents during hours of darkness can best be effected by road lighting even outside urban areas, but this method is very expensive and would only be justified in the case of very important night traffic.

The established tendency to avoid existing villages and towns by means of by-pass roads does not seem to be the right remedy against accidents. It is feared that the built-up areas will in the future tend to develop so as to reach these by-pass roads, and in spite of all restrictions against ribbon development, the mounting ground cost would finally swallow up the by-pass into the developed area. Through traffic should therefore be carried on independent roads built as trunk roads, as far as possible away from inhabited localities.

There seems to be little doubt about the fact that the construction of these two Forth and bridges would change considerably the lay-out of road transport throughout the County. Tay Road Bridges. It may therefore be necessary to consider the question of the location of the bridges. Before the construction of the Kincardine Bridge the whole traffic from Edinburgh to Perth and the North of Scotland was directed to the bridge at Stirling, as the ferries at Kincardine and Queensferry took only an insignificant part of the traffic. This situation was remedied partly by the opening of the Kincardine Bridge in 1937, but the North traffic from Edinburgh has still to make a detour of about 30 miles to reach Dunfermline.

A similar situation arises for the traffic from Dundee to the South, as apart from the ferry at Newport there is only the bridge over the Tay at Perth, a distance of 21 miles from Dundee. In the case of traffic moving South from Aberdeen through Perth this distance in mileage is admittedly less. The distance between Edinburgh and Dundee over the Kincardine and Perth bridges is about 85 miles, as against 53 miles through Queensferry and Newport.

As regards the position of the proposed Forth Road Bridge there is no dubiety. It is now definitely settled that it should run between South and North Queensferry, by way of the Mackintosh Rock. For the proposed road bridge over the Tay two alternative sites are in consideration, one near Newport and the other over Mugdrum Island to the north of Newburgh. These sites are about 13 miles apart, and the choice of one or other site would considerably affect the road system of Fife.

We now consider the relative claims of the two sites from the point of view of the County of Fife. On the financial side it may be noted that the Newport Bridge has been estimated to cost £3,000,000 as against £500,000 for the Mugdrum Bridge. The Newport Bridge would offer many advantages to the interests both of Fife and of the north-east of Scotland, including Dundee. Even under existing conditions the volume of road traffic carried by the Newport Ferry system is liable, on occasions, to create congestion, and this will be increased as the counties to the north and south of the Tay develop. At the moment, however, the cost of such a bridge is prohibitive and the interests of Fife as a whole are more intimately linked with an alternative scheme of a bridge at Mugdrum.

The opinion in the industrial areas in Fife and generally the region to the north-west is decidedly in favour of a bridge at Newburgh rather than one at Newport. From New Inn, an important road junction in the centre of the County, the distance to Dundee by a bridge at Newport is 19 miles, as against 24 miles by a bridge at Newburgh, a difference which is insignificant compared with the difference in the estimated cost of the two bridges. The road between New Inn and Newburgh leads through an area containing Small Burghs and villages, with small but prosperous industries, capable of development; and a bridge over the Tay at Newburgh would tend to favour further development. An alternative proposal has been put forward to construct the bridge at Friarton, one mile south of Perth and nine miles upstream from the Newburgh site. Although Friarton is at the northern end of the Glenfarg road from Kinross it would not help any region with already developing industries, and from its close proximity to Perth it could only serve as a by-pass to the existing Perth bridges. In addition to the importance a bridge at Newburgh would have for the County of Fife and the general traffic to the North, this bridge would furnish an important link between West and East, shortening the distance between Glasgow and Dundee. Ultimately both bridges may be necessary, but consideration of this point is for the future. In the meantime a bridge at Newburgh is of first importance for the County of Fife.

Railways — All the railways in the County of Fife belong to the London and North-Eastern Railway Company. The County is traversed by the main route connecting Edinburgh with Dundee and Aberdeen over the Forth Bridge. Another important section connects Edinburgh with Dunfermline, Kinross and Perth. From the main Edinburgh-Dundee line two loop-lines go to the east, one from Wormit to Leuchars, touching Tayport

THE PORTALS OF FIFE

Photos—Valentine, Dundee

BY ROAD

Kincardine Road Bridge, carrying some of the heavy road traffic from Fife to the South

BY SEA

The Harbour, Kirkcaldy, through which flows sea-borne traffic to the ports of the world

BY RAIL

Still one of the wonders of the world and a link in the main East Coast rail route between Scotland and England—the Forth Bridge

Not quite so famous except in relation to the disastrous collapse of its predecessor, the Tay Bridge carrying the East Coast rail route over the broad estuary of the River Tay

Photos—Valentine, Dundee

P

with its trade in timber and esparto grass, and the other from Leuchars to Thornton, serving the University town of St. Andrews, with its golf-links, and then leading along the north-east and south-east coasts of the peninsula through agricultural country to the seaside towns of Crail, Anstruther, Pittenweem, St. Monance and Elie. It then passes along Largo Bay, through Largo and a highly industrialised district to effect a junction with the main line at Thornton. To the west a branch line from St. Fort goes at some distance from the Tay, to Newburgh and Perth ; from Ladybank a connection is provided to Newburgh and another through Auchtermuchty to Kinross. A short goods line joins Leslie with the main line at Markinch. From Thornton a line leads westwards through the mining area, passing Auchterderran and Lochgelly, and at Cowdenbeath joining the line from the Forth Bridge and Dunfermline to Kinross and Perth. From Dunfermline a line runs to Alloa and Stirling. In addition, a great number of mineral and mining railways criss-cross the area of west Fife, connecting the different coal-pits with each other and with the main railway lines.

The existing railway systems of the County are shown in the map on pp. 124, 125, and it does not appear that many changes or improvements will be necessary on the railway system in the near future. Electrification, though desirable on the grounds of amenity, is hardly likely to become urgent so long as coal remains plentiful.

Passenger Road Transport Services

The first tramcar service in Fife was introduced in Wemyss in 1908, and three years later a tramcar service was introduced in and around Dunfermline, but this mode of transport had its disadvantages, and it was gradually replaced by omnibuses. The last tramcars disappeared from Fife in 1937. The map gives a picture of the network of 'bus routes, showing also the density of travel. We note that the main traffic is from Dunfermline along the mining strip of Cowdenbeath and Lochgelly towards Lochore, from Dunfermline towards Rosyth and the Dockyard at St. Margaret's Hope, and along the coast from Kirkcaldy towards Leven.

The average speed of the 'bus service varies according to the route, as in agricultural areas there are fewer stops than in densely populated industrial districts.

Length	Under 7 miles	7/10 miles	10/20 miles	Over 20 miles
Average speed	14·8 m.p.h.	15·5 m.p.h.	16·7 m.p.h.	17·8 m.p.h.

Taking the maximum travelling time for a workman from house to work as 45 minutes, and allowing 15 minutes of this time for the walk from house to 'bus stop and from 'bus stop to factory, we may assume that, if the journey is made by road and 30 minutes are consumed by travelling in a 'bus, this restricts the worker to a radius of 7 miles from his home to his place of work.

Here again it should be taken into account that although housing estate roads should not be provided for major traffic, they should be of such width that 'buses can traverse them and stop at appropriate places, as the absence of such roads would extend the walking time to the 'bus stop. It is assumed that a width of carriageway of 22 feet will meet the requirements of a housing estate road with occasional 'bus traffic. If possible the 'bus stop should nowhere be more than half a mile from a workman's house in unbuilt areas. Although the 'bus companies must make their own arrangements through the Traffic Commissioners in providing new routes to

COMMUNICATIONS

'Bus Station and Plan

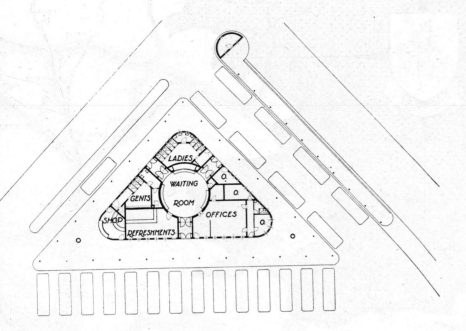

The 'bus station depicted above was erected immediately prior to the war. Stations of this sort, providing conveniences such as we look for at the more important railway stations, are very much needed at the principal points on the 'bus routes

COUNTY OF FIFE

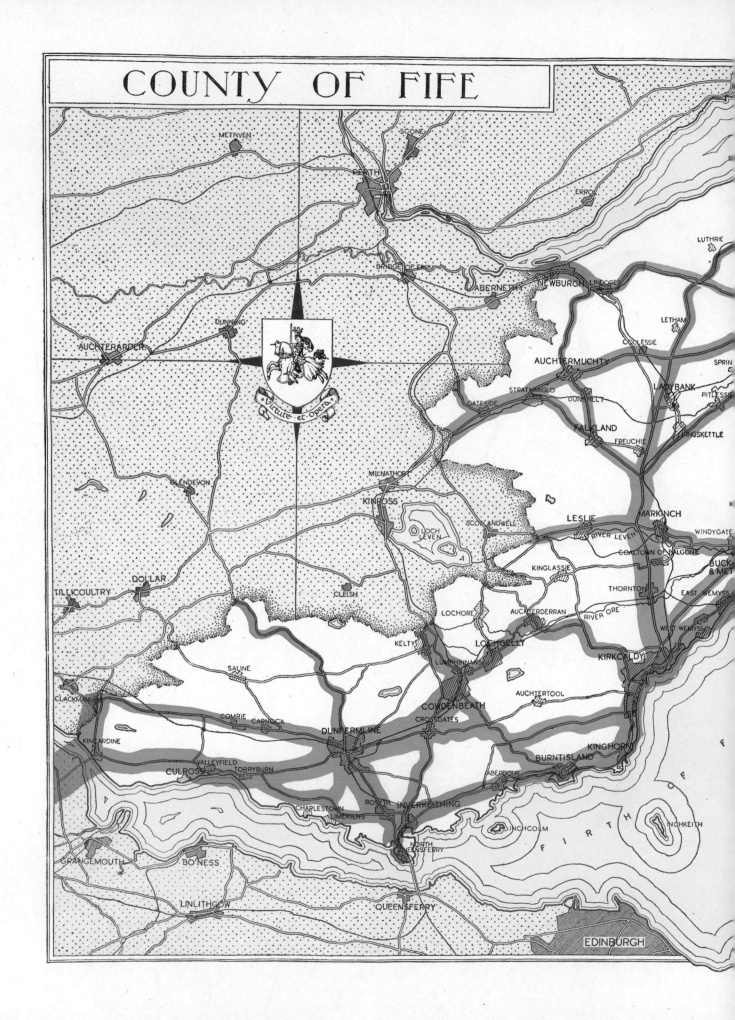

Virtute et Opera

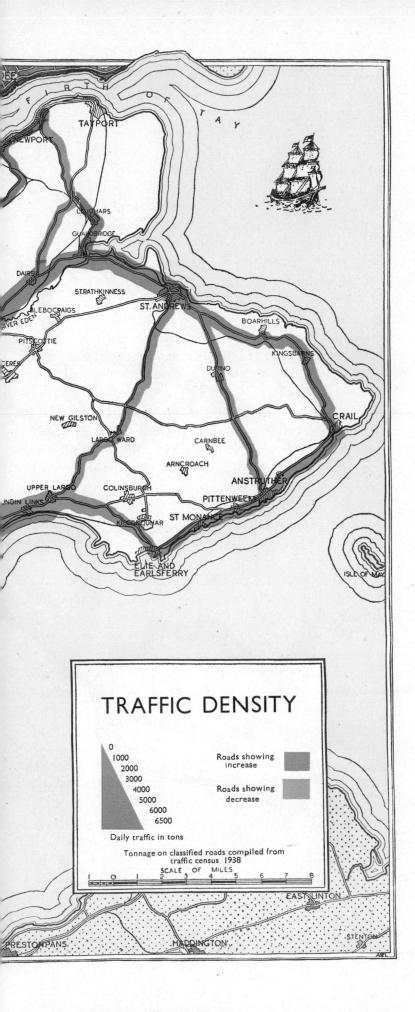

TRAFFIC DENSITY

THIS map, made up from the traffic census figures gathered in **1931** and **1935**, illustrates traffic density over the main roads within the County of Fife. On the roads shown pink there has been an increase between the two census periods, whilst on those shown blue a decrease has been recorded. It will be noted that in the industrial areas, Dunfermline, Cowdenbeath, Kirkcaldy and Leven valley, a considerable amount of traffic is recorded, indicating the necessity for a new through road by-passing these built-up areas.

factories or housing estates, contacts between local authorities or industrialists and these companies are of advantage to the general public.

Bus Stations

'Bus transport has increased very much of late years, and we see no reason to doubt that it will increase still further as time goes on. The existing system is unsatisfactory and it is distressing to see long queues of people waiting in all kinds of weather. It is to be hoped the County Council will approach the Traffic Commissioners and 'bus companies and secure agreement for the establishment of 'bus stations. At present in a single town there may be as many as six different points from which 'buses start for various directions. Co-ordination between road and rail transport suggests 'bus stations being in proximity to railway stations. A 'bus station should have waiting-rooms, left-luggage office, conveniences and, in the larger centres, a café. All 'buses should, if possible, start from the station.

Shipping Ports and Ferries

There are several harbours on the coast of Fife which are of importance, and in forming proposals for the future these should not be forgotten. The L.N.E. Railway Company are the proprietors of the harbours of Tayport, Methil and Burntisland, and except in the case of Tayport, traffic in the years before the war showed a tendency to increase. The traffic rests mainly on major industries, such as coal, linoleum, paper and timber. Coal is the main export from the harbours of Methil and Burntisland, and with the development of new pits in the east of Fife extensions of these harbours may become necessary. Such possibilities should be borne in mind. At Methil Dock the principal traffic in the meantime is effected by rail, but things may change somewhat in the future, and it might be advisable, with future possibilities in view, to consider the need for linking up the east end of Methil Docks with the main trunk road system.

The harbour of Kirkcaldy is outside the planning jurisdiction of the Fife County Council, but here an important part of the goods travels by road, and communications with the neighbouring industrial areas will have to be considered.

As to the ferries over the Tay and Forth, they are in the meantime an important link with the road system, but their importance will tend to decrease with the construction of the proposed road bridges. Except from the point of view of amenities, to which reference is made in another part of this Report, there does not seem, therefore, to be any need for special consideration of problems connected with the ferry system.

Throughout the County of Fife there are many harbours in various stages of repair and disrepair. Some are very little used, but it is our opinion that these harbours should not be allowed to be entirely neglected if they can be of service in any way. We consider that an appropriate authority should be charged with the duty of maintaining harbours at least to the extent to which revenue would be recovered from the harbours by way of dues.

Air Transport

Before the war there was no civilian airport in Fife. Two Service airports existed, at Leuchars and Donibristle, and these were supplemented during the war by two others, at Crail and Dunino. No information is as yet available as to the extent and suitability of these airports and as regards the alterations that would be necessary in order to convert them to civil use. As soon as information of this kind becomes available the survey will have to be continued for this purpose. It seems that the aerodrome at Leuchars is the best equipped and the one most likely, from its position, to be suitable for civilian use. Leuchars is 18 minutes from Dundee by rail, 1 hour 22 minutes from Edinburgh and

THE HIGHWAY BEAUTIFUL

Examples of good road lay-out and design from America. They show an improvement upon anything which we have in this country so far, and display a care and thought for the countryside and amenity generally that might with advantage be copied here

A "Gas" Station in the Westchester County Park system. No garish advertisements or unsightly pumps here!

' Tee " Junction on a trafficked road

The Road in the Country, merged with the rural beauty

Photo by courtesy U.S. Bureau of Public Roads

State Highway in Virginia

$2\frac{1}{4}$ hours from Aberdeen; and although there is no direct train to Leuchars from Perth, the journey can be effected in 45 minutes. By road the distance is 7 miles from Dundee (by an eventual Tay Bridge at Newport), 44 miles from Edinburgh by a bridge at Queensferry, and 27 miles from Perth. As the crow flies Leuchars is 6 miles from Dundee, 32 from Edinburgh, 20 from Perth and 60 from Aberdeen. The geographical situation, therefore, seems to be an ideal one for an airport suitable for traffic to the north and north-west of Europe, and as an auxiliary airport to Prestwick.

As to the topographical situation the general position seems to be as follows. The aerodrome is situated at the south-west corner of an alluvial plain which forms a rectangle, $2\frac{1}{2}$ miles by 5 miles, between the railway from Leuchars to Tayport and the sea. The peninsula is bounded on the north by the estuary of the Tay and on the south by the River Eden. The elevation above the sea-level varies from zero up to 25 feet. There are no major roads over the area and no villages. The aerodrome has therefore plenty of room to extend except for some wooded parts of the ground, which would eventually have to be felled and slightly levelled.

The retention of the aerodrome at Donibristle will probably depend on the maintenance of the naval base at Rosyth, and will in any case be of purely military importance. The other two aerodromes, at Crail and Dunino, will probably disappear now that hostilities have ceased. Eventually one or other could be taken over by private aeronautic societies.

So long as the future of the existing Service aerodromes is unknown it is impossible to state accurately what the future policy of the County should be as regards civil aviation facilities. In the opinion of the Committee it is better to have one well-equipped large centralised air station rather than numerous small units which would serve only limited local needs. If it be decided to establish one centralised air port it should be either in the neighbourhood of Kirkcaldy or of Ladybank where suitable areas of ground are available, but the situation might be profoundly altered if the Government decided to dispense with any of the existing Service aerodromes.

SUMMARY OF RECOMMENDATIONS

AGRICULTURE

1. That the County Council appoint an Agricultural Committee of seven members with knowledge and experience of agriculture and the management of land, four of which must be members of the County Council, the other three not necessarily members of the County Council, to be chosen by the Council because of their skill and knowledge of the subject ; that these seven have power to co-opt other three men of knowledge and skill from any area under review, making a Committee of at least seven and at most ten ; the duties of the Committee to include—
   (a) the review of rural housing and to advise in view of prospective Government policy in the near future ;
   (b) the formulation of plans for agriculture ;
   (c) a thorough survey of the ancient road system of the County with a view to the maintenance of such roads in the interests of agriculture.

2. That the County Council represent to the Department of Agriculture the need for the development of resources which are found to be neglected.

3. That it represent to the Department of Health the urgent need for making available once more the grants towards the reconstruction of rural housing.

4. That grants should be made available for bringing up to modern standards existing houses of farm workers as long as building costs are excessive.

5. That present grants in connection with the purchase of lime and improvement of drainage should be continued.

6. That farm workers should be encouraged, in connection with their work, to take practical courses of training at approved centres.

7. That the County Agricultural Adviser should keep all farmers in his area closely in touch with work being carried on at the Technical Agricultural Colleges throughout the country.

8. That the County Council be empowered to supervise the maintenance and efficient working of waterways. Under such powers, a County Officer should be appointed to make an Annual Report and exercise continual supervision over the state of streams and burns into which field drainage flows throughout the County, so as to ensure the proper functioning of field drains. [This matter is also dealt with in Recommendation No. 3 under the heading " Public Health."]

9. That a special transport service should be provided on specified days of the week to enable farm workers and their wives to visit the large centres in the County.

10. That the proposed County Agricultural Committee be asked to consider the possible advantages of establishing Training Farms, Institute and Research Station in the County.

11. That in view of the deposits of suitable clay known to exist the opening of tile works seems to be desirable.

HOUSING

1. That in order to secure co-ordination between the different housing authorities in the County there should be constituted a County Housing Association representative of County, Burgh and other appropriate interests, and that in the meantime co-operation be developed between the County Council and Burghs and between adjacent Burghs, with a view to avoidance of duplication and the encouragement of economy in provision of necessary services.

2. *Agricultural Housing.*—That the Joint Committee proposed in the recommendations of the report on Agriculture should give special consideration to the location of new houses for agricultural workers, keeping in view the best interests of this vital industry and the possibilities of road transport.

3. That in order to secure the preservation of agricultural land due consideration should be given to well-designed flatted houses in planning housing schemes, and to the use for development of derelict sites.

PUBLIC HEALTH

1. *River Leven.*—That consideration be given to increasing the flow of the river and that the proposed intercepting sewer should be constructed without delay.

2. *River Eden.*—That consideration be given to the desirability of constructing an intercepting sewer for the River Eden.

3. *River Pollution and Drainage.*—That there should be some authority responsible for the supervision of the various rivers and streams throughout the County and that legislation be introduced to bring this about.

4. *Industrial Waste.*—That the Ministry of Fuel and Power be invited to institute research for better disposal of pit refuse.

5. *Drainage.*—That a regional sewerage and drainage plan should be prepared for the County so that co-operation or amalgamation would be secured between the various authorities responsible for these services.

6. *Water Supply.*—That the scheme authorised by the Act of 1940 be consummated as soon as practicable and that there should be co-operation between water authorities.

7. *Hospital and Health Services.*—That the scheme described in the foregoing report and approved by the County Council be carried out with all convenient speed.

8. *Slaughterhouses.*—That the County Council should make inquiry on the subject of slaughterhouses with a view to centralisation and construction of modern abattoirs.

AMENITIES

1. That the Council adopt the policy of developing villages into community centres.

2. That suitable areas in the County be acquired (by lease or otherwise), by the appropriate authority, for recreation, week-end camps, etc. and made available under supervision for young people.

3. That steps be taken to prohibit the erection of unsightly poster advertisements.

4. That tentative zoning proposals of a flexible nature should be drawn up for the whole County so that future developments may proceed on systematic lines.

5. That the Planning Committee give careful consideration to plans submitted to them as Interim Development Authority.

6. That the Ministry of Fuel and Power be invited to institute research for better disposal of pit refuse. (See also " Public Health.")

7. That all possible measures be taken to see that the authorities concerned restore the sites of the opencast coal production workings to their previous condition.

8. That the " controlled tipping " system for the disposal of household refuse be extended.

9. That before any local authority chooses a new site for a refuse dump, the Planning Committee should be consulted in order to discuss how far the site may ultimately be made available for playing-fields or other recreational purposes.

10. That consideration be given, where it is economically possible, to the introduction of modern plant for refuse disposal.

11. That the Planning Committee approach the owners of the various golf-courses with a view to impressing on them the desirability of preserving the courses in perpetuity if possible.

12. That the County Council should prepare at an early date a coastal survey and draw up a plan for the preservation of the coast.

13. That in the preparation of the planning scheme, careful consideration should be devoted to the approaches to towns and that the architectural features of the immediate surroundings should be kept in view.

14. That all ancient monuments be surveyed and scheduled under the Planning Acts and that, in addition, buildings which by their design and character are worthy of preservation should be listed and every attempt made to preserve them.

The co-operation of owners in the preparation of plans will be appreciated.

MINES AND MINERALS

1. That the County Council provide as soon as possible the housing and other amenities required for the development of the mining industry.

2. That provision be made for the reservation of the land required for the development of new collieries essential for the exploitation of the minerals, and that the liability for compensation should not fall upon the County Council.

INDUSTRIES

1. *Forth and Tay Road Bridges.*—That the County Council urge forward by all possible means construction of the Forth and Tay Road Bridges.

2. *Light Industries.*—That having regard to the need for greater diversity of industry in Fife and to the likely surplus of female labour in the County, consideration be given to :—

(a) the formation of a Fife County Industrial Development Council representative

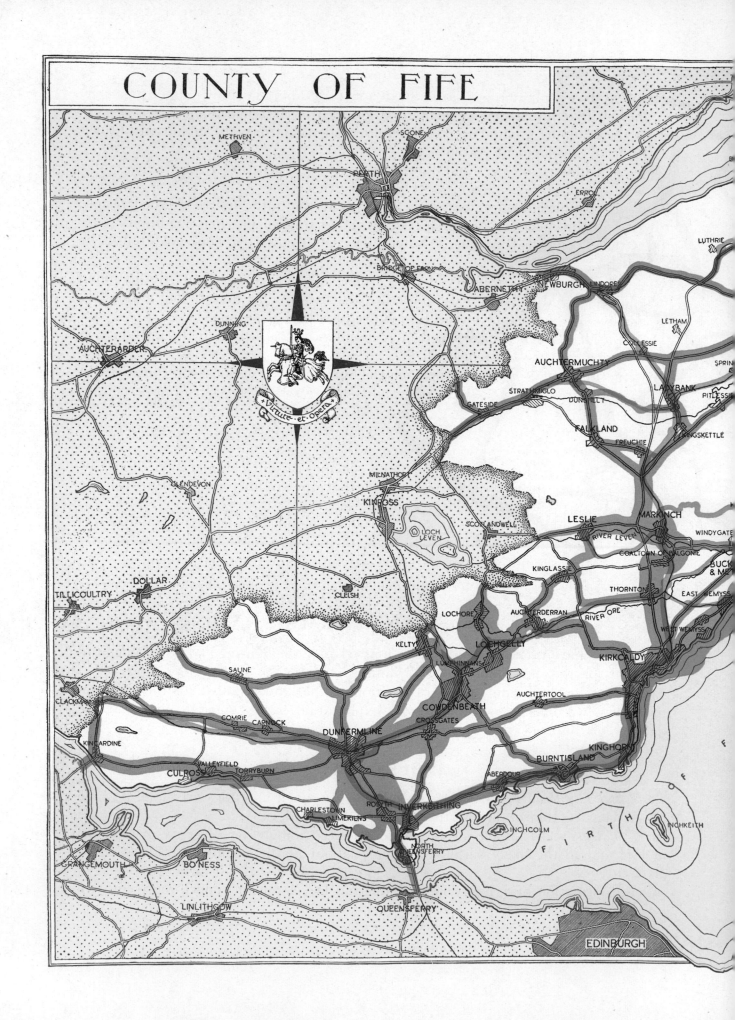

COUNTY OF FIFE

Virtute et Opera

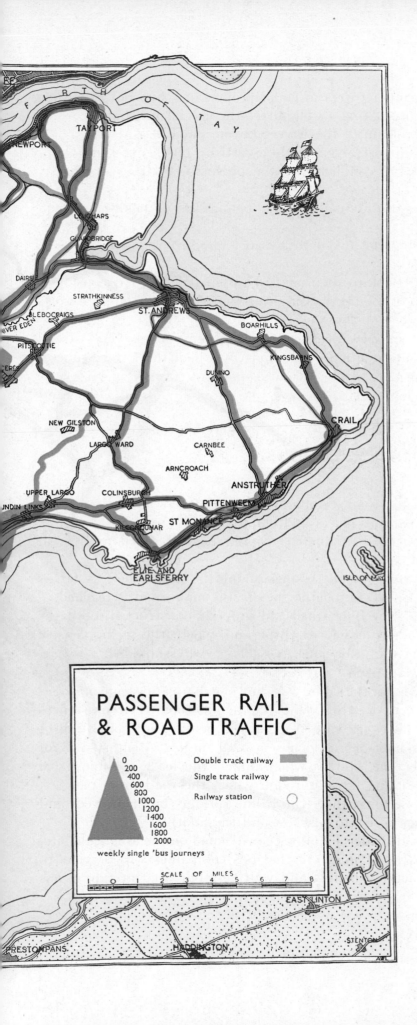

PASSENGER RAIL AND ROAD
TRAFFIC

MAP showing the Railway System
and Bus Routes in Fife.

of local authorities and manufacturers in equal proportions, but not exceeding twelve in number and incorporating a Committee the special function of which will be to deal with the problem of the Rivers Leven and Eden.

(b) the strengthening of the support given to the Scottish Council on Industry ;

(c) the means whereby industries conducive to the prosperity of the community could be introduced ;

(d) the preparation of a brochure annually giving particulars of facilities for industrial development.

3. *Housing.*—That all possible steps be taken to advance the provision of houses in the interests of industry.

4. *Holiday Resorts.*—That a Guide Book to the County be prepared and that consideration be given to the setting up of a bureau of information regarding holiday resorts in the County.

5. *Leisure Time Activities.*—That in view of the shorter working week very careful consideration be given to the introduction of methods by which the leisure time of workers can be profitably spent, *e.g.* by the encouragement of courses of study, the affording of facilities for development of hobbies, the provision of suitable entertainment, etc.

COMMUNICATIONS

(A) ROADS :

(1) That in the development of road communications it is essential that space be provided for markets, parking places and children's playgrounds.

(2) That shopping centres and residential areas should be segregated from main traffic roads.

(3) That in the interests of safety, road-crossings should be diminished as far as possible by joining points of access together before the main road is reached.

(4) That on main and busy roads well-designed and properly constructed footpaths should be provided, also side-tracks for cyclists, and, where the traffic density reaches 400 vehicles during the peak hour, the carriageway should, if possible, be divided into two one-way parts.

(5) That the revised road system for the County as shown on map appearing on pages 108, 109 should be introduced by the County Council as soon as circumstances permit, the utmost effort in every case being made before the final siting of roads, to ensure that the line of road chosen shall, unless circumstances of overriding importance intervene, be that which inflicts the least possible harm on the economic stability of the farms through which the road must pass.

(6) That the approach roads serving the Kincardine bridge be improved and widened to permit of speedy access to Glasgow and the South.

(7) That the proposed Tay Road Bridge should be constructed on the Mugdrum site.

(8) That a determined approach be made to the 'bus companies with a view to the inauguration of satisfactory shelters and waiting-rooms for intending 'bus passengers.

B) AIR :

That failing arrangements being possible for utilisation of one of the existing Service air ports in the County, arrangements should be made for the reservation of land in the vicinity of Kirkcaldy or Ladybank for the purpose of constructing a civil air port.

(C) SEA :

That an appropriate authority should be charged with the duty of maintaining the various harbours in the County, at least to the extent to which revenue would be recovered by way of harbour dues.

EDUCATION

1. That when a new housing scheme is being planned the Education Authority should be consulted with a view to the reservation of a suitable site for a school, and where deemed necessary, a site for a nursery school.
2. That in order to check the drift from country to town rural schools should be more adequately staffed and equipped.
3. That where, in the interests of country children, secondary education has to be centralised, travelling should be restricted as much as possible.
4. That secondary schools in rural areas should normally be expected to develop a rural bias so as to foster and maintain a genuine interest in country life.
5. That Bell Baxter School, which has already acquired a reputation for rural work, should be provided with more extensive facilities for the study of farm life.
6. That town children should be encouraged to make themselves acquainted with rural life and conditions through the establishment of school camps and camp schools.
7. That, for those over school-age, the Education Authority should provide adequate facilities for general culture and for recreation.
8. That the installation of community centres should be encouraged, and that as a beginning community centres should be started at once in, for example, Gateside, Kennoway, Woodside and Comrie, taking the greatest possible advantage of the grants available from the Home Department.
9. That in order to foster technical education there should be a further extension of the Pre-Apprenticeship Scheme in engineering and building, and that training schemes should be instituted for young mine workers and farm workers.
10. That the Education Authority through their Careers Council should, by the use of vocational and other tests, make suitable arrangements for guiding young people into appropriate employment.

THE REPORT

IN MAKING THE FOREGOING RECOMMENDATIONS
to the Planning Committee the signatories to this Report wish to
make it clear that they have not confined themselves merely to
plans which may be considered practicable in the immediate future,
but have also dealt with plans some of which perhaps cannot be
introduced for many years.

It has not been thought possible or wise to attempt to look
further ahead than 50 or 60 years at most. While the question of
cost is not one that the Committee has had to consider, it is obvious
that many of the recommendations put forward will entail large
outlay, and the timing of reforms will have to be most carefully
considered, especially when an increase of rates is concerned and more
especially when a given plan benefits a limited section of the community alone.

The signatories to the Report wish it to be understood that,
while they approve the Report generally, they do not wish to be
held as agreeing, individually, to every finding and recommendation. Some of the members had difficulty in approving the reports
on Agriculture, Population, Zoning and Housing, especially in connection with the zoning proposals, while others, although admitting the
strength of the case for a road bridge over the Forth, feel that
the arguments advanced in favour of a road bridge over the Tay
at Dundee are hardly strong enough to warrant the expense
involved.

We desire to express our thanks to the Provosts, Councillors and officials of the Town Councils, to the many individuals and societies who offered information and advice to us, to those who communicated written memoranda (Appendix IV), to those who kindly allowed photographs to be used (Appendix V), to the County Medical Officer and the Director of Education for information supplied by them, to the Editor—Mr. Neil S. Snodgrass, M.A., F.E.I.S.—for care and attention paid by him to the writing of the Report ; and we wish especially to record our gratitude to the County Clerk, the Senior County Clerk Depute and the County Clerk's staff for their unfailing help and courtesy, and to Mrs. Hannah Robertson, a member of that staff for her efficient services in carrying out the secretarial duties.

J. D. Crosbie.

John Whiteford.

R. L. Christie.

James T. Irvine.

C. Augustus Carlow.

Peter McArthur.

Michael Wemyss.

R. Officer.

George Prentice

J. Lorimer.

J. B. Rae

R. R Taylor.

J. M. Mitchell,
County Clerk.

Matthew Pollock,
Senior County Clerk Depute.

APPENDICES

on Reports of Preliminary Conferences, Initial
Surveys and Public Meetings, and Summary
of Suggestions made at Public Meetings

APPENDIX I
REPORTS OF PRELIMINARY CONFERENCES

CONFERENCE ON RURAL DEVELOPMENT
17th November, 1944.   2.15—4.20 p.m.

Present—

From Scottish Council of Social Services—Mr. A. M. Struthers, Miss Grace Drysdale.

From Scottish Country Industries Development Trust—Miss J. D. Bruce and Mr. W. Freckleton.

From Department of Agriculture for Scotland—Mr. T. B. Manson and Mr. A. J. Bean.

From East Fife Agricultural Executive Committee—Mr. J. K. Duncanson, Mr. J. F. McIntyre, Mr. A. Duncan, Mr. E. W. S. Balfour, Sir Robert Spencer-Nairn, Mr. Gordon Lennox, Mr. George T. Clark, Mr. John Arbuckle, Mr James Melville.

From Standing Sub-Committee of Fife Regional Planning Committee—Mr. John Sneddon, Bailie Blamey, Mr. W. G. Marshall and Col. N. E. Baxter.

From Planning Advisory Committee—Mr. C. Augustus Carlow, Mr. J. Lorimer, Mr. R. Taylor, Mrs. R. Officer, Mr. John Whiteford, Major R. L. Christie, Mr. Peter McArthur, Captain Wemyss and Mr. George Prentice.

Gen. J. D. Crosbie, County Convener, and Lord Elgin, representing Scottish Country Industries Development Trust and Scottish Council of Social Services, were also present.

Attending—County Housing Supervisor, County Medical Officer, County Engineer, County Planning Officer, and Mr. Jeffreys representing Mr. F. C. Mears, County Planning Consultant.

Mr. John Sneddon was in the Chair.

Apologies for absence were intimated from Principal Sir James Irvine and the County Road Surveyor.

The Chairman extended a hearty welcome to all those present and intimated that the Conference had been called on the suggestion of the Scottish Country Industries Development Trust, and thereafter named the bodies present.

In introducing Miss Bruce of the Scottish Country Industries Development Trust, and Mr. A. M. Struthers of the Scottish Council of Social Services, Lord Elgin expressed his thanks for the welcome extended and for the tribute paid to the Scottish Country Industries Development Trust in inspiring the calling of this Conference. His Lordship felt that the most important task before them was to provide healthy, happy homes for their people, so that they would be enabled to fulfil their duty as citizens. His Lordship intimated that there had been a distinct reduction in the agricultural population within the last few years, and he considered that the possibility of creating smaller industries which would attract people to remain in the country should be investigated.

The third interest of His Lordship was the Carnegie United Kingdom Trust which sets aside grants to assist the progress of the Scottish Council of Social Service and the Scottish Country Industries Development Trust. The Trust has also allocated certain sums for the development of village halls, and his Lordship expressed the hope that in years to come village halls and community centres might become available to all villages.

Miss Bruce explained the functions of the Scottish Country Industries Development Trust in assisting craftsmen, black-smiths, joiners, etc., in rural areas by procuring new plant, training them in its use, and helping them to modernise their workshops. She informed the Conference that in the past 171 blacksmiths and joiners in the County had been contacted, and that out of these 41 had been certified blacksmiths ; 16 were under training at present ; 14 were on the lists for the next batch ; another group was coming forward, and that approximately two-thirds of the 171 will be fully trained as oxy-acetylene welders. Miss Bruce went on to state that the Trust had started discussion groups in neighbouring Counties among the rural country craftsmen, and that these were proving most interesting. The Trust propose starting two discussion groups in Fife, one at Dunfermline and one at St. Andrews. Two years ago, with the help of the Education Authority, three very successful welding classes were started in Fife, one at Kirkcaldy and two at Cupar, and within the next two weeks the Trust hope to open a new welding class at the Fife Mining School, Cowdenbeath.

Miss Bruce further explained that a Technical Adviser had given advice to 311 inquirers in Fife, mainly in connection with plant problems and problems of reconstruction of their premises, and that there had been supplied to this County Council from the Rural Equipment Fund the sum of £450, this money being given interest free. The Trust's main interest in Fife was stated to be the development of brickworks and potteries.

The Chairman then called upon Mr. Freckleton to speak to the Conference on the subject of brickworks and potteries. Mr. Freckleton explained that they had found that there is existing in Fife quite a bed of clay which, for some reason or other, had not been developed and that there were also two brickfields which had not been developed. They had been unable to get people to take the necessary interest in their development, even although loans to instal new machinery could be supplied from the Rural Equipment Fund. He thought that Fife would do well to go deeply into this question and find out the possibilities of developing the raw material which lies at its door.

Thereafter Miss Bruce continued her address and gave statistics of the following communities :—

STRATHMIGLO—2 Linen Mills, at present making cotton, in which half the looms are idle. Approximately 80 workers employed, but this industry could be considerably enlarged. Housing is the difficulty.

AUCHTERMUCHTY—Already Cast Iron Works which they hope to develop, also very keen on developing light industry here. Suggest reopening old linen factory for other than linen manufacture.

FALKLAND—Linen and Linoleum Works used as War Department store—capable of development in its own lines. Approximately 500 male or female employees.

NEWBURGH—Large Linoleum Works and Oilskin Factories. Oilskin Factories employ female labour, while mostly male labour employed in Linoleum Works. Hope to increase so soon as housing available.

There is also a company building boats for the Admiralty, and they are most anxious to explore the possibility of the development of that industry at Newburgh.

Meal Mill—Have urged the people to open it and are helping proprietrix to instal electricity and machinery.

KEMBACK—There exists a wood-milling industry. New machinery has been installed, and the proprietor buys in saw-dust which is ground into wood flour and sold for the manufacture of plastics. Suggest that this industry could be developed, not necessarily at Kemback, but probably nearer Dundee.

132

GATESIDE—Existing Bobbin Factory which at present employs about 40 people. Efforts are being made to obtain post-war contracts for Indian trade, and the factory could then employ 90 or 100 if housing was provided.

The Chairman thanked Miss Bruce and Mr. Freckleton for their interesting addresses, and called upon Mr. A. M. Struthers of the Scottish Council of Social Services to speak.

Mr. Struthers said that the Scottish Council of Social Services were mainly concerned with the social aspects of planning. He stated that there were 159 fewer farmers in Fife in 1931 compared with 1921, and 1918 fewer farm servants than ten years earlier. The question was how could this drift from the land be stopped. Mr. Struthers stressed the fact that it was most important that agriculture should be prosperous and that every possible endeavour should be made to attract the necessary labour. He mentioned that there was a great need for better housing and that it would be of great advantage if the rural communities could be so grouped to enable the families to obtain employment on the farms or in local industries. Mr. Struthers went on to say that he thought consideration should be given to the setting up of a Rural Community Council in Fife, and he explained that the Development Commission and the Carnegie Trust have, in the past, made grants to such Community Councils. He also informed the Conference that the Carnegie United Kingdom Trust Village Hall Scheme have paid £10,000 for the provision of some 63 village halls, and paid from 1-6th to 1-3rd of the total cost of these halls. The scheme also provided loans so that it was possible for a village to have a scheme and repay a considerable part of the cost after the hall had been built.

Gen. Crosbie, Convener of the County Council, then addressed the Conference. He expressed the view that the primary source of wealth of a country is a healthy, happy population, and that to achieve this end there should be an alliance between housing and planning.

The next speaker was Sir Robert Spencer-Nairn, Bart., representative of the East Fife Agricultural Executive Committee. Sir Robert thought that it spoke a great deal for the East of Fife farmers that the number of people on the land is very much less than it has ever been before and yet they have under cultivation a greater acreage than has ever been known. He stated that there was always a great demand for casual labour, and suggested that small agricultural communities be set up in order that labour might be available for the surrounding farms. With the mechanisation of agriculture Sir Robert thought that it would be a great advantage if in each of these proposed communities there was a contractor who could hire out machinery to the smaller farms and assist the farmer in his work. In this connection the East of Fife Agricultural Executive Committee would be willing to help the Planning Committee in deciding where these communities should be. At present there are three such areas : at Craigrothie, Dunshelt, and Arncroach.

Sir Robert expressed the hope that in the near future there would be a plentiful supply of water to all farms, especially dairy farms. Another point which he raised was the making of roads. He stated that he had known of cases where the line of a road looked very well from a planning point of view, but if carried out would completely destroy the economics of the farm, and this was a point which he hoped would be given very careful consideration.

The meeting was then addressed by Mr. Manson, Utilisation Officer of the Department of Agriculture. Mr. Manson stated that naturally their interests were concerned with the preservation of agriculture, and in the planning of Fife great deference would have to be paid to the coast of Fife, which has been frequently referred to as a " fringe of gold," and this, he said, was no exaggeration. He stated that the Department had formed a nucleus of staff inside the Department—Land Utilisation Service—and that there was an Officer attached to this district, Mr. Bean, who has a unique experience of this County, and he hoped that the Planning Committee would consult with Mr. Bean on every possible occasion, when he might be able to direct our planning operations to less valuable agricultural land.

Mr. Jeffreys, representative of Mr. Mears of the Central and South-east Scotland Regional Planning Office, then addressed the meeting, and stated how interested they were in the rural problems of East Fife. He thought it might be of some interest to the meeting that Mr. Mears has promised to submit an interim report no later than January of this coming year, and this report would concern itself with many items which he thought would be of particular interest to the eastern part of the County. He was extremely interested to see the steps which this County have already made, and he felt that the County and the Region could be of great assistance to one another.

Mr. Hodge, County Engineer, then explained to the Conference the County Council's Regional Water Scheme.

After a full discussion the following resolutions were arrived at :—

(1) That District Councils should be asked to consider the desirability of setting up Rural Community Councils for the purpose of fostering and developing community life in rural areas by the provision of village halls and the encouragement of social amenities, with grant and loan assistance where desired.

(2) That it be recommended to the County Council that there be associated in an advisory capacity with the Fife Regional Planning Committee, the Land Utilisation Officer appointed for Fife by the Department of Agriculture for Scotland.

(3) That the Fife Planning Advisory Committee should consider the compilation and dissemination of information relative to the development of light industry in East Fife.

Approval of the above resolutions was given on the motion of Bailie Blamey, seconded by Lord Elgin.

CONFERENCE WITH INDUSTRIALISTS—CUPAR

9th July, 1945

Present—Mr. W. B. Robertson of Messrs. Hay & Robertson, Ltd., Dunfermline ; Mr. John Balmain of Messrs. H. Balfour & Co., Ltd., Durie Foundry, Leven ; Mr. James B. Rae of Messrs. Tullis, Russell & Co., Ltd. ; Provost Anderson of Messrs. Smith, Anderson & Co., Ltd. ; Lord Elgin and Mr. W. C. Kirkwood of the Scottish Development Council.

Attending—Mr. Carlow (Chairman), Sir James Irvine, Mr. Christie, County Clerk and County Planning Officer.

Mr. *Carlow* (*Chairman*) opened the meeting by explaining that its purpose was for the Committee to get in touch with industrialists in the County in order to find out at first hand what they desired in regard to trade and industry and how far the Committee could assist them in their plans for the future. The Committee understood that they could not plan for anybody else's industry, but they wanted to get an answer to the question " Can we, as a County Planning Committee, do anything to facilitate the expansion of your industry in our County, either by roads, by supply of electricity, by supply of water or some other thing which is entirely or partly under the control of the County Council ? " We had here, he said, representatives of engineering, paper-making and textiles.   If there was anything the Committee could do, they would be pleased to do it, and he suggested that the matter be dealt with now so that it would not be said later on that the Committee had missed something, that a silly report had been made, or that they had made an error in this, that or the other thing.   Anything that could be done the Committee wished to include in the Report, and they wanted the assistance of technical people in this matter.   Mr. Carlow then said they could deal with the frills later on—the houses, playfields, etc., and he did not minimise the importance of these—but after the foundation of a prosperous industry had been secured so far as it was humanly possible to secure it.

Mr. Carlow then referred to the representatives of the Scottish Council on Industry with whom the Committee would be conferring at a later stage in the meeting, and said that the Committee wished to get information from their valuable experience outside the County, so that every avenue might be explored which would lead to a successful result, viz. the expansion of industry in Fife.

Sir James Irvine then asked as to the particular method to be adopted.   Would the three concrete industries here represented be taken one by one in an endeavour to find common factors?

Mr. Carlow replied that there had been a proposal to interview representatives of industry individually, but personally he thought it more interesting for everybody and better, in case of any clashes, that they should all meet together and all hear each other's difficulties, hopes of betterment, etc., with a view to facilitating extension.

Sir James stated that he did not think they would feel any discord of interests.   He was, he said, desirous of finding any common factors which could be incorporated in the County Scheme.   They might hear from each representative his views as to extension of his own industry which he sees is coming and then get down to where County fails and where it can be improved.

The County Clerk suggested that the circular which was sent out to industrialists might be taken as a guide, and invited the views of those present on transport questions, etc.

Mr. W. B. Robertson (Messrs. Hay & Robertson, Ltd.) said he was almost ignorant of what this meeting was called for, and he rather anticipated coming along and sitting at the back of the hall to hear something about this planning business.   It was, he said, rather difficult for him to speak about the textile industry of Fife because he thought in Dunfermline his own firm was, and would be in the future, very much more interested in cotton and rayon than in linen, whereas Kirkcaldy, the Howe of Fife, etc., would, he thought, remain interested largely in Dundee spun linen.   Right away they got a considerable difference of outlook.   Then there were the silk mills in Dunfermline which would undoubtedly develop.   There was one, he believed, looking for additional accommodation at the moment and unable to get it.

With regard to public services, they were well satisfied in Dunfermline with regard to water ; they had electric power at a price which was considered very expensive ; they had coal.

Development, he thought, was almost certain to be along the lines of improved machinery—automatic looms and so on ; but automatic weaving machinery is almost out of the question on an 8-hours' day, and in the textile trade they were very strongly bound up to day-work only, which was a legacy from being the first industry to start female workers.   For the protection of the workers it was then decided that night-work was bad for them.   That ought to be overcome now.   If factories were to be modernised as they should be, an 8-hour shift would not pay for the difference in cost as between automatic machinery and the present hand machinery.   He had, he said, taken up some very rough figures a short time ago, and the difference in the weekly depreciation of the single loom was as between 4d. and 3/9, and that more or less washed out the benefit of the modern machinery.   That was, however, not a County matter but a national one.

In replying to the *County Clerk* as to whether a longer working day would be involved, Mr. Robertson said he, personally, would like to get two shifts, each with 40 hours a week—semi-night, semi-day.   That in his opinion was very important.   If modern machinery was not obtained, then he saw the textile trade (i.e., all except the silk trade, perhaps, which has already reasonably modern machinery) dying a slow death.   It simply could not compete against Lancashire, which was at least 20% below Fifeshire (cotton).

In reply to a question by *Mr. Carlow* as to what had happened to all the linen factories up and down the country Mr. Robertson said only one or two were defunct—at Kirkcaldy, Cowdenbeath and Ladybank.   The majority of the others were still working.   He was of opinion that rayon was one of the things that would be developed throughout the whole of Great Britain.

Coming back to County problems, Mr. Robertson repeated that they were satisfied with water, electricity and gas supplies.   Coal supplies were handy, and he thought it extremely desirable, from the coal industry point of view, to encourage such industries as will employ large numbers of female workers.   He thought all would agree that the satisfied collier was the man who had a family in reasonably good employment.   If his family could not get a job, then you had a dissatisfied man on your hands : if they were in reasonable employment, you had the man who did not want to shift and would do his best to stick to his job.   It was desirable for the Committee to keep in mind that the employment of families is not only directly beneficial to the families, but beneficial to the main industry, which is coal-mining.

Referring to roads, Mr. Robertson said he would probably be very unpopular, but he had never been a supporter of the Forth Road Bridge.   He could, he said, see no use for a bridge from the industrial point of view.   He thought it would have a disastrous effect on Dunfermline, break up distributive trades and give another wide-open opportunity for the expenditure of even more money on pleasure than is going on at present, and he, personally, did not want to see the Forth Road Bridge.

His firm's transport was a very important matter, particularly in competition with Lancashire.   All their cotton had to be brought up from Lancashire and the majority of the stuff had to go back to England for ultimate sale, and if the roads to the south of Kincardine Bridge were improved this would suit their purpose infinitely better than a Forth Road Bridge.   Rail transport was both expensive and slow : before the war they had had an excellent road service at a reasonable price by public hauliers.   Mr. Robertson here quoted as an example of nationalisation the experience of his firm in regard to transport.   The yarn is brought up from England and the empties have to be returned.   The haulier used to return the empties at 1/6 a time.   The other day, under the Ministry of Transport, the firm asked for transport for empties and were told that they could only get that done on a capacity load basis.   The lorry was filled up and the empties cost 14/8 as against the 1/6 previously.

With regard to the Tay Bridge, Mr. Robertson said this did not affect his firm in any way whatsoever.   The road plan which had been sent to his firm was not, in his opinion, going to help traffic in and around Dunfermline to any extent, and he had sent back a diagrammatic plan of how he would like to see the roads going.

Sir James Irvine said the main County problem seemed to be in having good road connections from Glasgow and the South.   The firm was not specially interested in the Forth Bridge nor were they interested in the Tay Bridge : the former might be some disadvantage, the latter neither an advantage nor a disadvantage.

Mr. Robertson in reply said the Kincardine Bridge route was for them the shortest road to England but that the roads south of the bridge, and especially the Lanark road, were disgraceful.

Continuing, Mr. Robertson said the only other point he had was about technical education. He was of opinion that Dunfermline attained and maintained its position in the linen trade very largely because of the success of the Lauder Technical School. It was now, he thought, a little bit old-fashioned, and he would like to see the technical educational facilities in Dunfermline brought up to date. It would cost money, but it would be worth it. They had no difficulty in their district of getting young entrants to the trade. A good many of them started and stopped very soon—they got other jobs, particularly at present—but they could get youngsters. The Education Authority were now giving classes for girls in addition to boys, and this was found very beneficial. The firm themselves ran a school in connection with their own works where practical training was given outwith the workshop, and Mr. Robertson said he should like to see the County Council being generous to the Technical School in bringing it up to date.

Mr. *Christie* asked if the cotton was treated before coming to Fife, and Mr. *Robertson* said that it came as yarn, and that there was no cotton-spinning in Fife. Mr. Christie then asked if this would not be an industry which would spring up, but was informed by Mr. Robertson that this was very unlikely as it was a very big job, and no new firm would ever think of spinning its own yarn ; they could buy it more economically.

Mr. *Robertson* replying to a question as to how his firm compensated for extra transport involved in the material coming from England to Scotland and back again to England stated that they could not compete on bulk production, but they were essentially Jacquard weavers and knew much more about this than they did in Lancashire.

The *County Clerk*, in further referring to road system, said the road on the Fife side appeared to be satisfactory, and it was a question of how far we could exercise persuasion on our neighbouring County. He thought this would be through the Ministry of Transport. Mr. *Christie* then said this point could be mentioned in the Report.

Sir *James Irvine* here remarked that in any national development of the road system one had got to remember that the weak links in the chain could spoil the whole chain, and we had a weak link, namely, from the Bridge to Lanark.

The *County Clerk* then said it was a very opportune time to mention it because the Government were considering a new trunk road policy.

Mr. *Carlow* said he was interested to know that Fife did Jacquarding better than other places, and Mr. *Robertson* added that at least they claimed to know more.

Sir *James Irvine* was interested, he said, in the plea for improvement of technical education. It was very clear that if firms were going to maintain their specialised work, technical education must move with them, otherwise they would be relying on experience of fifty years ago to deal with problems fifty years hence.

Mr. *Christie* in this connection then referred to the provision of a training centre in Fife for agriculture, and asked Mr. Robertson if he thought the same need applied in the training for agriculture as for technical education. Mr. *Robertson* said he thought there was need but hardly on the same lines, and Mr. Christie added that with regard to dairying and the scientific approach to it, they would be relying on the experience of 50 years ago.

Mr. *Carlow* then said the Committee were obliged to Mr. Robertson for his views on the transport question, the employment of girls, technical education, Jacquarding, etc., and in connection with the latter the County Clerk asked how far Mr. Robertson would like silence kept on the pre-eminence of his area on this subject, to which he replied that they had claimed that for a long time. Northern Ireland did similar work but Lancashire was not comparable. He thought reference might be made in the report to work being of a specialised nature.

Mr. *Rae* (Tullis, Russell & Co., Ltd.), speaking of the paper-making industry, said his company had six paper mills in Fife, one of which was closed at the moment (Fife Paper Mills, Leven). It was true to say that they, as a trade, did not visualise any spectacular expansion in the future, rather one of steady development as had happened in the past.

On the question of the transport of their materials, he said these were mainly imported. They had three mills which used large quantities of esparto grass imported through Burntisland, Methil and Tayport, and there had been no representations for improvement at any of these points. Wood-pulp supplies were, he said, also imported from the Scandinavian countries, and the three ports mentioned seemed to fulfil quite adequately the present needs. In reply to Mr. Christie, who asked if he foreshadowed any increase in importation of pulp from Russia, Mr. Rae said it was difficult to say because they did not know what developments in Russia would be. *Provost Anderson* said he was of opinion that that depended on what was going to be done with Finland.

Continuing, Mr. Rae said that with regard to their finished product, this went to England, and so far as he understood the present facilities by rail, road and coast steamer seemed to be quite adequate.

With regard to the bridges, Mr. Rae said the Tay Bridge was not of any great direct interest to the paper trade, nor was the Forth Bridge, although it might facilitate deliveries to the Edinburgh printers and publishers, but only to that extent. For Glasgow it would not help, and this was their exporting point for Australia and New Zealand.

There was one point of local interest in connection with transport—coal, and his company, he said, were concerned about what the effect is going to be on the railway line between Thornton and Markinch after the new pit is laid. There had been, from time to time, delays in delivery of coal simply because of the bottle-neck at Thornton. This had happened twice during the winter because coal seemed to be centralised at Thornton. They had to pass their coal supplies from Thornton along the main line to Markinch and from there to Leslie, and there seemed to be a bottle-neck at Thornton which held up supplies. The Company did not know if that would get worse when the new pit was laid. Mr. Carlow said that considering the possibilities of road transport by large lorries, it might be that coal would be transported from the colliery along to Mr. Rae's district by road if there was a good direct road. He said his own company were now just getting into the various points relative to road transport. Mr. Carlow was also of the opinion that there would be no more subsidence at Thornton. In reply, Mr. Rae said it was not a question of subsidence but of congestion. No doubt during the war there had been increase in war transport passing through Thornton, but delays had certainly occurred.

Referring to water supplies, Mr. Rae said there were no points in this connection to be raised by the mills ; there was a question of pollution, but this would be dealt with.

Mr. *Christie* then stated that they should concentrate on coal and paper-making, and the possibility that the River Leven might become an industrial area. What effect would it have on the supplies of water in the River Leven and surrounding ground if Loch Leven were raised another 8 ft. with the idea of borrowing water for washing materials through the pipes?

The *County Clerk* said that point was thoroughly explored in regard to the Provisional Order.

Provost *Anderson* said there had been no wastage of water during the last several years. The matter had already been discussed by the Trustees and others, but it would need very careful consideration, otherwise in raising the loch Kinross might be flooded.

Mr. *Christie* then inquired as to the raising of Loch Fitty.

Provost *Anderson* said there was a coal-pit there on the point of closing, and Mr. *Carlow* said that at present coal was being worked under the loch.

Major *Christie* said this might be a possible source of compensation for loss of water from the Ore.

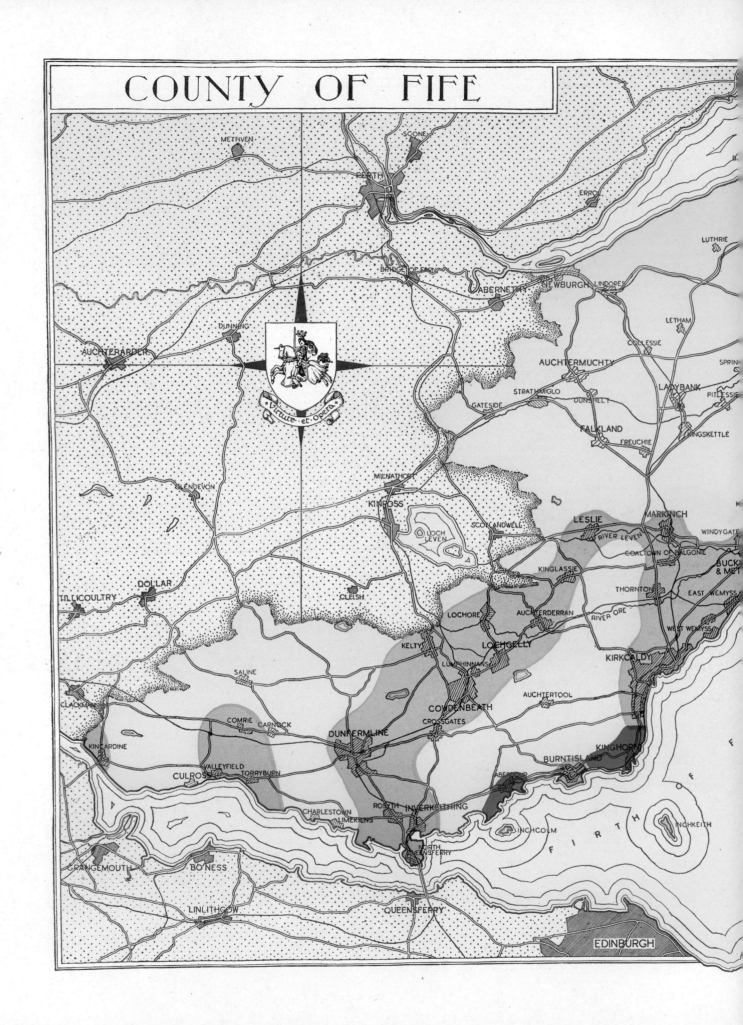

COUNTY OF FIFE

Virtute · et · Opera

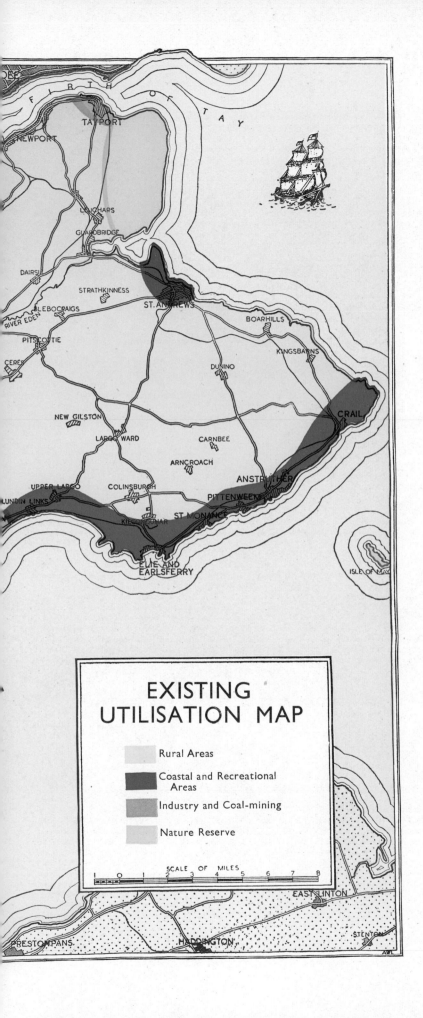

EXISTING UTILISATION MAP

OWING to geographical and geological features in the County, the predominating zones have already been defined; thus the coal industry is situated in the Wemyss area, between Kirkcaldy and Buckhaven, the Central Fife area around Cowdenbeath and Lochgelly, and in the Valleyfield-Comrie area to the west. Other industries are predominant in the Leven Valley and around the populous centres of Kirkcaldy, Dunfermline and Tayport. The residential areas of the County have naturally been determined by the employment of labour, the larger concentration being therefore in the above districts.

Agriculture is predominant in the east of the County, particularly within the "Golden Fringe." The residential areas in this section of the County are, therefore, mainly the villages and market-towns, although round the south-east coast fishing and holiday resorts predominate.

The proposals should keep these existing uses in mind, and safeguards, therefore, should be provided for their continuance.

Mr. *Rae* then supported Mr. Robertson's plea for increased facilities for technical education. The paper trade had its research authority and the Papermakers' Association had a technical section, but technical education would be very useful.

Mr. *Carlow* asked if the technical education which a boy could obtain in night-school would be of much importance to the paper companies in the sense that each paper-mill possibly had its own technicalities, and all one could learn in school would be the rudiments of paper-making?

Mr. *Rae* replied that you could not learn paper-making in school, but you had more technical control coming into the actual process of paper-making, and you got an intelligent workman better able to cope with the work.

Provost Anderson said his firm (Messrs. Smith, Anderson & Co., Ltd.) were different from Messrs. Tullis, Russell & Co., Ltd., in that they dealt with the cheap end of the trade. They were more dependent on local markets. They were going to be aced with importation from Scandinavia, and his firm wanted the cheapest transport possible, principally to Edinburgh fand Dundee. They would take paper to Edinburgh and bring back wastepaper, pulp or foreign paper which they may have to buy for economic reasons, and the same would apply to Dundee. They had a fairly good market there, and would bring back pulp and wastepaper from there also. At present they had to use the Ferry, which was costly, and for Edinburgh, Kincardine Bridge route was used, which was also pretty costly. In regard to connection to Kincardine Bridge, that was an important line of transport for his company, and they wanted a good service to Glasgow, because they exported from there and had also a large market for their own paper, and for bringing back raw materials.

Mr. *Rae* said Mr. Anderson's mill was not engaged in making esparto papers. This was regarded in the nature of a specialty for Scotland and was used for high-class printing paper. Scottish esparto paper was, he said, a very suitable medium for all sorts of publications, and there was a great demand for it from Australia and New Zealand. Question of export in esparto mills is greater than in Mr. Anderson's mill.

Mr. *Carlow* here suggested that there should be in the report a historical paragraph in regard to textiles and the paper trade.

Mr. *Carlow* then referred to the shortage of water experienced by the Guardbridge Paper Company and how this would hinder the extension of the mills and the building of houses.

Mr. *Rae* then reported that he had been in communication by telephone with Mr. Smith of the Inverkeithing Paper Mills, and he had no points he wished to bring forward.

At this point in the meeting Lord Elgin and Mr. Kirkwood arrived, and *Mr. Carlow* explained to them that the purpose of the meeting was to receive and discuss with representatives of the engineering, paper-making and textile industries in Fife what their hopes and fears were, what the County Council hoped to do and what was wanted in order to develop these three industries. The Committee would also, he said, be grateful for suggestions and guidance from those experienced in planning industry, e.g. The Scottish Council on Industry or the Scottish Development Council. They were trying to advise the County Council in the preparation of a report for the County—it was something new for the Committee, and he thought it was their duty to get together all the information they could and so assist and not impede progress.

Provost Anderson further referred to the Tay Bridge, and said his company wanted this because their work was local bulk work and would prefer it at Dundee. Mr. *Carlow* said the bridge at Abernethy would make the journey a few miles longer, but not much. Provost Anderson said they wanted the shortest way to Aberdeen and Dundee. Dundee was most important—they had mostly one-way traffic to Aberdeen, but raw material comes in at Dundee, and they sold material in Dundee. Speaking generally, Provost Anderson said the paper trade in Fife had done a good job during the war. Jute and flax had been used and paper produced to nearly full production, and it would make a wonderful story. Referring to the Report in course of preparation, Mr. *Mitchell* inquired if it was wished that the industries themselves give an account of their industry, and Mr. *Carlow* was of opinion that a few pages would be appropriate, and he thought the County Planning Officer should collect the information relative to the principal features. Mr. *Rae* here referred to a historical booklet which they had covering the trade for the whole of Scotland.

Mr. *Balmain* (Messrs. Henry Balfour & Co., Ltd.) then spoke in regard to the engineering industry. He had, he said, only got notice of the meeting that morning, and he doubted if there was much he could add as to what the various companies wanted apart from what had already been given in the replies to the questionnaire. Several firms were grouped together —Henry Balfour & Co., Ltd. and George Scott & Son, Ltd., Enamelled Metal Products Corporation and Hillside Foundry, Cupar. With regard to the companies centered at Leven, there was Henry Balfour & Co., Ltd. who had been there for over a century ; later they became associated with George Scott & Son (London), Ltd., also with Ernest Scott & Co., and later still with a newly formed company, Metal Products Corporation. Therefore at Leven there was an engineering industry giving products for almost every branch—e.g., glass-lined containers used in the milk and brewery industries and various branches of the chemical industry. Henry Balfour & Co., Ltd., so far as complete plants were concerned, specialised in gas plants in addition to their general engineering work. George Scott & Son, Ltd., specialised in the design of complete plants and did quite a lot for the paper-making industry and various branches of the chemical industry. Mr. Burns, he said, might comment about the road at the west side of Leven. He suggested that that road might be closed with a view to affording better access from the main works to the field at Levenbank. In replying to Mr. *Christie*, who asked if that would outbalance the development of the road over the bridge and into Methil Dock, Mr. Balmain said they did not use Methil Docks a great deal. There had only been one Russian contract pre-war. It was mostly road transport connecting up with the west of Scotland. All mild steel metals came from the west of Scotland, therefore good road transport was essential. It was the case, prior to the war, that if there was anything of exceptional urgency it was a decided advantage to get it by road. In normal times rail transport was all right. Mr. *Carlow* remarked that if raw material was taken from Glasgow and material taken back to Glasgow, there would be double haulage on materials. Mr. Balmain said the majority of materials was dispatched south of the Border by rail.

Referring to Mr. Robertson's point as to the charges made by the Ministry of War Transport, Mr. Balmain said that if there was a load going south and it was only three tons and there was nothing else for that particular customer or for customers in the area, the chances were that you would not get it away unless you paid for a five-ton or six-ton load. It was impossible to meet competition with a factor like that with which to deal. In fact on one occasion at Hillside Foundry he wasn't going to get the goods away unless he could make up the load. Mr. Balmain said there was also a desperate need for houses, especially in Cupar. Mr. *Carlow* then said they wanted better road transport, which included naturally the bridges over the Tay and the Forth. In replying to a question by Mr. Carlow, Mr. Balmain stated that he anticipated his company would extend, and with reference to the continuance of the manufacture of aeroplane parts, he said he thought the space used at the moment for such war products would be used as an extension for machinery in the works, and that their pre-war business would be extended by continuing in the same line. They anticipated continuous and reasonable expansion and increased employment. In reply to Mr. *Christie*, Mr. Balmain stated that they were contemplating the production of agricultural machinery at Hillside Foundry, Cupar. Replying to the *County Clerk*, Mr. Balmain said that as regards electricity, and speaking for all the companies, he would say the costs were on the high side. In this connection Mr. *Rae* said that Tullis, Russell & Co., Ltd. generated their own power, and the proportion purchased outside was very small.

Mr. *Carlow*, speaking again of the bridges, said he thought there was a slight vote in favour. He then asked Lord Elgin to speak, and explained that the Committee had been surveying the County and had visited Town Councils and Provosts. They had held public meetings in order not to miss any person or firm. All works appearing in the Valuation Roll in excess of £100 had been sent a questionnaire asking for information and opinions. Replies had been received from more than half. Then it was decided to take the industries one by one. Three industries had been dealt with to-day. They were then going to take agriculturists, and he wondered if Lord Elgin could suggest anything more that might be done, because planning was going to depend, not upon the imagination of any person who might like to see this done and that done, but on factual details. They wanted to get at solid facts. There was also the question of light industries, and they would be grateful for the assistance of those who had experience of this in other spheres. Mr. Carlow said he had always thought that the best way of getting industries into the County would be to get a pamphlet printed with vacant sites for factories, with particulars as to transport, water supply, electricity supply, population, etc., and have this advertised periodically.

Lord *Elgin* said that from what he had heard, particularly in Mr. Carlow's summing up, there had been the question of making known the facilities and possibilities for light industries. Before the war the Scottish Development Council had instituted a Bureau for people to make known particulars and facilities for factories and in order that the Council might contact possible development either in Glasgow at Headquarters or in the London Office. A good many inquirers had been put in contact with possible factories through that means. During the war years the Scottish Council on Industry, of which the Scottish Development Council is a constituent member, had taken over largely that part of the work and had recently sent out a questionnaire to all local authorities asking them to send in details of any available factories. His impression was that Fife had not replied to that questionnaire. It might have been premature but there was a possibility which was open to the County to have taken a course which was recognised, not only by the Secretary of State but by the Council on Industry which had been appointed by him and by the local authorities to co-ordinate the Scottish view and to help to bring Scotland before the public. He understood that some other Counties did take action and that the Council on Industry had visited them and inspected sites, but contact had never been effected with Fife until to-day, and that was why he felt obliged, from his own contact with the County, to make a special effort to be present to see if he could do anything to contribute. The opportunity had not been taken so far by the County of Fife. It might have been for a very good reason. He had gathered from a letter he had received from the County Clerk that it was largely because this Committee had been formed that the County Council were anxious to get details before making contact with the Council on Industry, but it had let others in ahead of the County in this particular line, and therefore Fife County were behind certain other local authorities who had, perhaps without the knowledge, definitely presented their case.

If he were tempted to go into the question of road bridges, Lord Elgin said he might take up an hour or two of the Committee's time, but he thought he preferred to leave it at this stage. There must be a large development of road transport, and there must be, if Scotland is to be developed at all, not only a question of bridges, but a question, seriously considered, of main roads. He gathered, he said, from some members' references and also from some information which he had gleaned from the Ministry of Transport, that some new main roads were projected through Fife, but whether or not we should see them was a matter for the future. As regards the question of bridges across the Tay, he did feel inclined to say one word here because he thought it might be of use. It seemed to him, in considering this problem, to be desirable to get the bridge across the Tay at a place more or less corresponding to the crossing of the Forth at Kincardine, at a cost of £300,000 instead of 2 to 3 million pounds, and this could be got in the neighbourhood of Newburgh and Abernethy at a stage where a link-up with the main trunk road from Dundee to Perth could be got, and thereby a link-up also to Dundee at approximately the same distance as having the bridge across the mouth of the Tay near Dundee. There was this further advantage, that when the traffic got across the Tay it could be distributed north, east and west. Traffic could go to Perth and the North, or by the by-pass road to Dundee and the North or into Dundee itself, whereas if the bridge were at Dundee traffic must go through Dundee. From these points of view Lord Elgin said he felt very strongly that the proper place, so far as Fife is concerned, is for a bridge in the neighbourhood of Newburgh or Abernethy rather than in the neighbourhood of the Tay Railway Bridge. That was his own view after careful study of the whole situation. Road haulage from Fife to the North across the Tay would be very much easier that way than right into the heart of Dundee. Mr. Kirkwood, he said, might be able to give help by furnishing details of the work of the Development Council and the statistics which were compiled before the war. Even coming here to-day Lord Elgin said he had had brought to his mind that there were possibilities in Fife—empty factories. They were a problem at the present stage because of the power of the Board of Trade under present legislation.

Mr. *Kirkwood*—On hearing of an industry requiring a factory, the Board offer a new factory on the terms of the Industrial Estate without the trouble being taken to look for an empty factory, even although it may be up to date. This matter had been brought to notice a few years ago—the factories were there and quite up to date but they were not on the priority list for occupation in the same way as priority is given to a firm going into a Factory Estate. The policy of the Government seemed to be focussed rather on certain areas where they wished industry to grow. Fife should consider carefully all those Small Burghs which had built up their communities with successful industries and who had the population and facilities in a good many cases available now, and which could be brought up to date. Unless the Council could, however, sit on the doorstep of the Board of Trade, he did not know how otherwise it was to be got. Mr. *Carlow* said the County could get old factories brought up to date without permission, and Lord *Elgin* advised that there should be contact through the Development Council or otherwise with the Board of Trade. Mr. Kirkwood said this was most important because Fife, not being a development area, could not participate in the benefits which the development areas would derive from the Act. The Act, he said, empowered Industrial Estates to build factories at to-day's prices— roughly twice as much as in 1939—and to let them to people on ten years' lease at 1939 rental values . . . It was, he thought, most important that those districts which are not designated as development areas should do everything possible to ensure that those factories which are vacant or likely to become vacant are put before potential industrialists. The time factor was very important. A great many people had been dispossessed of their factories, and as manager of an Industrial Estate he had seen people every day wanting factories. The cost did not matter, but occupation was required at the very earliest opportunity. It seemed to him that this was where districts like Fife should come in. It was up to the Committee, he said, to take a note of factories likely to be available, to get the fullest particulars about them, and to pass on the information to the Development Council and the Board of Trade. If this were done, and the information put before the people who are so urgently in need of accommodation, then Fife would be in a position to get factories. If it were left for a year or eighteen months, however, Fife might miss the boat!

Mr. Kirkwood then asked if the Committee had looked into the question of probable employment in the various districts. If an industrialist could be assured that the necessary labour would be made available for him, that was a great step forward,

It was a fundamental necessity that a survey of labour be made. This had been made for Dundee in conjunction with the local office of the Ministry of Labour. If it was a guess, it would be an instructed guess. An industrialist, he said, would not come up from the South unless he was reasonably sure that labour would be available.

Mr. *Balmain* said that if labour were assured the next question was where to find accommodation for the workers. Replying, Mr. *Kirkwood* said that unless factories were available and labour, there was little chance of starting new industry. Mr. Balmain said it was housing accommodation he meant, and the real problem, he thought, was going to be to find houses for key workers who would be brought from the South.

The *County Clerk* said there was difficulty about the 1939 level. He instanced a factory at Springfield which was under requisition by the War Department. Assuming, he said, that that factory was privately owned, anybody coming along would require to make a bargain with the owners of the factory as to rent, etc. How would the 1939 level apply?

Mr. *Kirkwood* replied that it was only in development areas that that applied. He had been trying to point out the advantages which the development areas enjoyed.

The *County Clerk* said that the Bill as originally drafted would have been very severe, but Clause 9 had been taken away, which relieved matters.

Mr. *Christie* asked Mr. Kirkwood if he actually had lists of people who were looking for factories, and Mr. *Kirkwood* said the Council did have them but they had been obtained from the Board of Trade, and he would not be free to make them available. There were at least 100 inquiring for factories in Lanarkshire who had not been directed. There were four development areas—South Wales, North East Coast, Cumberland and Scotland. People were given choice, but in certain areas they might have to wait ten years.

Mr. *Kirkwood*, replying to Mr. *Carlow* as to the chances of getting new industries in Fife, said unless the factories were already built it was not going to be easy. Mr. *Carlow* then asked if the Government could refuse a building permit and tell the builder to go to Glasgow or somewhere else, and in answer Mr. Kirkwood said that was the whole Government policy. You could always have extensions . . . One of the last things Dalton said was that if productive industry wanted to go into factory used for storage, then he would find storage elsewhere.

Provost *Anderson* said he had light industry but he understood from the Board of Trade that he had little chance of continuing his extension.

Mr. *Christie* asked if the activity of the Development Council would help, and Mr. *Kirkwood* said his Council were in daily touch with the Board of Trade. Mr. Christie then referred to one place in Fife where there was a thriving industry which wished to develop, but which could not get permission to extend and was therefore going to leave Fife. Mr. *Kirkwood* said this was a case for the Development Council to contact the Board of Trade.

Mr. *Carlow* said it appeared that new factories could not be obtained for Fife in the immediate future, and all that could be done was to make the best of existing factories and see if industry could not be enticed to existing buildings. Mr. *Kirkwood* advised that copy of these particulars be sent to the Board of Trade.

Mr. *Kirkwood* said that if it could be proved that the rate of unemployment had risen beyond a certain figure in Fife then Fife would qualify to be included in the development areas. He then referred to one new industry which had been fixed up for one of the Industrial Estates in Lanarkshire—manufacture of vacuum cleaners. There were also the following being made :—electric washing machines, cigarette cases and lighters, electric irons, and so on. Another firm were producing 50,000 cheap alarm clocks a week. They had been on aircraft production work but were now going to stay on as a purely peace-time company. Then there were also other people making aluminium hollow-ware pots and pans ; and others condensers for wireless sets, edge tools, equipment for automatic boiler feeders. All the money was found, he said, by the Government for these Estates. Hillington was started in 1936, and other Estates were about to be started, including Dundee. Mr. *Taylor* said he had a list of industries starting in Wales.

Mr. *Carlow* said that in the pre-war period, West of Scotland, Durham and South Wales were the unemployment areas. The reason for the unemployment in Lanarkshire was the finishing of the coal-mines. The point was to get employment to counterbalance the closing down of the coal-fields. The South Wales unemployment was also connected with the collieries. South Wales navigation coal had largely lost its markets through the navies of the world and the big passenger liners having gone on to oil. Even Anstruther fishing-boats, he said, had nothing but Diesel. This had hit South Wales. Durham for the same reason was a partly distressed area. The west part of Durham coal-field was, Mr. Carlow said, getting exhausted, and unemployment was particularly bad after the fall of France in 1940. Durham coal and South Wales coal were going to France at the rate of twenty million tons a year. France collapsed and that twenty million tons was not wanted.

Mr. *Kirkwood* again emphasised the need for sending particulars of available factories in Fife to the Development Council and the Board of Trade. Agreement *re* rental was one thing but urgency was another, and the time factor was of paramount importance.

Mr. *Carlow* said the best the Committee could hope for was for existing factories to be 90% occupied.

Provost *Anderson* remarked that his experience had been that he could not extend his new factory, and he could not get a permit from the Board of Trade.

Mr. *Robertson* said his firm had put up a drying plant and had had no difficulty.

Mr. *Kirkwood*, replying to Mr. *Carlow*, who asked how statistics could be furnished of the labour available, said this should be done in collaboration with the local Labour Exchange. He thought it was possible that these particulars were in existence now for report to Regional Headquarters, and it would only be a question of making these figures available to the Committee.

Mr. *Robertson* said that in this connection the official statement unfortunately was that Rosyth is short of skilled and unskilled labour. He said his firm could get unskilled female labour but skilled men were, of course, short at present.

Provost *Anderson* thought the only way was to offer them houses, and Mr. *Carlow* said new industry would possibly require unskilled labour.

Mr. *Kirkwood* said the Secretary of State for Scotland had laid particular emphasis, and was empowering local authorities to provide, a certain percentage of houses for key workers of incoming industries. The *County Clerk* said this created difficulties right away. Mr. Kirkwood stated the Minister might review the scheduling of the development areas, and at the end of three years areas which have brought unemployment down a certain percentage may be removed and districts where unemployment has grown might be scheduled.

Mr. *Robertson* was of opinion that the Trading Estates might be attracting big firms at the moment because of the lack of alternative accommodation, but in ordinary circumstances he thought firms would not normally go to Trading Estates where rents were high.

Mr. *Kirkwood* agreed. The only difference, he said, was that a company could choose a site anywhere within the development area and not necessarily in the Estate. The Industrial Estates tried to get a large number of small firms instead of a small number of large firms. There were 100 factories with communal playfields, canteen services, etc. Mr. *Robertson* said there was a proposition for Dunfermline in 1938 on the same lines as Hillington, but the war came along and prevented it. The

County Planning Officer referred to the morning and night trek involved and the competition between firms for labour and was informed that there was not much of that in Hillington. The *County Clerk* said he presumed the Industrial Estate existed because of the fact that it was within a development area, and this could not be had for Fife, and Mr. Kirkwood replied that this could not be had in Fife at public expense. The County Clerk said from planning authority point of view he thought it would be better to indicate to industry the possibilities with regard to accommodation, water, labour, etc., and if industry were induced to come, good and well. The new Planning Act arranged for local authorities providing building, and it was a start-off for industry. Mr. Kirkwood pointed out that the local authority must pay for it exclusively.

Mr. *Carlow* asked whether the Board of Trade would still refuse a building licence supposing the County Council were to offer to acquire a site.

Mr. *Kirkwood* took as an example a small town in Fife which had previously depended on one industry and was going to give up. If it could be proved that that area was likely to lapse into a state of unemployment, then under these circumstances licence would be granted.

The *County Clerk* in this connection referred to Leven and said he did not think the Board of Trade would stand in the way if a scheme were put forward for developing the area.

Mr. *Kirkwood* reminded the Committee that for the next few years there was bound to be a severe shortage of building labour and materials.

Mr. *Robertson* stated that modern factory accommodation did not need builders : all, or the majority of modern factories, are built of steel and asbestos, and that is entirely different from the building trade.

Mr. *Taylor*, County Planning Officer, said he was of opinion that if a factory in Leven were to be built to employ female labour then the Board of Trade would grant it, and Mr. Kirkwood agreed with this if it could be said there was unemployment to the extent of say 500 female workers. Mr. Taylor then remarked that this had already happened and permit had been granted in Leven.

Mr. *Carlow* said it was clear that lists should be made up of all existing factories, and a labour survey made and put forward pointing to the fact that there was female labour available.

Sir *James Irvine* said it appeared that Fife was not a scheduled area. On the whole he was rather glad, as he would rather be in an area which was earning its own keep than in an area with mass unemployment, etc. In Fife, so far as their plans went, it was common knowledge that there was likely to be a development in the coal industry. Industry in Kirkcaldy is thriving, he said, and Dunfermline was emerging from a period of some difficulty, and an age of prosperity lay ahead. Fife still had priority in paper-making, and in looking at this industrial problem it did not have any benefits as a scheduled area, but it was nevertheless advisable, wherever it was possible, to get planted here and there small subsidiary local light industries, partly to absorb female labour and partly as a kind of insurance against the major industries coming into a bad period. He recognised, he said, it would be a sporadic effort effected by the County themselves. He thought the point of view of urgency had been to him the greatest surprise. It was necessary to act now in order that it be made known that in certain places in Fife there were additional factories which could be brought into operation, that there was, even without the planning scheme of the future, a pretty efficient working County organisation, and, in short, in quite a brief space we could lay out the advantages of coming to particular parts of Fife. With that could be given the labour likely to be available. As had been said, this could only be a guess—at least it could be intelligent conjecture. Likewise with regard to the position of housing as it now stands. We would, he said, have to be frank and honest about that, and if we did that he suggested we had done our best for the immediate duty that lies before us without infringing in any way upon the Council's long-dated policy. It could not conflict with that, and that was, he thought, the immediate step that ought to be taken.

Mr. *Kirkwood* said it applied particularly to those companies depending for success on their export trade—delay there would be fatal.

The *County Planning Officer*, replying to Mr. *Christie*, said there were 12 factories of various shapes and sizes known to be unoccupied.

Mr. *Kirkwood* inquired as to the use in Fife of aerodromes to help housing shortage. Mr. *Christie* stated that at the moment there were very keen inquiries by a live young firm as to one of the aerodromes. Nothing had yet been decided with regard to the other two, and it was suggested that it might be worth while for the Committee to find out. Mr. *Carlow* said inquiry had been made of one of the Provosts, but he did not know and he did not want any new industries.

Mr. *Balmain*, referring further to labour, asked if the returns proposed would reveal any great figures. He was more concerned from the engineering point of view with regard to obtaining labour for the expansion of existing trade. There were contracts which could not be met because of the lack of labour. At Hillside Foundry there was a Ministry of Works contract, and the firm had agreed to make their best effort, but they could do more if labour were available.

Mr. *Christie* said it depended on how soon the local authority could supply houses, and Mr. Rae suggested that as demobilisation occurred labour would become progressively easier.

Mr. *Rae* said that as works were again being started, workers were being taken away and sent back to normal employment. The Ministry of Labour could not replace these men, and the situation would not improve until there was a larger amount of demobilisation. Young men of 18 were constantly being called up, so that there was the same number *in toto* in the country as in 1941 but spread over a greater area.

Mr. *Carlow* suggested that all labour exchanges should be contacted to see if there was surplus labour, and Mr. *Taylor* said they wanted to know what labour would be available in six months' time.

Mr. *Rae* said a form had just been completed for the Ministry of Labour in which was given the present employees, estimate of what would be in September and what they will have in December.

Mr. *Kirkwood*, referring to a statement made by Mr. *Carlow* that the Shell Factory at Crombie would be closing down, stated that this was where this Committee would be of use in contacting these Government Departments and going officially to Supply Department and Ministry of Labour. It might be ascertained when Shell Factory labour will be on the market.

It was agreed that an approach be made to the Ministry of Labour Headquarters in Edinburgh and the propositions put to them.

Mr. Carlow then referred to a plan which might be of interest showing works and factories, and Mr. Kirkwood drew attention to his Council's reports on light engineering, and on industry in Scotland.

Mr. *Carlow* then thanked everyone for coming to the meeting. It had, he said, been one of the most useful the Committee had had.

CONFERENCE WITH AGRICULTURISTS, CUPAR
16th July, 1945

Present—Mr. Christie (Chairman) ; Mr. Carlow ; Mr. J. Whiteford ; Mr. A. Dryburgh ; Mr. J. Paton ; Mr. F. W. Roger ; Mr. D. L. Buttercase ; Mr. P. T. Sutherland ; Mr. Fair ; Mr. G. R. McGarva ; Mr. J. C. McIntyre ; Mr. A. J. Cuthill ; Mr. G. T. Clark ; and Mr. J. Melville.

Attending—Mr. M. E. Taylor, County Planning Officer.

Mr. *Christie* explained that the County Council of Fife decided some time ago to produce a Report for the whole of the Kingdom of Fife, looking to the next 60 years : developments of all kinds—mining, arterial roads, agriculture, satellite towns, etc. No doubt they would have seen reports in the papers of some of the meetings which the Committee had been holding. In order to get an unbiased opinion upon the various questions the County took a very democratic way of appointing a Committee of about 14 who were not members of the County Council ; the only member of the Advisory Committee who was a County Councillor was General Crosbie, Chairman of the Committee. The Vice-Chairman was Sir James Irvine. An effort was made to get representatives from all the various industries and undertakings so that everybody would have a voice so far as the future was concerned. It was found that a smaller Committee was necessary to carry out the exploratory work, and a Sub-Committee consisting of Mr. Carlow (Chairman), Sir James Irvine and himself were appointed for this purpose.

Mr. Christie said it had now come down to this, that each of them was asked to write part of the Report ; he had been asked to prepare a report on agriculture. Mr. Christie felt there was a chance in the production of this Report for agriculture to make its voice heard, and so he had asked the Editorial Sub-Committee and Mr. Mitchell if they would call together a number of skilled agriculturists first of all to see if they could not air their views upon certain subjects regarding which the Committee wanted guidance, and then having got these views throw the meeting open to suggestions. The subject was so large and the amount of thought needed was so great, he said, that he was going to ask them if they would be good enough to turn these things over in their minds, and if they had any suggestions of a concrete nature which might lead to the betterment of agriculture in the future, would they put them in writing and send them in to the County Clerk. Mr. Christie went on to say that they had already received three most excellent reports, and he could not stress too strongly the value these were going to be in the preparation of the Report.

Mr. Christie stated that they were all aware that there had been a desperate decline in agriculture since 1875. Only twice during the period 1919-1939 had returns from agriculture at any time approached what they ought to be. Because of this tremendous depression of agriculture since 1875 they had been faced with a depopulation affecting the whole of agriculture and a great decrease in the number of skilled men. The young men did not want to stick it and they had all gone off to where they could get better jobs, better houses and better wages. Something would have to be done to improve the workers' houses and to bring the farm steadings up to the standards which were necessary to meet the competition which was going to come in agriculture. Some suggestions, he said, might be put forward during the afternoon. Mr. Christie had his own pet scheme which he said he would just touch on. People, he stated, said the days of landowners had passed, but his view was that they ought to have a very large increase in the number of landowners, because the man who owned his land and buildings looked after his property much better than anyone else. It was rapidly becoming impossible for landowners to keep their property in a good state of repair. Costs of maintenance had risen by 300% whereas rents were still at their pre-war level. They were therefore faced with the necessity of taking every chance they could get to better matters, and he thought this opportunity was one which they ought to seize. That, he said, was why they had called them together to consider one or two of the outstanding points and give the Committee their ideas.

First of all Mr. Christie took the question of depopulation. During the last half-century, he said, men had been leaving the land : the question was how was this to be stopped. There had always been a gulf between the wages of the industrial community and the wages of the agriculturist, and the time was coming when the agriculturist was not going to be willing to put up with the wages of the past, and he wanted his wages to be brought into line with the general wages of industrialists in the County. The farmer, said Mr. Christie, could not do that unless he got prices for his goods. Mr. Christie then asked if any of those present wished to say anything on that subject.

Mr. *Dryburgh* asked if the question of wages did not entirely depend on the Government's agricultural policy. It was really a matter of prices. Prices determined the wages to be paid to the workers. If the farmers were to get a decent price for their produce, he said, then in that way the flow from the country to the towns could be arrested. In the past agricultural produce had been paid a very low price. Farmers had been unable to pay a decent wage and landowners hadn't been able to reconstruct or do anything to farm-servants' property, but this was definitely a political matter.

Mr. *Carlow* said he was looking forward to listening with great interest to this conference about agriculture. What they wanted to get for their Planning Report from this industry, he said, was more a question of what the County Council could do in carrying out their planning to assist, or at least not to impede, the agricultural industry. He knew wages and prices were most important but doubted whether the planning of the County could influence prices or wages.

Mr. *Christie* quite agreed with what Mr. Carlow had said, but wished to bring out the point that the whole future of agriculture depended on the Government's agricultural policy. The prices of coal might rise and fall, he said, but to his mind for agriculture they must have a steady future to look forward to if anything was going to be accomplished in stopping the drift from agriculture.

Mr. Christie then took up the question of housing and hoped that there would be a certain amount of discussion. There was the difficulty of rehabilitating the rural housing. An effort had been made some years ago, with the assistance of a grant, in putting right the rural houses, and in many cases the money had been thrown away. He knew several cases where within 10 years the house had had to be pulled down. The standard of living expected by the worker had risen so rapidly that the man and his wife had been led to look for something very much better than they had had in the past.

The County, he said, had been advancing very rapidly in these little agricultural houses they had built at Craigrothie and Dunshelt, and Mr. Christie said he had been struck that in two of the reports they had received they both very strongly supported the encouragement and further development of these housing experiments. In fact they had found that nearly every industry in the County expected the Government or the County to supply houses, and agriculturists were about the only ones who expected the houses to be put up by the landowners. One report the Committee had received analysed the workers on 17 farms, and out of the 99 employees on these farms the report was that 34 could very well be spared to live in a central community and travel to their work. Some of the agriculturists he knew were rather opposed to the idea and thought that the houses should continue to be erected on the farms themselves and not concentrated in community centres. Mr. Christie then asked for the views of those present.

Mr. *Paton* said that some years ago he happened to be on a Commission regarding the wages question and they had evidence from a very well-known man in Aberdeenshire. They put this question as to whether he would like to have his workers on the farm or in the village, and his reply was he didn't mind, but the stock men must be housed near the steading. It was essential that the stock men should be on the farm. Difficulty had arisen in Aberdeenshire because some of the big sheep farmers could not get their sheep looked after because the shepherds would not go out to the outlying districts. In a case in his own area Mr. Paton said a farmer was building a house in the low country and the shepherd would have to travel up to the hills.

Mr. *Carlow* asked if that would not leave the stock men more isolated than ever. It would mean fewer people at the steading and they might not be so happy being more isolated.

Mr. *Paton* emphasised that cattlemen and all men driving horses would have to be at the steading. There weren't so many other men, the percentage wouldn't be very great. You might have in a whole district a considerable community of orramen but your diminution of men resident on the farm would be very small.

Mr. *Carlow* thought the County Council would rather build them in a village than at the steading, and that they would be able to do that as a policy to a certain extent.

Mr. *Roger* claimed to know something about agricultural workers. He had reconstructed 19 cottar houses for his 40 employees. He had talked with his employees and they agreed that the proper place was on the farm, with the exception of out-of-the-way farms where a tractor driver or orraman might be housed in the village, but it would be worse for those left on the farm if some were taken away to villages. There were, of course, some men's wives who would prefer to live in the village, and Mr. Roger thought it would be quite a good thing if houses were built in villages for these men and old age pensioners. Mr. Roger thought larger subsidies should be given to owners and occupiers to help them keep their property in good condition and to make better roads to the farms. He considered that a piped supply of water was essential. He knew that from personal experience, because he had one house which didn't have water in it and two different families had left because there was not water in the house. Mr. Roger thought the County Council's Regional Scheme was a very good idea. Their difficulty in East Fife was lack of water supply.

Mr. *Carlow* inquired how many agricultural houses had baths.

Mr. *Roger* said he had reconstructed all his houses before the County Council insisted upon a bathroom and hadn't had any demand for putting bathrooms in the houses.

Mr. *Paton* thought it was essential that there should be hot and cold water in all the houses. It was a great thing to have contented workers.

Mr. *Carlow* remarked there was a certain amount of feeling that part of the workers might be housed in villages and part on farms.

Mr. *Christie* said that one of the troubles was that the cost of building houses at the steading was so exorbitant. He had put up two himself, and they cost between £1100 and £1200 each.

Mr. *Melville* thought the cost of building had risen by 250%, but the subsidy given by the County Council was still at the pre-war rate.

Mr. *Sutherland* said that if one scanned the advertisements of people looking for jobs, in every case they would see that the situation must be near a 'bus route and the house must be modernised. A school was occasionally inquired about. Mr. Sutherland expressed the view that our system of education was rather to blame for the depopulation in our areas. The Education Authority in the last few years had closed a great many rural schools. In Newburn they had had the greatest difficulty in keeping their school open when the attendance was down to 5. Fortunately it was kept open and the attendance was now up to about 20. Where schools were 2 or 3 miles from the cottars' houses the employees simply wouldn't have it. The distance from the various schools was attracting employees from the farms to community centres, which was all wrong, because if a child had not a rural mind when he was a youth he would not have it when he came to manhood.

Mr. *Mitchell* asked the view of the gentlemen present on the question of the hostel idea for the housing of orra' labour. In these villages, he said, it might be suitable to meet the needs of labour on certain farms if hostels were provided for accommodation of the single men who were employed as orramen.

Mr. *Dryburgh* thought the idea would be quite good. It would, of course, depend on the number of young men who could be used to make it an economic proposition.

Mr. *Roger* stated that it was essential before to have these young men on the farms because they were nearly all ploughmen, but now the biggest percentage was tractor men and they could certainly be housed in a hostel.

Mr. *Christie*, answering the question as to how far mechanisation was going to take the place of horses, said it was very difficult to form a picture of the future. He thought it would continue that a large number of farmers would keep the number of horses at their present level.

Mr. *Clark* remarked that a great deal depended on the soil. On very sandy dry land tractors could be used, but on heavier land horses were required.

Mr. *Mitchell* asked if they could take it as the view of the meeting that the present educational system was responsible for a great deal of the depopulation.

Mr. *Whiteford* stated the whole question of housing on farms was a very difficult thing to form a suitable opinion about. From the farmer's point of view he would say that the more people he had housed on the farm the better. A man who was on his job had a tendency to be more efficient than a man who was a bit away.

From the worker's point of view he would like to be clear of the " tied " house, in many cases. Mr. Whiteford went on to say that he had spoken to all his men and found that the older men had no notion to leave their little country cottage, nor had their wives, but the demand for being in community centres came largely from orramen and young women who would not take a job on any farm. They wanted to get away where they could start late in the morning in a clean job.

In summing up, Mr. Whiteford thought that in their district there might be plenty of permanent houses on the farms because should a farmer see a need for another house he could quite possibly get a little wooden hut that would satisfy many people. It was very difficult for a landlord to grant every wish of his tenants.

Mr. *Carlow* asked if the general view was that the houses should all be built at the steading, or some in or near a village.

Mr. *Christie* thought they had got it from quite a number of people that so far as orramen were concerned there was no difficulty about their being housed in villages.

Mr. *Buttercase* said he had no trouble as a rule in getting people to go to his two farms in the Cupar district, but he had great difficulty to get them to go to the one in the Kilmany district because it was so far from 'buses. In all three places the workers wanted to stay on the farms if there was only a 'bus to take them away.

Mr. *Mitchell* then asked Mr. Buttercase for his own view.

Mr. *Buttercase's* own view was that they should all stay as near the farm as possible.

Mr. *Taylor* asked if he could put the case of housing workers in community centres. One of the prime aims of the Report, he said, must be to have a well-balanced agriculture. As had already been mentioned, there was a steady drift from the country to the town, and they would have to do something about it. Mr. Taylor said he was not quite certain how they were going to do it, but he would make certain suggestions which were brought out in the Scott Report, which was an English report and therefore slightly different. In Scotland, he said, they were fortunate in this respect that the " Jerry " builder had not come into the countryside as much as in England. There you had houses built up and down the countryside where development had been badly planned and uneconomic, and some of the best land had been used. This had made immense difficulties in regard to transport of children to school and also to the towns. The week's social life was improved by having community centres ; good agricultural land was not wasted for building purposes, and public services such as gas, water, electricity could be provided at an economic figure. It was also possible to provide medical services at an economic figure. In some rural areas, he said, they would find a doctor charged £1 per visit, but if the people were housed in a community centre it would be possible to bring him at a much cheaper rate. They could also get better shopping facilities, and Mr. Taylor felt that by giving the workers such things as a village hall and organising social life in keeping with the countryside they would get a return of the personnel to the basic industry of the countryside.

Mr. *Christie* thought the advantages of the community centre were quite obvious, but there was the difficulty of working it with the farming system here, and it was going to be a question of the balance between the two.

Mr. *Carlow* asked if it would be any use if he suggested that in order to give the farm-working community at the steadings a little more social life a 'bus should go round the farms, maybe twice a week at some time to suit the job, to take the people into the nearest village or town and then take them back again at perhaps 11 o'clock at night. That seemed to him, as a complete stranger, to be a way of cheering up the lives of the workers.

Mr. *Roger* remarked that there was something in that. In a great many cases the 'buses were packed before they got to the outlying districts and the people were forced to walk. If a 'bus could collect people from a certain number of the outlying farms it would be a great benefit. It might be as well, he remarked, to subsidise a 'bus as to subsidise a house.

Mr. *Christie* said the economic pressure of the future was going to force the landlord to do away with his smaller farms. He gave a concrete example of a farm on his own place which would be given up as from November next. He was told he could let it quite easily if he would spend £2000 on the steadings, which was just impossible, so out would go one small farm. Mr. Christie was quite positive that this would happen again and again, and they were going to lose these small training farms from which a man could work up.

Mr. *McGarva* agreed that there was no alternative to what Mr. Christie had said. It was quite hopeless unless they could get decent agricultural prices. Mr. McGarva said he had had to pull down a good many in his day for the simple reason that it was impossible to replace buildings.

Mr. *Clark* asked why couldn't the Department take over these small farms to make small holdings?

Mr. *Roger* thought it would be a mistake if those small farms were done away with altogether.

Mr. *Christie* remarked that as things went at present it was inevitable.

Mr. *Mitchell* then asked if the real difficulty was the cost of renovating the buildings.

Mr. *Christie* replied that the real difficulty was the cost of bringing the buildings up to modern standards. He was convinced that the owner-occupier was able and more ready to do what was needed.

Mr. *Taylor* remarked that a census had been taken, and it was found that farmers would rather have a bad landlord than own their own farms.

Mr. *Whiteford* stated that there had not been enough money coming into agriculture for landlord, tenant, or worker. The whole industry had been impoverished. They were all agreed, he said, that the kernel of the whole matter was prices of agricultural produce.

Mr. *Christie* then raised the question of the possibility of establishing a Training Farm to deal with the recruitment of younger people with a bent towards farming. His suggestion would be, he said, that it should be a residential farm ; that the people trained should be boys from 15 to 17 ; that at this Training Farm there should be both the arable side and the dairying side ; that there should be a centre for learning all the most up-to-date machinery ; and that at the age of 17 the brilliant ones should be given a year's travelling so that they could see the farming methods of countries such as Canada and New Zealand. Mr. Christie felt that Fife had its own farming problems, its own soil, its own rainfall, etc., and you couldn't get training in Fife farming by going to Auchincruive or Aberdeen. The idea had been growing in his mind as to whether it was practical or not, and he was anxious to have their views.

Mr. *McIntyre* said Aberdeenshire and Ayrshire were very bad comparisons. They were not getting a training in practical work there. The training was all in theory and the application of science to agriculture. This was an entirely different thing from learning to use their hands in agriculture. To his mind the application of science to agriculture was the same all over. What they wanted in Fife was the establishment of a Training School where boys and girls from the cities and towns could be recruited into agriculture to revitalise it. Mr. McIntyre was all in favour of the establishment of a Training School where people could get instruction in the ordinary everyday work of the farm, so that they could put into the farmers' hands people who were skilled.

Mr. *Buttercase* expressed the view that the most successful farmers were those who had had to work hard when they were young. Nowadays they were at school and they didn't care to work.

Mr. *Christie* then asked if Mr. Buttercase would be in sympathy in general with the idea of a Training School.

Mr. *Buttercase* replied " up to a point." If they start young enough at home they can get proper training.

Mr. *McIntyre* took the example of stacking. " How many men are there in the County of Fife under 30 who can stack? " he asked. The young men of to-day were getting no experience in stacking and very few were anxious to learn.

Mr. *Whiteford* was afraid with the " happy go lucky " methods of a Training Farm they would take very bad with the rigours of farm service.

Mr. *McIntyre* stated that if a young boy was imbued with the idea of doing a job he could get satisfaction out of doing the job well.

Mr. *Fair* thought there were youths in the cities and towns who were really interested in farming, and if they had a Training School it would be possible for such boys to go there and learn all they could about the job in which they were interested.

Mr. *Melville* said that in the period between the two wars they had lost a very large proportion of their skilled farm workers and these had been replaced by a class of people who were mainly seasonal workers. He knew quite a number of farms into which the families of these people drifted as workers, and they were not of a particularly high intellectual type. What they wanted to do was to bring the proper type back to the farms, and he thought Mr. McIntyre's idea was the only way they could do so. He was prepared to support the scheme.

Mr. *Carlow* wondered if they would not get better results if it was done to a co-operative plan so that gentlemen like themselves would control the teaching of the youths and not leave it to some educated person who would not be such a practical man. He explained that the Fife Coal Company had training pits where all boys and men coming from outside the industry received training by qualified managers.

Mr. *McIntyre* said they could work quite well in the County of Fife because they had the Executive Committee and they had Agricultural Colleges which could help with the theoretical side, and he visualised that on this farm staff they would have recruitment of farm workers who could build a stack and who could plough and do all the skilled work of a farm.

Mr. *Mitchell* thought Mr. Carlow's point would be met by what Mr. McIntyre had said. The Agricultural Department and the Education Authority would control the Model Farm, and Mr. Mitchell thought it should work well.

Mr. *McGarva* said to make sure of their family farms. He took for his example the very splendid type of man from round about Kilmarnock. " If you want men with secondary education, leave them until 17, but if you want a worker you must begin at 13," he said. Mr. McGarva expressed the view that it was up to this Committee to try to save these family farms.

Mr. *Christie* then raised the question of the upkeep of farm roads. This, he said, was a point where the County could help. Many of the farms in Fife had been put down near old main roads, new roads had been made, and the County had dropped the old roads. Mr. Christie referred to an estate of over 100 farms where the farmer and owner had to keep up 6000 yards of road. These were simply farm roads and nothing else, and they couldn't claim the County had any interest, but in addition they had to keep up 13,000 yards of roads—County roads, the old main roads. It was becoming quite impossible for the landlord or the tenant to keep up these roads. Mr. Christie thought they were justified in putting forward a very strong suggestion that the County should take up the macadamising of these roads. He thought that if he could get statistics from any farmers placed in the same sort of position it would help the case.

Mr. *Sutherland* asked if the roads referred to by Mr. Christie were through roads, to which Mr. Christie replied in the affirmative.

Mr. Sutherland was of the opinion that where a road supplied 3 or 4 farms it was not the proprietors' affair to repair that road. The roads were used by heavy vehicles, the proprietor got no benefits, but the tenant looked to the farmer for repair. He suggested that where a road did supply more than two farms the County should at least contribute to the upkeep.

Mr. *Christie* suggested they put it to the County that they should have a census of all the old roads to see if it would not be possible to keep them up.

Mr. *Mitchell* thought it might be helpful if those present saw the map showing the proposed new roads in the County. A copy of this map was handed to each gentleman present.

Mr. *Christie* then mentioned the question of forestry, but didn't think they need bring it up. Mr. *McGarva*, however, remarked that it was a very important question.

Mr. *Mitchell* thought it was very important because before the appointment of the Advisory Committee Mr. Mears, the County's Planning Consultant, pressed very strongly for the County Council to consider the forestry question. He said there were many acres which might be suitably planted by the County Council and be quite an economic proposition in time to come. If that was the view of this Committee Mr. Mitchell thought they should express it now.

Mr. *Christie* said they had received a very special report dealing with the question of forestry which he thought covered all the ground, and they needn't discuss it further at the moment if Mr. McGarva had no objection to a copy of the letter going in. (The letter is contained in the Appendix to these notes.)

Mr. *Whiteford* thought it was certainly one of the things which the Planning Advisory Committee should consider as being a likely means of employment for the future of the County.

Mr. *Roger* wished to raise a point about Methil Dock. The Government, he said, had made them send all their seed potatoes by ship, and he discovered that they couldn't get them into Methil because the dock belonged to the railway company and they wouldn't allow potatoes to be sent into the dock unless in railway waggons, with the result that the potatoes had to be taken to Kirkcaldy and Dundee.

Mr. *Dryburgh* explained that there was only the one wharf, and it was not handy for the shed where they loaded the potatoes. Buckhaven and Methil Development Committee were taking up that point.

Mr. *Christie* remarked that there was a suggestion of driving a new road into the east end of the dock. This would necessitate the building of a fly-over bridge.

Mr. *Dryburgh* said the Potato Marketing Board were anxious to curtail the shipment of seed potatoes as much as they could as they were more liable to frost.

Mr. *Christie* explained the map showing the proposed arterial roads which had previously been handed to the gentlemen. There was a suggestion that the road linking up the Forth Bridge and the Dundee bridge might be swung round towards Newburgh and cross there instead of at Dundee, he said. Perhaps they would be reporting along the lines of a bridge at Newburgh as against the Dundee bridge.

Mr. *Roger* raised the question of the type of houses which they proposed to build. He remarked that there has been a lot of talk about building tenements to save agricultural land, but it seemed to him that a tenement was a kind of God-forsaken building and that a little bungalow with a garden was a far more suitable place to live in, and that instead of building tenements to save agricultural land they should develop the land in the centre of the County. There was a great mass of land, he said, which could be utilised. At present it was standing in secondary grass. This land of low-grade fertility stretched from the vicinity of Fife Ness across Fife towards the Lomond Hills. At one time it had been used for the grazing of agricultural horses and young horses from the East Coast side. Now there was no demand for the young horses, but a dairying industry had sprung up round the coast, and Mr. Roger was wondering if this land could not be developed to make it first-class grazing land.

Mr. *Christie* said dairying was a growing industry in Fife. There were 310 dairies in Fife, and he thought they were going to see a steady increase in heads of dairy cattle.

Mr. *Taylor* then explained two maps. Map 1 showed the agricultural value of the land in Fife, and Map 2 proposed rural zoning.

Mr. *Christie* said the question periodically arose at their meeting as to whether there was anything they could do to ensure the carrying-on of the training of people who would be able to shoe horses. He had been talking to a blacksmith who had informed him that between 1911 and 1921 he had trained 11 men ; only two completed the course, and they both said they wouldn't shoe a horse. They were up against a real problem, Mr. Christie said. When the older blacksmiths went out what were they going to do?

Mr. *Carlow* asked if the time wasn't going to come when the blacksmith's shop would have to be portable and travel to the farms. Mr. *Dryburgh* said they were doing that already, but the trouble was there were too few of them.

Mr. *Christie* was inclined to think that the trouble was the apprentice system, and asked if anyone had any constructive suggestions. Mr. Roger gave as one suggestion better pay for apprentices.

Mr. *Christie's* next question was whether there was any area in Fife which needed draining on a large scale. Mr. McIntyre said practically every farm had pieces of land which needed draining. Mr. Christie had in mind an area somewhere near Edenshead which could be greatly improved by a drainage scheme. Mr. McIntyre informed the meeting that the area at Edenshead had all been surveyed by the Department of Agriculture, but the trouble was that the remainder of the work required to be done further down.   Mr. *McGarva* said that was not the whole trouble.   There was the question of the valuation of the land.   Mr. *Melville* stated that at the present time it cost £50 to drain an acre.

Mr. *Buttercase* didn't think enough attention was paid to main burns.   He took as an example the Motray Burn, which, he said, was now almost level across.   That, said Mr. *McGarva*, was brought about by people not agreeing.   Mr. *McIntyre* said the trouble there was the area of ground which would be improved by deepening the burn.   The Government only allowed £5 against every acre that could be improved, and if the scheme was costing more then compulsion could not be used on proprietors to get the job done, but the Department of Agriculture were trying to use their persuasive powers on the people who were not willing to pay their contribution.   Mr. *McGarva* was of the opinion that the situation had not been improved by the County Council reinforcing the bridge with concrete.

Mr. *Mitchell* stated that the County Council had been informed that the invert at the road bridge was not an impediment here.   He thought one man was holding up the whole thing, and if he could be persuaded to do his job the matter would be solved.

Mr. *Christie* wondered who was to bring pressure to bear on owners who would not do jobs.   Mr. *Mitchell* thought that if it was simply noted that the Department of Agriculture should be given compulsory powers and that if these should be used, that would be sufficient.

Mr. *Christie* then spoke on the question of resuscitating the Seafield Tile Works.   Mr. *McIntyre* said the Ministry of Works had asked the Department of Agriculture to requisition the works, but the trouble appeared to be largely a case of the proprietor not wishing to have his amenities destroyed.   Mr. *Roger* remarked that there had not been any hold-up for want of tiles, and Mr. *McIntyre* explained that the Department had tried to get over any difficulty by importing tiles from Angus and having these stored in dumps from which they could be drawn when required.

Mr. *Christie* expressed appreciation of the work which had been done by the Agricultural Executive Committees, and held that in the future there should continue to be something in the nature of the Agricultural Executive.

Mr. *Mitchell* then asked if the gentlemen present were satisfied that the new County water scheme would serve all needs of the farming community.

Mr. *Christie* thought the proposed scheme was a very good one and would bring water within fairly easy distance to nearly every farm.   There was a pipe, he said, passing near one or two farms he had in mind, and it would be a heavy cost to bring in the water.   The question was whether the County was going to bring the water in or whether it was the duty of the landlord.   Mr. *Mitchell* explained that the obligation was on the County Council to give a piped water supply practically to every inhabited house in the County if it was reasonably practical to do so.   That was the problem the County Council were faced with, and they had tried to carry it out in their new scheme.   Mr. *Roger* stated that he understood the scheme stopped at Boarhills, but there was an extensively farmed area about 4½ miles from St. Andrews which would not get any water, and he wondered what could be done about that.   Mr. *Mitchell* replied that it might mean they would have to extend a branch pipe from the other main to supply the area.   If there was a community in that area requiring water it was up to the County to get it there.

Mr. *Mitchell* then asked if the gentlemen were satisfied that the transport system for the bringing of goods to the farm and the transport of farm produce to the nearest markets was adequate in Fife.   Mr. *Christie* thought that if the roads were put right it would meet a considerable amount of the present trouble, and there didn't seem to be a great shortage of transport when one needed it.   Mr. *Roger* said that was one of the troubles, but the lack of warehouse accommodation was another.   He was thinking about Methil.   If they could get bigger warehouses erected it would be a great advantage.   Even if the shipment of seed was stopped, he said, they would likely send a considerable quantity of produce to the London market by boat.   Mr. *Carlow* then asked how Kirkcaldy would do for that purpose, and Mr. *Roger* replied that the warehouse accommodation was very limited, and at Methil it was practically non-existent.   Mr. *Carlow* expressed the view that if there was enough trade they would get the warehouses, but if there was not enough trade to make the warehouses self-supporting then that would be the difficulty.

Mr. *Christie* inquired if the slaughtering arrangements were quite satisfactory.   Mr. *Roger* said the matter was being considered.   They didn't know whether cattle were going to be sold on the dead-weight scheme or whether they were going back to the old system.   Mr. *Christie* wondered if from a medical point of view it would not be better to have fewer slaughterhouses.   Mr. *Paton* stated that it was a question of policy.   If the policy was to be on the dead-weight basis it would mean building about 80 slaughterhouses, but if they were to go on the present system of live-weight basis, then the present slaughter-houses were pretty adequate.   If they went back to the pre-war way every local butcher would have his killing house, which was not very desirable.

Mr. *Carlow* proposed a vote of thanks to the Chairman and to Mr. Mitchell and his staff for their presence and assistance.

There is also contained in the Appendix to these notes a report received from Mr. A. J. Cuthill, Easter Kincaple, St. Andrews.

APPENDIX REFERRED TO

Balcarres Estate Office,
Colinsburgh, Fife.
15th January, 1945.

Royal Scottish Forestry Society—Post-War Forestry

Several weeks ago a copy of the Joint Report on Forestry Policy recently prepared by the Royal Scottish and Royal English Forestry Societies was sent to all Members of Parliament.   The membership of these Societies exceeds 3,000.   As senior Vice-President of the former Society, I am asking your support of the views in the Report when this very important subject comes up for discussion in the House of Commons.   In the East Fife constituency there are so many interests demanding your consideration that I can well imagine you have had little time to peruse the Report.   It was issued after eighteen months of much discussion, controversy, negotiation and many meetings between the members of the two Societies.   It can now be accepted as the considered opinion of the private woodland owners of Britain.   After full consideration to all important questions affecting the continued existence and prosperous development of private estate woodlands and stressing the need of extension, the Societies maintain that future success depends entirely on a continuity of policy.   This means that a sound financial basis unaffected during periods of depression is absolutely necessary.   Many woodland owners will, if reasonable terms are available, undertake the task of making their woodlands more productive and extending areas where the ground is favourable.

The small size of Britain's forests and her dependence in peace-time on a vast importation of timber proved a serious embarrassment to transport in the two world wars.   These war needs have been met largely by laying waste nearly all the better woodlands in this country.   Their rehabilitation and extension have become urgently essential for our future national policy.

The last war gave rise to the Forestry Commission, which directs now nearly 500,000 acres of State forests.   This war has shown very clearly a national demand for a fuller utilisation of the 2,500,000 acres of privately owned woodlands. The Commission was set up in 1919. Recently it was announced that Major Sir Samuel Strang Steel of Philiphaugh, Selkirk, and Mr. J. M. Bannerman, Aberdeen, have been reappointed the two Scottish members, but no reference is made to any specified term of office. It is assumed these appointments will be for the usual period of five years. Sir Roy Robinson is reappointed Chairman and Sir George Courthope, M.P., is again the Spokesman in Parliament. In the proposed post-war plan for forestry practically one-half of the planting programme will be in Scottish woodlands. Surely Scotland is entitled to have a larger representation of Commissioners with a Scottish outlook than only two out of a total number of ten and a separate Scottish Committee as suggested under Head 4(c), page 24, of the Report.

There is, however, another point about the Commission to which I wish to draw attention. In the past there had been an unfortunate antagonism and lack of helpfulness shown by it towards the private owner. It has dealt neither sympathetically nor understandingly with private estate forestry. It will be a sorry day for Scotland if the only planter should be the Commission. This is why the Report recommends ministerial control from the centre and devolution of responsibility to Local Committees in the provinces. Not only will the Commission be the most powerful competitor against the private owner in the sale of woodland products but will also be a serious competitor for employees. It is therefore absolutely essential that private woodland owners have a reliable assurance that the future administrative power will be sympathetic towards their needs.

The very large clear fellings, particularly in Scotland, which have taken place since September, 1939, make replanting very urgent. The Societies are most emphatic that very definite remedial measures must immediately be taken to improve the situation, which must be most acute for many years. They also recognise that the job is so comprehensive that no government department can tackle it single-handed.

In your constituency, in the early days after the last war, there was ample evidence of the large clearance of timber during the war. For various reasons, chiefly uneconomic, many of them unfortunately have not been replanted. Further, and later, numerous other fellings have taken place generally to meet the increased incidence of taxation, death-duties, etc., and also for estate maintenance. Heavy taxation and insecurity are powerful deterrents to private forestry. Indifference and ignorance also come into this question. The two last ailments would no doubt respond to educational treatment, a policy urged on the Forestry Commission by the Societies.

In 1939 the Timber Supply Department was set up to control the production of sawn timber. Now the countryside is completely denuded of all mature timber and timber approaching maturity. Prior to this war the *per capita* consumption of timber was larger in Great Britain than in any other country, whilst our stock of growing timber was lower per unit of population than anywhere else. We grow a wider range of timber trees than any other country of equal size. The foresters of the past saw to it that our excellent soil and climate were used to produce many non-indigenous varieties to cover a wide range of indigenous trees. Further, we practise a closer utilisation in working up grades of timber into useful commodities. Almost anywhere else these grades would be regarded as fuel wood only. Further, the standing value of our home-grown timber grade for grade is much higher than in any other timber-producing country.

The controlled maximum prices of standing timber are practically unchanged since the beginning of the war. If control is to continue the maximum prices should be materially raised because the cost of forestry work and estate maintenance have approximately doubled. By and by the Forestry Committee, being the largest woodland owner, will become the chief competitor of the private owners in regard to sales. On that account it is necessary that the Commission should co-operate with the private owner in marketing and fixing standard prices of woodland products.

Since 1914 the traditional system of land tenure in Britain has tended to break down. Until recent years the Government showed little interest in forestry and in agriculture, with the result they became depressed industries. Their traditional markets were invaded by imports from other countries. This competition will require to be met by a more determined local efficiency. The heavy taxation already referred to has necessitated the breaking up of many estates which were formerly large enough to maintain an efficient staff of foresters and to carry out a regular annual planting programme. Many forest areas consequently have been left derelict and are now incapable of supplying even local requirements. It is futile that the importance of woodlands in the national economy can only have public recognition during a world-wide war. An acre of well-grown woodland can carry 100 tons of timber. In doing so it saves that amount of shipping when transport is difficult. Standing timber is the ideal method for storage because for many years it continues to grow and improves in storage. No other commodity does so. The Forestry Commission, I understand, allows about 1 man per 100 acres of forest area. Many more operatives are required when the yield of 100 acres comes along to the sawmill. When Britain is so favourably placed for the rapid growth of trees it is surely a hopeless policy that necessitates so much dependence on foreign imports.

Twenty years ago planting could be carried out at £8 or £9 per acre. Owing to the gradual rise in prices the smaller size of plants last year cost between £9 and £10 per acre, to which must be added labour, netting, etc. The result was that the average cost per acre of a fairly large enclosed area could not be undertaken for less than about £20. Many planters talk of a much higher figure, but my experience is this is moderate, provided, of course, there is no open ditching nor brush nor broom clearing required. To encourage planting, the Forestry Commission is authorised to give a grant of £2 per acre for conifers, which, of course, is now hopelessly inadequate.

Generally the Report endorses the Commission's recommendations for planting and maintenance, but many members consider an additional grant should be available for clearing brush and the debris of war fellings. The Report recommends a planting grant of £7, 10/- per acre to all private woodland owners. Many members pressed for a higher sum, but in the course of lengthy negotiations with the Commission it became evident that a higher figure would be sternly resisted by Parliament. Then there is a maintenance grant for fifteen years of 2/6 per acre per annum, where new plantations are properly maintained and a grant of 2/6 per acre per annum from the date of dedication of all productive woodlands other than new plantations. These grants will be a great help to the larger and more opulent owner, but only to a small extent can they induce the small hard-up owner to plant. The result will likely be that in the end the Commission will take the small man in hand. Such a step cannot be objected to, but it would be most unfair to effect compulsory acquisition before these owners were afforded by grants the opportunity to carry out what is desired of them. At first the Commission was inclined to leave out small woods, the area of which is not clearly defined but which might represent approximately one-third of the private woodland area. Now it is proposed to recommend a planting grant of £7, 10/- per acre but no other help. This is a very important point to be yet cleared up.

Conifer timber-growing in Scotland is a highly specialised work. Whilst a good number of planters held the view that Scottish forestry cannot be placed on a satisfactory footing so long as controlled from Westminster and Whitehall with an outlook designed primarily for England, this point need not be stressed here. The general feeling is that the Government control of forestry affairs will be tacked on to the duties of the Minister of Agriculture. The Societies would like a Ministry of Forestry, and overtures were made some time ago to ascertain if the formation of a Forestry Ministry could be entertained. The reply was, this simply could not be done as no new ministries were to be established. On that account it was decided to let the suggestion drop. Strange to say, since then two ministries have been formed.

I recently read the following reference to Germany, which is highly instructive :—

"Clad in fabrics produced from wood, living on wood sugar, wood protein, and meat and cheese from wood-fed "cattle, with a schnapps ration made from grain alcohol obtained from sawdust, German soldiers move to the battle-"lines in wood-gas-driven trucks. These trucks are greased from tree-stump lubricants and run on Buna tyres made "from wood alcohol. Explosives are manufactured from the waste liquors of wood-pulp mills, also squadrons of "plywood planes and war films from wood cellulose acetate."

When timber in enemy hands can yield so many vital supplies, surely afforestation is an enterprise that the British nation need not grudge to support in the future.

The private owner in the past knew and did his job well. There is abundant proof. Take the last war. It was the enterprise and efforts of private owners generations ago which saved this country so far as timber was concerned, and again in this war, excepting for the supply of pit-props by the Forestry Commission. Somewhat similar problems have been solved in other countries in a manner consistent with their national political genius. This country can overcome the difficulties standing in the way of full-scale forest activities by goodwill, courage and endeavour. A broadly based forest policy is now one of the major economic needs of the day. On these grounds I feel justified in asking your support in the House at a later date for the terms suggested for the private woodland owner. If you can see your way to support generally the views set forth in the Report it will indeed be very much appreciated by your interested constituents.

If there is further information desired, I shall be pleased to supply it to the best of my ability.

I am,

Yours faithfully,

(Sgd.) GILBERT R. McGARVA.

Easter Kincaple,
St. Andrews.

MR. CHAIRMAN,

I think we require to sift out the reasons that have prompted the building of houses in their present positions, and see how many of the reasons could be changed to suit modern times, and how many could not. Before changing a practice which has been followed for so many years one must be very careful that the new scheme is absolutely essential.

The object in building workers' houses where they are at present must have been to be near their work. Many advantages can be quoted for a man living beside his work. A man wants to be well rewarded for his work, and he will give the best return when he does not have to use energy to get to and from it.

If not housed near their work the workers will have to bear their own cost of transport, which, if by cycle or on foot, is not very nice in bad weather, and if by motor, either 'bus or car, is very expensive.

We cannot allow the present to blind us as to what may come if we have changes of government and agriculture is allowed to fall back into the serious plights that are so short a distance away.

A new government might take away subsidies, and what is left to give increases in wages and provide transport of say 3 or 4 miles twice per day and four times per day if the man is to get a cooked dinner at his own home—and why not? What is a ploughman's wife going to do with herself when her husband goes out in the morning and does not come in till 5.30 afternoon? Her duties are certainly going to be less. Her preparing of a dinner for her husband is a most necessary occupation which she will not be able to carry out, and the man is faced with the alternative of eating a piece (which is not a dinner to a manual worker) or having some other one preparing and cooking what his wife has plenty of time to do. The farmer's wife would be asked to do this extra cooking, and how many have time to tackle it, and why should they? Instead of encouraging men to stay on the land this would be encouraging them to look for work in the town or near where they live.

The education of the children is a vexed question. Take Gateside, for instance : 11 of them are hustled away every day—4 of them all the way to Cupar. They will surely have a long enough day. These children should not be conveyed away this distance unless they show some special aptitude for something other than farming. It would be very interesting to know how many of the 11 children attending secondary schools will come back to the land. The children as they grow up on a farm are semi-skilled at 14 years of age, having had a trial at most of the jobs their fathers work at and trying to copy them. Many not having this incentive will fail to hear the call of the land.

Pleasure, such as pictures, football, etc., cannot thrive in a small community, so they must still journey to the larger centres as at present. For instance, even Auchtermuchty cannot hold their interest, and they travel to Cupar, Kirkcaldy, or Perth for entertainment.

Traders' vans would find it uneconomical to go round the few remaining houses in the outlying country districts, thus isolating and penalising the key-men who remain on the farms. A cattleman or dairyman would simply be non-existent, and that would seriously affect those living in towns or villages if they had no meat or milk.

If the half of the men are having the time of their lives in communities it will be very difficult to get the right type of men to be grieves, horsemen and cattlemen.

Imagine a community of 25 new houses accommodating, say, 35 workers who have to go in all directions to their work. How could transport be provided? and distances are too great for the outside ones to cycle. Working hours will become shorter, and to get through the work extra people will have to be engaged. Therefore labour will be at a ransom on the poorer farms. This will determine the policy of farming by forcing land to grass and causing the drift from the land to continue.

If Gateside is symbolical of country districts in this area and 27 houses have been reconditioned, leaving 15 still to do, the work of improvement has gone two-thirds of the way, and with more effort being applied greater results might be expected.

By the end of 10-12 years countries which have been suppressed by war will be working like niggers for little more than a bellyful of food. Are we able to finance this scheme and all it involves by that time? I would counsel you to go slow with any drastic change.

With all these points of view before us I am thoroughly convinced that community housing is not the attraction that is to encourage the people to work on the land. Give them a nice cottage with all modern conveniences near their work, and no man will ask for more.

To stimulate agriculture and prevent the drift from the land the agricultural worker requires, besides his cottage, to be paid at least as well as the mason's labourer, the town scaffy, the railway surfaceman, the coal carter, etc., and there would be no need for further planning on their behalf.

Give him a house near his work with modern conveniences, his garden and perquisites, and the king will hardly be claimed as a cousin.

I am,

Yours faithfully,

(Sgd.) A. J. CUTHILL.

148

APPENDIX II
INITIAL SURVEYS AND PUBLIC MEETINGS

NOTES TAKEN AT INITIAL SURVEY OF ST. ANDREWS AREA
26th February, 1945

County Buildings, Cupar, 2 p.m.

The County Clerk outlined the programme for the afternoon, and intimated that after the various County Officials had given some ideas of the development of this particular area from the public health point of view, roads side, educational side, etc., the members of the Editorial Sub-Committee would make a tour of the area and meet with representatives of Newport Town Council at Newport and then go on to Tayport to meet the Provost and Members of the Town Council.

Mr. Taylor said he had hoped to have a 6-in. map of the area available in order to let members see exactly where they were going, but unfortunately he had not managed this. By the next meeting, however, he promised to exhibit such a map.

He went on to state that he had some statistics of this area, and unfortunately from an agricultural point of view it was on the decline as far as population was concerned. From a planning point of view, he said, we must lay out this area in such a way as to entice people to live there from the agricultural side, but on top of that we will have to reserve certain areas for industries allied to agriculture in order to get the people to remain there. Mr. Taylor said he had analysed what everybody did in the towns of Newport, Tayport, Leuchars, Guardbridge and St. Andrews, and was having the analysis stencilled for circulation to the members.

The main thing from the planning point of view was to centralise the areas where development was to be allowed so that public services could be supplied economically.

Mr. Carlow intervened to enquire whether agriculture in this area was any worse than in any other. Mr. Taylor said he thought it was much the same all over and was due to the lowness of wages and the living conditions.

Dr. Fyfe spoke of the vary bad condition of many of the farm cottages. He said grants were being paid to farmers to have these houses reconditioned, but that in his opinion the whole matter would require to be reconsidered. In a great many cases the houses were much too near the farm buildings, and it would be better to help the farmers to build new houses at a distance from the farm.

At this point Mr. Carlow asked how far people ought to be asked to travel to their work. In his opinion it was necessary to have men, such as cattlemen, at the farm.

For cycling, Dr. Fyfe said a convenient distance was considered to be $1\frac{1}{2}$ to 2 miles and for travel by 'bus 6 miles.

Dr. Fyfe stated that in the East of Fife we have no less than 6 hospitals—4 Infectious Diseases and 2 Cottage. 43% of all sickness is treated in Fife hospitals; 10% in Dundee; 6% in Perth and the rest in Edinburgh, so that the bulk of the hospital needs of the County are supplied by the County itself and by Edinburgh. Dr. Fyfe thought that there should be another Infectious Diseases Hospital near Cupar so as to dispense with small uneconomic units in the County.

Major Christie asked if there was a long delay in Fife for getting into Edinburgh Infirmary. The answer was yes. There was a long delay, particularly in the early part of the war, but now to meet the delay Fife cases are being taken into E.M.S. Hospitals.

Dr. McIntosh ventured to suggest that the area under discussion was perhaps the most interesting from the point of view of education because it has within its circuit St. Andrews University, which is the first and perhaps the best Scottish University. He said that in one way this was the simplest area which had to be tackled from an educational point of view, but in another it was the most difficult. It was the simplest because of the declining population, and the existing accommodation is quite able to cope with the entire population. It was the most difficult from the point of view of advanced education, which is between 12 years of age and school-leaving age, and there, he said, we are having that vexed question of centralisation. You must have children in fairly large numbers, and where population is scattered the children must travel, and the question is how far should the children have to travel. Take Newport, he said, it is a fairly small area yet is near Dundee—where should we centralise—in Cupar or St. Andrews—or is Newport more akin to Dundee? The really acute problem is in St. Andrews, where accommodation is very limited. Roughly for the area, therefore, the existing accommodation would meet demands because of decline in population, with the exception of St. Andrews, where a new Primary School and two Secondary Schools will have to be built to meet existing needs.

The County Engineer explained to the meeting that in the East of Fife water is rather a difficult problem in so far as it is flat area : there is no good catchment area for water supply, and rainfall is very low.

Mr. Hodge went on as follows :—The County fortunately have 3 large reservoirs in the Ochil Hills, the largest being on the River Devon itself. There is a tributary of the Devon called Glenquey, and on it we have a reservoir. The third reservoir is at Glenfarg.

Our reservoir at Glendevon, which supplies one thousand million gallons, was built for the West of Fife, but there is surplus water for the requirements of West of Fife, and we have a scheme to carry water through the length and breadth of East Fife. One line of water main goes through Cupar and on by Dairsie to Guardbridge with a branch to Strathkinness. The north section of the line goes by Letham, Luthrie, Rathillet, Kilmany, taking in Gauldry and Balmerino. Newport and Tayport are within Water District of the City of Dundee, and there is a large pipe over the Tay Bridge which is not running to anything like full capacity.

We also have pipe line running round the coast by Largo, Colinsburgh, Crail, Kingsbarns and Boarhills. There is a high piece of ground between the coastal and the central line at New Gilston and Largoward, and it is not possible to reach these places by gravitation, but we have a scheme whereby water could be pumped into a tank and then distributed westward to Woodside, Peat Inn, Radernie and round to Dunino and Stravithie, covering small villages in the high level area.

Drainage presents its problems because in addition to tanks and filters the final stage is dilution in burns, and for this you require a burn which is running fairly strong, and these are very difficult to get in East Fife.

In answer to Mr. Carlow's question as to how far water would have to be pumped to get to the top of the hill Mr. Hodge replied, from above Colinsburgh, $2\frac{1}{2}$ to 3 miles.

Major Christie then enquired when the work of water mains was likely to be started, and Mr. Hodge replied that so far as commencing the work was concerned we were in the hands of the Department of Health and that Mr. Mitchell was pressing the Department to allow us to proceed as soon as possible. Mr. Mitchell said that he thought he should add that the County Council attached so much importance to proceeding with this work that it told the Department they should proceed without grant to enable them to get materials, but this was not allowed.

Mr. Boyd explained that the County Planning Committee had made certain suggestions about planning roads, and these suggestions coincided to a great extent with the proposals of the Ministry of Transport to extend the trunk road system.

So far as St. Andrews is concerned the main road from Dairsie by Guardbridge to St. Andrews and down the coast to Crail is the planning road and proposed trunk road. From Crail westwards the proposed planning road and trunk road follows an existing unclassified road to Easter Pitcorthie, thence by B942 to the west of Colinsburgh. From this point an entirely new road is contemplated, passing between Largo and Lundin Links to join Kirkcaldy District near Blacketyside. From the road between Crail and Colinsburgh spur roads would be made to link up with the coast burghs.

There are certain difficulties in connection with the scheme suggested by St. Andrews Burgh. Mr. Boyd said there had been some criticism about the increase of traffic which would be the result of an arterial road running through St. Andrews, and he thought the only way to overcome that would be to by-pass the town, and the Planning Committee have already given this matter some consideration.

Coming northwards one must consider the possible extension of the aerodrome at Leuchars. Traffic at the present moment was not permitted to pass through the aerodrome, and it would be necessary to lay down an alternative road. Such a line had been suggested by the Planning Committee which would run from the top of Seggie Brae to join A92 a short distance north of St. Michaels. From this point the existing road would be used to Newport with a spur from somewhere in the neighbourhood of Forgan school to the south of Newport to link up with a proposed Tay Bridge, if, and when, such a bridge were built.

The Committee then proceeded to Newport, where they met with the Provost and representatives of Newport Town Council.

Mr. Mitchell briefly explained to the representatives the task undertaken by the Planning Advisory Committee and the Editorial Sub-Committee.

Mr. Carlow then called upon the Provost to put forward any suggestions which the Town Council had in mind regarding the development of their Burgh.

The main points put forward on behalf of the Burgh were as follows :—
    (1) that no industries be brought into Newport but rather that it should be left as a residential area ;
    (2) that Newport might be developed as a seaside resort ;
    (3) that the proposed new road bridge over the Tay should be nearer Abernethy than Newport ;
    (4) that the pier should be improved.
The population is very stable, about 3,200.

About 30 acres of the best building land in the Burgh cannot be supplied with water. This ground is between 200 and 230 feet.

Mr. Mitchell asked if the Burgh would be prepared to come in with the County Water Scheme, as a new main would be brought through Fife very soon and it might be possible to give them a bulk supply. The Provost said this was rather a big question as Newport came within the Water District of the City of Dundee.

After discussion it was agreed that the first public meeting in the St. Andrews area should be held in the Town Hall, St. Andrews, on Tuesday, 20th March, at 3 p.m.

The party then carried on to Tayport and were met by the Provost and representatives of Tayport Town Council.

Here again Mr. Mitchell explained briefly the task undertaken by the Planning Advisory Committee, and Mr. Carlow called for suggestions towards the improvement of the Burgh.

The Provost informed the Committee that apart from sawmills, Tayport had a spinning mill which employed about 400 people ; a jute factory employing about 550 ; and a foundry which employed approximately 40 people. There is one vacant factory which formerly manufactured bobbins. This factory has not been functioning since India, to which country all the bobbins were shipped, commenced to manufacture her own. Then there is the harbour which used to take boats up to 2,000 tons and which supplied the Guardbridge Paper Company with esparto grass and pulp. Since the war, however, the harbour has not been used to a great extent, but it is hoped that when hostilities cease the trade will return.

Tayport Burgh would prefer to have the proposed Tay Road Bridge further up the river than the present railway bridge, and thereby have transport facilities which would encourage development round this area of the County.

Mr. Carlow said he thought it would be a very good idea to have a booklet published showing all the places in Fife with a list of industries which might be attracted to these different places, and also showing the local rates, cost of ground, availability of transport, etc., all which points would be taken into consideration by any prospective industrialist who wished to establish a light industry.

So far as water is concerned the Burgh is fairly well served, said the Provost, but he wondered if they would not be better to switch to the County scheme in the event of this passing near. Mr. Mitchell explained that water was coming as far as

Gauldry and as far as Leuchars, but that as the Burgh came within the compulsory area of Dundee any arrangement would have to be through Dundee Corporation.

Mr. Carlow expressed appreciation on behalf of the Committee of the hospitality extended to them, and the party proceeded to inspect the improvements carried out by the Burgh on the water front.

NOTES TAKEN AT INITIAL SURVEY OF KIRKCALDY AREA
1st March, 1945

Mr. Taylor exhibited to the Committee a map of the Kirkcaldy area.

This area, he said, is well known for its linoleum. There are only two of this type in this country, Lancaster and Kirkcaldy, and, therefore, that is a consideration which wants keeping in mind—that is one of the things we don't want to lose, and we want to try to encourage the industry to stay and expand here. The other industries of Kirkcaldy are, I believe, mainly concerned with the allied trades of the coalfields.

We want to plan not only for coal, but for subsidiary industries so that when bad times come in coal we can offset them, and that is why we should do everything in our power to encourage linoleum to stay, and we should make suggestions as to how the amenities of the district might be improved—better transport facilities, better roads—and I think it is up to us to find out all we can about what the people in this area want, it is what we are here for to-day.

One thing about this area—we have in contemplation 3 new collieries—that was in the Scottish Coalfields Report—they are all in Kirkcaldy area. First pit is to be sunk west of Thornton Junction, and we bought the Estate of Strathore for the purpose. The second is at Dysart, the third at Seafield at south end of Kirkcaldy, so there are 3 new pits in course of planning.

Mr. Taylor—I should say I was aware of these 3 pits and it has been remitted to my Department to lay out new villages for these areas.

Mr. Carlow—There is one fact I do wish to emphasise, that we, the Fife Coal Company, do desire the County authorities to reserve sufficient land for these 3 pits. I am getting plans prepared, but you can understand that in the case of Seafield it may be some considerable time before the pit is started, and mining engineers 30 years after this may have different ideas from those which we have to-day. We are making plans to the best of our knowledge and belief, and there is one thing I do wish to emphasise—and I cannot put it in too violent language—and that is there is no other place by which these millions of tons of coal can be attacked than Seafield and Dysart. Thornton might be moved a mile here or a mile there, but Seafield cannot be moved a mile anywhere. Dysart must go on Dysart land, a plan of which I will give you. These sites must be reserved for these pits. Each pit will take anything over 100 acres—we would never start a pit with less than 100 acres. I think in future it may be considerably more, and all that ground has got to be earmarked and reserved. I think we have enough at Strathore as we bought the estate, but there may be bits beyond our estate.

Mr. Taylor—Well, these will want reserving for industrial purposes in the planning scheme.

Major Christie—Can you envisage in what way this coal is going to be used? Will it be for internal consumption, for export, or for both?

Mr. Carlow—For both.

Major Christie—The question is, if it is going to be exported could Kirkcaldy Harbour be utilised?

Mr. Carlow—Methil or Burntisland Docks would be used. Burntisland can take nearly as big ships as Methil. The harbour of Kirkcaldy is not suitable.

Major Christie—Could it be made suitable?

Mr. Carlow—I should not recommend development of Kirkcaldy Harbour. It has a very bad entrance for transport. I think there is sufficient facility at Methil and Burntisland to export as much coal as is likely to be available for export.

Dr. Fyfe—This area south-west of Kirkcaldy has its problems. They are a little different from what was discussed last time. You will see population has gone up by leaps and bounds—similar increase in Burntisland—fall back in Kinghorn.

The County area which corresponds is falling back in Kinghorn ; Auchtertool is holding its own and Burntisland is increasing. (The maps exhibited give population from 1811 onwards.) You have got a future in this area so different from St. Andrews area.

Dr. Fyfe pointed out the area in question, which he said was completely surrounded by industry, and he said the proposed new pits at Seafield and Thornton were going to make matters worse. There must be open spaces where people can get away from the smoky atmosphere and get their lungs filled with fresh air.

The Seafield pit, he said, was on the only good piece of agricultural land in the vicinity. At this point Mr. Carlow said he was still uncertain whether it would be possible to get the pit on the seaward side of the railway, in which case it would not interfere with agriculture very much.

Dr. Fyfe said in his opinion the new pit at Thornton was going to jeopardise Thornton Hospital, which is becoming a Mental Defective Home, with about 100 children in it, and he asked if it was contemplated that other ancillary industries would gather round the pithead. Mr. Carlow replied that he did not think so.

Mr. Hodge—I don't think there is really much to say about water supply. Chief industries mentioned are linoleum and coal in Kirkcaldy Burgh area. There is aluminium and shipbuilding at Burntisland.

Burgh of Kirkcaldy have water supply reservoirs of their own and Burntisland also have reservoirs of their own and Kinghorn. We have been in contact with the Town Councils and we propose to give each of these Burghs a supplement from our Regional Scheme in order to safeguard their supplies for next 20 or 30 years. In the County area there has never been any problem regarding water supply. We have no pipes nearer than Chapel and Auchtertool. These pipes are at the tail-end of our system, but between them and the coast there has been no serious demand for water.

The new pits might want water. So far as Strathore is concerned we should be able to supply you. For Dysart and Seafield you would require to contact Burgh of Kirkcaldy.

With regard to drainage, Auchtertool and Chapel have been dealt with, but otherwise there have been no problems. If there is a new village at Seafield there should be no difficulty about drainage. It would be an outfall to the sea. Thornton —it would be taken into our regional sewer.

Mr. Carlow—I think the most important matter is to form an opinion as to whether Kirkcaldy should gradually increase or whether we should establish a new centre and leave green belt between.

Mr. Taylor asked Mr. Carlow if he had ever formed his own opinion of what should be the ultimate size of a town and Mr. Carlow replied that he had not, but that it would be better for them (the Fife Coal Company) to see Kirkcaldy increase with a pool of miners there, which could go from there to any of the 3 pits in the area,

KINGHORN

The Committee then met with the Provost and representatives of Kinghorn Town Council.

The representatives did not think there was prospect of any new industries. At present Kinghorn has a bottle works and wood flour mill, the wood flour being used as a base for linoleum. The Old Tannery, which is a fairly substantial building with a railway line leading into it, is now being used as a naval store. Before the war rug skins for motor cars were being made—only about 12 men employed.

Water Supply.—Not too happy about that. Have to depend on Kirkcaldy some parts of year.

Housing.—Going in for a number of houses.

Population increases about threefold in summer.

Might prefer to be residential town with green belt between them and Burntisland and green belt between them and Kirkcaldy on the other side.

Majority employed at Burntisland Shipyard and Aluminium Works.

BURNTISLAND

The Provost extended a cordial welcome to the Committee on behalf of his Council. He went on to say that in Burntisland they were not so far ahead as they had hoped to be owing to shortage of staff and the illness of their Burgh Surveyor, but that now the Burgh Surveyor had been told to put roughly on a plan the improvements they proposed to carry out, which scheme would then be submitted to County Council for approval.

Mr. Carlow thanked the Provost for his kind welcome, and said that whatever might be the outcome of these meetings they would at least have a wonderful effect in bringing together the central body in Cupar with the Burgh authorities.

Mr. Mitchell explained briefly the duties undertaken by the Editorial Sub-Committee, and intimated that two public meetings would be held in Kirkcaldy in the near future.

The main places of employment are :—

Docks—which will come back to their own after war.

Aluminium Works—Very well handled concern employing about 600.

Feeding Stuffs and Oil Cake Mills.

Mr. Carlow asked if it was any trouble for people to work in Burntisland and live at Kinghorn, and if it would be a detriment to Burntisland if we were to favour building residential houses at Kinghorn and have the people travel to Burntisland, with a green belt between Kirkcaldy and Burntisland and between Kinghorn and Kirkcaldy. A member of the Town Council replied that 9 out of every 10 people living in Kinghorn work in Burntisland. Mr. Carlow thought that it might be that places like Cowdenbeath and Burntisland, and many others, would be places for industry to be centred, and that there might be other places where it would be better for housing schemes to be set down so that people would get away from the smoke of their industry.

The Provost replied that he thought the suggestion put forward by Mr. Carlow was ideal, but it was only natural that they should want as many of their work people round about them as possible.

The question of how far people should have to travel was discussed when Mr. Mitchell explained that it wasn't the distance so much as travelling time. At present 12 to 14 'buses take men to Kirkcaldy every night and a good percentage travel east.

Major Christie then asked " Doesn't Burntisland rather pride itself on its residential side as well as its industrial?" to which a member of the Town Council replied that the eastern part of the Burgh was suited for residential purposes and was still attractive to summer visitors, while the west end was industrial.

Hospital Accommodation.—Kirkcaldy, Dunfermline and Edinburgh.

Education.—Require another school.

Water Supply.—At the moment Burgh is fairly well off, but recognise there may be difficulty in the future, and are negotiating with County for a supplementary supply.

Housing.—Quite a few sites available for development.

Playing Field.—Trying to acquire 6 acres of land to be reserved for recreational purposes.

There is a natural belt on north and west of town which should be preserved.

Burgh are in favour of the proposed Forth Road Bridge.

NOTES TAKEN AT INITIAL SURVEY OF CUPAR AREA
6th March, 1945

Mr. Taylor.—The area to be dealt with to-day includes Newburgh, Auchtermuchty, Falkland and Ladybank, and with the exception of Newburgh and a small strip along the Firth of Tay the whole of this area drains into the Eden Valley. I think you will agree that this area is perhaps one of the most picturesque in Fife for rolling countryside, and the valley is closed by the Lomond Hills. On the east there are many vantage-points looking out into the bay. You will find that this area is rich in historic monuments, and there are many country mansions. Unfortunately many of them to-day are empty, but we are still left with some very beautiful groups of trees and avenues of trees, regarding which I think this Sub-Committee could do well to make some recommendation. The area is mainly agricultural ; I have studied all the various industries in the area, and with a few exceptions the whole of them are connected with agricultural pursuits. The majority are of an agricultural nature.

Major Christie.—The land round about Strathmiglo and Auchtermuchty has been marked down as the richest land in Scotland.

Mr. Taylor.—The main centre is Cupar. You will find 5 classified roads all converging on Cupar, and within a radius of one mile there are over 15 roads of various descriptions all entering at various points.

The population is decreasing, which is not surprising when you come to look at some of the houses. They are not houses, they are hovels. One begins to wonder whether it is worth while beginning to recondition some of the hovels in this area. They have no amenities such as gas, electricity and water, therefore you don't wonder that this area is decreasing. The people are moving away to where there are better houses and better wages. Through the planning scheme these conditions can be arrested by arranging the grouping of villages so that each group comes within easy reach of a larger centre, suitable centres being Ladybank, Newburgh, Auchtermuchty, and naturally Cupar, Cupar being the focal point in the area. One or two of the villages are so small that it will be necessary to choose a suitable village in which to provide a village hall or institute common to the group, the remainder of the area being zoned for rural purposes.

Major Christie.—There are two little points I should like to raise—two outstanding needs in Cupar. A by-pass is badly needed and I wouldn't be surprised if we don't come to recommend two. Mr. Taylor intervened to say that the difficulty was to obtain a suitable line. Major Christie continued—Another thing is, in Cupar we are badly in need of a site for light industries. I should like the Planning Committee to make reservation of a site for light industries in agriculture, and I have searched this area and up to now I have been unable to find a site which I like. If you could give these two points consideration I would be greatly obliged.

Mr. Carlow.—I think we agreed that we should have a list of the main features for every town, giving particulars of water supply, railway transport, road availability and that sort of thing so that Light Industries could have a lot of places to choose from.

Major Christie.—There is one point which I would very much like to see brought up—the possibility of urging the provision of an Agricultural College in Dairying in the East of Fife, perhaps linked up with college for experimental purposes. Then we could have trained byremen, which one rarely finds to-day. If there were 10 or 15 trained byremen produced by this college every year then the farmers would be better served and would know what they were getting.

Dr. Fyfe.—I really haven't much to add to what has already been said. The area concerned is agricultural, and I think always will be. There are no mineral resources.

Regarding houses, Mr. Taylor's suggestion seems opposed to renovation of houses. I would be canny about that, because you have got to remember your features, and any house you build is going to stand out unless you build a house at great cost which will fit into the landscape.

Regarding industries, Mr. Taylor is quite right, most are allied to agriculture. There is one which I want to draw attention to and that is livestock industry. Just now it is scattered all over the shop. I think you might consider centralisation of cattle sales in Cupar, the County town, so as to make this really the market town for the whole area. And also allied to that is question of the slaughtering of cattle. It is not so bad with the restrictions in force just now, but we have an awful job in peace-time with the number of slaughterhouses. You will find slaughterhouses at Newburgh, Strathmiglo, Cupar, and nearly every village will have a slaughterhouse once restrictions are lifted.

Then there is the question of having sites for light industries, and already local garage proprietors are considering extending their premises to deal with repair of tractors, etc. Local industry is taking a step in the right direction.

Mr. Boyd.—Cupar district has an excellent road system, and the planning proposals coincide with existing roads. There are two planning roads in Cupar area, viz. :—

    (1) From Burnside (Kinross boundary) by Auchtermuchty and Cupar to Dairsie (St. Andrews boundary). This road (A91) is also part of the Ministry of Transport's proposed trunk road extension scheme.

    (2) From New Inn (Kirkcaldy district) by Melville Gates, Parbroath, Kilmany and St. Fort (St. Andrews district).

On A91 it is intended to by-pass the Burghs of Auchtermuchty and Cupar. At Auchtermuchty the by-pass road will be on the south side of the town and at Cupar on the north side.

NEWBURGH

The Committee was met by the Provost and representatives of the Town Council and was given a very hearty welcome Mr. Carlow thanked the Provost for making the necessary arrangements to meet the Editorial Sub-Committee, and called upon Mr. Mitchell to explain the purpose of the meeting.

Mr. Mitchell thereupon explained that the Planning Advisory Committee had been appointed for the purpose of preparing a report which it was hoped would be a guide in the planning of the County for the next 50 or 60 years, and that the Editorial Sub-Committee would be responsible for collecting the necessary information to complete the report. He then intimated that two public meetings would be held in Cupar to which the Town Council would be asked to send representatives.

Mr. Carlow then spoke of how the Committee wished to see Fife County leading the way in the matter of planning for the future rather than lagging behind.

Major Christie spoke of the opportunity which was being given them to-day to plan for the future and of how the Committee particularly wanted long-range suggestions which might be embodied in their report. He then mentioned how interested he was in the question of hospital accommodation in Fife and the need for the provision of maternity centres, which he thought would probably be dealt with under the forthcoming social legislation.

Major Christie then asked whether there was a need or otherwise for the introduction of light industries into Newburgh and whether they would prefer to have the proposed Tay Road Bridge at this end of the County or the Dundee end. Bailie Lyall replied that " for cheapness and safety this is the place where the road bridge should cross. You have high ground at west end, you have Mugdrum Island and high ground on the Carse side. You could almost put that bridge across with 2 or 3 spans."

The Provost then remarked that before they could think in terms of long range planning they would require extension of the Burgh boundaries as they had no room for development. At present, he said, they had one housing scheme laid down which was pretty well advanced and just awaiting approval. On Mr. Carlow asking if the houses would be required for housing newcomers or for reducing overcrowding, Bailie Lyall replied that there were about 400 away serving in the Forces and most of these had been married and had no homes to come back to. All these people, he said, were employed in Newburgh.

The main industries are :—

    Tayside Floorcloth Company.—Employing between 400 and 500 before the war.

    Oilskin Factory.—Employing about 100 people.

    4 Quarries.—Employing over 100 (a member of the Town Council remarked that before the war the Quarry Company was putting away as many as 10 boats a week).

    Salmon Fisheries.—Employing in normal times between 200 and 300 people, half of whom came from Harris.

In answer to Mr. Carlow's question as to whether they used any building stone for building a member replied that brick was quicker but there were a good many whinstone buildings in Newburgh.

Newburgh used to cater for between 100 and 200 summer visitors, but now there is no accommodation available.

A member of the Town Council then raised the question of the harbour and said he thought the piers could be improved, and in fact the whole of the foreshore. Three of the piers belong to the Tayside Floorcloth Co. ; one to Alexander's 'Bus Company ; and one to a Mr. Cameron.

The Floorcloth Company have a boat of their own running between Dundee and Newburgh. Before the war a great number of Dutch boats called at Newburgh purely for linoleum and most of these boats took between 200 and 600 tons. They plied between Newburgh and the Thames.

In answer to Mr. Carlow's question as to what size of steamers the harbour could take, a member replied that he had seen boats leave with a cargo of 800 tons.   Bailie Scotland said motor boats were by far the best because although there was a good depth of water at the harbour, further out in the river there were many sandbanks.

Spring Tides ...... 14 ft.   Neap Tides ...... 9 to 10 ft.

A member spoke of a very fine walk by the foreshore which was becoming dangerous because the tides were eating away the path, and expressed the opinion that this part could be made attractive as a promenade.

Nearest Agricultural Markets—Cupar and Perth.

Water Supply—Plentiful, have loch of their own.

AUCHTERMUCHTY

The Provost welcomed the Editorial Sub-Committee on behalf of the Town Council, and Mr. Carlow thanked the Provost for his kind welcome.

Mr. Mitchell explained briefly the purpose of the meeting and reported that two public meetings would be held in Cupar in the near future, to which the Town Council would be asked to send representatives.

Mr. Carlow then asked if they would let the Committee know what industries they had in the Burgh, if there were any empty factories, if there was any accommodation available for industries coming in, and if there was water supply, drainage, electricity, gas and anything else which might be wanted for industries.   Fife, he said, has got to be in the forefront of all good movement.

The main industries in the Burgh are—

    Foundry and Engineering Works—Employing 100.

    Foundry—About 50 employed.

    Linen Factory—40 employed.

    Hosiery Factory—Employing about 20 girls.

There is also a factory at present being used as a military store, which could be utilised for some light industry after the war.   It is in very good condition and very up to date.

With regard to housing, the Provost said that the Burgh was very overcrowded and badly in need of houses.   The Burgh's initial housing scheme is for 80 houses, but to meet requirements between 400 and 500 would be necessary.   There are plenty of sites available for development.

In answer to Mr. Mitchell's question as to how the Burgh was placed as regards water supply, the Provost replied that it had an ample supply of its own and that it was probably the distribution which was at fault.

On the question of recreational facilities being raised the Provost intimated that the golf-course had been ploughed up and would not be reopened.   The only other facilities available are a bowling-green and a town's green for the children.   The Provost said they were in need of a playing field for the children.   He also mentioned that the Army Cadets were going to get a hut and that the young people of the town would have the use of this for billiards, etc.   There is one hall in Auchtermuchty which is open on Saturdays for pictures and is available for concerts and dancing, but the majority of the inhabitants travel to Cupar, Kirkcaldy and Perth for entertainment.   The Provost, however, thought that if there was a suitable hall for pictures it would be well patronised.

Major Christie raised the question of hospital accommodation and maternity services, and in reply the Provost stated that Auchtermuchty had a Fever Hospital, but for other services they depended upon Dundee, Kirkcaldy and Perth.   Mr. Mitchell mentioned that this was in the post-war public health programme.

FALKLAND

Mr. Carlow thanked the Burgh representatives for meeting the Committee, and Mr. Mitchell explained briefly the purpose of the meeting.

Mr. Carlow said the Committee would like to hear about industries which Falkland has and industries which might possibly come to this neighbourhood, or in what way the Committee could help in the Burgh's planning work.

With regard to industries the Provost stated that they had a linoleum factory and a linen factory, both belonging to the S.C.W.S., but that since 1940 the Linoleum Factory had been closed and was at present being used as an Admiralty and Ministry of Supply Store.   Before the war, however, over 300 people were employed there.   In answer to Mr. Taylor's question as to what proportion of male and female labour was employed the Provost replied that it was all male labour.

Major Christie asked how the goods were transported, and was informed that they were taken by heavy lorry to Falkland Road Station, and that London goods went to Kirkcaldy for the weekly boat.   Lorries at one time were going direct from Falkland to Manchester and even to London.

The Linen Works, said the Provost, in pre-war time employed between 85 and 90 people—about 30 men and 60 women.

The Provost expressed the view that the existing industries would be sufficient as the extension of both factories after the war was being contemplated.   Major Christie asked if the S.C.W.S. would be going to house their people locally, but the Provost said he did not think so as they never had been in favour of housing their workers.

    Housing.—The Burgh require between 50 and 60 houses, and there is plenty of ground available for that number.

    Water Supply.—Have good supply from two springs in the Lomond Hills.

    Hospitals.—Kirkcaldy, Perth and Edinburgh.

With regard to recreational facilities, the Provost said that they had a hall and an institute, the institute having a billiard room and reading room.   The hall, he said, was out of date, but they were contemplating building a new one after the war, which would be fitted so as to have accommodation for a cinema.

Mr. Carlow asked what type of linen thrived in Falkland, and was informed that it was mostly towelling and tablecloths prior to the war.

LADYBANK

In the absence of the Provost, Bailie Opdahl extended a hearty welcome to the Committee and hoped that they would have a pleasant and constructive discussion on the arrangements to be made for the future planning of this area.   He then put forward what he termed his own line of thought and that of the local population to this important subject of planning as follows :—

"Situated as we are in the centre of a large and presently prosperous agricultural area, and having importance as a Railway Junction, we are probably better suited for future planning than many other districts in Fife, and can offer more immediate and ample services in the way of electric lighting and power, gas, water and drainage.

"The principal industries presently carried on within the area are Agriculture, Malting, Railway Engineering, Building contracting, Sawmilling and Timber manufacture. Fruit growing on a large scale is also in prospect immediately the present restrictions on building are withdrawn.

" The large War Department buildings at the top of Melville Road and at Annsmuir Camp offer considerable scope for industry after the war, or they might usefully be taken over by Messrs. Alexander & Sons, 'Bus Proprietors, as a main 'bus station and workshop. Ladybank's situation between the Forth and Tay Ferries suggests it as an ideal site for such a station, giving easy contact with the Counties of Angus, Perth, Kinross, Midlothian and Edinburgh City. An enterprising firm of agricultural engineers might also do well to consider the position here. It is also within the bounds of possibility that present plans for the growing of fruit on a large scale might encourage the setting up of a Jam Factory.

" With regard to the Social Services, I must first speak as to the housing needs of the community. Applications for houses presently number close on 70 and will tend to increase, as against a post-war allocation of 30 houses. The immediate post-war prospects at Ladybank for attracting new industries make it imperative that this allocation be reconsidered by the Department of Health and that it be generously increased.

" The introduction of the Education (Scotland) Bill providing for the ultimate raising of the school-leaving age to 16 years, and the present congested arrangements for higher education at Cupar clearly indicate that a much larger and more modern Secondary School is now required in this part of Fife, and Ladybank would most certainly be the ideal site for such a building, accommodating as it would pupils from Newburgh, and the North of Fife, Auchtermuchty, Dunshelt, Freuchie, Falkland, Strathmiglo, Gateside, Kingskettle, Cults, Pitlessie, Markinch and Ladybank."

Mr. Carlow thanked the Bailie for his very kind welcome and for the hospitality extended to the Committee. Thereafter Mr. Mitchell explained very briefly the duties undertaken by the Planning Advisory Committee, and intimated that two public meetings would be held in Cupar to which the Burgh would be invited to send representatives.

On Mr. Carlow asking for some idea of the size of the building which the Burgh thought might be utilised as a 'bus station and workshop the Town Clerk stated that it was the biggest military workshop in Scotland and the best fitted-up in the British Isles.

Major Christie then raised the question of the Forth and Tay Road Bridges, and the Town Clerk said that the question of the Forth Road Bridge was a sore point in Ladybank as they had not been invited to send representatives to the many meetings which had taken place. They were most certainly in favour of this bridge. With regard to the Tay Road Bridge the Town Clerk said he did not know whether the Dundee authorities had had many meetings, but here again Ladybank had not been consulted. Major Christie asked whether they would favour the bridge at Newburgh, Abernethy or nearer Newport, and Mr. Mitchell said he thought the representatives should know that this question had been put to Newport and Tayport, and that Newport favoured a bridge at Abernethy while Tayport wished to see it nearer Newport. Quite a lot of discussion took place on the matter, and the general opinion seemed to be that a bridge over the Tay at Newburgh or further west would not benefit Ladybank as the main arterial road would be considerably west of Ladybank, but it was really immaterial to the Burgh where the bridge was situated.

The question of housing was then raised when Mr. Mark, the Burgh Surveyor, stated that they had a site earmarked at the top of the town for development of 120 houses. The number of houses allocated to the Burgh was only 30 although they had made application for 70. Here Mr. Rolland, the Burgh's Architect, said he thought that the reason for Ladybank being allocated so few houses was because they had built very few since the inception of housing schemes. To cover the Burgh's needs the Burgh Surveyor was of the opinion that between 200 and 300 houses would be required. At this point the Town Clerk stated that there were a number of agricultural workers in the district who wished to live in Ladybank and travel to the different farms. It was thought there was a possibility of some houses being built by private enterprise after the war, and there was already a small development at Monkstown, which, however, had not proceeded very far.

Major Christie then brought up the question of fruit-growing, and the Town Clerk explained that it was proposed to build 40 glass-houses, each 100 feet in length. He thought that in the height of the season there would be employment for at least 50 people.

In answer to Mr. Mitchell the Town Clerk said the principal industry was agriculture—a good deal of dairying.

They had in Ladybank a blacksmith's shop, he said, which was being fitted with modern machinery. He thought there was a good deal of room for development in this type of repair shop, and described to the meeting how a man in Evanton, Ross-shire, had developed his blacksmith's shop into a large agricultural engineering concern employing a number of black-smiths and motor engineers. Mr. Carlow raised the question of the possibility of having a travelling servicing lorry for mending tractors and agricultural implements and even shoeing horses. He thought this could be so readily combined with a concern such as the Town Clerk had mentioned, and would save the farmers' time to a very great extent. He thought perhaps a travelling forge with headquarters at Cupar could shoe all the horses in the east of Fife.

Major Christie said there was one point they would have to deal with, and that was those agricultural workers who desired to live in Ladybank. He asked if this was due to the state of their houses, and the Town Clerk replied that to a great extent it was. The Town Clerk thought it would be a great advantage to the people to stay in Ladybank, whereupon Mr. Carlow asked if he had thought of the key-men, such as cattlemen, who had to be on the spot. Having the other workers living away from the farms would leave these key-men and their families more isolated than ever, he said.

Main industries are—
Agriculture.
Malting—About 50 people are employed in normal times.
Railway Engineering.
Building Contracting.
Sawmilling.
Timber Manufacture.

Recreational Facilities.—Have good golf-course and bowling-green. Cadet Forces are going to build a Nissen hut somewhere in Ladybank.

Water Supply.—Have their own supply. In the water tower they have storage for 60,000 gallons. The large pump pumps 8,000 gallons per hour and the small one 4,000 gallons per hour. The windmill draws 150 gallons per hour.

NOTES TAKEN AT INITIAL SURVEY OF ANSTRUTHER AREA
13th March, 1945

ELIE

Mr. Carlow thanked the Provost for arranging to meet the Committee, and explained that the Editorial Sub-Committee had been charged with the duty of preparing a report for submission to the Planning Committee in connection with the planning of the County for perhaps the next 50 or 60 years. They were anxious, he said, to obtain all the information possible to assist them in their work.

The Provost said that Elie was really a seaside resort and had no industries whatsoever. The people were mainly concerned with letting their houses in summer, when the population increased by 3 or 4 thousand. He personally would like to see Elie the County's playground. A good train service from Glasgow, Edinburgh, and other centres would be a great help to Elie.

The Town Clerk intimated that for years the Town Council had been trying to get another golf-course along to the east of Elie on land belonging to Waideslea Farm. They tried to buy the land from both Mr. Baird and his son, but neither would sell at any price. Now the land belongs to Sir Michael Nairn, and he will not part with it. Mr. Cook thought it seemed a pity that the land should not be adapted for the purpose for which it was most suited. The land was mostly sand dunes, he said, and not suitable for cultivation. Part of it was used for grazing a few sheep. The proprietor's objection to the use of the land as a golf-course was injury to amenities. Mr. Mitchell explained that the County Council had power to earmark land for certain purposes, and the Town Clerk expressed the desire to have this land earmarked as a golf-course. In answer to Mr. Mitchell's question as to whether there were any building on the site, the Town Clerk replied there were a look-out station in connection with the Coast Guard and a hut which was built as a hydrophone station in the last war and thereafter let as a dwelling house, the rental of the farm being £157 ; of the signal station £4, 10/- ; and of the dwelling-house £8. To lay out a golf-course some 180 acres would be required.

Major Christie expressed the opinion that within the next 30 or 40 years the East of Fife round the coast by Largo, Lundin Links, Elie, St. Monance and Crail would probably become the Riviera of Scotland, and stated that in Leven they had found that accommodation for summer visitors was grossly under what was required. He thought something ought to be done to procure more houses. In Leven certain areas were being set aside for municipal housing and other areas for building by private enterprise, and he thought this policy should be adopted elsewhere.

The Burgh possesses 9 hard tennis-courts ; a bowling-green ; putting-green and golf-course.

The question of boating was raised when the Town Clerk stated that the coast was rather dangerous for boating.

ST. MONANCE

Mr. Carlow opened the meeting by saying how happy the Committee were to visit St. Monance and how they hoped to get the Town Council's views with regard to the development of the place and to help them in every way possible.

The Provost said that St. Monance was probably a little bit different from most of the small villages in that the whole of the community was an entirely working one.

There were two industries, namely, fishing and boat-building. Other than that there was no industry except small repair shops. Unfortunately fishing before the war was bad, but during the war it had been indifferent, and after the war the prospects were definitely black. When the boat-building got back to normal it would employ 60 or 80 men. If we want to see our Burgh advancing, said the Provost, we have got to try to encourage some other trade to come in to employ the population. At present they had to go round the coast to find employment at Elie and Anstruther. Labour was there if they could get an industry. Mr. Carlow then asked what type of industry they had in mind, and the Provost said that Mr. Henderson Stewart had visited the village and suggested the setting up of a dehydrated fish factory, but the Provost did not greatly encourage such a factory. There were no empty factories for anyone to come to, he said ; they would have to build. The conditions were very favourable, he thought, so far as water supply, drainage, electricity, accessibility to main road and railway were concerned, and an industry could be quite a financial asset to the Burgh. He was very anxious to see an industry of some kind come to the place as the young men would be coming back from the Forces with no trade at their finger-ends and nothing to do. There was one big difference between fishermen and, say, miners. Miners were supplied with all their necessary equipment, but fishermen had to provide their own nets, boats, etc. Mr. Mitchell then asked if the men were supplied with equipment would they come back. The Provost was of opinion that they would provided the Government could guarantee them a market for their herring. At the moment herring fishing markets had simply disappeared. Before the war the main markets were Germany, Austria and the Balkan States. The real problem was the marketing of the herring. There was a reasonable market for white fish. They had a nice little harbour which could take boats up to 100 feet long, he said. The harbour belonged to the fishermen and was run by Harbour Commission, which was constituted under an Order made in 1885.

In answer to a question as to type of boats used, the Provost replied that motor-boats were in use now, some of which accommodate 6 persons. The Provost thought that after the war the cost of boats would be so great that the men would most likely go in for smaller ones. Boats could not be mass produced but had to be built to suit their particular harbour. Mr. Carlow expressed the opinion that if a market for the herring could be got the rest would solve itself, but the Provost thought they would require some other industry quite separate. Mr. Carlow thought that as the natural industry of the place was fishing it would be better if they could do something with the herring to secure a regular market.

With regard to boat-building the Provost remarked that St. Monance was very badly situated for any building development as there wasn't a single foot of room on the seashore. There were two boat-building firms in St. Monance, and before the war one built mainly yachts, while the other concentrated on fishing-boats. Now they built a type of Government craft.

A member then stated that there was any amount of coal in the district, but Mr. Carlow said they might get a little local sale for it but for practical purposes it was not any good.

Housing—Require 120 houses to meet overcrowding.
Recreational Facilities—Bowling and putting-greens.
Also bathing-pool, which had been great asset to the town.
Population—1,600.

PITTENWEEM

The Provost welcomed the Committee and Mr. Carlow returned thanks. He then asked for any information regarding industries, etc., in the Burgh and in what way the Committee might be of assistance.

The Provost said that the main fishing was herring, but that this had been a complete failure this year, the first catch being landed to-day—30 barrels. The herring fishing season, he said, only lasted for three months in the year and this was practically the end of the season. He thought that the number of restricted areas probably accounted for the shortage of herring. Before the war there were about 200 fishermen and 30 boats. 65 feet sailing-boats used to be in operation, but now it was mainly motor-boats. A member stated that the harbour was very dangerous owing to its exposed nature, and the Town Clerk said they had been trying to get a scheme to improve the harbour and to make it safer, but before the war the estimated cost was £7,000, and the Town could not rise to that. In answer to Mr. Mitchell's question as to whether the harbour was a good revenue-producing subject, the Town Clerk replied that it kept itself.

There were no other industries, said the Town Clerk, but there were 4 small holdings extending to between 80 and 100 acres.

Major Christie asked if the position here was the same as at St. Monance, and the Provost expressed the opinion that if the fishing were more prosperous they could have a building yard at Pittenweem. At present, he said, boats were repaired at Anstruther and St. Monance, small repairs being carried out by the local engineer.

Major Christie then enquired if there would be sufficient waste from fish to keep a manure factory going, but the Provost did not think so, and a member of the Town Council suggested that a cannery would be a much better industry.

The Provost remarked that there was plenty of coal round about Pittenweem. Mr. Carlow stated that the coal stretched from Elie right along to Pittenweem, partly under the sea and a little bit on land. He had examined the coal at Grangemuir many years ago, he said, but it was of no value. Major Christie then asked if there was any possibility of coal being opened up on a small scale, but Mr. Carlow thought not. He said they did not wish to encourage anything which was not going to pay its way.

Mr. Mitchell suggested that what Pittenweem would want would be an industry connected with fishing or farming, and Mr. Carlow expressed the view that if they could get a good market for their hearing, ancillary industries might be induced to follow. A member of the Town Council pointed out that Pittenweem used to manufacture salt and barrels. Major Christie wondered why these industries had died out and the Provost thought that it was because no one else would take the premises when the proprietors gave up. The wood for the manufacture of the barrels came from Norway in ships measuring 120 ft. or thereby, and these vessels could carry 100 tons. The nearest barrel-manufacturing firm was in Aberdeen.

Major Christie was interested to know where the farmers took their tractors to be repaired, and the Town Clerk informed him that the local garages carried out the necessary repairs.

During the months of June, July and August there were quite a number of summer visitors. Pittenweem had a putting-green, bowling-green, tennis-courts, 9-hole golf-course and a bathing-pond.

The population is 1,700.

ANSTRUTHER

Mr. Carlow thanked the Provost for arranging to meet the Committee and explained the work undertaken by them.

Anstruther was a fishing community, said the Provost, and the future of the fishing industry must be their first concern for that reason. With the help of the Fishery Board for Scotland the harbour was put into a condition which had made it better than nine out of every ten harbours.

But the great difficulty immediately facing Anstruther is the getting of a fleet of new boats. Before the war Anstruther had 46 steam drifters, but these had all been sold and not one was coming back. In a way the Provost was not sorry because steam drifters had become entirely out of date. Diesel motor-boats were much more economical and could be built at home and serviced in their home port, thus preserving the life of the community. The Provost went on to say that these boats would be 50-55 feet in length with about 80/100 h.p. engines and could be run comfortably on one-third of the running expenses of steam drifters.

Mr. Carlow asked what chance St. Monance and Pittenweem would have to compete with Anstruther, to which the Provost replied it was not a case of competition but co-relation. These ports had an equal chance, and it would preserve their communal life also.

Provost Carstairs went on to say that probably the big difficulty would be to persuade the orders to come from the fishermen. If they thought there was a future in the fishing industry they would support it, and with any improved financial benefits would attract the younger and on-coming generations to the industry. This would depend on the helps in the way of grant and loan, and the Provost thought that it was certain that substantial helps to suitable fishermen up to 33⅓% on the cost of a boat would be available. The price of a boat was reckoned to be £3,250/£3,500 and towards this about £1,000 might be paid by way of grant. There was no use in helping fishermen over 55 years of age. He was keen on helping young men who had been in the services, Merchant Navy, etc., on a deck hand's pay. They would be coming out of the services with small savings but without capital. They should be helped. At the end of the last war men had £50 or £60 saved up and there were no grants then. This sum they put into nets which were very perishable.

The Provost continued that without help to the young fellows the industry was going to get a very big set-back. He thought it likely that they would be asked to put down 10% of the value of a boat and the balance could probably be arranged on the annuity system of principal and interest spread over 20 years. The Provost felt that he had been able to be of some assistance to the recent Herring Industry Commission of which he was a member, by making suggestions for promoting the interests of the industry. The Bill put before Parliament followed very closely the Report of the Commission.

Anstruther Harbour, said the Provost, was available in practically all weathers and was the biggest winter herring port in Great Britain.

The Provost told the Committee of his attendance at a Conference in Aberdeen presided over by Col. Walter Elliot, when they sampled fish cakes made of dehydrated herring and kipper. These cakes, he said, had the real taste of herring and kipper, and were just the thing to be taken up by potato chip and fried fish shops, as well as grocers, throughout the country.

Major Christie asked if there was any chance of getting a dehydrated factory for Fife. The Provost thought this would be a real asset. Herring, he said, were the most quickly perishable fish taken out of the sea and new scientific methods of dehydration or refrigeration must be brought into the industry. Whitefish, he said, could also be preserved and stored by refrigeration. Major Christie enquired if the Provost had any idea of the outlay which would be involved in such a scheme. Provost Carstairs replied that to fit up a room the same size as that in which the meeting was taking place, as a refrigerator, would have cost £587 before the war.

Then Major Christie raised the question of fishmeal or manure. The Provost thought a fishmeal factory could be run in conjunction with the dehydration and refrigeration. Before the war fairly large quantities of herring oil and meal were imported from Norway and practically none made in Great Britain.

The question of boats was again raised by Major Christie, who wanted to know whether the production of these would be held up until there was a demand for them or whether they would be built on the assumption that there would be a demand. The Provost thought that there would be a possibility of chartering some of the vessels which the Admiralty had built during the war, for two or three years, and this would tide the fishermen over while they were having their own boats built.

The Provost then told the Committee of a model which he had of a boat which was adaptable for three purposes—drift net, ring net and seine fishing. He thought in the near future the fishermen would require to go further afield for seine net fishing and the present ring net 45-feet boat could not very well undertake that. In some of the most important Scottish ports the difficulty in the past was that the drifter and fleet of herring drift nets were only being used seven months in the year, whereas this new three-purpose type of vessel could be employed all the yea r round. Such a boat could be made locally. The Provost said that in 1935 he built two 52-feet-long vessels to serve two kinds of fishing at a cost of £1585 each.

The Provost gave particulars of the fishing seasons as follows :—

January to March—Winter Herring fishing at Anstruther.
March to June—Whitefishing—seine.
June to end of September—Summer herring fishing.
October to November—East Anglian herring fishing.

Anstruther has a fish sale-room and rest-room for the fishermen.

Major Christie asked whether there was a demand from farm workers for houses in the Burgh, and a member replied that he did not think so.

There is a cattle market in Anstruther.

(Particulars sent by the Provost to the Co-operative Wholesale Society in Glasgow in an endeavour to get them, as possessors of unlimited capital, interested in providing the nucleus (say at least 6 vessels) of a fishing fleet for the port are shown in appendix to these notes.)

CRAIL

The Provost welcomed the Committee and Mr. Carlow thanked him for agreeing to meet the Committee. He explained the duties undertaken by the Editorial Sub-Committee and called upon the Provost to put forward any suggestions which he might have for the improvement of the Burgh.

The Provost did not think that the Burgh would want very much in the way of industry. Crail was purely a summer resort, he said, and should be developed under that heading. There was the air station nearby, but they did not know what the future of that was to be. At present, said the Provost, the Burgh had enough ground for housing development, but a great deal would depend on the future of the air station. If it was retained after the war no doubt they would require a great many houses.

The population is 1100, but during the summer months it increases to about 2500. Crail, the Provost said, had sufficient recreational facilities to meet the needs of the Burgh just now. They had four hard tennis-courts ; a bowling green ; putting-green and golf-course.

A member of the Town Council said that the fishing carried on at Crail was mainly inshore fishing for lobsters and crabs. In normal t mes about 16 or 18 boats were employed, but now there were only about 10. Only three boats were employed on herring fishing. The member went on to say that there was quite a good railway service from Crail, and crabs and lobsters sent off by the 4 p.m. train reached the London market by 5 o'clock the following morning. London, he said, was the chief market, but they also sent consignments to Liverpool and Birmingham.

In answer to Mr. Carlow's inquiry regarding the harbour the Provost stated they had a very quaint harbour on the improvement of which they had spent considerable sums of money.

Another member told of how large quantities of potatoes used to be shipped from Crail and he looked forward to a revival of the coast traffic.

With regard to water supply the Provost said there were 20 houses outside the Burgh which they supplied with water, but, of course, if Crail developed to a great extent they might require water from the County.

Major Christie asked if there was any demand for building by private enterprise. The Town Clerk stated there was a demand for a number of years but since the introduction of municipal housing the demand had not been so great. They had given grants, he said, to 21 houses built by private enterprise under the 1923 Housing Act and these were nice bungalows which were let for summer visitors. Pinkerton Farm, said the Town Clerk, has been purchased by the Murrayfield Housing Company who built 13 houses with grants of £100 for the first six and £120 for the second seven. They had intended to build more, but the war came.

Mr. Mitchell asked if there were any agricultural shops in the Burgh, and in reply the Provost said there were a blacksmith and engineer who did all the repairs for the farmers round about Crail. Mr. Carlow then said his idea was that they should have a travelling forge which would go out to the farms. A member of the Town Council remarked that Crail did not want that as it would be to the detriment of the small man in the town. You have got to think of the men who are away fighting for their country, he said.

General Crosbie asked if there was any clay in the district and the Town Clerk replied that there was quite a lot of blue clay.

The question of light industry was again raised, and the Provost expressed the view that a light industry connected with fishing, farming, or golf would be welcomed.

With regard to entertainment the Town Clerk said that Crail was very much in need of a cinema.

APPENDIX REFERRED TO

Memo. by Provost of Anstruther to Scottish Co-operative Wholesale Society, Glasgow

The Port of Anstruther is very conveniently situated in connection with the fishing grounds. Some of the finest seine netting grounds are just outside the May Island—a matter of three hours' passage from Anstruther Harbour. It is now also the largest winter herring fishing port in Britain, and there is a likelihood that the port may be made one of the centres for refrigeration and/or dehydration depots.

In any case, it would only require a comparatively small capital for you yourselves to erect a modern small, but efficient, refrigeration house. This would enable " graded " consignments of all kinds of fish to be despatched, and at the most favourable marketing times, thus giving maximum economic chances of income to the vessels.

The harbour is one of the best on the East Coast of Scotland, very safe, and can be taken by vessels, in bad weather, long after most other ports are impossible to take.

A few years ago the harbour had spent on it £58,000 (grant and loan) by the Fishery Board for Scotland, deepening it by 8 feet more water, and cement—topping all the working piers, thus making it one of the most up-to-date harbours, from the point of view of handling the fish, and also from the hygienic point of view. Unusual facilities are offered for handling large quantities of fish at the harbour, and it is most conveniently situated for Edinburgh and Glasgow markets, as well as for quick distribution over all the populous middle belt of Scotland. It is 100 miles nearer the large English markets than Aberdeen, and far more advantageously situated from the markets point of view than other Scottish ports.

The harbour is nicely lit with electricity and the great winter Firth of Forth herring fishing is just right on its front doorstep.

Boats.—Of all the fleet of steam drifters we had belonging to the port, not one is coming back to the port after the war. They have all been sold on service, except two—the two newest, which are now owned in North Shields.

From the point of view of fishing vessels, perhaps this is none the worse for the port, as the steam drifter has become "outmoded" and has become a most uneconomical fishing proposition.

The only consequent difficulty thus brought about—and it is a most serious one indeed—is that, while the men will be coming back from the Navy and Auxiliary Services, after doing their bit well, there will be no boats for them to go in. A very fine class of men will thus be lost to the port and industry which we can ill afford, either as a community, or nationally.

In pre-war days fishing vessels were mainly only one-type fishing vessels, prosecuting one of the following types of fishing :—
 1. Great Line (for cod, etc.) or
 2. Drift Net (for herring), or
 3. Ring Net (for herring), or
 4. Seine Net for whitefish (mainly flat fish such as plaice, lemon sole, etc.).

A number of the vessels followed out two modes of fishing ; but there is now possible (I have developed this type very carefully) a type of Diesel vessel which can be made a four-purpose boat, viz. :—drift net ; ring net ; and seine net, or local great line vessel, thus ensuring that the vessel (the capital) can be employed the whole year round. Being a four-purpose boat, gives it at all times the maximum earning chance.

The Diesel vessel of about 50/53 feet long has proved herself the most economical type of fishing boat ever placed in the hands of the fishermen.

Such a vessel can be built and engined ready for sea to-day at about £3250. At the ring net type of fishing the vessels generally work in pairs, so that, say, six of these vessels—three pairs—would represent a capital of £19,500 to £20,000.

In the fishing industry there will always be fluctuations in the seasons, but given ordinary average fishings and with the right men in charge, the return on the capital should be adequate—perhaps substantial.

I have been very keen on these new type wooden vessels from the point of view of preserving such communities as Anstruther; as the vessels could be built locally—local carpenters, local painters, local engineers, local blacksmiths, local ship chandlers, etc.—thus keeping such communities alive and prosperous.

Crews.—The majority of these men are worth doing something for, as they are a fine lot of men, and in both wars have lived dangerously—very substantially helping to save Britain.

Gear.—The vessels could buy all their gear and all their stores, amounting to a rather substantial figure, in a twelvemonth, from your own organisation—a live branch of which is already established in the town.

Catch.—Besides co-operative buying, it is a simple matter to co-operatively sell the product too, as the fishing fleet grows in numbers.

NOTES OF PUBLIC MEETING HELD IN COUNCIL CHAMBERS, ST. ANDREWS
20th March, 1945

Provost Bruce, St. Andrews, opened the meeting by thanking all those who had come from a distance, especially those from Tayport and Newport. He explained that the meeting would really be concerned with the planning of the landward area—Tayport, Newport, etc. He wished it to be understood that in St. Andrews they were a Town Planning Authority but that there were certain matters, such as roads, which affected both the Town and County Councils and in regard to which his Council had been co-operating and would continue to co-operate with the County Council.

Mr. Carlow also expressed pleasure at the good attendance and then gave a list of the various organisations, etc., which had been invited to be represented at the meeting—Local County Councillors, District Councillors, Agricultural Executive Committee, Youth Organisations, W.R.I., W.V.S., Co-operative Guilds, and Rotary Club—and emphasised that without the co-operation and help of everybody all the Committee's planning efforts would be entirely useless. The area concerned, as had been stated in the public press, included Newport, Tayport, Guardbridge, Leuchars, Balmullo, Strathkinness, Radernie, Lathones, Wormit, Kingsbarns and Denhead. Mr. Carlow further stated that another meeting would be held on 3rd April for the purpose of putting forward suggestions which would be considered by the Planning Advisory Committee in preparing its Report on the future planning of the County for submission to the County Council.

Mr. Carlow then explained that the County Council had a Planning Committee consisting of County Councillors who had very serious duties to perform in regard to the future planning of the County. Reasons for the urgency of planning were numerous—things moved more quickly and on rather a larger scale than had been customary in the past and it was necessary therefore to look forward and plan so as to ensure that nothing would be done to obstruct the natural and proper development of this part of the County in the next, say, 50 years. Mr. Carlow then illustrated from his own industry—the colliery industry. Three new collieries were to be sunk by the Fife Coal Company, one at least on ground not belonging to the Company. Each of these collieries might cost anything up to one million pounds. Surface arrangements, he stated, were very important and 100 to 200 acres of reasonably flat ground would be required adjacent to the railway as material cannot go by road. Roads, houses, water and drainage schemes would also be required as a large population would have to be provided for in these places. He explained that where there was a place suitable for underground and suitable for surface, as a rule there was only one possible site for that coal. If that site were covered with a planning scheme, etc., the whole of the underground minerals would be rendered useless, and it was therefore essential to look ahead for many years in regard to the planning of collieries. Mr. Carlow indicated that it was nine years since he had asked the County Clerk to see that whatever happened, certain areas were earmarked for collieries. Mr. Johnston, Secretary of State, and various other people had also been told that there must be legislation to give somebody powers to prevent certain ground being taken away from the mining industry, otherwise the minerals would be rendered useless. The position was similar in other industries. A road bridge was wanted over the Firth of Tay, and how silly they would all look if a housing scheme were placed on the foreshore at the only place suitable for a bridge. That would be the absence of planning in a most unfortunate fashion.

With regard to roads, Mr. Carlow said that they were all aware that there were roads skirting towns and centres—by-pass roads. There was one not very far away under contemplation. Planning would prevent such roads being obstructed by something else.

Mr. Carlow then explained that he represented the mining industry but that any person who joined public organisations for the benefit of his own industry was looked upon without complete approbation, and one had got to take the unselfish line. He had offered his services every Tuesday until the end of July. The County Planning Committee were not experienced in all the various industries, and this was where the Planning Advisory Committee came in. The Planning

Committee, therefore, had expressed a desire to have representatives of the different industries to advise them of their views on developments for the next 50 years, with regard to, for example, the coal, paper, fish and agricultural industries, etc. The Advisory Committee was therefore representative of landowners, agriculture, history and culture, coal industry and miners, railway, and independent representatives.

In further referring to the three new collieries, plans of which had been lodged to-day, Mr. Carlow stated that the Fife coalfields were in some respects the richest in Great Britain, and some of these contained more coal per acre than any other coalfield in Great Britain. Development, therefore, in Fife was going to be very great indeed, reference to which could be found in the Scottish Coalfields Report.

Mr. Carlow then said that the Advisory Committee was considered too big and a smaller Sub-Committee had been formed to carry out the detailed work. That Sub-Committee consisted of Mr. Christie, Sir James Irvine and himself.

With regard to what the Sub-Committee had been doing, Mr. Carlow here referred to the possibility of a road bridge over the Firth of Tay, and emphasised that the facts of the case would determine the site to be chosen. He also said that the Sub-Committee had visited every Provost on the coast and every Town Council beginning with Elie, St. Monance, Pittenweem, Crail and Anstruther. They had also conferred with the Provost and Town Councils in the Newport and Tayport district. Newburgh, Auchtermuchty, Falkland, etc., had also been visited and information collected which would assist in deciding where the bridge was to be. The Sub-Committee hoped to complete their survey by the end of August and have a report issued for the information of the County Council and the County as a whole.

In closing, Mr. Carlow again emphasised the need for the help of the public and expressed the hope that ideas would be put forward even before next public meeting, and that a scheme would ultimately be prepared which would do justice to the present generation and be for the good of the community for the next 40 or 50 years.

Mr. *Taylor* explained the object of the Planning Scheme and said that the word " planning" had been much to the fore in recent years and much overworked. Nevertheless, many people did not understand its meaning. Some thought that by planning, social evils would disappear overnight, others connected the word with housing, or a large building programme, while others were under the impression that it was merely concerned with the appearance of buildings. The scope and meaning of town and country planning is set out in the Town and Country Planning Act, 1932, as follows :—

" With the general object of controlling the development of the land comprised in the area to which the scheme applies, of securing proper sanitary conditions, amenity and convenience, and of preserving existing buildings or other objects of architectural, historic or artistic interest, and places of natural interest or beauty, and generally of protecting existing amenities whether in Urban or Rural portions of the Area."

He further stated that the preparation of a scheme did not imply any intention to promote active building development on the land to which it referred but merely to control and guide development when it occurred and preserve existing features of value. Its aim, in short, was to lay out the area concerned to the best advantage of the present and future population. The area under consideration was mainly agricultural and a healthy and well-balanced agriculture was a vital necessity to the well-being of the nation. Serious damage had been done in the last 20 years to the amenities of the countryside and to the basic industry, viz., agriculture, by sporadic building over the face of the rural areas. The best land from the agricultural point of view had been chosen for building purposes. Difficulties had arisen in connection with the transport of residents to adjoining towns ; existing village centres had not grown in population and their development had been retarded. It was intended that development should be encouraged into defined centres thus gaining advantages with regard to protection of amenities and agricultural land, provision of public services, village crafts, better shopping centres and recreational and educational facilities, etc.

Allied to this question was that of encouraging industries in rural areas, and it was evident that these industries should be closely connected with agriculture, *e.g.* canning, jam-making, agricultural implements, fertiliser production, furniture, and glove-making, etc., and food processing. In the past, he said, industries had been found more often in large cities mainly on account of reasons connected with labour, housing, markets, and perhaps a psychological one in that industries were nervous of moving further afield. In future, therefore, he thought industry would require to be looked on as one unit and not as in detached landward and burghal areas, as to obtain a balanced agriculture, one was dependent upon the other.

Mr. Taylor then dealt with coastal preservation. A considerable stretch of the area under discussion to-day was, he said, along the coast line of which the County was justly proud, and this question required to be carefully considered. The popularity of this area increased building value and with it increased the difficulty of directing development without giving rise to compensation claims. The task of preservation was of national as well as local interest, and there might be a case for making part of the cost a charge on national funds.

With regard to the chief recreation of the area, namely, golf, Mr. Taylor said there was no need for him to emphasise the fact that St. Andrews was known throughout the length and breadth of the whole land for its famous golf-course. In the planning scheme, therefore, existing recreational facilities required to be preserved, and provision made for facilities being improved.

In referring to the aerodrome situated in the area and to the future of travel by air, Mr. Taylor expressed the hope that the aerodrome would not be left in a derelict condition after the war but would be retained in view of its ideal situation in relation to Northern Scotland, Norway, Sweden, etc. Careful thought should be given to the provision of aerodromes in planning for the future as air transport would probably become as popular as road transport. On account of lack of planning in the past, public authorities were faced to-day with huge expenditure in trying to accommodate traffic, and were thus putting the cart before the horse. It was necessary to assure that in all future plans the horse came first.

Mr. Taylor then dealt with roads and asked that suggestions be made on this question. He had been amused to hear that Newport would like the Tay Bridge further up stream while on the other hand Tayport would like the new Bridge at Newport.

Dealing next with public services, Mr. Taylor stated that it was essential that public services and development should go hand in hand. If development was encouraged into defined centres, necessary services could be economically provided.

In closing his general remarks, Mr. Taylor made reference to historic monuments in regard to which this area in particular, and the County of Fife in general were particularly rich. It was through the medium of the planning scheme that not only these monuments would be protected but also their surroundings which were as important as the monuments themselves.

Mr. Taylor then made mention of the three main centres in the area—Newport, Tayport and St. Andrews.

Newport seemed to be mainly residential in character and the question might be asked whether it was to remain so or would light industries be wanted. There might be suggestions for a new park or promenade. A more utilitarian suggestion might be the consideration of the Burgh's water problem. The situation of the burgh was admirable with ideal building sites, the future development of which, however, would be held up on account of lack of water supply, and this was where the planning of public services came in to assist in the correct location of housing. Too much emphasis should not be placed on the rateable value question where land referred to might be outwith the Burgh Boundary as in all likelihood the people would shop and spend their money in the burgh.

Passing by Tayside to *Tayport*—a beautiful road which Mr. Taylor said he hoped would be preserved and not dotted with bungaloid growth at irregular intervals like mushrooms, one came to a thriving populace hiding its light under a bushel in regard to its various activities. There was a thriving sawmilling industry, and also flax works. There had been engineering works and allied industries in existence in the past. There was also the harbour with its immense possibilities. Mr. Taylor then paid tribute to the fine piece of planning which had already been carried out and was still developing, namely, the promenade and park produced by use of refuse and controlled tipping method. The same difficulty as to water supply existed in Tayport as in Newport.

Coming to *St. Andrews*, Mr. Taylor said that in these few remarks it was hardly fair to try to do due credit to St. Andrews. It deserved a lecture on its own and he doubted then if it would be complete. The city was known all the world over for its golf-course, University, etc. It was in addition an architect's paradise. It had a heritage of which it was justly proud. It had been well-planned already with its three wide streets and pleasing vistas. It would no doubt be agreed, however, that it was not possible to stand still. If progress was to be made, therefore, there must be a plan in mind in order that progress did not injure the amenities—a plan which would enhance existing possessions. Questions which might be asked were—if a light industry came to St. Andrews, where would it be established ? Or, again, if the Gas Company decided to reorganise their works, where would these be placed ? Could more be made of the land immediately behind East Sands ? Could better facilities be offered at the harbour ? . . .

Summing up, Mr. Taylor explained that the Advisory Committee was anxious to lay before the County Regional Planning Committee an outlined plan for the provision of a convenient, healthy and pleasant physical environment which would react to the economic social and cultural welfare of the inhabitants, and it was to the inhabitants the Committee appealed for suggestions, for it was on their behalf that the Committee was planning.

Mr. *Christie* said he did not propose to say very much as they were there mainly to gather information and ideas. There had been explained a great deal of the general scheme that was running round the minds of the Advisory Committee. There was always, he said, a stage of gradual approach to a conclusion, ideas began to crystallise and then it was found that these were progressing very rapidly. Of the two main industries in the County—coal and agriculture—he was of opinion that the latter was the more important—one could not eat coal but everybody had to eat food. The agricultural industry was in a bad condition. The real difficulties were perhaps not very evident but were mainly due to the fact that for so many years agriculture had been a depressed industry with the result that young people would not go into it. At the present time, 300 land girls and 600 Italian prisoners had had to be called upon to keep the industry going. When these workers were not avilable it was anticipated that great difficulty would be found in obtaining the services of a man who knew how to build a stack. He was of opinion that the question as to how this problem was to be met and dealt with would enter very strongly into the planning scheme, and that great as were the difficulties with which the coal industry was faced, agriculture was faced with much greater.

Mr. Christie mentioned that a Royal Commission had sat lately and he understood that there was a proposal to establish a Farm Institute for Scotland—possibly situated in Fife. There was a great need for the training in agriculture of boys from 15 upwards. Farmers at present were so overburdened with work themselves that it was impossible for them to give very much in the way of training.

With regard to recreation, Mr. Christie said that it was essential that facilities on a much wider scale than ever before should be made available. There was a rural population growing up who had no interest in the land. This was more evident in the west of Fife and possible suggestions as to this might be forthcoming.

Mr. Christie then referred to the area at Tentsmuir and to the possibility of discussion taking place at the next public meeting on the question of this area being acquired and retained as an open space for the nation. He stated that his suggestions were perhaps vague and amorphous but the Sub-Committee wanted to get the reactions of the public. He further explained that this was the first public meeting which had been held and that it was justified for one or two reasons, one being that St. Andrews was one of the most beautiful towns not only in Scotland but in Great Britain. He had seen St. Andrews spoiled. One of the questions that would face the planning authorities would be as to whether St. Andrews was going to grow and develop with bungalows to the south, or would it be decided that there should be satellite towns. Suppose, he said, that if there came to be large numbers of people in Guardbridge and Leuchars, were they going to be housed in modern bungalows in St. Andrews or should there be a fresh satellite town somewhere to the west near Strathtyrum ? There was a chance being given to make a report which might help to guide the future and he appealed to the public to help the Committee not to miss the opportunity that was being offered.

Mr. *Whiteford* said he failed to see many of his fellow agriculturists present. He had been flattered by the remarks of the Chairman and the County Planning Officer in regard to the industry he represented which had been referred to as the greatest industry in the land. It was a splendid industry to look at and behold, but sometimes it was thought that it was not so fine an industry in which to participate . . . It was very fine to be in an industry which was flattered from all sides, but in the County Planning Scheme an endeavour must be made to preserve for agriculture the various areas that were now reserved to it in the country. He stated that it was an alarming fact that since the war started between two and three million acres had been taken up by housing and aerodromes throughout Great Britain, and that in future it must be the aim of the planning scheme, as far as possible, to get aerodromes and housing schemes to go where they will not occupy good agricultural land.

With regard to the remarks of the County Planning Officer with reference to the housing of agricultural workers in villages, Mr. Whiteford stated that as a guide for the forthcoming public meeting, he wished to say that agriculturists did not view with pleasure and happy anticipation the idea of placing agricultural workers in village communities. They regarded it as an entirely impracticable suggestion and that no good would come of it.

Mr. Whiteford went on to say that he was pleased to hear the Chairman admit that he first of all was here to further the interests of his own industry. That was an honest admission right away. He was also pleased to hear him say that they were there as brothers and that an endeavour would be made to satisfy and ameliorate every section in the community . . . Perhaps by next meeting other views would emerge, and there might be good suggestions from various interested parties.

Mr. *Carlow* then indicated that later in the meeting plans would be available for inspection by members of the public present, and that meantime any suggestions or questions would be welcomed.

Q.—Mr. Ritchie, Secretary, St. Andrews University said there was a point on procedure he would like to have cleared up, and that was as to the relationship of the Planning Advisory Committee to the local Town Council.

A.—Mr. Carlow replied that as Planning Authority the Town Council of St. Andrews had equal rights with the County Council, and the County Council did not wish to intervene in any way in the internal affairs of St. Andrews. They hoped that the Town Council would be well advised and well guided. It was impossible, however, for a man to live without regard for his neighbours, and it was extremely unlikely that schemes would be developed without these affecting County interests, and the County would wish to collaborate with the Town Council for the general good.

General Crosbie then expressed on behalf of the Committee their thanks to the members of the Town Council for having made the Council Chambers available for the meeting. He said the meeting was a historic one and was simply a desire on the part of the elected representatives to make contact with the public on matters in regard to which they were well informed so that in co-operation there might be secured for St Andrews, Fife and the whole of Great Britain those potential advantages that are in mind. The Advisory Committee had been created because in the past it had been felt that there had not been sufficiently close contact between important burghs and important industries, and that it was desired to develop that to the utmost so that they might work together in a spirit of brotherhood and friendship for the best advantage of all concerned.

Bailie Imrie, St. Andrews, said that his Council quite recognised in St. Andrews that although they were Town Planning Authority, yet St. Andrews, as the ancient ecclesiastical capital of Scotland, belonged to the nation, and as the Mecca of golf it belonged to the whole world. They quite recognised also that others outside St. Andrews were quite as much interested in the future of the place as they themselves were. They were delighted to discuss matters of so great importance as those which had been mentioned to-day with the Authority that is nearest to their Council's planning authority.

Bailie Imrie on behalf of the Provost, Magistrates and Councillors of St. Andrews, then thanked the Committee for the meeting and hoped that out of it something of very considerable importance to St. Andrews and the County would emerge.

Bailie Fraser, St. Andrews, proposed a vote of thanks to the Chairman, Mr. Carlow, and opportunity was then given to the public to inspect plans and proposals.

NOTES OF PUBLIC MEETING HELD IN COUNTY OFFICES, KIRKCALDY
27th March, 1945

Mr. Carlow (Chairman) :

Mr. Carlow thanked the audience for their attendance. In the first place, he said, he would like to say how sorry the Committee were at the absence of the Provost through illness and he thought it would be appropriate for the Secretary to send him a note from the meeting expressing regret at his illness and their hope for his speedy recovery.

Mr. Carlow then went on to explain what the Committee meant and were trying to do and how they proposed to do it. First of all, he hoped that people would not think that the Committee were trying to interfere in matters which were better left alone. On the contrary, a certain amount of planning was necessary for the future development of the County, and that amount and no more was what the Committee wished to do. Matters, he said, were moving on a bigger scale than ever before, and while, for instance, they were all so interested in the crossing of the Rhine, there was also the crossing of the Firths of Forth and Tay to be considered. Schemes of that magnitude were in contemplation—no more than in contemplation—and at least they would like to see that neither the Burgh nor the County had made a mess of things by erecting a housing scheme or something else in the path or at the place where the bridge must terminate ; or that a housing scheme or something else had been put down on the only line for an arterial road to meet those bridges ; or, coming to his own industry, that a housing scheme had been erected on a site appropriate for a coal pit and nothing else. It could be seen, therefore, that a certain amount of planning was necessary, and the Committee wished to suggest that that amount be done and no more. He could assure the audience that the Committee did not wish to waste time needlessly in doing things which most practical people thought would be better left alone.

Mr. Carlow then went on to explain that the County Council had a Planning Committee, but the County Council was quite necessarily a body of business people who were actively engaged in the prosecution of the business of the County, and were, he thought, quite entitled to say, " Yes, we approve of something, but we want you from the coal industry to come and tell us what you think should be done because we don't know. We wish you from the paper industry to come and tell us what you want done in the way of planning," and so on from the various industries which thrived in the County. Therefore, the County Planning Committee invited a number of business men and others to form an Advisory Committee. From the mining industry they said they would like to have nominated an owner and miner to represent the two sides of the coal industry, and similarly from the Railway Company and paper industry and so on. There was now, he said, an Advisory Committee of people spending a great deal of time in the work under consideration. This Committee, of course, was too big and a Sub-Committee of three persons was appointed—Sir James Irvine, Principal and Vice-Chancellor of St. Andrews University representing tradition, history and culture ; Mr. Christie of Durie, representing land and agricultural interests, and himself representing the coal industry. This Committee had already visited a great many towns and had had meetings with their Provosts and Town Councillors, and it was hoped to have a draft report prepared by the autumn of this year. Mr. Carlow then said he appealed for the fullest co-operation between the parties—the Committee knew well that Kirkcaldy was its own Planning Authority, and they had no wish to interfere in the slightest with anything that happened within its boundaries. Their duty was in the County, but he pointed out that there was a combined duty on the Burghs and the County to work together co-ordinating their efforts and co-operating in order that nothing might be done in Fife which would be injurious to the future development of the County as a whole within the next 50 years. . . .

Mr. Carlow went on to say that Kirkcaldy was a very important centre indeed, because, as was known from the Scottish Coalfields Report, three large collieries were planned which were not very far away—Thornton Junction, Dysart (which he thought was actually within the Burgh boundary) and Seafield—one of the richest coalfields in this country, if not the richest unexplored coalfield in Great Britain. Obviously this would mean considerable development. There must be housing for the people, which involved water and drainage and many other things. There must also be reasonable amenities. This was where the Burghs and the County must co-operate. Mr. Carlow said he had had the pleasure of visiting the Provosts of Kinghorn and Burntisland, and had discussed with them the development south of Kirkcaldy. He had come away with the impression that there should be explored the possibility of Kinghorn being regarded as a residential area with a green belt a mile or two wide between Kinghorn and Kirkcaldy on the one side, and Kinghorn and Burntisland on the other, and that a goodly proportion of workers in the new area of Kirkcaldy, and perhaps the additional workers at Burntisland, might, instead of being housed in the immediate vicinity of their work, be conveyed in buses to Kinghorn and thus make the centre at Kinghorn a residential place for a considerably increased population in this part of Fife. It was, he said, only an idea which required working out.

In closing, Mr. Carlow again emphasised that the Committee came in the most friendly way to see how far they could work together for the general good of this part of Fife.

Mr. Taylor outlined the aims and objects of the Planning Scheme and emphasised that it did not imply any intention to promote active building development on the land to which it referred but merely to control and guide development when it occurred, so that the area would be laid out to the best advantage of the population as regards economy, beauty and health. To obtain this, he thought the County Council had approached the question in a most democratic way by appointing an Advisory Committee to ascertain the views of the inhabitants of the areas concerned and which the Committee would thereafter report to the Planning Committee.

In referring to the plans displayed, Mr. Taylor pointed out that although the area under consideration to-day was mainly industrial in character, there was a considerable hinterland which was still agricultural in character. There was some of the best land in the County between Kirkcaldy and Kinghorn. To the north of Kirkcaldy the land was still of good quality but not so good as that already mentioned, while that to the west, although good also, did not come up to the quality of the other two classes. It was necessary, therefore, in view of the scarcity of good agricultural land in the country, to protect that which they already possessed. It had been found that good-class land was good-class building land, and in that way much land had been lost to the nation—it was essential that the planner should see to it that the best agricultural land was retained and, where possible, poorer land used for building purposes. There was also, he said, a large agricultural area behind the coastal belt and it was necessary to see that this area as well as the industrial area was also well planned.

Due to the proximity of large towns, there was always the danger of sporadic development in the surrounding agricultural areas, and difficulties then arose as to services, transport, etc., for these scattered areas. It was thought that development in the countryside should be encouraged into defined centres thus obtaining advantages in regard to public services, transport, education, shopping, recreation. etc.

In the area under consideration, Mr. Taylor said there were two agricultural centres—Auchtertool and Chapel—which if development was guided properly, might become thriving agricultural communities serving the needs of the area. There might also be established there allied industries such as implement repair shops, carpenters' shops, etc.

Mr. Taylor then referred to the proposals the coal companies had in view and the prosperous future envisaged for this area in respect thereto. Collieries designed on clean and pleasant lines, and lay-out of houses, shops, etc., were visualised. In this connection, Mr. Taylor then mentioned the booklet issued in regard to Comrie Pit.

In this area in the future, it was known that there was going to be a considerable increase in population over the next 50 to 100 years. Should there be new towns in the area or should this increase in population be accommodated in the existing burghs of Kirkcaldy, Burntisland and Kinghorn, which have existing facilities in the way of public services, electricity, gas, water, sewers, schools, libraries, etc., and in addition, a civic pride which would take years to develop in new townships. Suggestion on questions such as this would be welcomed by the Advisory Committee.

Allied to this question was the question as to what should be the ultimate size of a town. A considerable number of English industrial towns were between 100,000 and 200,000 population. London had 8,000,000 and to say the least had become unwieldy. Kirkcaldy's counterpart in England, viz. Lancaster, in so far as it was the only other town of any size manufacturing linoleum, had a population of about 50,000. A town could be either too big or too small.

In connection with the three Burghs in this area already mentioned—Kirkcaldy, Kinghorn and Burntisland—if it should be ultimately decided that the increased population should be accommodated there, it would be very necessary to ensure that there was not a continuous spread of buildings from Kirkcaldy to Burntisland so that each town lost its individuality. This was particularly noticeable, he said, in the Lancashire cotton towns. Between towns there should be preserved a green belt. Kirkcaldy, he thought, was fortunate in this respect, and if a diplomatic approach were made to the landowners in the district it might be possible to preserve a green belt without much difficulty—Raith Park being a good example in this connection.

In Chapel area, to the north, it was thought there might be suitable land for the siting of an aerodrome, and forming part of the green belt mentioned. A town of the size of Kirkcaldy would in all probability in the future not be complete without an aerodrome or at least a landing-ground. Should consideration be given now for the reservation of land for this purpose? This might be a question on which the Town and County Council should co-operate.

Other questions which might be considered were whether burghs concerned wished to remain industrial. Ships would still be needed in Burntisland and with the glowing prospect of aluminium there was the possibility of it being a thriving industrial town.

What about Kinghorn and Aberdour? Would they grasp the opportunity of becoming high-class residential areas or endeavour to reintroduce industry?

Mr. Taylor then referred to the area of the coastal road which should remain unspoiled, and to the holiday industry. He felt that the coastline and the countryside behind should be preserved, and the Committee would welcome observations on this matter.

He then referred to the question of roads and the amount of traffic passing through Kirkcaldy, Kinghorn and Burntisland. Was it desired that this should continue, necessitating perhaps large widening schemes, etc., or should it pass to the north of the towns?

The question of public services was then dealt with—the services which are always taken for granted, but which required careful planning. The County Council and the Burgh of Kirkcaldy had already, he said, had preliminary discussion on this question, and "tentative agreement had been reached on all points to date."

Mr. Christie explained that the main object of the Committee's visit was to elicit information rather than give it. The method chosen was one which provided the Advisory Committee with the opportunity of putting out a few ideas and explaining their work, and at a future meeting—on 17th April—the Committee very much hoped that there would be a keen discussion and exchange of views. This work of producing a plan by the end of the summer was, he said, exceedingly onerous and difficult.

Fife had some of the finest agricultural land in Scotland. It had been exceedingly well looked after. Following the very difficult time due to the depression between the two wars and even going farther back than that, the brighter and more intelligent youths of the country left the farming industry, the result being that there was not the farming population coming in that there would have been had the industry been more prosperous. He had been told by the Agricultural Executive that they were working with 900 people—Italian prisoners and land girls—who would depart at the end of the war and everything would have to be done to retain the industry in a prosperous condition. People in this country had not yet awakened to the fact that it was possible that for the next 20 years Europe might be faced with semi-starvation and every single acre of ground was going to count. He knew of a town round which a green belt had been decided, but the local council saw fit to dot the green belt with one or two buildings, with the result they lost dairy farms and then wondered why there was no milk, etc. In another similar town, known to him, building development had just killed two dairy farms. Another dairy farm which was going to extend had to stop, a fourth was being absorbed and a fifth was dying—and people asked why there was not a plentiful milk supply, etc., in the community. Everything possible, he said, should be done to preserve the dairy farms—by-pass them, build beyond them, but they should not be wiped out. We were going to need all that ground very badly before we were finished.

Mr. Christie then explained that the Committee's report had to deal with the whole County. There were many things which came up which were not yet decided. The line of the new road, for instance, from the Forth Bridge going north.

Was it going to the west of Loch Leven? Was it going to skirt through the coalfields of the future? Was it going to drive right across to Dundee? Which was the best route? Mr. Christie asked that if there were any reasoned ideas for next meeting they should be brought out. As far as he could see there were three main areas in Fife :—

(1) purely agricultural where light industries would probably be blacksmiths' shops, creameries, etc.
(2) where you had industry and agriculture intermixed—e.g. Kirkcaldy and surrounding area, and where it was obvious that there was going to be a great increase in population on account of the three new pits to be sunk. Where was the increase to be housed? Would Kirkcaldy grow, or would the public prefer to have satellite towns?
(3) The coastal belt which was the best coastal area in Scotland. It was hoped this would be preserved as a residential area—apart from the fishing industry which had to be treated separately—and that a large number of holiday-makers would be attracted from the west of Scotland.

Mr. Lorimer (Railway Company) appealed for co-operation with the Railway Company. If Kirkcaldy, Burntisland and Kinghorn were planning any development or new industries he hoped they would let the Railway Company know what they had in view so that the company could take the local authorities with them. The company on their part would not hesitate to let them know what they had in view.

Mr. Carlow then gave the audience the opportunity of asking questions and referred to the maps displayed. He reminded them also of the public meeting to be held in a fortnight's time.

Provost Meldrum, Burntisland, proposed a vote of thanks to Mr. Carlow, Chairman, who, he said, had conducted the proceedings and given his point of view on the planning question very efficiently. To this gathering of Fife people, he thought it was most appropriate that he should say that the County Council had approached them in a very accommodating spirit on this question of planning. The County Council were asking them for their co-operation, and in view of the appeal that had been made from the three speakers he thought they would be ungrateful if they did not give the County Council all the help they possibly could. They would take home the opinions they had got to-day and come back on the 17th with their official point of view.

NOTES OF PUBLIC MEETING HELD IN ST. ANDREWS
3rd April, 1945

Mr. Carlow (Chairman) said this was now the second of these meetings to be held in St. Andrews, and it was a great pleasure to his colleagues and himself to know how much interest was being taken in this matter in St. Andrews. It would be very nice if the same degree of interest were to be found all round the County. It would make their Report very much more interesting and their journeys more agreeable. Referring to the powers and duties of the County authorities and the City of St. Andrews authority, Mr. Carlow said he was not an expert in these matters and he would require the matter to be settled in a friendly manner between the Town Clerk and the County Clerk, but the County Clerk was not present this afternoon so he hoped the matter would not arise . . . The Committee hoped they had the goodwill of everybody with them ; otherwise it would not be possible to make a Report which was worth while. At the last meeting the Committee, he said, had done most of the speaking ; on this occasion they would like to do most of the listening.

Mr. Carlow then reported that he had received in writing, since last meeting, suggestions from the undernoted bodies, and for which suggestions the Committee were very grateful.

(1) St. Andrews Preservation Trust Ltd.
(2) St. Andrews Citizens' Advisory Council.
(3) St. Andrews Women Citizens' Association.
(4) St. Andrews Boys' Club.
(5) St. Andrews Co-operative Women's Guild.

(The letters are shown in the Appendix to these Notes).

In addition, Mr. Carlow said he had received a very informative letter in connection with Guardbridge Paper Company requirements which he did not think would clash with anybody else's. The Company were very short of water, not only for dwelling-houses but for processing purposes, etc., in their works, and it might be said that these works were being cramped and stultified for the want of water. Whatever houses were to be built should be built near the works and not in a satellite village. Even if the houses were connected by telephone, it would not compensate for the inconvenience of having their people housed several miles away. The works ran 24 hours a day, and particular employees were required for certain processes. Even apart from breakdowns, changes in certain things in their works required certain men to be available. Mr. Carlow said it would be necessary to compromise between the strictly utilitarian aspect and the aesthetic and amenity aspect. It might be better for people in certain cases to live a mile or two away from their works if these works had an objectionable odour, or if the atmosphere was contaminated. It was a good thing, he said, to have people living with a green belt between their works and their homes. In Kirkcaldy, additional population might be housed in Kinghorn and carried by 'bus for two miles from their work in Kirkcaldy to green country, morning and evening. Even people working in Burntisland might be carried by 'bus to the seaside resort at Kinghorn. On the other hand, he did not know whether Guardbridge could be considered as undesirable or if any place half-way between Guardbridge and St. Andrews would be better than Guardbridge. Personally, he favoured the economic point of view, because if a works could not pay its own way it would fail. Mr. Carlow then said the Committee would like to have suggestions in addition or in supplement of those already heard.

About the Tay Road Bridge, Mr. Carlow said it might help if he reported that Newport was opposed to the bridge being constructed there. With reference to Crail, the Burgh wanted to have nothing to do with heavy traffic or works, business or commerce of any kind. It wanted to be a golfing seaside resort. The Provost had said he might look favourably upon a factory making golf-clubs—a suitable appendage to the golf-course.

Elie was in the same position exactly. They wanted another golf-course but no works or factories.

The only places which wanted encouragement were Anstruther, St. Monance and Pittenweem. They were in need of development with regard to better utilisation and preservation of herrings and whitefish. These were the only serious developments they had been able to find in the East of Fife which would require to be considered in the way of future planning—facilities for disposing of excess catch, freezing of whitefish and selling when market was good.

When the Committee went to Newburgh further up, near Mugdrum Island, they found quite another atmosphere. They were anxious to have the bridge there. That, Mr. Carlow said, was as far as the Committee had been able to go in connection with the bridge.

Mr. John C. Henderson (Tayport Town Councillor) said that Tayport was a semi-industrial area and there were several long-established industries. Some of these during the last 30 years had gone back, one or two had closed down or partially closed down, and it was suggested that assistance might be given in the creation of some light engineering works—probably in connection with agricultural machinery. At present there were small firms and others who specialised in the service of farm machinery, but what they did want was something established which would take up the manufacture of some definite article. There was scope for that in Tayport—they had the population and skilled labour. Apart from that, Tayport some 50 years ago was in a certain way a shipbuilding centre, chiefly in the manufacture of small boats, and it was considered that there was scope in Tayport for that in the future. Siting was good and there was deep water . . . It might not be amiss to say that Dundee Corporation did have in their minds a scheme for heavy building on the Tayport side, and it might be well to keep this in mind. There might also be scope for a civil aerodrome in the vicinity. There was poor agricultural land which might be used for that purpose if it were thought needful. Another point which, he said, might be mentioned was the large area of mud flats, and it was not beyond reasonable thought to consider that these—some 600 acres of land—might be at some future time reclaimed. Tentsmuir was quite near with its fine collection of natural sand which might be suitable for glass-making. The vast resources of sand might also help to solve housing difficulties in the future if someone could find solvent or binding properties.

Miss Kidston (*St. Andrews Preservation Trust*) asked a question about the preservation of old Scottish architecture and the housing of people. There were no grants, she said, for the reconditioning of old houses. There had been until recently a grant up to £100 for houses which were used by agricultural labourers or people of that status, but that limited the extent very much, and many houses had deteriorated, which, if reconditioned, would be very much better than temporary houses costing £600 or more. Would it be within the Committee's scope, she asked, to endeavour to get a grant for the reconditioning of houses in the immediate future ?

On being asked whether she referred to old dwelling-houses or to houses of architectural value, Miss Kidston replied that she meant both types.

Mr. *Carlow* said that no doubt grants would be made available for the building of new houses, but whether grants would be made for restoration was a matter about which he would not like at this stage to give a definite reply.

Mr. *Pollock* said there were certain powers under the Housing (Rural Workers) Act which at the moment could be utilised for the purpose of repairing houses. Artistic or historical interests could be dealt with under the express planning powers referred to this Committee, but the Committee would require specific indication for reference in their Report.

Mr. *Roger, Farmer, Kenley Green*, referred to the question of the housing of agricultural workers. He thought the correct place to house agricultural workers was as near their work as possible, and the same should apply to most work. He thought it was a wrong principle altogether to put the social benefit of wife and children before the man who was going to do the work. Work should come first. He knew by experience how difficult it was when he wanted to get a worker from another farm. He thought there should be 'buses or transport, and a worker should be paid wages so that he could afford a motor car to enable him to go to social activities.

Mr. *Taylor* in reply said that in rural areas houses should not be dotted about at random but should be grouped in village centres. That suggestion had been put forward by the Scott Committee, who had considered the question of the use of rural land. We had heard the side of the farmer but there was the other side. He knew by experience the difficulties of having to walk four miles to school and four back. It was better, he thought, that the man should have to cycle to his work rather than that his wife and children should have to walk long distances to schools and shopping centres. Country people saw nothing but work and seldom got any cultural facilities, and town people were apt to look down on country people. If people were congregated together in a centre this would allow of the County Council providing public services, etc. Everybody was not as philanthropic as regards his workers as was Mr. Roger, and a social life should be available in the countryside. Social facilities must be provided in the way of a village hall, etc. He was of opinion that there was everything to be gained by having agricultural workers in village communities.

Mr. *Christie* said he represented land-owning interests, but had always refused to accept that limitation . . . This idea of housing agricultural workers in communities was new. It was going to go very deep in the near future, and he felt it could not be adequately dealt with that afternoon. In the old days, companies such as coal companies, railway companies, S.C.W S., etc., housed their own workers. No longer was this happening. The work of housing these people was being put on the community and our very slow-moving farming system was definitely breaking down. The landowners were no longer able to put up the cottages on the farms and to keep them up to standard and the farmers had not the power of housing workers. The solution has not yet been found.

Dr. *J. Paton* (*St. Andrews Boys' Club*) said he would like to add some data to the letter which Mr. Chalmers and himself had submitted in connection with the by-pass. He apologised on behalf of Mr. Chalmers for his absence and said he had been asked to read a statement in regard to the proposition.

At present, even under the existing conditions of restricted motor traffic, Abbey Street and Abbey Walk created major safety problems for children and drivers alike, owing to the school lying alongside the main highway. Nearly 500 pupils were in attendance at the Abbey Walk School and these pupils could not avoid using Abbey Walk on their way to and from school. It was only to be expected, then, that with post-war motoring in full operation dangers would be much increased. There was no possibility of a rear exit from the school being available, by which pupils could go to their homes without having to use Abbey Walk, and no steps could be taken to counteract risks. In addition, pupils attending the East School (120) could not reach school without having to cross the main road at some point or other . . . Safety measures should be taken at present in the vicinity of school premises. He strongly urged that traffic passing through these channels should be kept to a minimum. This could only be done by means of a by-pass road.

It was not generally known that some years before the war St. Leonard's School had to construct, at considerable expense, a subway at Abbey Walk in order to enable those pupils who lived on the south of Abbey Walk to reach school in safety . . . On his own behalf, Dr. Paton said he would like to add some data relating to the subject. The number of native child population was between 1,300 and 1,400. He had arrived at this figure by adding the population attending the Burgh School, East and West Schools and Madras College, and 70 day girls attending St. Leonard's. In addition to this, St. Leonard's and St. Katherine's School had 400 boarders for 9 months in the year, all of whom, to reach the centre of the town, *e.g.* Post Office, had frequently to cross the main traffic route at one point or other. 56 day children attended St. Katherine's and had to cross North Street every time they came to school. The number of child visitors who came to the city could not be less than 1,000, which was an extremely conservative estimate. Every one of these must cross North Street in order to reach the Links, West Sands or Step Rock. There was no means of estimating the youth population, but it must be considerable. Dr. Paton said he did know that 600 students attended the University from outside St. Andrews and were resident for 8 or 9 months in the year. All of these must use North Street frequently daily. When these were added to the total it was evident that the youth and child population of the city was between 40% and 50% of the total population. St. Andrews was in quite an unusual position as regards its child and youth population. Dr. Paton said he hoped education would remain the chief industry of the city and that the holiday population would not be diminished. For safety, they urged that as a first objective in road planning, through traffic and especially heavy traffic should be diverted from its present route by means of a by-pass road.

Ex-Provost Fairweather, Newport, asked if any census had been taken of the traffic which would use the by-pass road. St. Andrews was a very important centre in this part of Fife, and he should have thought much of the traffic going along the coast would naturally come through to do business on the way, and if such were the case, the by-pass road would not be used to the same extent as it would be if there were no business to be done in St. Andrews.

Mr. J. W. Kinnear said that a body in the town, the Citizens' Advisory Council, had considered the question of a by-pass road. He did not think he was giving anything away when he said that a survey had already been made at the cost of the Citizens' Advisory Council, and in due time the plans would be placed before the Planning Authorities. With regard to what had been said about a census of traffic, it would be very difficult to take a census at the present time because far and away the biggest percentage passing through the town to-day was in connection with war works, such as the aerodromes at Crail and Dunino. In normal times, the traffic was seasonal. Towards the end of the year the farmers in the East Neuk came to St. Andrews with beet loads for the Corporation at Cupar. If there were a by-pass, it would be quite unnecessary for that seasonal traffic to come through the town. Again, there was the haulage of herring from Anstruther—which went North—mostly to Aberdeen and Peterhead, and was carried by Aberdeenshire contractors. This traffic would not require to go through St. Andrews. There was a big haulage firm in Pittenweem, but most of the loads were taken from points in Dundee ; it only happened that the headquarters of the firm were in Pittenweem. This contractor would use the by-pass road. There were a few farmers who had vehicles. He had counted 9. They, on an odd occasion, might have to come to town. There was also a Crail carrier who operated in the town, and 'bus traffic, but apart from that a very small number of vehicles came in to St. Andrews. A by-pass road would be used by all seasonal traffic.

Mr. Carlow said that people from a distance would come to golf, shop and spend the afternoon, and therefore a by-pass road would be of no use to them. What proportion that would bear to the traffic which needlessly came to St. Andrews and would be taken by the by-pass road was a matter on which he had not the slightest indication or information whatever.

Sir James Irvine said it was of no moment what the present volume of traffic was—it was what the future traffic might be. What they were afraid of was the utilisation of that corner of Scotland connecting the east coast roads with those running to the North. Through traffic was not wanted, and it was desired to leave the historic streets as they were.

Mr. Taylor referred to a narrow strip between the road and river along the Newport-Tayport Road on which it would be a desecration to build houses. He said it would also be a violation of the terms of the Restriction of Ribbon Development Act.

Ex-Provost Fairweather, Newport, said Newport was a residential burgh, often called the " Dormitory of Dundee." They were quite satisfied to be a residential burgh and to be called the " Dormitory of Dundee." They did not know where the Tay Road Bridge was to be situated. He was afraid in Newport they would have very little say, but it was an important matter, and the County Planning Authority should co-operate with their friends on the north side of the Tay as the situation of the bridge was bound to affect any future planning in Fife, especially in the north-east corner. With regard to Mr. Taylor's remarks in connection with the road between Tayport and Newport, Ex-Provost Fairweather said that that question at the moment was a County matter which was outside the jurisdiction of both burghs.

Mr. J. Henderson, Tayport, reminded the Committee of the fact that Dundee definitely had their eyes on Tayport as a shipbuilding area and for housing schemes.

Mr. Philip Boase then proposed formally that in any road planning a by-pass road should be outside St. Andrews. He said he thought he was rather preaching to a convert, because he had been interested to find in a map which the County had drawn up they had proposed a by-pass road.

This was seconded by Dr. Paton and carried unanimously.

Colonel Alford said he had had a letter in the *Citizen* in regard to the proposal, which was to cut across from the north-west corner to the south-east corner and it was to start near the Eden Course and to come out to join up with the Crail Road. That would get over the difficulty about which so many had been talking to-day as regards school children and the taking of traffic from the east part of St. Andrews. There should be a 'bus station near the railway station. In a by-pass road it would solve all the problems, and it would land people at a convenient centre in St. Andrews. He entirely supported what was suggested except that the road should curve round and come into a point near the railway station, so as to have a 'bus station.

Mr. Philip Boase said St. Andrews Advisory Council had a scheme in which that point was provided for—while the main road went outside St. Andrews, there were roads radiating therefrom. A 'bus station did not negative the suggestion of a by-pass, and it was the unanimous opinion that no through traffic should be carried through St. Andrews.

Mr. J. Angus (St. Andrews Merchants' Association) asked if, in view of the letter sent by St. Andrews Merchants, they would be able to meet the Committee again in St. Andrews, where the members of the Association would have an opportunity of speaking. They would prefer also that the meeting should be held at a time suitable to the Merchants and not in the afternoon.

Mr. Carlow said he personally would be very pleased to come at any time to St. Andrews, or alternatively, if the Association sent in a written communication the Committee would consider it and thereafter decide whether another meeting should be held.

Sir James Irvine said he had been thinking over the proposals—not from the City's point of view but from Fife County Council's point of view. For good or ill, the planning within the Burgh area was the problem of the Town Council of St. Andrews. The planning of the County was the province of the County Council. It was really as representatives of Fife County Council that they were considering the various projects and as to how far they would impinge on County schemes. They had heard that citizens did not want their old town cut into pieces by traffic, and they had suggested—rather appealed—that any road scheme should include a by-pass. Other points had been mentioned, the desirability of having light industries in the neighbourhood for example, on which question there might be more than one opinion. One had always to remember, he said, if you planted an industry there was the economic background to be considered. Natural laws could not be defied, and St. Andrews was peculiarly poor in economic resources. All kinds of difficulties would have to be surmounted, and he doubted whether small factories could be provided. Nevertheless, if the County scheme involved the arrangement of areas in which such industries could be developed and the provision of the necessary facilities, no serious objection would be taken provided the essential part of St. Andrews was retained.

The first practical suggestion was in regard to a green belt. A green belt was definitely wanted round the city. This was not a new idea but was about 20 years old. The town was overflowing to the south to meet the needs of housing—it was filtering out to the west, and it was necessary to see that any further proposals did not impinge upon the green belt surrounding St. Andrews.

Another plea was that the historic views of St. Andrews should not be impaired—over the hill from Largo, Pilgrim's View, St. Nicholas Brae, from Ceres Road, etc. It was, Sir James said, the easiest thing in the world to ruin a view.

Mr. Kinnear asked why, if no industries were to be introduced, houses should be built. People had to live, and how were they going to live if there was no industry.

Sir James Irvine replied that that depended on the size the town was going to be.

Mr. *Kinnear* said that in the past they had put the cart before the horse. Houses had been built without considering where those who lived in them were going to obtain a livelihood, with the result that there were more people than there was work. He thought they would be falling farther into the trap by providing more houses without a means of livelihood, and therefore if housing was to be developed industry should be introduced. If houses were to be built, they had to be let ; they had to be subsidised. What was the difference, he asked, between subsidising a house and subsidising industry ?

Mr. *Carlow* in reply said he hoped that it would never be suggested that industry should be subsidised. It should be able to stand on its own feet and hold up its head. They wanted to be masters in their own house.

General Crosbie then proposed a vote of thanks to the Town Council for having made the hall available and for the support which had been received at the meeting.

APPENDIX REFERRED TO

(1) *Letter from St. Andrews Preservation Trust Limited.*

THE COUNTY CLERK,
    FIFE COUNTY COUNCIL,
        COUNTY BUILDINGS,
           CUPAR, FIFE.

90 SOUTH STREET,
ST. ANDREWS,
2nd April, 1945.

Fife Planning Advisory Committee

DEAR SIR,
    On behalf of the Preservation Trust I am desired to express to the Planning Advisory Committee of the County Council our appreciation of their frank and friendly approach to the whole question of planning in the St. Andrews area.

Representatives of the Trust will be present at the meeting on 3rd April, but in view of the suggestion that any recommendations should, if possible, be made in writing, we should like to draw attention to the following points :

(1) As regards the planning of trunk roads in the St. Andrews area, the Trustees are opposed to the passage of heavy through traffic by way of the town, and sincerely hope that the scheme for a by-pass road indicated in the draft County Plan will be carried into effect.

(2) On the more general question of the planning of the area the Trustees, while favouring the development of St. Andrews as a well-balanced community, are strongly of the view that there is a natural limit to the growth of the city, and that any undue expansion would destroy its distinctive character. The existence of a natural green belt round St. Andrews is, moreover, one of its most attractive features, which should, as far as possible, be maintained.

(3) May we further suggest that as Fife has a distinctive and very attractive type of rural architecture this should also be maintained in any future development.

(4) We also express the hope that the adjacent coast-line should be preserved in its natural state.

The general standpoint of the Trustees regarding the future development of St. Andrews and its neighbourhood is set out in the Trust Handbook, *Old St. Andrews,* of which I enclose a copy for reference.

Yours faithfully,
(Signed)   R. G. CANT,
Chairman of Trustees.

---

(2) *Letter from St. Andrews Citizens' Advisory Council.*

J. M. MITCHELL, Esq.,
    COUNTY CLERK,
        COUNTY BUILDINGS,
           CUPAR.

11 ALEXANDRA PLACE,
ST. ANDREWS,
2nd April, 1945.

Fife County Council Planning and Advisory Committee

DEAR SIR,
    The St. Andrews Citizens' Advisory Council, consisting of representatives from the University of St. Andrews, the Merchants' Association, St. Leonards and St. Katherine's Schools, St. Andrews Preservation Trust, the Women Citizens' Association, St. Andrews Co-operative Association and the St. Andrews Ratepayers' Association, wishes to inform the County Council that it is very much in favour of the construction of a road by-passing St. Andrews. Such a road would make it unnecessary for heavy vehicles to pass through any part of the old city and would obviate the need for widening of existing streets.

The Advisory Council would also like to ask the County Council to endeavour to preserve the views on the approach roads to St. Andrews. At present these are very fine and give a delightful impression of the town to incoming vehicles. It would be most unfortunate if buildings were erected which would spoil or screen these views.

Yours faithfully,
(Signed)   D. RITCHIE,
Secretary.

---

(3) *Letter from St. Andrews Women Citizens' Association.*

J. M. MITCHELL, Esq.,
    COUNTY CLERK,
        COUNTY BUILDINGS,
           CUPAR.

ST. ANDREWS.
(Undated).

DEAR SIR,
    May I say how glad we are to have had the opportunity of meeting the County Planning Advisory Committee at the Meeting held on 20th March in the Council Chambers, Town Hall, St. Andrews. A meeting of the Committee of the Women Citizens' Association was held on Tuesday, 27th March, and in response to your invitation to send in suggestions to the Advisory Committee, they have asked me to send in the following for your consideration :—

1. A by-pass should skirt St. Andrews and no wide roads for traffic should pass through the city.
2. Any light industries which might spring up in or near St. Andrews should be placed on the Guardbridge Road beyond

the golf-courses, and buildings erected should be pleasing to the eye. We envisage a satellite town here which would be adequately served by the proposed by-pass road.

3. We are strongly in favour of bridges over the Forth and Tay.

4. Leuchars Aerodrome should be retained as an air port. If this aerodrome is needed for the sole use of H.M. Forces a civil air port for this district should be provided.

5. If it comes within your jurisdiction, we ask you to prohibit long-time parking for chars-a-bancs and 'buses in North Street.

May we point out that the time of the meetings (3 p.m.) arranged by the County Council prevents a great many interested people from attending.

Yours truly,

(Signed) ELEANOR SCOTT,

Hon. Secretary.

---

(4) *Communication on behalf of St. Andrews Boys' Club.*

The main route by road from Cupar and from the Tay to the East Coast Burghs at present passes through St. Andrews by way of Pilmour Links, North Street, Abbey Street and Abbey Walk.

As representatives of one of the Youth organisations in St. Andrews we wish to put forward two outstanding objections to this route.

1. All pedestrians wishing to go to the Links, the Weat Sands or the Step Rock bathing-pool must cross it. And we would emphasise that in the term " pedestrians " must be included the children of residents and of summer visitors.

2. The Burgh School is situated in the Abbey Walk. Every pupil, to reach it, must pass along the Abbey Walk and many must cross it.

In view of the increase in traffic anticipated by your speakers last week, we plead, as a matter of urgency, for safety of children alone, for the provision of a by-pass road round St. Andrews, to divert this coastwise traffic, and especially heavy traffic, from its present route.

(Signed) T. CHALMERS,
Headmaster, Burgh School,
Hon. Sec., St. Andrews Boys' Club.

(Signed) J. HUNTER,
P. PATON,
Representing St. Andrews Boys' Club.

---

(5) *Letter from St. Andrews Co-operative Women's Guild.*

(Undated).

The above Guild respectfully submits the suggestion, that the Town Planning Committee use the power and influence they have to encourage factories to be built for light industries, such as glove-making, lace-making, cigarette lighters, jam-making, etc.

The Guild also suggests that now is the time to start on these new schemes to enable Service men and girls to start work immediately on their return to civilian life.

Factories could be built around the town, without interfering whatsoever with the old-world atmosphere of the town itself.

(Signed) Mrs. A. MITCHELL,

38 Chamberlain Street,
St. Andrews.

Secretary.

NOTES OF PUBLIC MEETING HELD IN COUNTY HALL, CUPAR
9th April, 1945

Mr. Carlow (Chairman) :

Mr. Carlow thanked the audience for their attendance and said how glad they were to see such a large turn-out of people interested in the planning of the County, and so anxious to know in what way they could assist.

Mr. Carlow went on to say that planning was a word which had been greatly abused. A certain amount of planning was necessary in view of the future developments, but the word could be very much overworked. They did not wish to plan in detail such things as they knew would never be carried out.

Continuing, Mr. Carlow spoke of the industry in which he was interested, namely, coal industry. They knew quite well beforehand, he said, where new pits were going to be. That was determined by underground situation and surface situation, and how stupid they would all be if, when pits were required and this was the only place where pits could be sunk, it should be found that the fields had been occupied by a housing scheme or something else. Therefore, it was necessary to plan ahead and so avoid making stupid mistakes. The question of the road bridges over the Tay and Forth was another example. Arterial roads would require to be planned to deal with the traffic expected to be attracted by those bridges. There might only be one or two alternative routes for these roads, and how foolish they would all look if the routes for these roads were covered with housing schemes, etc.

Mr. Carlow then went on to say that the County Council had a very difficult task before it in that members of the Council did not necessarily know about the industries on which the future prosperity of the County was going to depend. They therefore called together a number of industrialists and others to come to an Advisory Committee to advise the County Council as to what might be required by industry, agriculture, and other interests in the County and so help the County Council to plan aright. On the Advisory Committee, he said, there were representatives of railway employers and workers, agricultural employers and workers, and various others from the major industries in the County, and the Advisory Committee was as well prepared as it could be to represent the industries, on which, as he had said before, the future prosperity of the County would have to be founded. The Advisory Committee was considered to be too large, and it was decided that Sir James Irvine, Mr.

Christie and himself, who now had the honour to appear before them, should be charged with the duty of preparing a report for the approval of the parent Committee. They hoped to have their report completed by the autumn.

Mr. Carlow then went on to explain that the County had been divided into different areas, Cupar area including the Burghs of Cupar, Newburgh, Auchermuchty, Falkland and Ladybank, and that a tour had been made of the area with a view to obtaining the views of the different Burghs. The purpose of this meeting was to explain to all interested what the Committee had in view, and to invite their suggestions so that these might be brought before the Committee at the next public meeting to be held in the County Hall in about 10 days' time. Mr. Carlow appealed for as many concrete suggestions as possible and hoped that all interested would co-operate to the fullest extent. The Committee proposed to send out a questionnaire to industrialists and others and Mr. Carlow hoped that these questionnaires would be answered.

With regard to the Tay Road Bridge, Mr. Carlow said he thought the Provost and Councillors of Newburgh were very anxious to have the bridge in their district. It seemed reasonable to the Committee that the bridge should be placed so as to serve the purpose of industry to the best advantage. They proposed, therefore, to have a plan prepared showing the industries according to their character and magnitude so that they might plan the roads to be of the best possible service to the industry of the County.

In concluding his remarks Mr. Carlow again emphasised the need for the help of the public and expressed the hope that they would send in all information possible so that it might be considered and decided upon. He then called upon Mr. Taylor, County Planning Officer, to speak to the meeting and to explain the plans which were exhibited in the hall.

Mr. *Taylor* began by stating that the Committee was an Advisory Committee and therefore there to receive the advice and suggestions of the public. Great stress had been put on the word " planning " in recent years, but even though this had been the case there were many people who did not understand the proper implication of the word. Many seemed to be under the impression that if we planned the social evils would disappear overnight ; others were under the impression that it had something to do with housing, or again that the Planning Authority were going to embark on a large building programme; and there were others who were still under the impression that town planning was merely concerned with the appearance of buildings. The scope and meaning of town and country planning is set out in the Town and Country Planning Act, 1932, as follows :—

" With the general object of controlling the development of the land comprised in the area to which the scheme " applies, of securing proper sanitary conditions, amenity and convenience, and of preserving existing buildings or " other objects of architectural, historic or artistic interest, and places of natural interest or beauty, and generally of " protecting existing amenities whether in urban or rural portions of the area."

Mr. Taylor said he would like to stress that the preparation of a plan did not imply that the authorities who were preparing the plan were going to embark on a large building programme. In brief, he said, the object of planning was to lay out the area to the best advantage to its population. The County Council was dealing with the question in a most democratic way by appointing an Advisory Committee to obtain the views of the inhabitants of the different areas of the County. As the Chairman had already said, the County Planning Department had compiled a considerable amount of information as could be seen from the different maps on the walls. The County Council had no final scheme as yet and they were holding these public meetings in order to gather as much information and as many suggestions as possible from the people. Mr. Taylor said he was in the unfortunate position of not knowing the area as well as some of those present, and therefore any remarks which he made were merely suggestions for their criticism and might give them a lead to suggestions for the betterment and future planning of their area.

In continuing, Mr. Taylor referred to Cupar area as the " agricultural hub " of this County, and emphasised that a well-balanced and healthy agriculture was a vital necessity to the well-being of the nation. Therefore in the planning of the countryside the interests of those living in the country must be the first concern, and any attempt to reconstruct or plan the countryside would fail unless this was done. Fife, he said, had not been desecrated as many of the English counties had by the building of sporadic development. The building of isolated dwellings up and down the countryside would lead to many unnecessary and uneconomical problems for the public authorities in the way of transport of children to school and the laying of public services such as water, electricity, etc. Something would have to be done to stem the drift of population from the country which, if it continued much longer, would prove disastrous.

Mr. Taylor indicated a map on the wall showing the layout of two villages. The map showed where development should go. It also indicated where the shopping centre should be located, the playing field, the site for light industries and for a village hall, making altogether a very nice community. At this point he referred to the Cambridge Village College built by the County Authorities just outside Cambridge. In the daytime it was used as a school and in the evenings any person could go to classes or to the library and on Sunday evenings discussions on various subjects were held. It was too big a thing to be sponsored by one village and accordingly was so placed that surrounding villages could come in of an evening. This college had worked very well in Cambridge and he saw no reason why a similar one should not meet with success in this County.

Mr. Taylor went on to say that there were many points in favour of as well as some against attracting development into community centres. The main point in favour was perhaps that they would encourage people to return to the basic industry of the countryside by the provision of reasonable living and community conditions in the villages provided. Along with this question of rural planning came the question of what industries should be encouraged in rural areas. He thought that if they were to encourage industries into agricultural areas these should have a rural association. In other words the industries should be closely connected with agriculture, such as—canning, jam-making, agricultural implements, furniture-making, glove-making or hosiery, etc. In the past the majority of industries had been found in large cities. If they were to encourage these industries in rural areas or in smaller burghs they would have to see that these were properly placed so as to fit in with the surrounding countryside.

Continuing, Mr. Taylor said he could not pass over this agricultural area without making reference to the beautiful countryside. In it there were some very beautiful rows and groups of trees, but unfortunately they were being felled, he thought, indiscriminately, and whilst they did not in any way wish to be accused of holding up the war effort he felt that a little more thought could have been given to the trees which were being felled, particularly on the Kinross-Cupar road. There were also some very nice country houses and mansions, but many of these were becoming derelict owing to the high taxation and the difficulty in running such large houses. This was a pity, because along with those large estates one found in the adjoining villages the village blacksmith, the joiner, and other tradesmen. These trades were unfortunately dying out, but he hoped to see them return on a modern scale.

Mr. Taylor said he was surprised to note that all the burghs in this purely rural area had their quota of industries, the majority being allied to agriculture. He thought they were well served with industries and asked whether they thought it would be better to press for more, only perhaps to find that if they did get some these would be to the detriment of the industries which they already had, or whether they should press for better living conditions, better housing conditions, for the people who were in those industries at the present time.

169

With regard to roads, Mr. Taylor said that until the site of the Tay Road Bridge was fixed with some certainty there was little use of laying down a cross country route from the Forth. There seemed to be some difference of opinion as to where the site of the bridge should be, but he sincerely hoped that a site would be agreed upon which would do most good to the County of Fife and its industries and also to the counties to the north. The road should skirt any existing towns *en route* and connections should be made therefrom with the various towns. According to reports in the press, he said, someone seemed to have an entirely wrong idea of the Planning Committee's work. Roads were only a part of the plan. The paper stated :—" Roads are a favourite plaything with these planners. Give them a map of an area and they get busy right " away by-passing some places, diverting roads for little apparent reason, building new bridges, and widening roadways to " 100 feet.

" The energy devoted to this job would suggest that Britain's most pressing need was roads. We all know that it " isn't.

" Houses come first " ; and so it goes on.

Mr. Taylor said he thought they all agreed that houses were their first concern, but they must also be considered in connection with industry. They had all to be considered and that was the aim of the Planning Committee. No undue preference was being given to roads.

Another question which Mr. Taylor thought would be brought up when the question of roads was being discussed was the transportation of the people from the rural areas. He thought that question could be given more consideration.

Mr. Taylor then dealt with the question of recreational facilities. Every village ought to have a site for a playing field and also a small village hall. Or, if a village was too small a village should be chosen in which a hall could serve a group of villages.

Concerning Cupar Mr. Taylor said they would have to guard the amenities as Cupar was in a beautiful situation. The most important function of the town was its use as a market centre, which therefore made it dependent upon the prosperity of the farmers and farm workers from the adjoining rural areas. Whilst the economic prosperity of the inhabitants of rural areas was dependent upon the Government policy both national and international, much could be done by means of the planning scheme to assist in maintaining a prosperous agriculture consistent with good planning. Development should be encouraged in the market town or villages where it would be economically grouped. In a burgh like Cupar it was most important to ensure that facilities for shopping and trading were available for the large number of people who came into the town on market days for that purpose.

The second function of the town was as the centre for Local Government of the County, which made Cupar a residential town and accordingly the reservation of sites for residential property should be carefully considered.

Here, Mr. Taylor said, there were two points upon which he would like their observations, firstly, if they were going to encourage industries in Cupar (and by industries he meant those allied to agriculture), where would they suggest these should be placed so as not to spoil the amenities of the town ? The second point was that if Cupar was going to function properly a ring road to the north should be provided. There were two sites for such a ring road—one to catch the traffic on the Cupar-Kinross road outside the town and divert it to come out near the sugar factory. This was a feasible proposition. There was also a considerable amount of traffic from the Kirkcaldy direction, and if they were to divert that it would mean cutting through behind the station, crossing the railway and the river. That would be an engineer's dream—or nightmare.

Mr. Carlow then called upon Sir James Irvine.

Sir James Irvine said he would like to reinforce what had been said and to emphasise that a great amount of work had been done by the County Council before the Advisory Committee came into being. For the matter of two years the County had applied itself through its officers to make a survey of the whole of the County showing contours, water mains, sewerage, etc. All that was ready, and therefore the services required for community, for village, or for town life could be directed under the County's plan to wherever it was needed. All that work had been done very thoroughly and very ably. He said he would not like people to think that the County Council had in any way been losing time in this matter. It had all been well directed and very well done.

Another point made by Sir James was the drifting of the population during the past 120 years. It was common knowledge that the population in certain parts of Fife had increased and in others it had decreased, and was still decreasing. The causes had been fully explored and now they knew more or less why it had happened, and that would be a guide in determining what might happen in the next 50 years. Planning, he said, was an endeavour to avoid mistakes.

Sir James then referred to the dividing of the County into areas for the purpose of the Preliminary Survey. In their own particular area, he said, east and north-east, they had, for good or ill, no economic minerals and were dependent on the land. Accordingly, everything dealing with agriculture must have priority ... He drew attention to the point made by Mr. Taylor when speaking on that same issue where agriculture must be fostered, encouraged, and where people must be tempted to live on the land. Mr. Taylor raised the question as to where and how these people were to live. Were they to live in small cottages scattered about in the neighbourhood of the farms, or were they to be centred in community centres ? Sir James knew there would be two opinions about that, as was seen by the report of the Highland and Agricultural Society. There must of necessity be people to live immediately in the vicinity of the farm. Those who took care of the animals could not be housed in the community centre, but there were others who need not actually live on the spot. An entirely new type of country life would be available if these others were gathered together in community centres. All this, he said, was outwith his line until he became interested in the Pilgrim Trust. This Trust was a body in the happy possession of a large sum of money which they utilised for improving conditions of life generally, and while working for that Trust he had seen the advantages which followed from these small community centres, which were arranged in a most artistic way, with a little hall where dramatic performances could be given, where music could be heard, where children, and at week-ends their parents, were taught, if they so desired—in other words the Cambridge Village College. This was a great success. It was something very real and an entirely new type of country life was available there, and he saw no reason why something like it should not develop in Fife. " Do you like the idea or do you not like the idea ? In this we want your advice."

Sir James said there was another side which they must not lose sight of, and that was the better education of those who worked on the land. Their education should have the purpose of making their work more interesting. If we wanted a man to do his work well and feel he was serving his part in the country he must be educated in every aspect of his work.

Sir James then referred to his visit to the West Indies, where he was given the extremely interesting job of creating a new University. While there he saw many good examples of the Farm Institute and Farm School in Porto Rico.

In continuing, Sir James referred to minor industries, or rather forms of employment. He thought it very desirable that these should be associated with agriculture, and that so far as possible they ought to guard themselves against any form of employment which was based on one kind of industry only. Some forms of light industry, he said, would be quite out of place in this area.

Mr. *Christie* also referred to the enormous amount of spade-work which had been done by the Planning Department of the County Council in obtaining information about the different parts of the County. He thought the Advisory Committee had been asked to do rather a difficult thing, and that was to look into the future. If they were to plan for the next 50 to 60 years they would need all the concrete suggestions they could get from the public. Wherever the Committee went they found people with a long-range view, and it was in the hope of getting many of such suggestions that they were travelling about the County.

In continuing, Mr. Christie said that the Alness Committee had agreed that a Farm Institute should be provided for Scotland and there was just a chance that it might come to Fife. If it was built elsewhere he hoped that the County Council would do its utmost to provide an Institute for Fife, preferably in the Cupar area. It was essential that their children should know all about the soils in their own County and not be sent elsewhere to learn.

In concluding, Mr. Christie emphasised the need for a ring road at Cupar.

Mr. Carlow then intimated that Mr. Taylor would explain to the audience the maps exhibited and that meantime any suggestions or questions would be welcomed. It would be a great advantage, he said, if they would kindly write out their suggestions and forward them to the County Clerk so that they might be considered before the next meeting on 24th April.

NOTES OF PUBLIC MEETING HELD IN KIRKCALDY
17th April, 1945

Mr. *Carlow (Chairman).*

Mr. Carlow said that a great deal was said about light industries at the meeting convened by Kirkcaldy Town Council last week—these should be set up here, there or elsewhere, in order to find employment for certain grades of workers. The Location of Industries Bill was definitely something which should be very carefully considered. Those in charge of industry knew where industry should go and the Government was taking a very serious task upon itself by trying to direct industry. Mr. Carlow was in favour of leaving light industry to go where it thought it would prosper best. Wages were the most important thing so far as the workers were concerned ; amenities took second place. Mr. Carlow said that when he was a member of the Grand Council of the Federation of British Industries this question of location of industry was exercising the attention of the Government and many industrialists. It was felt at that time that Greater London was becoming too great and that the drift to the South had exhausted itself. The Federation suggested that lists should be prepared showing the advantages of different sites up and down the country in regard to matters such as local rates, water supply, electricity supply, transport, nearness to main roads, and all advantages and circumstances which an industrialist wanted before he decided where to place his industry. That was with a view to attracting industry to the most likely places where it would flourish, rather than forcing it to go where the Government thought it ought to go.

There had been a great deal of talk about collieries and Mr. Carlow thought that everybody knew the position in regard to the new pits. A considerable number of houses would be required, and the question was whether these houses should be erected to a greater extent within the Burgh of Kirkcaldy or whether part of the population should be housed in places like Kinghorn or Woodside, or whether a village should be developed about 7 miles north of Kirkcaldy, where the larger number of houses might be built instead of constantly increasing the number of houses in Kirkcaldy. That was a matter, he said, upon which he would express no opinion at present.

Mr. Carlow thought it might be of interest to the meeting to know that he had to-day received the report of independent engineers on the coal round about Dunnikier House and west of it, and he feared that it would not be so satisfactory as the Burgh of Kirkcaldy had hoped. There was a considerable quantity of coal in that site, and to sterilise that quantity would cost Kirkcaldy a good deal of money. This was a matter which would no doubt receive the careful consideration of the Town Council.

Another matter on which Mr. Carlow wished to have the opinion of the public was arterial roads. Would the industry of Kirkcaldy be advantaged if there was a direct road to Dundee with a bridge at Newport ? Would the industry be advantaged if that bridge were placed at Newburgh ? The cost of the bridge at Newport was estimated to be at least six times the cost of the bridge near Abernethy or Newburgh and it was a matter for serious consideration whether the extra cost was worth while. Would it be an advantage to have an arterial road between Kirkcaldy and the West of Fife coalfield ? The road to Bowhill, Lochgelly, Kinglassie, etc., was at present a narrow and tortuous one. These, he said, were some of the points upon which the Committee wanted to get their suggestions.

Mr. *Dall, Kirkcaldy Town Council,* said he would like to correct the Chairman on one statement. He did not think it was the intention of the Government to compel industrialists to go to certain places. What they did say was that industry could not go to certain places. The fact that coal-mining located itself determined the location of the coal-mining industry, and the different uses to which coal could be put were well known. You therefore had a large variety of industries developing round about the coal-mining industry, for example gas, electricity, chemicals, and it seemed to be desirable that the location of these industries should be near the source of the raw material. It was also a well-known fact, he said, that iron and steel works were located near coal-fields. He thought the Government's action in encouraging industry to go to developing areas was a good move both socially and industrially. They all knew what had happened as the result of allowing private enterprise to go where it wanted to go. It had simply meant that all sense of social obligation had been lost and large areas had been left derelict, and the Government could not assume responsibility for a high level of employment and condone a state of affairs like that.

With regard to roads, Mr. Dall thought that as the arterial roads in this area would have to be linked up with roadways in a much wider region the question would have to come under a wider planning authority, such as the South-East Scotland Regional Planning Committee, whose report would be submitted to the Secretary of State in consultation with the Minister of Transport.

With regard to development of Kirkcaldy Mr. Dall said that when they extended the Burgh boundaries they told the County that additional acres were needed for future development. They did not extend the boundaries just to leave them as a green belt. They visualised that Kirkcaldy was a growing town and therefore made provision to meet that growth, but at the same time they were determined that Kirkcaldy was not going to lose its identity by being linked up with Burntisland and Leven. They were going to have a green belt round their town.

According to the Report of the Central and South-East Scotland Planning Advisory Committee Kirkcaldy area was likely to attract between now and 1974 an additional population of approximately 42,000. That, said Mr. Dall, was almost the same population as Kirkcaldy had already—an overcrowded town with something like 18,000 families living in approximately 13,000 houses. Therefore, if this additional population was to be housed on standards which were higher than present-day standards a very large number of houses would be required, and in Mr. Dall's opinion to spread these houses over Balgonie, Kinghorn and Markinch would not meet the position. He thought the best way to deal with the situation would be to create a completely new town within the area to house something like 25,000 inhabitants. Kirkcaldy, he said, had sufficient ground to provide for 16,000.

Mr. Dall went on to say that they did not come to the meeting to offer suggestions, but to invite the Planning Advisory Committee to meet Kirkcaldy Town Planning Committee, when they could go into matters in greater detail.

Provost Meldrum, Burntisland, said that since the Committee visited Burntisland and since the subsequent meeting held in Kirkcaldy last month they had approached the subject in Burntisland both with the Town Council and at a meeting with the various industries in the town. They welcomed the opportunity to express local opinion, he said. Provost Meldrum went on to say that certain questions had been addressed to them at the last meeting for local opinion on such matters as ribbon development. Burntisland, he said, were whole-heartedly with the Committee in their attitude against ribbon development. They felt that that form of development should not be encouraged.

They had also viewed the possibility of the growth of Burntisland, he said, and had come to the conclusion that Burntisland would always remain a self-contained locality and the fear of the green belt disappearing was not in their mind. They felt that no matter how the Burgh developed the green belt which existed just now would remain.

With regard to the suggestion that the extra housing requirements should be met at Kinghorn or Aberdour, Provost Meldrum stated that Burntisland's answer was in the negative. They definitely felt that they had ample accommodation to house all workers employed with the Burgh, and that, he said, was also the opinion of industry.

The next question, namely, to what size would their town develop, was a much bigger question and simply could not be answered. It would all depend on the development of industry. The Provost stated that as everyone knew, the British Aluminium Company and the Shipbuilding Company were Burntisland's two principal industries at the moment. Representatives of both these firms indicated that they did not anticipate any appreciable development on present undertakings. They further stated that it was their view that the number of employees presently engaged could be taken as a static figure. At the meeting between the Town Council and industries Mr. Lorimer of the Railway Company indicated that certain improvements were to be effected at the docks, but did not indicate to what extent. Provost Meldrum did not think it was appropriate to say anything at this meeting as Mr. Lorimer might not have the liberty of saying anything further on the matter, but he suggested to Mr. Lorimer that a lot could be done to improve the appliances and facilities both with regard to loading and discharging cargoes.

Provost Meldrum then referred to the three new pits to be sunk in the Kirkcaldy area. Burntisland, he said, felt that this would probably mean a large increase in export of coal, and he would be delighted if the Chairman could give them any idea of the probable increase in that direction. With the present facilities he thought Burntisland would be capable of exporting 8 million tons per annum, but that if the figure was going to be greater the possibility was that they might require extra dock accommodation to cope with the traffic. If there was a possibility of extra export trade the Provost wished the Committee to keep the claim of Burntisland before them. As Burntisland was quite close to the Comrie pit and also quite close to the proposed new pits at Seafield and Dysart he felt that they should receive some consideration. Further, they had a good roadstead and quite a number of ships came there to anchor prior to going to Leith. 300 yards south of their present pierheads there was sufficient water to float the largest vessel afloat without any dredging. There was 30 feet of water at lowest neap tide, he said. These were factors which he thought the Committee should know and keep in mind should the possibility of dock extension arise.

Speaking of light industry Provost Meldrum stated that light industry would be very welcome in Burntisland as at present their industries were all heavy. The Provost said he would like to tell this meeting that about two months ago, prior to the issue of the White Paper on the Location of Industry, he had a communication asking if Burntisland was interested in further industry and if they could supply a site of between two and three acres. After discussing the matter with a Committee the Provost replied that Burntisland would be very glad to provide a site, but just on the back of that the Government's White Paper was issued and the matter was now in abeyance. The proposed work was to employ between three and four hundred women, and that was just what Burntisland was in need of. In view of the Government's White Paper the Provost thought it was probable that Burntisland would lose this industry.

With regard to housing, the Provost stated that the immediate requirements of Burntisland were 500 houses. The Burgh would develop to that extent as soon as possible after the end of the war, but further development depended on the possibilities of the docks and light industry.

Bailie Beath of Kinghorn said that Kinghorn, as they all knew, was mainly residential. They only had a bottle works and cleek works and the remainder of the population was employed in Burntisland. He thought it would be a great help if they could get some form of light industry. Their present housing requirements were 80, for which they had ample ground available.

Mr. Cameron, Thornton, said he was very much interested in Thornton. They had always thought of Thornton as a most important centre both as a railway junction and as a mining centre. In fact the inhabitants had visualised that some day Thornton would grow to be a second Cowdenbeath, but owing to the mine workings this was not possible.

With regard to the proposed new pit near Thornton, Mr. Cameron wondered if it would be possible to store away the refuse rather than build it up on the surface.

Mr. Sutherland of the Burntisland Aluminium Company then spoke. He thought that the Provost had given all the answers so far as his firm was concerned. As the Provost had said, the number of people employed at the works was likely to remain the same for some time to come.

Mr. Sutherland said he would like to say a word about housing. He had listened to Mr. Christie at the last meeting when he very forcibly brought into the picture the number of dairy farms and lands which were going out of existence owing to housing. Since he had gone to Burntisland two farms had gone out of existence and another was going that way. That meant that when Burntisland got her 500 houses there would not be sufficient dairy farms to supply the needs of the people. He was of the same opinion as Mr. Christie that it was most unfortunate that so much good land had to be taken up with housing, and the question was what could be done now. He had asked Mr. Taylor, the County Planning Officer, privately how he felt about building flats instead of the present type of bungalow. Mr. Sutherland thought there was too much ground attached to these houses. It wasn't everybody who wanted a garden, and even during these past six years when it had been so necessary to grow one's own vegetables certain people had done nothing to their gardens at all. This type of tenant didn't want gardens attached to their houses and would be far better housed in flats. Mr. Sutherland said he would like an opinion on the building of flats of about three storeys, with modern conveniences. " How do you consider that from a housing point of view, and would it tend to save agricultural ground which is proposed to be taken for housing purposes ? "

Mr. Howie, Grange, Aberdour, said he felt a bit diffident about speaking on the matter of housing because he farmed land between Kirkcaldy and Burntisland. He didn't put the matter before the Agricultural Executive Committee because so far as he could see the authorities were trying to avoid taking the best land for housing purposes.

The land round about Kinghorn was A1 land and ought to be preserved.

With regard to Auchtertool, he said, it was mentioned in the Committee's proposals that Auchtertool might be developed into an agricultural village. At the request of the Agricultural Executive Committee four of the County's rural houses had been built in Auchtertool. Mr. Howie said he would just like to point out that the Agricultural Executive Committee were not consulted as to a site, with the result that in the middle of the war these houses were erected on the very best land in the Parish of Auchtertool—land which was capable of being highly productive and capable of being developed as a market garden.

From an agricultural point of view Mr. Howie was very anxious to know whether the coal at Seafield was on land or under the sea. (Mr. Carlow replied that it was under the sea.) Mr. Howie hoped that from the point of view of Kinghorn it would not contain washings and screenings. He was thinking of the Wemyss-Buckhaven area where all these beautiful little villages had been put out of sight with coal-pits and refuse stored in enormous bings.

Mr. Howie went on to say he did not know where they proposed to house the mining population, but it would not do to house them alongside agricultural population. If this was done they would immediately sap the confidence of the farmer by the many types of trespassings which would inevitably take place.

Regarding the siting of agricultural light industries in Auchtertool, Mr. Howie said that at present most of the agricultural requirements were met from large city firms, and there was only one blacksmith serving the whole of the area.

Mr. *Carlow* remarked that the proposals of the Advisory Committee had got to be vetted by the Regional Committee, but naturally the Advisory Committee had to put forward their suggestions. In order to do this it was essential to have the views of the public, and if the public didn't say what they wanted then neither the Advisory Committee nor the Regional Committee could be held to blame for producing a scheme which did not turn out to the satisfaction of Kirkcaldy. The Advisory Committee wanted to work with the Planning Committee of Kirkcaldy and not usurp their powers as a Planning Authority, and if they did not want to express an opinion the Advisory Committee might make arrangements to drive an arterial road so far away from Kirkcaldy that it would not be of any use to the Burgh whatsoever.

Mr. *Dall* said he could give the Committee an assurance that once they met the Planning Committee of Kirkcaldy they would give them their views on the question of arterial roads.

Rev. *J. H. Michel Dabb, Burntisland*, said there were one or two points which he would like to mention, firstly with regard to housing. It had been his privilege to visit the Scandinavian countries and to see the blocks of buildings with their own community kitchens, playing rooms, and cinemas, all within their own blocks, and he felt that something could be developed in Scotland along those lines.

In Burntisland they had come up against a serious problem with young people, who seemed to be in a destructive mood. This was largely due to the fact that children and also grown-ups had no very definite interest. He expressed the desire to have the planning experts' views on the question of building something on the lines of Community Housing Schemes, so giving people an interest in their own centres.

Mr. Dabb stressed the great need for playing fields and other accommodation outdoors for youth. It was one of the tragedies of his experience that, after 16 years in Burntisland, he had not been able to secure a place where the Boys' Brigade could play a game of football on a Saturday afternoon. If they did not set aside a place where the youth could go for sport then he thought they were raising very great problems for themselves in the future. He spoke of his own congregation who had erected a suite of halls so that youth could have all the indoor winter work they could possibly have, but that was not sufficient. It was necessary to encourage young people to go out of doors, and unless they could find areas in which their youth could play he did not think there was any point in asking if Burntisland was going to increase its area.

So far as the workers were concerned, Mr. Dabb said his experience of industrial people was that they liked to get home as quickly as possible and didn't like travelling in their working clothes. The number of workers in Burntisland was not going to increase to any great extent and Burntisland was capable of housing their own workers rather than have them travel to and from Kinghorn.

Mr. *Struan Robertson*, a native of Kirkcaldy who is now working in London, thought there was one important industry in this district which had not been mentioned at all, and that was the holiday industry. This part of Fife had attractions equal to many places of much wider renown, he said, and every effort should be made to preserve these amenities and encourage holiday makers to visit the area. Mr. Robertson referred to a feature of the Aberdeen Regional Planning Scheme. There they had an area between the railway and the sea, a very narrow strip, very similar to the strip between Seafield and Kinghorn, and that small area had been scheduled as an open space. He thought this Committee would do well to take similar steps to preserve the amenities of the coastline in this district.

The next point dealt with by Mr. Robertson was the question of arterial roads. He said he had done quite a considerable study of the development of roads in Scotland throughout the ages and thought he could claim to know as much about the subject as anybody. He thought that the planning authorities should go all out to build good roads where they ought to be. It was not sufficient to widen a corner here and there and have wide roads leading to villages through which there was only a narrow track. There should be adequate communications between Kirkcaldy and the west (*i.e.* Kincardine Bridge), whether or not a Perth Road Bridge is built. " Suppose you were at Kincardine Bridge and wanted to go to Leven," he said, " one way is to go through Dunfermline, Cowdenbeath, Leslie and Windygates—quite an appalling thought— and the other way is to go through the coast towns, which is equally terrible." There was need for a trunk road from Kincardine Bridge, perhaps three miles inland from the sea, and Mr. Robertson thought that such a road, by providing access to the other industrial areas of Scotland, would be of the greatest value to this district.

Mr. *Beaton* (*Kirkcaldy Town Council*) said the Chairman had mentioned the fact that three new pits were to be sunk in this area, which as far as Kirkcaldy was concerned was practically underneath and round about it. He was anxious to know what effect these pits were going to have on the areas which would be required for building purposes.

Councillor Waddell, Burntisland, said Burntisland had had a great deal of difficulty in regard to housing and he felt that in view of this difficulty Burntisland Town Council ought to be allowed to plan their own areas. They in Burntisland had been the football between the Department of Health for Scotland and the County Council.

A great deal had been said about a green belt, but what was the use of a green belt to a man who was hurrying home to get a meal and get back to his work if he had to cross it every time ? What use was a green belt to a worried housewife if she had to cross it to get her shopping done ?

It had been remarked that it was possible to use 'buses to travel to and from work, but it must be remembered that 'buses meant cost and loss of time to the workers.

Again, taking up the question of the green belt, Councillor Waddell said they had quite a lot of open spaces about Burntisland, for example they had " The Binn " and Grange Hill which ought to be saved from interference, and if these were not sufficient for green belts they could go further afield to Auchtertool where there was good agricultural land. If there was to be a green belt it should be between these areas so that land within could be left for building purposes.

173

With regard to a playing field, they had had great difficulty in obtaining possession of land. They were told it was valuable feuing land. If that was to be part of the green belt, he said they were going to get it cheap.

Mr. *Henderson, Kirkcaldy,* thought that they should keep in mind that no amount of planning was going to attract light industry to any area. The first thing to do was to attract the light industrialists, and the only way to do that would be to create conditions which would be favourable to establishment of light industry. No town council or county could create an industry in any locality. In his opinion the Bill which was at present before Parliament would create in this area conditions unfavourable to light industry, by providing artificial attractions elsewhere. If they hoped to attract light industry to this area then that clause would have to be deleted from the Bill and thus prevent unfair competition by other localities. Mr. Henderson went on to say that it appeared to him that under the Bill in its present form it would be practically impossible to attract to this area sufficient light industry to provide the ancillary employment which would be desirable to the development of the coal industry which was envisaged. Another point was that the development of the coal industry had rendered places unsuitable and liable to subsidence, and it seemed to him that some definite delimitation of areas would be advantageous to persons considering the establishment of light industry so that they could be assured that there was no danger of their factory falling down about their ears.

With regard to housing, Mr. Henderson remarked that he was very keen on the idea of blocks of flats such as he had seen abroad with every kind of communal centre, but he found that in this country the people didn't want them. The average person preferred to have his house from the ground up. It might be unreasonable but there it was. It might be an advantage to have a greengrocer's shop near the house, but when a woman wanted to buy a hat she liked to have a jaunt. " The people of Kennoway shop in Leven and the people of Leven shop for Kirkcaldy," he remarked, " while the people of Kirkcaldy when they lose a collar stud go to Edinburgh." He felt that a shopping expedition was a bit of a treat and included a jaunt, and he was convinced that a community centre of about 20,000 people built with shops and everything else would not in fact work.

Mr. *Wishart, Burgh Engineer, Kirkcaldy,* who said he was expressing his own views and not those of his authority, was of the opinion that if miners were housed in the country villages there was a great danger that these villages would lose their identity entirely. He thought they should have miners alongside other types of workers in places where there would be other work available for members of a mining family who did not wish to work in the mines. While he did not think all the miners could be accommodated in Kirkcaldy, he thought a great number must live in this district.

Mr. *Christie (Advisory Committee),* thought that all the ground had been covered with the exception of roads, and Kirkcaldy Planning Committee were anxious to discuss that matter with the Advisory Committee.

Mr Christie then went on to speak of the question of recreational centres for the young people. He suggested there was a possibility in considering the future of organisations working in close conjunction with the Education Authority, for the acquisition of several fairly large sites in the County which would be looked upon as areas to which young people could go for week-end camps, holidays, etc. He had suggestions which he intended to bring up at a future date for these purposes, principally for areas such as parts of the Lomonds, Norman's Law, Tentsmuir, etc. The idea might be considered visionary, but it was not beyond the bounds of possibility, and he thought a community might set aside a fairly large area of ground where the young people might go and disport themselves. He thought that young people were forced from the land because there was no facility for them to enjoy themselves in the country and therefore there ought to be ground provided for them.

Mr. Christie considered that the question of the layout of roads in the County was a very difficult problem. There would be an immense mass of traffic appearing after the war. Within two or three years there would be an increase of traffic of which they had no conception. The County would require roads for the purpose of developing its own interests, and a decision would have to be made as to how near the collieries or Kirkcaldy the road from the Forth to the Tay would require to be. The Tay Road Bridge could cut across just to the east of Mugdrum Island, but it might be that it would not be necessary for the next 50 or 60 years.

Mr. *Carlow* in summing up dealt with the most important points raised by the various speakers.

With regard to arterial roads, he said, they would have to consider ways and means as to the planning and cost of these roads. He was going to leave the matter of these roads to the Planning Authorities and their staffs, and he understood they were going to have a conference.

It had been said by one of the speakers that they had to consider the likes and dislikes of the people, while another set out drawbacks of the green belt between works and stated that the workers did not like the cost of travel but preferred to get home as quickly as possible. Another advocated the building of houses near the works. Mr. Carlow said he knew they had to consider the likes and dislikes of the people, but reminded them that they were trying to plan for a better world than that in which they were living to-day. He knew that 50 years ago people would have said they could not touch the slums because they wanted to live in them. It was necessary to be very very wise and to draw wise lines between the likes and dislikes of the inhabitants of the community. Fifty years after this their planning might be considered very bad practice, just as if they looked back 50 years they thought the planning of their grandfathers was very bad practice. They had to take a view of 50 years ahead and try to visualise what would be considered good practice at that time. They had not only to consider the ideas of the people of to-day, but the ideals of the children of to-day 50 years hence.

Replying to Provost Meldrum regarding the future of Burntisland Docks, Mr. Carlow said that nobody liked to be a prophet, least of all himself. If they got back to the maximum export of 1913, which was in the region of 83 million tons of coal, they would not need to worry, and if the dock accommodation was sufficient at that time he thought it would be sufficient for the future.

With regard to the coal round about Dunnikier, Mr. Carlow said there was a considerable amount of coal there and it must not be sterilised without due consideration. If it was sterilised, and Kirkcaldy was prepared to meet the cost of doing so, then their housing scheme would be safe and secure from subsidence. These were matters which those responsible for the Kirkcaldy Burgh Planning would have to consider.

Speaking of Fife's attractive coast, Mr. Carlow remarked that there were places for holidays and places for industries, and " if you want to play in a workshop and work in a playground you are trying to do the wrong thing." If people were working in Kirkcaldy and wanted to be near their work and have the advantage of living in a town they would be living perpetually in the atmosphere of their work. It was with a view to enabling people to spend their evenings in an atmosphere miles away from their work that they were considering the question of housing people at a distance from their work.

Mr. *Sutherland* cordially thanked Mr. Carlow for presiding.

NOTES OF PUBLIC MEETING HELD IN THE TOWN HALL, ANSTRUTHER
20th April, 1945

Provost Carstairs said he was very pleased to see those present, but that he had pointed out earlier that afternoon to the Committee that 3 o'clock was not an appropriate hour to get a big turnout. He then introduced Mr. Carlow, Chairman, of the Editorial Sub-Committee.

Mr. Carlow stated that a Sub-Committee consisting of Sir James Irvine, who could not be with them to-day, Mr. Christie, Durie, Leven, representing employers and workers in agriculture, and himself, who could be taken as representing industry, were touring the County with a view to ascertaining the wants, wishes, hopes and aspirations of the people in regard to planning. They had therefore come to Anstruther to find out what the people of Anstruther and district (which district covered the region from Lundin Links to Crail and Kingsbarns) wanted in regard to planning. The word "planning," said Mr. Carlow had been very much abused and some people thought things were being entirely overdone. It was ridiculous to build "castles in the air," but what the Committee did want to know was along what lines industry, agriculture and all the other activities were likely to flow. They didn't want to do anything in 1945 which would stand in the way of development. They did not want to lay out a housing scheme where an arterial road or colliery ought to go, and they didn't want to have people pointing to them 40 or 50 years hence as very stupid people. That brought them up to the present position and that was why the Committee was there to-day. The Committee had interviewed the Provost in a good many Burghs by way of breaking the ice and introducing themselves. Mr. Carlow went on to say that the Committee had decided to hold two public meetings in each centre ; one at which to explain the Committee's purpose and a later meeting to which they wanted people to come with concrete suggestions which might be embodied in the Committee's Report which they hoped to have in the hands of the County Council before the end of the year. The success of that Report would depend on the public. It was up to everyone to put any views or objectives before the Committee for consideration and probable inclusion in their Report. The Committee had prepared a questionnaire which was to be issued to firms of a rateable valuation over a certain figure, and Mr. Carlow hoped that these firms would answer the questions as well as possible and so enable the Committee to collect as much information as they possibly could.

In continuing, Mr. Carlow said that he hoped the people of Anstruther would correct him and let him have their views should he say anything about the fishing industry which was not true to fact. They desired the fishing industry of Anstruther, Pittenweem and St. Monance to work together. The Committee knew some of the difficulties, such as boats not being suitable, steam drifters not being wanted and the desire for all boats to be fitted with Diesel engines and to be 55 feet in length in order to be useful for all types of fishing from that part of the coast. It seemed that what was wrong with the fishing industry was that if a boat came in with a good catch everybody rushed to buy that fish ; when a second boat came in the demand was not so great, and by the time the last boat landed its catch there was no sale at all. In Mr. Carlow's opinion it was obvious that some method had got to be developed in order that fish might be stored when plentiful and sold when there was a scarcity. He thought it would be a good commercial proposition. While that applied to whitefish, herring were in a different position. Herring were very perishable, and while they could be sent to Hamburg in four days he felt that something better ought to be done so that a buyer could be found for every single herring and at a reasonable price, while leaving a good profit for the fishermen. That could be done by processing the herring by dehydration and making the fish into powder which could be used for making fish-cakes, etc., which Mr. Carlow understood tasted like real herring, and naturally the fish would last a long time. The vitamins of herring were well known. They were valuable body and bone builders and also, he was told, brain builders. Herring oil was another substance which was in great demand.

Mr. Carlow went on to speak of the Herring Commission, of which Provost Carstairs was a member. This Commission had made many recommendations which would no doubt be carried out. They recommend a minimum price for herring ; grants by the Government for the purchase of boats, nets, and gear ; research in method by which herring would be processed, etc. Mr. Carlow said that if this country did not carry out necessary research work on fish other countries would, and research, whether in coal-mining or herring, was one of the necessities of the present day, but especially in coal, and it required to be carried on with great energy so that past misdeeds might be recouped.

Speaking on the number of people employed in the fishing industry, Mr. Carlow said that in 1913 somewhere in the region of 9,000 men were employed, but that by 1938 this figure had dropped to 7,000. It was the same in every industry. This might be due to the fact that wages were so high that employers were compelled to reduce the number of employees by introducing labour-saving devices.

In concluding, Mr. Carlow hoped that sugestions would reach the Committee so that they might correctly represent the views of this area. He then called upon Mr. Taylor, County Planning Officer, to speak to the meeting.

Mr. Taylor, County Planning Officer, said that the main object of a Planning Scheme was to lay out an area to the best advantage to its population. It was no use preparing a Planning Scheme without taking into consideration the views of the people in the area. If they did not do this the scheme would be a failure.

In continuing, Mr. Taylor said that so far as he could see this area had 3 main industries : (a) fishing ; (b) holiday attractions ; and (c) agriculture.

Mr. Taylor said that a major difficulty seemed to be how to dispose of the fish. Mr. Taylor said he would like to help them in their difficulty, and in that connection, he added, since he had met the Provost he had been in touch with Dr. Reay of the Department of Scientific and Industrial Research, the Ministry of Agriculture in London, the Ministry of Agriculture in Edinburgh and the Royal Institute of British Architects. All these people were trying to obtain information for them on refrigeration plant and offal. While awaiting this information Mr. Taylor thought they could be giving consideration to the question of a site on which these buildings could be put. As the Chairman had said, there was no use in allowing a site to go now for some other purpose if it would be just the right thing for a dehydration plant. Mr. Taylor went on to say that he had given some consideration to the question of a site. It would require to be in easy communication with the harbour, close to the railway and main road, and not placed in such a position as to be a detriment to the surrounding residential area. The site would also have to be sufficiently large so that if, at a later date, it had to be extended, the extension could be carried out in the same locality. In the past they had been prone to choose sites which had proved to be too small. It seemed that the Committee could help the people of Anstruther area most if they could get them a refrigeration or dehydration plant, and they would like suggestions from the public as to the type of plant, etc.

With regard to the holiday industry, Mr. Taylor remarked that before the war greater use had been made of the coast than ever before and he didn't see any reason why that should not increase. The coast-line of Fife was one of the main assets of this County, and they ought to see that the coast-line was used aright. The holiday industry had brought about many new towns, especially on the west coast, and in many cases the natural features which made that town had been lost for ever. They must see that that did not happen in Fife.

175

Mr. Taylor then put forward one or two suggestions for the observations of the people of Anstruther—that no buildings should be allowed between coast road and the sea ; that the parking of caravans and shacks, which had a habit of springing up overnight, should be controlled and proper sites located for the purpose ; that private and local development would have to be carefully vetted to see that the design fitted in with the locality. The design of buildings in places like Crail would require careful consideration to see that they harmonised with the surrounding property.

With regard to the roads, Mr. Taylor suggested that if they were going to build new roads these should be made well inland. He would not like to see the coast road widened to 180 feet, because people passing along that coast liked to spend a bit of time looking out into the bay.

Mr. Taylor said there was a period of the year when they could do with some industry to tide them over until the summer season came again, and he had been working out what type of industry would best serve this purpose.

Another point which had not received enough consideration was catering for the holiday population in wet weather. None of the resorts of to-day had originally been resorts ; they had sprung up from little villages. Many of them would fail to keep pace with the changing times, but through the medium of the Planning Committee they could assist these towns to a better livelihood. He said he would like the public to turn the position over in their minds and criticise the suggestions made.

Mr. Taylor said he could not leave this area without mentioning agriculture. He explained two maps showing the agricultural land in the area. They would be surprised at the decline in population of East Fife, he said, and something would have to be done or else they would find themselves in a deplorable state. He suggested that they ought to give the people living in the country better living conditions, and the only way that could be done was by trying to develop larger village centres instead of allowing development to be scattered up and down the countryside. The population could then be given public services, such as water, electricity, drainage, which had been so long lacking in the rural areas. Mr. Taylor then spoke of the Cambridge College, which was used not only as a school in daytime but as a place where people could go in the evening to classes, if they so desired. It was in a rural area and was so placed that it was central to about 8 villages. This college had been a great success and Mr. Taylor did not see why something of a similar nature should not be a success in this County. The people were drifting away to the town, he said, and something would have to be done to encourage them to stay. There was criticism from the farmers of the suggestion to have community centres, but they could either have their cottages on the farms and no people to fill them or have their workers in a centre. These were just one or two suggestions, and if the Committee's plan was going to be a success it would have to take in the views of the public. These remarks had been said to stimulate suggestions.

Mr. *Christie* said they had found that the population round about Kirkcaldy was likely to increase by 40 to 50 thousand, and Mr. Christie felt that the people would simply pour into the marvellous coast-line in this area. Before the war, he said, they used to have 8,000 people pouring into Leven in the summer season, and in the rush period people were sleeping in 3 hour shifts and many used to sleep on the shore. The demand for recreational facilities was going to increase, and Mr. Christie felt that the area from Lundin Links to Kingsbarns would be very popular if there was somewhere for the people to go, and he was almost inclined to say that during the next 40-50 years the holiday industry would be the most important in this area, but as they all knew the priority just now was housing. Mr. Christie thought the inevitable result of having a bridge over the Tay near Dundee would be the pouring of people into this area and boarding-houses and houses for letting would simply be at a premium.

Perhaps the best way the Committee could help the people of Anstruther, as Mr. Taylor had already said, was by helping them to obtain a dehydrating plant. They were not going to get a dehydrating plant from the Government, from the County, or from anybody else, he said. It would have to come by private enterprise. Such a plant would be a tremendous possibility for this area.

Mr. Christie said he would like to refer to the agricultural side before sitting down. He had been told by an Executive Officer of the Agricultural Executive Committee that it was just impossible to obtain the services of a man who could build a stack. Farmers were all busy and they had no time to put off in training. The result would be that in 20 years hence, unless a move was made now, there would not be a trained agricultural population. There was a possibility of a Farm Institute being supplied by the Board of Education for Scotland, and Mr. Christie believed there was just a chance that it might come to Fife. At all these meetings he took the opportunity of appealing to anybody who was interested that if the Institute did not come to Fife they should have a Farm Training School where their own children could go from the school to learn about the soils of their county.

In concluding, Mr. Christie said that the production of this Report, which Mr. Carlow hoped to have ready by the end of the year, was a very difficult task if they considered the amount of ground which had to be covered, and he hoped that as many concrete suggestions as possible would be forthcoming to help them in their work. He made reference to a very valuable report which the Committee had received from the Auchtermuchty area.

Provost *Carstairs* remarked that much that had been said, as most of the audience would know, required some qualification. He could not speak very well on agriculture although at one time he had a very great notion for a farm. He would never think of putting up any opinion of his against such keen agriculturists as Bailie Fleming and Mr. Edie. They could speak for themselves. What he did claim to know something about, however, was the fishing industry. Provost Carstairs spoke of the offal factory which used to be at Cove. This factory was now falling into decay and had been taken down, and the offal factory was right in the centre of the city of Aberdeen, which showed that there was a very big difference in the scientific handling of offal for meal and oil. He did not think the smell would be a formidable difficulty. The great difficulty in this locality was undoubtedly to be the procuring of a fleet of boats. The steam drifters had been sold and were not coming back. The fishing industry had gone down very definitely, and that had been almost wholly due to economic reasons. After all, he said, it was very simple arithmetic to say that if you could get a job which offered you £4 and one which offered £8, you would definitely take the one which offered £8. That was what had happened to the fishing industry. There was not a living in it. Fishermen prohibited their sons from following in their footsteps and going into the fishing industry. With the coming of the new type of boat and modern methods of fishing there was an economic chance for fishermen. Even in the old days there was a very poor living in the fishing industry, but to-day he had known of boys of between 15 and 16 getting £30 a week as their share, and if there was an economic return in the industry undoubtedly sons would follow their fathers. The big difficulty was the obtaining of new boats. That, of course, was not so much a matter for the Planning Committee as for the Herring Industry Board.

With regard to dehydration and refrigeration, Provost Carstairs said that such a plant would be a real asset to the district. In the past the difficulty of the glut had always been a serious problem, but with dehydration and refrigeration this difficulty would be solved. He had seen, in the Aberdeen market on a Wednesday, boxes of sizeable haddocks sold for £3, 5s. a box, while on Thursday the price per box would drop to 12s. The difficulty was that one day there was a scarcity while the next there was a glut. This could be levelled out by means of refrigeration. So far as Anstruther was concerned, the Provost said, if they could get a fleet of boats undoubtedly there was a future for the industry in economic returns.

With regard to the tourist industry, Anstruther reckoned that during the Glasgow and Edinburgh fair weeks they doubled their population. That information was mainly from the records of the Railway Company. A very great difficulty was housing. A great deal of the shortage of housing in their community had come about as follows : A father had downstairs and let the upstairs to his son ; then they all found that they could get more out of a few weeks' letting in the summer than for a whole year with a tenant, so they had been keeping their houses to themselves, letting them stand empty for the sake of the letting in the summer. But there they had an opportunity in that, if a sufficient number of houses were provided they would have just that letting in the summer which quite frankly gave Anstruther a great deal of municipal rent and rates. Provost Carstairs went on to say that Anstruther was far better situated than St. Andrews, by a long way. Anstruther had a southern exposure and had the opportunity for tourists which was very valuable. The whole coast, he said, had a south lie.

If Anstruther got a sufficient provision of houses they could pull up the community in its economic position by the second form of industry mentioned. Without any question there was an opportunity for the fishing industry which had never been before, and with more houses Anstruther could have a very fine future.

There was one difficulty, said the Provost. Anstruther did not have an 18-hole golf-course, which was one of the best assets that any community could have, but he hoped that the Town Council would take its courage in both hands because a golf-course did bring the best type of visitor.

In concluding, Provost Carstairs remarked that was all he could say about the two industries, and he would rather leave the matter of agriculture to Bailie Fleming or Mr. Edie.

Col. Baxter (Local County Councillor) said there were many different views about housing, and he found himself at variance with the Chairman on one point at least. The Chairman said wages and industry were of the first importance, but what was the use of wage earners if you didn't have houses ? In Col. Baxter's opinion houses were everything. He was rather interested in that point because he had learned at Cupar that West Fife was to get 97% of the houses allocated to Fife while East and North East—Anstruther, Cupar and St. Andrews areas—were to get a miserable 3%. The country villages required houses far more than the bigger areas. He hoped the Advisory Committee would press for more equal distribution of houses.

Col. Baxter went on to say that he represented a purely agricultural area and was trying to look after the interests of the smaller country villages—villages without a school, without water, without lighting. They had been promised that the villages in the Riggin of Fife would be supplied with water when the Regional Scheme came into operation, but he did not like to be fed on promises. He would also like to see lighting come to the villages.

Rev. J. A. Inglis Carnbee (representing the Youth Council) said he would like to support Col. Baxter in what he had said about housing in the rural areas. Housing was definitely of first importance. He did not think that it was wages that drove rural workers into the towns, but the housing. He had had the happy experience of seeing great improvement in housing in his own particular village, and it was his impression that it was the young married woman who drove her husband away to the town for the superior amenities of the town. Now, he found that certain of these young married women who would not consent to live in certain of the houses on the farms, were perfectly happily settled down in the type of houses supplied in recent improvement schemes. Housing in the country areas, especially in the villages, was of the first importance and was a point which the Planning Advisory Committee ought to bear very strongly in mind.

Mr. Gatherum, Upper Largo, stated that certain of the villages in the Anstruther area were almost deserted because of the bad housing conditions. These houses could not be reconstructed because there was no water. He wanted to ask what efforts the Planning Advisory Committee were making to try to get houses for those rural areas. They had heard about residential houses being provided for people from Glasgow, Edinburgh, and Dundee, he said, but that didn't concern them so much as their own people. People would be coming home from the Forces and would have nowhere to live except with their fathers and mothers. Anstruther area lay on the fringe of an industrial area and the people were prepared to travel to and from their work so that they might bring up their families in the rural area, and after all the Chairman was bound to know that the rural areas were the life-blood of the community.

General Crosbie then spoke of the County Council's Provisional Order in which arrangements were made whereby not only places like Springfield, Largoward, Dairsie, would be supplied with water, but every single house in every part of Fife except the north-west would be accessible to water supply. The scheme had been held up because it was just impossible to obtain the necessary materials. So far as water supply was concerned there was nothing to prevent housing development.

The General then made reference to the valuable report made by the Committee of the Herring Industry, of which the Provost was a member, and remarked that it would be very desirable for every member of the community to read and study the Report. If they did not they could not fully realise that the potentialities of the fishing industry in Anstruther were such that it would be very foolish not to develop it. The people of Anstruther should put forward concrete suggestions about dehydration and refrigeration plant and not talk about them continually in the abstract. It might be that they needed Government subsidy ; it might be that the County Council could do something to help, but they could not help if they kept talking about the subject in an abstract way.

Bailie Fleming in referring to the drift of agricultural population said that the Education Authority were at the bottom of the whole thing. Children could not be taken away from country schools and retain an interest in agriculture. The children had to leave early in the morning and did not get back home until late at night with the result that they had no time to go into the fields to learn to drive a horse. Some children had to leave before 8 o'clock in the morning to attend school at 9.30 a.m., and did not get home until after 5 o'clock. If the country schools were opened again it would help the children to take an interest in farming. He mentioned that Kilrenny School was the one which he had in view. There was need for more transport facilities. If the country children had to go to town schools why should town children not have to attend country schools ?

Rev. J. A. Inglis remarked that what Bailie Fleming had stressed was of interest to Youth Organisations, and the Young Farmers' Club in Cupar had backed it as had the Young Farmers' Club in Anstruther. "Why should country children be taken to school in towns?" he asked. They lose rural contacts which are of very great value to them. "Why cut out the country ?" "Why cut out agriculture ?" he asked.

Mr. Gatherum remarked that in his village they had a housing site where the roads and everything else were prepared and the need for houses was very great.

Mr. Carlow said he did not think this line of country was their business at all. They were not a " House of Lords " over the County Council. They were not dealing with houses under their authority from the County Council (here Mr. Carlow read the terms of remit to County Planning Committee). The housing of the people was a matter of much interest not only in our County but in every County.

Mr. Carlow went on to say that when he referred to wages being the first desideratum he was thinking of new industries which must be self-supporting, otherwise things which flowed from industry would not be available. He wanted to see industry on a sound footing. If it was, the amenity side and the education side would follow, but unless industry was self-supporting all their planning would come to naught.

Further, Mr. Carlow stated that the relief of overcrowding was a matter of interest for the whole County and not matter for the Planning Advisory Committee. If he were asked the reason for the shortage of houses and the solution of the difficulty he would be very happy to tell them these things if they could give him half an hour.

Likewise the question of the transport of children to school did not come within the scope of the Advisory Committee.

One thing was within their scope in regard to housing, however, and he suggested the housing of agricultural workers in a central point instead of having so many of them close to the farm steading. Everybody had their own views on this matter and he knew that certain of the farm workers simply had to live on the farms to look after the animals, but there were others who did not necessarily have to live at the farm. There was no reason why these men should live at the farm any more than the miners should live at the pit. In the future they might find that a farm contractor, holding so many tractors, a large stock of implements and a large number of workers, would contract to do their land work for so much an acre, and thereby workers would not be staying 2 or 3 at the farm steading, but might be collected in a central village where there would be a certain amount of community life.

Mr. *Edie, Cornceres*, spoke of the great difficulty experienced in obtaining drain tiles or bricks or roofing tiles. He had had to purchase his from a firm in Laurencekirk. If they could get the brickworks in the County opened up again he thought there would be plenty of trade for them. Mr. Christie remarked that he understood that the County Council had done its utmost to try to get someone to open up the Seafield Works, but without avail.

Before the meeting closed arrangements were made to hold the second meeting at 7 p.m. on 30th April, instead of at 3 p.m., as this was the most suitable time for the inhabitants of the Anstruther area.

Provost Carstairs proposed a vote of thanks to Mr. Carlow and thanked the Committee for visiting Anstruther.

NOTES TAKEN AT PUBLIC MEETING HELD IN THE COUNTY HALL, CUPAR
24th April, 1945

Mr. *Carlow (Chairman)* recalled the meeting held a fortnight before when he had explained the Committee's purpose and informed them of their visits to the various Burghs. Since then they had received suggestions in writing from the undernoted parties, for which suggestions the Committee were most grateful :—

(1) Michael G. Black, Esq., Edenwood, Cupar.
(2) Messrs. G. T. Clark, and W. G. Leburn, Gateside.
(3) Springfield W.V.S.
(4) Miss Janet Low, Blebo, Cupar.
(5) Miss Annie Moon, Edenfield, Springfield.
(6) Rev. David Laird, The Manse, Springfield.
(7) Falkland Town Council.
(8) J. K. Hutchison, Esq., Kinloch, Collessie.
(9) Royal Burgh of Auchtermuchty.
(10) Ladybank Town Council.
(11) Freuchie W.V.S.
(12) Cupar W.V.S.—Letters from M. S. Proctor, Cairnie, Cupar, and Mrs. C. R. Normand, Bishopgate House, Cupar.
(13) Newburgh Town Council—Memo from Provost.
(14) Burgh of Cupar—Memorandum by Town Council.
(15) Parish of Monimail—Letter from Mrs. Hutchison-Bradburne and Rev. W. McCraw.
(The suggestions are shown in the appendix to these notes.)

The Committee had visited Newburgh and were received by the Provost and a considerable representation of the Council, said Mr. Carlow, and were given a very interesting report on what was happening in Newburgh. They referred to the floorcloth works, oilskin factory, quarries, salmon fisheries, etc., and to the importance of their harbour which could cope with vessels of a reasonable size. Since visiting Newburgh the Committee had received in writing from the Provost a further note in which they favoured the erection of a bridge across the Tay in the vicinity of Newburgh ; facilities for boating, fishing and bathing ; the provision of a new Junior Secondary School, etc. and reconstruction of the Gas Works. Mr. Carlow remarked that the Committee would shield themselves behind the Education Authority in any questions dealing with schools and that the question of the increasing of the capacity of the Gas Works did not come within their sphere.

The suggested new industries for Newburgh were canning factories for fish and fruit. The Committee had come across the same suggestion in Anstruther regarding fish. Dehydration and refrigeration appeared to be the best methods of dealing with fish to overcome the difficulty of the losses suffered by fishing people when there was a glut, and *vice versa* when there was a demand for fish and no fish to be had. Mr. Carlow expressed the view that Anstruther would have prior claim as the fishing industry was their principal livelihood. He thought there would be enough pioneers in Newburgh to set up a fruit-canning factory.

At Auchtermuchty the Committee were surprised to find that there was a foundry and engineering works, and a foundry which did not make engineering parts but was merely for casting. Then there was a linen factory employing 40 people, hosiery factory employing 20 girls and a factory being used as a military store. Mr. Carlow suggested that in regard to unlet factories a list should be prepared giving particulars of the factory, such as floor space, nearness to road and railway transport, water supply, gas and electricity supply and so on, so that any person intending to develop light industry could, by applying to the County Clerk, obtain a list showing precisely where the factories were and giving the information which any industrialist would want before deciding to establish a light industry. He also suggested that the particulars should be advertised in the press perhaps once a week.

The Committee found that Falkland had a linen factory and a linoleum factory both belonging to the S.C.W.S. and both of considerable magnitude. Before the war some 300 people were employed, but at present there were not quite so many. Mr. Carlow, however, saw no reason why these factories should not at least come back to pre-war position.

Mr. Carlow went on to say that at Ladybank they found a very prosperous community very well able to hold their own against any adversities. Since visiting Ladybank the Committee had received a memorandum from the Town Clerk on the future development of Ladybank and district.

Mr. Carlow said one reason for his dwelling on these points at some length was because he wanted to know if a bridge was put over the Tay would it be better placed where it would serve these works and factories and get their products more quickly delivered to markets in Perth and Dundee or the South, rather than take the arterial road through the County and build a bridge over the Tay at Newport where the cost would be 6 times greater than at Newburgh? He was merely mentioning that point because he wanted the criticism of the public.

At this point Mr. Carlow made special reference to a most valuable report which had been received regarding the development of the Gateside area.

Mr. Carlow then touched on different suggestions contained in letters which had been received. One point which interested him very much was contained in a letter received from the Parish of Monimail—"why should we encourage the expenditure of money on bridges and arterial roads and such like, when so much remains to be done for the improvement of the amenities of our agricultural workers at home?" Mr. Carlow said he did not know what proportion of the roads and bridges would be paid by the Ministry of Transport and he did not know what proportion of the cost of improving cottar houses would be paid by a Ministry and how much was paid by the owner of the land, but perhaps they could get more information on the subject.

Another point was the question of advanced education for farm workers—whether it would be possible to improve their minds and their general position in life by providing a little more education which could be absorbed in their working time. This was exactly the same suggestion as had been made in other industries, where newcomers into the industry would receive a certain training and education, naturally at the expense of their employers, and the time spent on education would be taken out of their working hours for which they would receive the usual remuneration.

There was a suggestion that local Advisory Committees might be set up in districts in order to get more closely in touch with the Planning Committee before the Report was prepared. Mr. Carlow said that the Advisory Committee would be delighted to go and visit any locality without the necessity of setting up any local committee, if they would just tell them when they wanted the Committee to go.

The W.V.S. stressed the need for housing while a member of the W.V.S. stressed the need for a new Primary School in the place where she lived. Another member of the W.V.S. spoke of the need for covering up a stream which ran through part of the village of Freuchie, but Mr. Carlow did not think that was within the scope of this Committee.

Bailie Walker, Cupar, said that this was the Cupar area but he had not heard any mention made of Cupar Burgh, one of the oldest Burghs in the County and the market town. Cupar had a certain amount of industry, but the important point was that they wanted more.

They had mentioned the question of having a bridge at Newburgh. If a bridge was built at Newburgh, Cupar would certainly not subscribe to it. If they were going to have a bridge across the Tay it must serve the interests of St. Andrews, Leuchars, where the airport was to be, and Cupar. Cupar, he said, was a district which was important. In his opinion there was an intention to sidetrack the industrial development of Cupar and put it up to Newburgh. Cupar was anxious to develop. They had been challenged by landward members that they had stood still for centuries and if Cupar was to make any headway and to advance they must have light industries, and the only way to get these was to extend the Burgh boundaries. Cupar's greatest difficulty was the acquisition of housing sites and having a considerable surplus of labour they were in a very good position to supply labour for light industries.

Provost Robertson, Newburgh, had no fault to find with what had been said for Newburgh. Cupar could look after itself. He thought that industries were required in Cupar, but Newburgh required them more. In Newburgh there were only a few industries such as linoleum manufacture, salmon fisheries, etc.

It would be important to have the foreshore opened up. Long ago Newburgh was a famous shipping port, and coal, manure, slates, paint, etc., were imported from Russia. The sand industry could be developed by making concrete blocks to supply housing.

Mr. Sloss, Town Clerk of Ladybank, spoke to the meeting on the memorandum prepared by him on behalf of his Town Council for the future planning of Ladybank and district, a copy of which memorandum is appended to these notes.

Bailie Peebles, Auchtermuchty, said that Mr. Mark, the Burgh Surveyor, had prepared a very fine report on Auchtermuchty which had been submitted to the Committee. Their great need in Auchtermuchty was housing and certain improvements could be carried out to the general amenity of the Burgh. The Reedie Den, for instance, could be made into a real beauty spot. Auchtermuchty had practically no facilities for recreation, he said.

In Auchtermuchty they felt that something could be done by way of introducing light industries. Mr. A. M. White was doing fairly well with Government Orders, but there was always a danger of falling off and there might be some unemployment and if some form of light industry were introduced it would help Auchtermuchty. At the present time the old Reedie Den Factory was being used as a military store. Bailie Peebles stated that this factory was in a good condition, had good water supply and drainage and was only about 10 minutes' walk from the station and adjacent to the public road.

Provost Robertson, Falkland, stated that Falkland was well off for industries. The problem was housing of the workers. The linoleum factory employed between 300 and 400 and the linen factory over 100, and there was a proposal to extend both factories after the war.

Another point mentioned by Provost Robertson was the need for a community centre. Falkland was not very well off for halls, and a community centre would have to be provided as the population were drifting away for lack of entertainment.

Falkland was on the main Perth-Kirkcaldy 'bus route, but they were anxious to see an improved 'bus service to the east of the County, to Cupar and St. Andrews. At present there was only one 'bus to Cupar per day.

Falkland was not concerned whether the bridge over the Tay was erected at Newburgh or Newport.

Mr. Bonthrone, Newton of Falkland, stated that they must make sure that private enterprise led the way as it had always done. They must make certain that if private enterprise was going to take an active part in developing industry it was not, sooner or later, absorbed into some type of State control. Rural industries did require development, but he thought if he might speak in a humble way, that the greatest drawback to the development of these industries was in the form of State interference. He felt sure that private firms would not be found lacking in developing their own industries if there was not the fear of State interference.

Mr. Bonthrone expressed the view that if a summary was made of the chief materials imported into Fife information might be used as a basis of what might be done to compete with these imported articles. Then these articles could probably be replaced or partly replaced in Fife itself.

Miss Low, Blebo, spoke as representative of a very rural area. Their great difficulty was want of water and light, and until these facilities came the housing problem would never really be solved. She understood that the water scheme was on its way and hoped that it would visit the really remote areas. Lighting was also coming, but Miss Low wondered if anything could be done to help the provision of electricity to a really poor district.

Another suggestion made by Miss Low was the provision of telephone kiosks in the little country villages. It was all very well to feel there was a private telephone not very far away, but this was not always available.

Miss Low concluded by saying that the provision of water, light, kiosks, and help in the providing of playing fields for the children would do very much to help in her particular area and also in many others.

Miss Haig, Clayton, Dairsie, said that water was also Dairsie's biggest difficulty. They knew that the water scheme was coming and would be very glad to get it. Dairsie was very fortunate so far as light was concerned as the cable passed right through the village.

Miss Haig went on to say that she supposed they could not move the main road from the middle of Dairsie, but it was a very dangerous road for children and the playground was just at the side of the main road.

The people of Dairsie felt that one of the reasons for the depopulation of the countryside was the fact that children were being taken away in 'buses every day from their country homes to school in the towns. They got the idea of being in a big community of scholars and their idea was to get back to the towns. If the village schools could be developed and children kept there longer that would be one of the things to keep people in the country districts.

With regard to the question of putting people in villages instead of on farms, Miss Haig thought this might be successful in some cases. There were some cases where it was very difficult for a mother to wheel her pram down to the main road in order to get to the village, so that in that case it might be an advantage. In other cases, however, they found that people would prefer to be at their farms.

Mrs. Lindsay, Craigsanquhar, stated that the village of Logie was 3 miles from the 'bus route and they only had a 'bus on a Saturday. Housing, lack of water and transport were their main difficulties.

Mrs. Hutchison-Bradburne, Cunnoquhie, remarked that they had heard a great deal about Newburgh, but Monimail as a very small community wanted to remain as a country and rural community and were very much in favour of having more educational facilities for their agricultural workers. Monimail was also in need of better housing conditions, water and light.

Rev. W. McCraw, Bow of Fife, referred to the suggestion made that local Advisory Committees might be set up in the different districts, for consultation, if necessary. Mr. McCraw felt that such a Committee would be of value to the Advisory Committee, having, as it would, a knowledge of its own particular area. He referred to a factory which had been built on good agricultural land and expressed the view that had such a Committee been consulted another equally suitable site might have been obtained.

Mr. McCraw went on to say that the national purse was not bottomless and the County Council's purse certainly was not bottomless, and he felt that if they embarked on big schemes like road bridges and arterial roads the time might come when suggestions would be put forward about houses and they would have to say that they were very deeply involved with these bridges and roads and couldn't tackle the question of housing.

Dr. Arthur, Dunbog, said he would like to stress the things which had been said in regard to water, electricity and the improvement of village halls for community centres.

One thing which had not been mentioned was the need for cheaper electricity. It was all very well laying cables, but by the time these reached the farms the cost of the supply of electricity was simply prohibitive. Something ought to be done to provide cheaper electricity so that the country places might share in its benefits.

Mr. J. S. Brown, Redriggs, Ceres, began by saying that he represented a parish which had no industries whatsoever—the parish of Ceres. He did not know in what way the Advisory Committee could help Ceres unless they could do anything in the way of helping to improve it as a resort for people spending their holidays. They had electric light, but no water or drainage.

Recently some officials had visited Ceres looking for a suitable site for a factory. There was a nice place there with a dam with lots of water and a good many buildings, but whether they looked at it or not Mr. Brown did not know. The factory had been erected at Uthrogle where there was no water supply. That would have been a chance for setting up a village industry.

Mr. Brown said he had asked his son, who was home on leave, how the boys in the Forces felt about matters, and he replied that what they wanted was to be sure of a job to come home to and a house to live in.

W. G. Leburn, Gateside, said they had heard a lot this afternoon, and he thought it would be very nice if they saw in Fife parks and new schools and new industries, but his point was that Cupar had said they had a surplus of labour and Newburgh wanted new factories and Auchtermuchty wanted new industries, and he thought the long-term view was a very good thing, but he thought that before that they should help the industries which they had. Many good industries in Fife were being restricted for the want of labour and housing, and he felt that the Committee should press very strongly that housing should be put where the industries were at the moment and not placed where industries were speculative, and where new industries were being started.

In Gateside it was felt of great importance that as many agricultural workers as possible should be moved in to community centres so that the wives could be on the 'bus routes and children could walk to school.

Bailie Scotland, Newburgh, said he did not think there was anyone present from the Balmerino district. At the present time there was no 'bus service, and he stated quite frankly that if it had not been for the Stand Still Order, ploughmen and their families would not have stayed in the area. The district referred to extends from Newburgh right along the Tay to Gauldry, a distance of some 8 miles.

Mr. Carlow wished to apologise for any seeming discourtesy to Cupar or any other Burgh if he had not mentioned the written communications which had been sent in. These were only received by him at a quarter to three and he just referred to the few which happened to be in his hand.

Mr. Christie, in referring to the Report by Cupar Burgh, thought this was very well rounded off and exact, and he didn't think much needed to be said about it except to take note of all the points put forward by the Burgh and take them into consideration with regard to the new proposed by-pass roads.

He would like to differ from the Chairman on one thing. When Newburgh spoke of the possibility of the development of a canning factory or refrigerator Mr. Carlow said that Anstruther should have prior claim. Mr. Christie held that the person who had prior claim was the person who got going first. One thing which came out quite clearly was the need for private enterprise in the whole of these developments. There seemed to be an idea that the Advisory Committee was going to bring Utopia. They were not going to get anything from the Advisory Committee but a Report.

In continuing, Mr. Christie referred to the evident possibilities and need for the development of those light industries which were spoken of so much. Canning factories and refrigeration plants were light industries, and they must hope that there were some far-sighted people who would see that there was going to be a very large profit in the development of them.

Mr. Christie went on to say that they had heard references made to community centres. These centres were a most excellent idea. He did not know whether they had read the Government report on community centres, but the first thing was to form a Community Association and he thought that was the answer to Mrs. Hutchison-Bradburne and Mr. McCraw. Mr. Christie said he spoke with a certain amount of knowledge on this subject as he had been busily engaged in forming a Community Association in Kennoway. In Kennoway, there were a good many separate organisations working. First of all they got 33 members, but decided that was not enough so they waited a fortnight and got 147. They then sent out voting papers and within a week had 140 papers back without a spoilt paper among them. Now they had a very live organisation which could speak with knowledge on matters concerning their district. Mr. Christie expressed the view that if Community Associations of that kind were formed the County Council would get a great deal from those rural areas.

With regard to the question of light industries the report from Gateside was an extremely good one, and the point brought out by Messrs. Leburn and Clark, that where there was a light industry in existence this should be saved at any cost, was worthy of note. In the coming years everything available would go into the building of houses and there would not be much left for the building of anything else.

From the Gateside report also came the first suggestion from a member of an agricultural community of the possibility of farm workers living in community centres. That was a question which was going to be a very large problem in the future. Mr. Christie thought that the Advisory Committee should have a meeting with some of the outstanding agriculturists in the County to thrash the matter out, because it was a matter which would have to be settled.

Mr. Christie then asked if Ladybank was thinking of forming a community centre, to which Mr. Sloss replied that the thought had passed through his mind because, as Mr. Christie had said, it was the only way to get what was really required. Mr. Sloss stated that the question would probably be discussed at the next meeting of their " Welcome Home " Committee.

Mr. Christie was very pleased that the representative from Dairsie had raised the question of farm roads. So many farms long ago came into existence beside the existing County roads and they went there because the roads were there. About 1828-30 we entered the time when new roads were built and farms were left high and dry, and gradually the County had dropped these old roads and now farmers had to keep them up. On one small property which Mr. Christie had to do with they had 4 miles of these roads and it was utterly impossible for farmer or owner to keep these roads in good condition.

With regard to Mrs. Hutchison-Bradburne's and Mr. McCraw's reference to the bridge, they said that improving the amenities of Fife must have first call. This Committee was appointed to make plans for the future and the question of the bridge was of importance economically. Mr. Christie thought he went further than his Committee, as he thought there was an absolute necessity for a bridge at Dundee and also at Newburgh. He thought there would be three main roads—one from the Forth direct to the North; a second road passing through Lochgelly, Cowdenbeath, and up through Falkland, Auchtermuchty, and Newburgh, to contact with that area where industries were going to be established, especially the huge coal-mines at Kirkcaldy ; and thirdly, a great through trunk road by Dundee to Angus and the North. He thought that rather than having disputes about the bridges they should look forward to having at least two in 60 years' time.

Mr. Carlow then summed up on one or two points. It was interesting to note that at Gateside there were not enough houses for the workers. That more or less applied to every part of the County, and there were not enough workers for the work.

With regard to the bridges over the Tay and the Forth, Mr. Carlow thought it would be a good thing to get a plan made by the planning expert, having marked upon it factories which are working now and if the main roads were to be for the purpose of serving industry the position of the industry would give a very good indication as to where the road should be. If the road was to be for pleasure purposes then that was another matter.

There were things like Burgh boundaries which Mr. Carlow said did not come within the scope of the Committee. So far as telephone kiosks were concerned, he quite agreed with what had been said, but here again such matters did not fall to be dealt with by the Advisory Committee.

Speaking on the question of cheaper electricity, Mr. Carlow asked what was the grid put up for but to give people cheaper electricity. If it had not done so it had failed in its purpose. He did not think they would ever see electricity cheaper than it was to-day.

Mr. Carlow said he agreed with those people who said that people coming home from the war wanted houses to live in and a job.

The water supply scheme for the County was devised many years ago and was now held up because of war conditions, but no doubt soon after peace came the County would be able to get ahead with the scheme.

Again he emphasised that light industries would go where they would prosper, and the way to attract light industries was to compile a list showing water supply, gas, electricity, etc., all the information necessary to a prospective industrialist.

APPENDIX REFERRED TO

(1) *Letter from Michael Black, Esq., Edenwood, Cupar.*

EDENWOOD,
CUPAR,
FIFE.
12th April, 1945.

J. M. MITCHELL, Esq.,
COUNTY CLERK,
CUPAR.

DEAR SIR,

I was much interested to have the opportunity of attending the Meeting called by the Planning Advisory Committee in Cupar on Monday, 9th April.

I have given some consideration to the points which were raised and have much pleasure in submitting my suggestions, which I am of opinion should have the early consideration of the County Planning Committee.

I think, first of all, that the improvement of the living conditions in the area under review should be given priority and that little else should be attempted until such time as reasonable water, drainage and lighting facilities are provided in the homes of the people. I am not of opinion that more industries should be encouraged to settle themselves in our district, but I do feel there is a possibility of modernising certain auxiliary industries which could give a distinct service to agriculture.

I have in mind particularly the modernising of the village blacksmith's shop, which although it still functions in its hereditary way, requires nowadays to be more comprehensive. I visualise that in every rural village there should be a combined garage, blacksmith's shop, agricultural repair shed and joinery establishment. It seems to me highly important that such small industries as I have described should be well conceived to do immediate repairs to the agricultural equipment, which is quickly becoming motorised and modernised. I would expect such an industry to carry small stocks of vital replacements so that farmers would be able to get quick repairs done during the busy times of the year. In the area in question it should not be forgotten that there are in existence many buildings which were at one time prosperous linen factories and with little alteration it seems to me that these could be readily adapted for the purpose I have in mind.

I am very much in favour of the development of community centres and am in favour of such centres being in many cases adjacent to, if not part of, the village school, so that the facilities which are available for the teaching of school children could be used for adult education and recreation. I am a little hesitant in making the above suggestion as I fear the control by the County Council over such buildings might seriously hinder the effort of the people to run their own show.

There were references at your meeting as to the reasons why there had been a drift from the country to the towns. There is no doubt, to my mind, that the meagre agricultural wages conditions of the past twenty-five years and more have been largely responsible for this ; but now with better conditions and wages on the land there seems to be no reason why this drift should not be stemmed, if the housing conditions are made satisfactory and there are reasonable opportunities for social recreation in the village centres. The question of adequate transport is obviously an important feature.

It is perhaps not realised that a considerable proportion of the rural population is made up of elderly people who have worked in the towns and have bought a cottage in the country in which to spend their retirement in quiet surroundings. Such people can bring with them in many cases considerable talent and experience, and I believe it is important to cater to quite an extent for this class of person.

Although I am in favour of there being adequate trunk road facilities throughout the country and where bottle-necks exist provision being made for through traffic, I am not in favour of, nor can I see the urgent necessity for, the construction of either Forth or Tay Road Bridges at the present time. I would even go so far as to say that for the area in question neither of these bridges would be an economic asset. In fact, I believe they would tend to bring in many more people and motor-cars, particularly at week-ends, which would add not only to the danger of our roads but to the disturbance of our peace. It is clear that these projects are having the support of all parties purely as electoral tactics and they are not necessarily the desire of the thinking population. It seems to me that the spending of vast sums of money for these conveniences can be well shelved until such time as the housing conditions of the people are brought to a reasonable standard.

Yours faithfully,

(Signed) MICHAEL E. BLACK.

(2) *Memorandum on the future Development and Planning of Gateside by Messrs. G. T. Clark and W. G. Leburn.*

Having heard the proposals of the Advisory Planning Committee at the public meeting held in Cupar on April 9th, we beg to submit our suggestions concerning the future planning and development of Gateside.

In the first place, we should like to emphasise that the following remarks which we have to offer are made entirely as individuals and not as an expression of the views of any body or committee of the village. If, however, the members of the Advisory Planning Committee should consider our suggestions as either helpful or feasible, we propose to hold a public meeting or meetings in the village to explain what has so far been done and to ascertain the views of the members of the village thereon. Should this come about we should naturally communicate to the Committee any divergence of opinion from our own, and any further suggestions which might be offered.

Furthermore we would like to make it clear that our future livelihood depends on the village of Gateside and that therefore we are interested parties in any future planning and development. Moreover, having been born and bred in Gateside we have a natural love of the village and countryside, so that the interests of the village may be said to be synonymous with our own. At the same time we have genuinely tried to take a dispassionate outlook on the problem so that the memorandum may be of real value to the Committee.

Before dealing with specific problems concerning the village of Gateside, we would like to record our admiration for the way in which the Committee are approaching the general subject of planning for Fife and to say that by and large we endorse the schemes so far outlined to us at the meeting on April 9th. We are particularly enthusiastic over the idea of concentrating on community centres as we believe that therein lies the best hope for the future welfare and happiness of the people. Here we would like to make the point that while agreeing that in the Cupar area emphasis should be on agriculture we do not feel that in all instances it should have priority over industry. Industry, particularly where its manufactures are for export, is, we believe, of equal importance with agriculture, and we are of the opinion that the ideal is for such industry and agriculture to work complementary to each other.

One further point we would like to make : it is our strong conviction that where possible it is better to develop existing industry rather than to try to create new and unproven ones. We appreciate that in Fife there may be certain areas which have dead or dying industries, where it may very well be advantageous to introduce new ones, but in an area where a flourishing industry exists—and Gateside is such a one—we repeat that we are of the opinion that it is better to concentrate on the existing industry.

In making our suggestions and proposals we have at all times tried to be essentially *practical*.

In considering planning and development in any particular area or community centre we believe that the logical approach to the subject is :—

Firstly, to confirm that there is a desire, a need and a demand for development ; and secondly, having established the existence of such a desire, need and demand, to confirm that the area or community centre in question is one which is worthy, in the broadest sense, of development.

Based on these assumptions, we accordingly give our suggestions and proposals for Gateside in three parts : Parts I and II showing that the desire, need and demand for development exists, and Part III showing that Gateside is a village worthy of development.

Part I deals with the industry of the village, namely the Gateside Mills Company Limited, and Part II with agriculture. It will be noticed that Part I goes into more detail than Part II, but this is not because any greater importance is attached to it, but merely because little is known of this particular industry, and of necessity much of the information is technical, whereas the subject of agriculture is more widely known and its difficulties more generally understood. In dealing with Part III we have purposely restricted ourselves to the broad outline of suggested planning, for the obvious reason that detailed planning entails architectural knowledge, both for the design of any buildings and the laying out of new sites.

PART I.—THE GATESIDE MILLS COMPANY LIMITED
1. GENERAL

The Gateside Mills Company Limited are manufacturers of bobbins, shuttles and wood-mill stores of a similar nature for the textile trade. Eighty per cent. of its trade is for export.

The firm was established in 1870 and in 1922 was formed into a limited company. It has developed apace with the textile trade since the advent of the power loom and spinning frame.

The industry of bobbin and shuttle-making demands highly skilled workmen, whose training in many cases takes five years. The work produced is that of the craftsman. It is essential if the industry is to continue that a steady flow of trainees should be established. This point is of the first importance.

In 1939 a serious fire gutted the main mill. At the time this was a severe blow to the Company, but happily a completely modern mill was built and equipped by the middle of 1940, before the full force of Government restrictions came into being. All machinery is now electrified, every machine having its individual electric motor.

In the rebuilding and re-equipping of the mill, possible expansion was foreseen and the new mill was designed to give a much higher output than that possible previously. This in turn has meant that where the old mill employed some 60 or 70 workpeople, the new mill now has a possible capacity to employ over 100.

The foregoing gives an outline of the Company and it is now proposed to consider various factors affecting its present and future development.

Under discussion will be such factors as demand, present and potential production, raw materials, labour, wages and housing.

It will be appreciated that it is desirable to give, for the information of the Committee, certain figures. Some of these are of necessity of a confidential nature, and for this reason they are given as appendices, with the request that they will not be made public.

2. RAW MATERIAL

The raw material for bobbins is Scotch hard-wood. Scotch timber had during the war been brutally slaughtered, to an extent which leaves reserves so diminished that there is a very disheartening outlook for the home timber trade after the war. This applies, however, entirely to soft-wood and not to hard-woods—large quantities of the latter are still standing and in many cases much is requiring to be cut. There is no lack of suitable Scotch hard-wood for the requirements of the bobbin trade.

We would here like to make the point that we strongly condemn any disfigurement of the countryside caused by the felling of hard-wood, knowing that there are adequate supplies mature and waiting to be cut, in areas from which it can be taken without detriment to the beauty of the land. We are also deeply interested in the replanting of timber, and consider that all planting should be planned so as to enhance the beauty of the countryside without encroaching on arable areas.

For shuttles, persimmon—from the U.S.A.—is the raw material, of which there is no shortage. It might be of interest to note that not even shipping restrictions during the war have prohibited the import of this valuable timber, the reason, of course, being that shuttles are of sufficient importance to justify the allotting of shipping space for all the persimmon that has been required. With such a position in war, no undue difficulties can be anticipated in peace conditions.

Therefore, as far as raw material is concerned, there is no reason why the mill should not go on to full production right away ; and no shortage can be foreseen in the immediate or distant future.

3. LABOUR

In Appendix A are given the figures concerning labour at present employed, together with the labour which would be required to step up production to full capacity.

It will be seen that there is a deficiency of :

  2 administrative ;
  22 skilled ;
  9 semi-skilled ;
  7 labourers ;
  4 boys and women.

NOTE.—While boys and women are interchangeable, it is necessary that at least 50% of this number be made up of boys so that they may be trained and form the nucleus of future skilled labour. At present all of this class of labour is female.

There is at present an acute shortage of labour, and although the firm has been granted second preference by the Ministry of Labour very little additional labour has been procured, solely because it is well-nigh impossible to get accommodation for any labour which may be drafted to the firm. There is, of course, less labour available, due to war, but again when labour becomes available houses will be required. The result of no new labour being introduced is that many workers are getting old and due for retirement and unless labour can be got within the next year or two it will not be possible to train it before the older men retire, so that there is a grave danger of that craftsmanship, perhaps the industry's greatest asset, being lost.

This fact will be borne out by a study of the ages of skilled men given as a note to Appendix A.

It is suggested that after the war all the labour that is required will be available if houses are available.

Appendix B shows the numbers of workers who come from Gateside, from Strathmiglo and from Milnathort. It will be seen that a comparatively small number come from Gateside, and it is suggested that it would be to the advantage of the whole community if the main centre of labour were Gateside. This would make for a much happier community and would be of inestimable value to tradition and morale.

This question will be further discussed in the following paragraph dealing with houses.

From all the foregoing it would appear that the only way to put production up is more labour—and the only way to get more labour is by additional houses. *Therefore we must have houses.*

4. HOUSES

In considering the number of houses that will be required for the employees of the Gateside Mills Company Limited, it is assumed that no houses will be required for women and boys, as these will presumably be the wives, sons or daughters of the male workers.

It will be seen from Appendix A that if the mill is to go on to full production, 40 additional workmen are required. For these it is estimated that 30 new houses must be built. This average of three houses being required for every four men is based on the present situation.

In addition, it will be seen from Appendix B that if Strathmiglo and Milnathort workers are to be housed in Gateside, a further 22 workmen will require houses, the number of houses being required for these being, say, 15.

The total number of new houses required for the workers of Gateside Mills is therefore 45.

There are no houses available in Gateside at the moment, and in fact certain workers are already living in houses which are condemned.

PART II.—AGRICULTURE
1. GENERAL

Gateside, being the first village in Fife after crossing the county boundaries from Kinross and Perth, is the village centre for a widespread agricultural district.

It lies in the valley of the Upper Eden. This area is covered by 17 farms, this being the number which use Gateside as a centre. The farmers use its station and the children attend the Gateside school.

The 17 farms have an acreage of just under 6,000 acres.

Three of these have always been engaged on milk production, while a fourth, under the management of the Agricultural Executive Committee, went into production in 1940 and two more are in the process of starting.

The other farms are mainly concerned with general arable agriculture, the land being ideal for seed potato growing and cereals—though parts of it are on the light side for wheat and barley ; 7 quarters, however, have been threshed off land in this district.

A considerable acreage of roots is also grown, as the dry nature of the land makes it ideal for winter sheep-feeding.

2. Horses and Tractors

There are at the present time over 100 horses being shod at the village smithy, and this, along with general jobbing, keeps two men fully employed.

On the 17 farms in question, 21 tractors are at work on the land, 14 of these having been acquired since 1939.

Though some of the smaller farmers do not work their tractors to full production, it is not visualised that they will ever return to former methods, even if the acreage tilled is to some extent reduced after the war. It is, therefore, anticipated that at least the above number of tractors will continue to be used in this district.

In passing it is interesting to note that with this number of tractors there is an opening for someone to start a local repair service.

3. Labour

In common with most agricultural communities at the present time, labour is short.

In Appendix C is given the present position of labour which it is considered will be required after the war, allowance having been made for the possibility of a smaller acreage being tilled.

It will be seen that in all 78 workers are at present employed and that 84 workers will be required after the war. The apparent present shortage of labour is made good by approximately 20 prisoners of war, and a further 12 Irish workers, who are earning their living throughout the year on these farms, instead of merely coming spasmodically at crop and harvest times. In addition 7 potato workers travel daily from Milnathort and during potato-lifting time five lorry-loads of potato gatherers are brought in each day from Fife mining districts.

To revert to the figures of 78 and 84, it must be assumed that a certain number of men will always be required to live on the farms to tend the animals. Such men include shepherds, cattlemen and horsemen.

Based on this assumption Appendix C also shows the number of men of the 84 who will be required to live on the farms and the numbers who could live within the community centre of Gateside.

It cannot be too strongly emphasised that it is considered essential as far as possible to move workers from the outlying farms into the community centre so that the wives and families may be on a 'bus route and the children within easy walking distance of the school. It is interesting to note that there are in this area two reconditioned houses two miles from the village, which have been refused by agricultural workers, these workers having taken in preference an old house on the 'bus route.

It is also suggested that the practice of having workmen living in bothies should be strongly discouraged in the future.

4. Houses

There are at present no unoccupied houses in Gateside and therefore, if agricultural workers are to live in the community centre, there must be new houses for them.

From the information given in paras. 2 and 3 above it will be seen that at least 21 tractor drivers could be moved into the village, and in addition it is calculated that a further 14 men who do not have to look after stock, but who work on the farms, could live equally well at Gateside.

This makes a total of 35 and *it is considered that 25 houses* would be required to accommodate this number.

PART III.—THE VILLAGE OF GATESIDE

The first thing that strikes any visitor to Gateside is its beauty, its neatness and its healthy situation.

The village is at an altitude of 320 feet above sea-level and for the most part faces south.

To turn to more concrete facts about the village :—

1. Communications

(a) *Roads.*—The main St. Andrews-Cupar-Kinross-Stirling road runs through the village, with a main junction road branching to Perth, which is part of the main Kirkcaldy-Strathmiglo-Perth road. It would also appear from plans that Gateside will be well placed to any trunk road which may be built as a result of the Forth and Tay Road Bridges.

(b) *Railways.*—There is a station less than a quarter of a mile from the village on the Ladybank-Kinross line.

(c) *'Buses.*—There is an hourly 'bus service both ways on the main road from St. Andrews to Stirling and a two-hourly 'bus service on the Perth to Kirkcaldy route.

2. Public Services

(a) *Electricity.*—The village is connected with the Fife power.

(b) *Water.*—The village is connected with the Strathmiglo water supply.

(c) *Sewage.*—Unfortunately the village has no sewage scheme, but whether or not any building is undertaken, this service is long overdue and would in any case have to be installed immediately after the war. To do this is not a big undertaking as the village drains downhill to a centre point from which there is an excellent " tail " down to the bed of the River Eden.

(d) *Gas.*—There is no gas supply, but it is considered that having electricity this can be dispensed with.

3. Village Amenities

(a) *Church.*—The village has its own church and manse, both of which are in a state of good repair. The church would be capable of seating all the additional numbers involved by the building of new houses, even if there was a return to the stricter church-going habits of former days.

(b) *School.*—There is an excellent school and school-house, standing at the west end of the village. Again, this would be large enough to cater for any increase of pupils which additional houses might cause. There is at present one empty class-room. Attached to the school is a soup kitchen and an extensive grass playground.

(c) *Hall.*—The village has a Memorial Hall built after the last war, which is up-to-date and has all the necessary offices.

(d) *Public House.*—There is an adequate public-house.

(e) *Recreation Ground.*—The village has no park or recreation ground, apart from the school playing ground. There is, however, at least one and possibly two excellent sites, which might be developed for this purpose. If one particular site were adopted for new houses, the site most feasible, a very nice park could be made in the ground surrounded by these new houses.

(f) *Houses.*—At present there are in the village proper, excluding all farm cottages nearby, approximately 30 houses. Of these it is considered that 23 are in good repair and 7 unsatisfactory.

There are no fewer than six possible sites well suited to take new houses. No one site would be large enough for all the houses required, but this would not seem to matter.

When new houses are built it is considered most important that care be taken to build houses suited to those already there and in harmony with the general surroundings. To achieve this it is strongly recommended that self-contained houses of 3 and 4 rooms each would be a long way the best. This point cannot be too strongly emphasised and any attempt to put up large 4 and 8 house buildings—tenements—should be discouraged.

Normally it would be recommended that an additional number of houses of the three-room type should be built for the retired people to live in and these naturally would be very welcome, but at the same time, in view of the number of houses already visualised, this would seem to be an unreasonable demand at the moment.

The people of Gateside are exceptionally enthusiastic about village affairs and take a keen interest in the well-being of the community.

We cannot think of any village more worthy of development, nor more likely to repay a handsome dividend for any developments undertaken.

We believe it will make an ideal community centre.

CONCLUSION

We hope to have established the fact that there is a genuine desire, need and demand for houses in Gateside, and furthermore that Gateside is a village indeed worthy of development.

We accordingly beg to make the following suggestions for the future planning and development of Gateside :—

(a) that Gateside should be made a community centre, both for the agricultural and the industrial labour of the district ;

(b) that agriculture and industry should be treated with equal priority ;

(c) that the existing industry should be developed, rather than that any attempt should be made to introduce a new one (the present industry is particularly important in view of the fact that 80% of its manufactures are for export) ;

(d) that as far as possible workers from outlying farms should be concentrated in the village and that only those workers necessary for tending stock should be left on the farms, so that the families of farm workers should have the advantages of community life, including proximity to 'bus routes and to school for the children ;

(e) that 70 new houses be built in Gateside ;

(f) that any new houses should occupy the sites available and that they should be self-contained houses of 3 and 4 rooms of an architectural design to fit in with the present attractive surroundings ;

(g) that a sewage scheme should be undertaken in the village at the earliest possible moment, whether new houses are to be built or not ;

(h) that a recreation ground or park be made ;

(j) that bothy life should be discouraged.

We would earnestly plead that an early start be made with the building of new houses in Fife, not only to improve present living conditions and to alleviate labour and housing shortage, but also to ensure that the best type of persons be attracted to and selected for our village community centres in the County.

We would cordially invite the members of the Advisory Planning Committee, together with their architect, Mr. Taylor, to visit Gateside, when we would be very pleased and proud to show them THE BEST VILLAGE IN FIFE.

GATESIDE,
April, 1945.

Appendix A

LABOUR SITUATION

	At present Employed	Required for full possible production	Deficient
Administrative	6	8	2
Skilled	22‡	44	22*
Semi-skilled	5	14	9
Labourers	9	16	7
Boys and Women	16†	20	4
	58	102	44
Total Number of Men (excluding Boys and Women)	42	82	40§

Appendix B

WHERE PRESENT EMPLOYEES LIVE

	Gateside	Strathmiglo	Milnathort
Administrative	4	2	—
Skilled	10	12	—
Semi-skilled	3	2	—
Labourers	3	5	1
Boys and Women	4	3	9
	24	24	10
Where Men live (excluding Boys and Women)	20	21	1

* Greatest shortage is of skilled labour.
† At present are all women ; essential to get at least 50% boys to train as skilled labour for the future.
‡ Ages of skilled men—Under 40 years 5
Under 40/50 years 3
Under 50/55 years 1
Under 55/60 years 5
Under 60/65 years 5
Over 65 years 3
—
22
=

§ Of this figure only 4 can be expected to be found from employees at present in H.M. Forces

Appendix C

LABOUR AND HOUSING SITUATION OF FARMS

Key:—F, Farmer; FH, Farm House; W, Worker; C, Cottage; B, Bothy; N, New; R, Reconditioned; MP, Milk Production.

(a) Serial	(b) Farm	(c) Acres	(d) Miles from Gateside	(e) Houses on Farm	(f) Condition of Cottages	(g) Number at Present Employed	(h) Number Required after war	(i) Number who must stay on Farm	(j) Number who could live in Gateside	(k) Remarks
1	Gospetry	1,350	2½	FH, 9C	4N, 3R	F, 16W*	F, 16W	F, 9W	7W	
2	Lappie	292	2	FH, 2C, 1B	1R	F *	F, 3W	F, 1W	2W	Both houses empty. Inc. being considered
3	Lacesston	181	1	FH, 1B		F, 2W*	F, 3W	F, 1W	2W	
4	W. N. Urquhart	152	1	FH, 1G, 1B	1R	F, 2W	F, 3W	F, 1W	2W	
5	E. N. Urquhart	244	1	FH, 1C, 1B		F, 2W*	F, 3W	F, 1W	2W	
6	W. U. Urquhart	176	1¼	1C, 1B	1R	F, 2W	F, 2W	F, 1W	1W	
7	F. U. Urquhart	830	1½	FH, 3C, 1B	3R	7W*	7W	5W	2W	A.E.C.M.P. (1940)
8	Corston Mill	181	1½	FH, 2C		F, 2W	F, 2W	F, 1W	1W	
9	Wellfield	500	1¼	FH, 7C		F, 8W	F, 8W	F, 5W	3W	
10	Leden Urquhart	163	2	FH, 1C	1R	F, 3W*	F, 3W	F, 2W	1W	
11	Corinzion	202	1½	FH, 1C, 1B		F, 3W*	F, 3W	F, 2W	1W	MP (starting)
12	Balcanquhal	270	1½	FH, 3C	3R	F, 5W*	F, 5W	F, 3W	2W	MP (always)
13	Carmore	225	2½	FH, 1B		F, 2W*	F, 2W	F, 1W	1W	
14	Bannaty	315	2	FH, 4C, 1B	4R	F, 7W*	F, 7W	F, 3W	4W	MP (starting)
15	Bannaty Mill	88	½	2C	1R	F, 2W	F, 2W	F, 1W	1W	MP (always)
16	U. Pitlochy	370	½	3C, 1B	3R	6W*	6W	3W	3W	MP (always)
17	N. Pitlochy	440	¼	FH, 6C	6R	F, 9W*	F, 9W	F, 9W	Considered Gateside	
	Total	5,979		14FH, 46C, 10B	4N, 27R, 15 not Re-cond.	15F, 78W	15F, 84W	15F, 49W	35W	

* Farms employing Italians.

NOTES—Serials 7 and 16 farmed from Serial 17.
Deficiency between (g) and (h) made up at present by Italian P.O.W. and other imported labour.

Appendix D

CHILDREN IN GATESIDE DISTRICT ATTENDING SCHOOL

Serial	District	Miles from Gateside	Gateside Primary School†	Auchtermuchty Junior Secondary School	Bell Baxter School	Total
1	Gospetry	2½	2	1	—	3
2	Burnside*	2	5	—	—	5
3	Lappie	2	3	—	—	3
4	E. N. Urquhart	1	2	—	—	2
5	E. U. Urquhart	1½	6	2	—	8
6	Corston Mill	1½	2	1	—	3
7	Wellfield	1¼	4	—	1	5
8	Corinzion	1½	3	—	—	3
9	Balcanquhal	1½	5	1	1	7
10	Westfield*	1	2	—	—	2
11	Bannaty	2	1	—	—	1
12	Bannaty Mill	½	2	1	1	4
13	U. Pitlochy	½	1	—	—	1
14	N. Pitlochy	¼	7	—	—	7
15	Gateside	—	9	1	1	11
	Total	—	54	7	4	65

* These are not farms, but Burnside men usually work on Bannaty ; and Westfield men usually work on U. Pitlochy.
† Gateside School has two lady teachers. The school has 3 classrooms, but only 2 are at present in use.

186

(3) *Letter from Springfield W.V.S., per Mrs. Black, Edenwood, Cupar, dated 17th April, 1945.*

J. M. Mitchell, Esq.,
   County Clerk, Cupar.

Dear Sir,
   I was asked by the Cupar Branch of the W.V.S. to represent Springfield at the Town Planning meeting, which was held in Cupar, on Monday, 9th April.
   I have had considerable experience in connection with my W.V.S. work during the war, and am well acquainted with the urgent needs which may be of interest to the Planning Committee in the village and district of Springfield. I am of the opinion that the majority of the women are looking forward to better housing conditions. As you are no doubt aware, the ordinary services of running water and drains are non-existent in Springfield. These amenities, we feel, should be given first priority in any improvements that are likely to be made.
   Relevant to that there is an urgent need for improvement in design and size of the existing houses, many of which I know to be badly overcrowded. I would like to suggest next that provision should be made for a comprehensive playing field. By that I mean there should be provision for not only a suitable and safe place with appliances for the children to get recreation, but also that provision might be made for a bowling-green and other facilities, where young persons and grown-ups can spend their leisure in a healthy way. We are not in favour of there being established in the village a basic industry, but we believe there are opportunities for small rural industries, which could give service to agriculture in the district, and we feel sure that, given prosperous conditions in agriculture, there could be maintained such development as would be of advantage to the people. We also feel that adequate transport facilities are essential to the well-being of the people.
   There has been great publicity over the proposed Forth and Tay Road Bridges, but my opinion is that these bridges are not a real necessity while so much else is required to be done to benefit the health and well-being of the people in this district.
   I do hope that these very urgent necessities for Springfield will receive early consideration by the Planning Committee.

Yours faithfully,
(Signed) G. T. BLACK.

---

(4) *Letter from Miss Low, Blebo, dated 18th April, 1945.*

J. Methven Mitchell, Esq.,
   County Clerk,
      County Buildings, Cupar.

Dear Mr. Mitchell,
   Following the request that suggestions for rural improvement should be sent in in writing prior to the meeting on Tuesday, 24th, I send the following notes for the Parish of Kemback :—
   (a) *Dura Den.*
      (1) That water and lighting should be available.
      (2) A telephone kiosk in the Den. The nearest is at Pitscottie.
   (b) *Blebo Craigs.*
      Assurance that the County water supply will pass through the main street.
      There is already a telephone kiosk here.
      Each village has a hall, but both may apply to the Carnegie Trust for assistance in improvement.

I am,
Yours faithfully,
(Signed) JANET L. LOW, *District Councillor.*

---

(5) *Letter from Miss Annie Moon, Edenfield, Springfield.*

Dear Mr. Mitchell,
   I think it is essential for the health of Springfield that the Crawley Burn be put in a sanitary condition. It comes along the south of the village, going through the railway embankment, then between my land on the east and Crawford Priory land on the west side, to the Eden, except for a septic tank at the Manse, and I believe one or two other houses. All the sewage and soapy water just comes into the open burn. When the weather is warm the smell is such that my men have to stop their work. Messrs. Shiell & Small, my solicitors in Dundee, complained about it. My gardener has often cleared away the sludge along my ground. Last year the smell was so bad that my men left the field very sick, then the gardener cleared sludge to the depth of about 3 feet. He also went over the railway and cleared slush which was running over the grating and bits of branches and about 200 tin cans, etc., which he put on the bank. When he went back later to see if it was still clear he found the old tin cans had been thrown back again. Thanks to all the rain there has been, the burn is running clear just now. A conduit would require to be put in, going right down to the river, and a large septic tank, near where the burn goes through the railway embankment, as a good number of sewers with soapy water and sewage go into the burn on the east side, near there.
   When building any more houses, would it not be wiser to do so with bedrooms upstairs? It has always been considered more healthy to do so. Usually they are more sunny and get more air and a better view, which also helps eyesight. When built 2 or 4 together (semi-detached) it saves time in building, labour, material and expense, as well as a great deal of valuable land for the nation's food for people and animals.

Yours sincerely
(Signed) ANNIE MOON.

---

6) *Letter from Rev. David Laird, The Manse, Springfield, dated 19th April, 1945.*

The County Planning Officer,
   Cupar, Fife.

Dear Sir,
   In response to the invitation at the meeting on County Planning, held on Monday, 16th April, it is my strong conviction that we need water, drainage and electric street lighting, but above all some industry in our local mill, in which jute-spinning ceased about ten years ago.

Yours faithfully,
(Signed) DAVID LAIRD, *Parish Minister.*

(7) *Letter from Town Clerk, Burgh of Falkland, dated 19th April, 1945.*

THE COUNTY CLERK,
    COUNTY BUILDINGS,
      CUPAR, FIFE.

Fife Planning Advisory Committee

DEAR SIR,

    The Town Council met last night to consider the report of the meeting held in Cupar on 9th inst.

    The Town Council are informed that extensions to both factories are envisaged after the war, but at the moment the exact nature of these extensions is not known. The S.C.W.S. Ltd. have also recently purchased a property at Liquorstane, with a view to reconstruction. These developments will in all probability necessitate the erection of more houses, in addition to the 50 or so to be erected at Back Dykes, the layout plan of which has been approved by the County Planning Committee. The Town Council has earmarked provisional sites at South Street and on the south side of the road leading to Newton of Falkland.

    The Town Council have also in view the laying-out of a children's playing field at Back Dykes to the south of the housing scheme there, but there is need of a site for a playing field for adults—particularly for bowling and tennis.

    A suitable hall for entertainments and social gatherings will also have to be provided and there is at present in the hands of the Town Council the nucleus of a fund for the purpose.

    Reference was made to one point—the lack of an adequate direct 'bus service between Cupar and Falkland. It is felt there is much need for improvement here.

I am,

Yours faithfully,

(Signed) A. B. GALLOWAY
Town Clerk.

---

(8) *Letter from J. K. Hutchison, Esq., Kinloch, Collessie, dated 20th April, 1945.*

J. M. MITCHELL, Esq.,
    COUNTY CLERK,
      CUPAR.

Fife Planning Advisory Committee

DEAR SIR,

    Referring to last Monday's meeting, it occurred to me that there are things which are urgently required immediately after the war, and things which are *not* urgently required until the country settles down. Under the first category I would classify:—

    (*a*) Water supply.
    (*b*) Drainage.
    (*c*) Extension of electric supply.

    Further, in agricultural areas there is urgent need of better-equipped blacksmiths' and joiners' shops (combined), where repairs to agricultural implements could be done promptly.

    Housing.—Many two-roomed houses, which are owned by elderly retired people might be greatly improved with moderate expenditure. I do not think many of this class of owner wish or require additional accommodation.

    Country schools of not less than 15 pupils would benefit by having a gymnasium and a small playing field, if possible, near the school.

    Under the second category—expenditure of a lot of money on bridges (such as the Tay and Forth) and big alteration of roads ; these can wait for a year or two after the war.

Yours faithfully,

(Signed) J. K. HUTCHISON.

---

(9) *Royal Burgh of Auchtermuchty—Memorandum on Post-War Planning.*

    The Royal Burgh of Auchtermuchty is situated in the centre of a purely agricultural area, and although dependent to some extent on agriculture it has had for many years basic industries in weighing machine manufacturing, iron foundries and linen and hosiery manufacturing. In addition to these there is also grain milling and quarrying.

    The present population of the Burgh is in the region of 1200 and approximately 65 per cent. of the working population is employed in local industries.

    The general amenities of the Burgh are however negligible in that there are no proper facilities for recreation, public meeting place or place of public entertainment. Such amenities have to a major extent to be sought in larger towns in the County and outside the County. There is therefore a definite population drift to these centres for pleasure and recreational facilities which has the unfortunate trend to influence the drive for a large community or town life, in preference to urban or semi-rural. It is with this aspect in view that the Council are desirous of developing Auchtermuchty on such lines that there will be a minimum drift of population and that the major portion of the populace may not only obtain employment locally but also all recreational facilities and other amenities.

    The problems facing the Council at present can be classified under the following headings :—

    (1) Housing.
    (2) General amenities.
    (3) Recreational facilities.
    (4) Development of local and introduction of new industries.
    (5) Transport facilities.
    (6) Educational and Child Welfare Services.

HOUSING.

    Although provision has already been made to meet the immediate post-war needs there is the general planning or redevelopment of certain areas in the Burgh which must be undertaken. These areas can be regarded as heirlooms passed on by " short-sighted planners " which have been with the Council for many years. The problem is one which will need very careful consideration if general features and improved amenities of the Burgh are to be maintained, and is therefore one in which Fife County Council as Planning Authority can offer valuable assistance and guidance. Contemplated road improvements of classified roads, for instance, may materially affect internal Burgh roads and may therefore influence any redevelopment.

GENERAL AMENITIES.

General amenities are meantime inadequate, and to make provision for the Burgh community such public buildings as (1) Public Hall, (2) Club and Recreation Rooms, (3) Library and (4) Picture House, would require to be developed.

Within Burgh boundaries there is an attractive " Den " which the Council had at one time considered developing. In conjunction with other ground available at a higher level it is considered that a public park and den could with advantage be provided and so help not only to improve this area but also maintain to some extent existing natural features.

The Burgh being centrally situated in an agricultural area could in effect be developed to serve as a community centre for the landward population. If developed on such lines it would not only serve as a shopping centre but also provide recreational and educational facilities.

RECREATIONAL FACILITIES.

The only recreational facilities are a bowling-green and up to the outbreak of war a golf-course. No other provisions exist, especially for the youth. In considering, therefore, any planning scheme for the Burgh regard will have to be given to :—
  (1) Playing-fields,
  (2) Tennis-courts, and
  (3) Revival of golf-course.

Such plans could quite attractively be laid out and should have the object in view of providing every suitable means of recreation.

INDUSTRY.

It is anticipated that there will be after the cessation of hostilities a revival in local industries. It is known that in local existing industries development is contemplated, but despite such hopeful signs there is still scope for the introduction of new industries.

There are sites and buildings available in the Burgh which are already serviced or could with very little expense be serviced. Being surrounded by agricultural land Auchtermuchty could with advantage be a centre for fruit-canning and preserve manufactory. While the percentage of fruit grown in the vicinity is small this branch of food production could be developed.

In addition, such light industries as the manufacture or repair of agricultural implements should be encouraged. With the existence of two foundries actually in the Burgh the whole manufacture and maintenance of equipment could be undertaken.

It is not desired that the Burgh should develop into an industrial town but it is felt that its location lends itself to the development of industries allied to agriculture.

TRANSPORT.

The Burgh is suitably serviced with main roads from all centres of the County. It is felt, however, the location of the suggested road bridges over the Forth and Tay would have a direct bearing on any development. To site the Tay Bridge, for instance, in the vicinity of Newburgh would improve considerably industrial facilities of the Burgh. Road transport for both industrial and public purposes can be considered fairly satisfactory, but railway facilities and the cost of such facilities could be improved considerably.

Auchtermuchty is a changing point for 'bus services to Perth, Stirling, and other areas, and in any planning scheme provision should be made in conjunction with the transport authorities for some form of waiting shelter for the public.

EDUCATIONAL.

It is felt that the present school is not sufficient to meet the needs of the Burgh and surrounding districts and that in any contemplated re-allocation of school centres Auchtermuchty is advantageously situated for a secondary school to serve a larger area. In addition to this factor the present school does not adequately provide for recreational facilities, or dental and other clinical services.

For some time past dental and other child welfare services have been carried out in a small room in the Town Hall, and children not only in the Burgh, but also from the surrounding landward areas have been attended to in this manner. It cannot be disputed, therefore, that clinical and other child welfare services are not sufficiently provided and in any planning scheme the County authorities should consider this aspect.

The members of the Town Council have welcomed the opportunity of briefly expressing some of the aspects relating to the planning of the Burgh and trust that any expression of opinion will be helpful to the Committee in compiling their Report and formulating their ultimate recommendations.

(10) *Burgh of Ladybank—Future Planning. A Scheme for Ladybank and District prepared and submitted on behalf of the Town Council by Mr. William Sloss, Town Clerk.*

Possibilities as to Future Planning of Ladybank. — Situated as we are in the centre of a large and presently prosperous agricultural area, and having importance as a railway junction and marshalling yard, we are better suited for future planning than many other districts in Fife, and can offer more immediate and ample services in the way of electricity, power, gas, water and drainage ; there are also large modern and other workshop and factory buildings which with slight alteration could be adapted to house new industries.

Outline of Present Chief Industries.—The principal industries presently carried on within the area are as follows :—agriculture, railway engineering, building construction, timber manufacture and malting. A start has also been made with fruit-growing, which is likely to be developed on a larger scale immediately present restrictions on building are withdrawn.

Future Prospects.—The large War Department buildings at the top of Melville Road offer considerable scope for industry after the war, as do the buildings forming the old linen factory and maltings in Commercial Road, and the market enclosure at Golf Street. The War Department buildings, erected in 1939, are of the most modern design, with central heating, and air-conditioning plant. The workshops have power fittings, air compressors, concrete pits, and neon lighting is installed throughout. There is also room for considerable extension of the buildings. The place is ideally suited for motor car manufacture, agricultural engineering, or for use as a main 'bus station and workshop. Industries for the other factory and market buildings might include jam manufacturing and canning.

The location of industry and the distribution of the industrial population has been the subject of investigation and report by many Committees which pointed out the dangers of having industry concentrated in a few large places, and the present war has brought home in tragic manner the strategic disadvantage to a country having its industries so planned. Concentration of industry in towns has also the effect of causing a drift of labour from agriculture, with the consequence that land goes out of cultivation, and the war has brought home to us the serious consequences of being dependent to a large extent on foreign-grown food. It is essential, therefore, that agricultural development should be encouraged, and how better can we do that than by spreading industry to townships such as Ladybank ?

Housing.—The present P.O.W. Camp at Annsmuir could, with slight alteration, offer temporary accommodation for any increase in the local population resulting from new industries. Electric light, water and drainage are laid on.

Annsmuir Camp.—This camp also suggests itself for development as a holiday camp, and this in itself might constitute a new industry. Features such as a swimming-pool, open-air theatre and boating-pond could be added to provide the additional attractions necessary for such a venture.

Racecourse.—The proposed industrial and social development in the area surrounding the Forth, and the extensions approved for the Dundee area, demand some national and suitable sport to interest the increased population, and we suggest the sport of kings. Annsmuir offers the ideal spot for a racecourse. The subsoil is excellent for the purpose and the flat nature of the area would allow a full view of the progress of the races throughout the course.

Transport.—While presently good, could be improved by the addition of a local service connecting Kingskettle, Freuchie, Falkland, Strathmiglo, Auchtermuchty, Dunshelt and Ladybank.

School and Community Centre.—The provision of a new school for secondary education, the inclusion in present facilities of a day nursery, clinic and welfare centre. The erection of large hall and buildings to be used as a community centre for the area would be a boon and might in some respect arrests the drift from the rural area.

---

(11) *Letter from Freuchie W.V.S., per Mrs. E. G. Adamson, Home Cottage, Freuchie, dated 21st April, 1945.*

DEAR SIRS,

The following are suggestions which I consider would be a great improvement to the village of Freuchie :—

(1) That part of the stream entering the village be piped, or a decent road bridge be erected, so that Lomond Road could be continued to Dykeside. At present there are two foot bridges over the stream which, in bad weather, are at times under water. A through road would be a great benefit to farmers, vanmen and public generally.

(2) That public lavatories be erected at the earliest possible moment. Such conveniences are long overdue here.

May I also suggest that hospital accommodation in Fife be largely extended. The County Council already have a very excellent place at Cameron Bridge which to my mind has great possibilities.

Yours faithfully,

(Signed) E. G. ADAMSON (Mrs.).

---

(12) *Cupar W.V.S.*

CAIRNIE,
CUPAR.

DEAR SIR,

I think that the provision of a new Primary School in Cupar should have a prominent place in any replanning scheme for Cupar. The present school is quite inadequate for the needs of either pupils or teachers. Owing to lack of accommodation my daughter, who started school in April of last year, attended for only a half-day until February of this year.

(Signed) M. S. PROCTOR.

M. E. TAYLOR, Esq.,
TOWN AND COUNTRY PLANNING OFFICER.

DEAR SIR,

After discussion Cupar W.V.S. think that the housing question is most important at this time.

Yours faithfully,

(Signed) C. R. NORMAND,
Burgh Leader.

---

(13) *Burgh of Newburgh—Memo from Provost Robertson.*

TO THE CHAIRMAN AND MEMBERS OF
THE PLANNING ADVISORY COMMITTEE,
CUPAR AREA.

Newburgh Town Council

GENTLEMEN,

With reference to the County Clerk's letter of 28th March, 1945, I beg, on behalf of the Town Council of the Royal Burgh of Newburgh, to put forward the following suggestions for the post-war development of our town for your consideration :—

1. The erection of a bridge across the River Tay in the vicinity of Newburgh, for the development of post-war transport and the widening of part of the Main Street.

2. *Development of Foreshore.*—Promenade and facilities for boating, fishing and bathing.

3. *Playing Fields.*—Public tennis-courts, putting-green and hockey-field.

4. New Junior Secondary School, with facilities for all kinds of sports, swimming-pool, etc.

5. *Housing.*—Extension of Burgh boundaries to enable further sites being procured.

6. Reconstruction of Gas Works and relative services and development of electricity.

The local industries, meantime, are :—

The Tayside Floorcloth Co., Ltd. (Linoleum Factory).
Robert Watson & Co., Ltd. (Oilskin Factory).
The Tay Salmon Fishings.

Suggested new industries—Canning factories for fish and fruit.

I am, Gentlemen,
Yours, faithfully,

(Signed) ANDREW ROBERTSON,
Provost.

---

(14) *Burgh of Cupar.—Memorandum by Cupar Town Council of Suggestions to the Advisory Committee of the Fife Regional Planning Committee in connection with the future development of the Burgh of Cupar.*

Preservation of Local Amenities.—Cupar is of ancient origin and besides being the County Town of Fife and the centre for administration and judicial functions, it is also the centre of an extensive agricultural area. Everything possible, therefore, should be done to maintain the character of the Burgh.

St. Catherine Street, Crossgate, Bonnygate, Kirk Wynd and Kirkgate should be maintained with continuous frontages.

Common ground at Carthaugh, Hood Park and Nicholson Park, Fluthers, Moathill, Blalowan and Common should be maintained as open spaces.

Trees, as far as safety and free air-space will permit, should be continued. Where timber has been cut down new planting should be carried out to make good the loss.

Improvement of Local Main Roads. Short-term Policy.—Construction of new road from Bonnygate at St. John's Church to Burnside Square and the widening of East Burnside by bridging the Ladyburn to obviate the bottle-neck at Bonnygate. Linked with project is the widening of Ladywynd.

North Union Street, Skinner's Steps and Back Lebanon be widened to form loop from Bank Street to Bonnygate and for the development of Kinloss Estate district.

Brighton Road and Westfield Road are likely to be built on at an early date and these roads should be widened to 40 feet in continuation of the policy of the Town Council up to 1939.

Long-term Policy.—Kirkgate should be widened to 40 feet when reconstruction of property is required. In view of the difficulty of widening Kirkwynd at Duncan Institute, it is suggested that it be restricted to one-way traffic and Short Lane utilised for other line of traffic.

Areas for Residential Purposes.—Areas earmarked for Local Authority housing purposes—Braehead, field east of Westfield House, Westfield Farm and Blalowan Park, sufficient for 150 houses.

Areas for Private Building.—Bowling Green Road, west of West Park Road and west of Hillbank, between Brighton Road and Cupar Mills.

Areas for Industries.—Areas to the south-east of Burgh adjoining railway and River Eden, viz. ground between Cupar Mills and railway. The wards between railway and South Road and Tarvit Ground, south-east of station.

Light Industries.—Area in or near General Commercial Area, viz. Bonnygate, Burnside, Haymount and West Port.

Shopping and General Commercial Areas.—The Sub-Committee feel that the shopping and commercial area should be as concentrated as possible and that there is sufficient frontage in St. Catherine Street, Crossgate, Bonnygate and Ladywynd to serve the needs of Cupar, even if the population should increase considerably.

General.—The area lying north of Bonnygate between Castlehill and Ladywynd contains a considerable quantity of old property and it is felt that a great improvement could be made by cleaning up this area. The Sub-Committee feel that the remit should be continued so that this matter might be considered further with other areas in the same position.

The remaining unbuilt-on areas in the Burgh consist of Dalgairn Policy Park, Kinloss Estate and ground between Brighton Road and Westfield Road. It is suggested that Dalgairn Park be left as an open space meantime and that the other two sites be reserved for other purposes such as Primary and Junior Schools, which are urgently required.

As the number of houses requiring to be built within the next 10 years is approximately 300, it will be necessary to consider an extension of the Burgh boundaries to accommodate half of these as well as normal development after that period.

(Signed) D. M. BAIRD,
Town Clerk.

20th January, 1945.

---

(15) *Letter from Mrs. Hutchison-Bradburne and W. M'Craw, Parish of Monimail.*

It is considered that the Fife Planning Advisory Committee should press for improved amenities for the existing population of the County, especially those in rural areas, before expenditure is undertaken on schemes such as the Forth and Tay Road Bridges, which will result inevitably in an invasion of Fife from Edinburgh and Dundee.

It is not thought that there is justification at this time for other than essential domestic expenditure, when there is so much that needs to be done to " put our own house in order."

" Fife first " might be our current policy, and far from being a purely isolationist policy it is one that will enable us to be ready for the changes that planning of a more national character will inevitably bring.

In addition to the obvious need for new houses, modern amenities of sanitation and lighting and power should receive high priority in the long neglected rural areas.

Educational facilities for the big agricultural population is another urgent and vital need in the interest of our farming future ; and it is recommended that a plan is formulated for the establishment of centres of advanced education to cater for the farm workers in the country districts throughout the County.

Prior opportunity of employment to local people in local factories in the rural areas is another point that justifies consideration for the benefit of those returning from war service.

As a first step towards continued co-ordination of ideas throughout the County and of ensuring that local opinion can always be heard, it is recommended that Local Advisory Committees to the Central Advisory Committee be appointed in every parish.

Urban and rural needs must often be at variance and many remote districts feel that they are overlooked to the advantage of those nearer to authority. Local Advisory Committees should help to obviate this and to give a better chance to outlying communities of their fair share of post-war planning. That their general amenities of life fall deplorably short of those in town districts cannot be denied ; and it is felt that it is of the first importance to the post-war agricultural prosperity of Fife to keep our country dwellers from migrating to the towns by facing up to their comparative discomforts and improving them as a priority measure.

(Signed) RUTH HUTCHISON-BRADBURNE
W. M'CRAW.

23rd April, 1945.

NOTES TAKEN AT MEETING HELD IN THE TOWN HALL, ANSTRUTHER
30th April, 1945

Mr. Carlow (Chairman).

Referring to Provost Carstairs' speech at the last meeting, Mr. Carlow said that one of the things mentioned by the Provost was the procuring of boats. It seemed to Mr. Carlow from the Herring Report that the Government had set aside, or intended to set aside, a very considerable sum to be used as grants for the purpose of boats and gear, and perhaps the Provost might be good enough to say a few words in regard to that later on in the meeting. They knew there would be great fluctuations and, rightly or wrongly, it was previously reported that sometimes boys of 16 and 17 got up to £30 while at other times they got £4 or £5, and it was hoped to get rid of these fluctuations by dealing with the herring by dehydration or some other method, in regard to which Mr. Carlow wished the Provost to inform them. It was necessary to get some means of taking up the glut and giving it out to the public when there was a scarcity, and it was quite clear to anyone what an improvement that would be. Mr Carlow said he would like the audience to contradict and criticise his statements.

Speaking on the question of rural depopulation Mr. Carlow remarked that this was due to the fact that there were better houses in the towns than in the country, and the wives wanted to live in the towns in order to obtain these better conditions. Another reason given at the last meeting was that children were taken to schools in the bigger towns and were brought up with a sort of idea in their minds that everything is better in the towns than in the country. At the last meeting General Crosbie explained that a good deal of the trouble in regard to housing conditions was due to the want of necessary materials. It was also stated at the last meeting, in regard to schooling, that some children had to travel so far to school and transport was so inconvenient that they spent an hour and a half each way in getting to and from school. Mr. Carlow went on to say that he had received a list of the miles to schools from the various little districts in the surrounding country, which went up to 2½ miles. That was rather a matter for the Education Authority. He appealed for as many suggestions as possible on the question of rural depopulation.

Mr. Carlow went on to say that he had been accused of being too strong on the question of getting wages before amenities, and explained that what he meant was that industry mus tpay its way otherwise they would be building houses and amenities for a population which might fade away because of the failure of industry. The most important thing was to get industry remunerative and permanent and then they could see about amenities, etc., for the people.

In concluding, Mr. Carlow asked for as many suggestions as possible from the people of the district in order to enable the Committee to complete their Report.

Mr. *Christie* remarked that he was only going to speak for a very short time to-night because they all knew that the Committee's object was to ask for suggestions.

This method of going round the County and gathering suggestions would, Mr. Christie thought, lead to some very useful results. Wherever the Committee went they found there were one or two far-sighted people who could foresee some of the changes which were likely to take place in the next 50 or 60 years. These changes were coming more rapidly than they realised, and it was very difficult to judge the ultimate changes which were to be, changes such as housing of farm workers in community centres instead of on the farms. This suggestion would be met by a great deal of opposition, and probably it would be necessary to come to a compromise between the two points of view. Mr. Christie went on to say that he had been talking to someone just that day on that subject, and he thought the general opinion was that the present method of providing houses was just breaking down, and that some other method would have to be adopted. What that method would be he did not know. The County had been producing some very good ideas for experimental work and perhaps approaching the matter in too hesitant a manner. He was not quite sure whether the houses which had been produced were just up to standard and hoped that the County would loosen its purse-strings and build buildings to last two centuries instead of 70 years. "If we are going to build here, it doesn't matter whether it is refrigeration plants or houses, let us build to last," he said.

With all this talk about refrigeration and dehydration it might be that there was an idea that the Government would come along and build a plant. It might be possible to squeeze a small subsidy from the Government, but if Anstruther wanted any of these plants they would have to be built by far-seeing people who saw a profit in them.

Mr. *Carlow's* next remarks were in the form of questions—" Why don't we get dehydrating and refrigerating plant to equalise surplus fish and the want of fish ?" " What stands in the way ?" " Why can't we get some of these numerous grants the Government is going to give—loans up to £1,300,000 and grants up to £820,000 for boats, gear, etc. ?" " Why couldn't they get on with the provision of these plants either entirely independent of Government assistance or with Government assistance as the need might be, if refrigeration and dehydration were the things necessary to restore prosperity to the fishing industry ?"

Provost *Carstairs* began by saying that in the first place he would have liked a very much bigger meeting and was quite frankly disappointed. He could not be blamed for being a pessimist so far as public meetings were concerned. The reason he suggested that the meeting should be held in the evening was to take the " grouse " out of the mouths of a good number of individuals. The first complaint would have been that the meeting was held when they could not attend, and yet none of them had turned up at this meeting. The Provost said he was pleased to see Captain Symon present, as he felt the last meeting had not received the support it deserved from the local press.

The Provost went on to say that it was like telling them if it came on rain the pavements would get wet, to say that the future was going to be immensely different from what had ever been before.

He had preached for quite a long time that the Burghs of St. Monance, Pittenweem and Anstruther ought to be in a better position in the future than they had been for many years in regard to fishing. That morning he had received a letter which he was very interested to read to the meeting :—

" SHEERNESS.

" DEAR SIR,
I have heard your name mentioned very often in connection with fishing and boats, and now that we, my brother and I, intend to make our home in your locality I would like your advice and help, if you please, in our problem.
Briefly, my brother and I want a job and a home in Anstruther.
Why do we pick on Anstruther ? Well, because the boat we are out to get—providing, of course, that the Fishery Board plans to aid fishermen mature—is one of those Government boats capable, during the summer months, of competing with the Danes and Swedes at seine-net fishing in the North Sea. From many conversations with Moray Firth fishermen who have tried the fishing grounds in your locality, I have come to the same conclusions as they, namely, that Anstruther will be one of the principal seine-net fishing ports.
My brother and I have been employed at the west coast for 14 years previous to the war and do not intend to go back there. I was skipper and my brother engineer (Diesel engines). We are both experienced in all methods of fishing such as seine-net fishing ; drift-net fishing ; trawling ; ring-net herring fishing and lines, in that order of efficiency.
That's it as briefly as I am capable of putting it. Well, what can you do as a public-spirited man to help us coming off the Services ? We have both married since war began.

Yours faithfully,
.... "

The Provost was of the opinion that the fishing industry was going to have a much better chance after the war. Mr. Carlow, he said, wondered why there had not been that intensive cultivation of the fishing industry which one would have expected. A Herring Industry Board was appointed by the Government some 15 years ago, but unfortunately that Board did not come up to expectations and the Government dismissed the Board. That Board was in place of the Fishery Board for Scotland, of which the Provost was a member for 12 years, but the Government saw fit to take the handling of the herring industry out of the hands of the Fishery Board. Then a completely new Herring Board was appointed consisting of three members and they were in the process of handling the matter just when war broke out. For the war period that Herring Industry Board was absorbed by the Ministry of Food. After further agitations and conferences the Government appointed a Committee to deal with post-war problems, of which the Provost was also a member. That Committee issued a Report, and it was a very striking fact that the Report was hardly altered at all when incorporated in the Bill which went through Parliament. Provost Carstairs said that he had received an invitation to go to Edinburgh to-morrow with reference to boats. They could rest assured, he said, that he would do everything in his power to endeavour to obtain a new and modern type of fleet. The first Herring Board's powers were somewhat limited, but the new Herring Board have been given very wide powers and need not be reluctant to go forward. If they liked to handle the situation with boldness and imagination the fishing industry would have a chance which it had not had in the past.

It must have been a very sad fact to many of them, he said, that so much of what was good fish was dumped because of glut. It was not only because the markets could not absorb them. The thing was that on Monday, Tuesday, Wednesday, there might be a scarcity of herring, while on Thursday, Friday, Saturday, there might be far more than the whole port's organisation could handle. Refrigeration certainly would help them a very great deal. Provost Carstairs then mentioned the well-known methods of treating herring—(1) freshing ; (2) " klondyking " ; (3) curing ; (4) " redding " ; and (5) meal and oil.

Speaking on boats, the Provost stated that the steam drifter had been a very fine boat and could take weather that vessels twice its size could not take, but it was only suitable for two forms of fishing. The new type would be very much more economical and would also be a boat adaptable and suitable for drift net ; seine net ; and great line within a certain distance of the shore. The Provost was anxious to see the three burghs in Anstruther area benefiting from the new conditions which were going to be very much improved. There were great opportunities for young men if they would just have courage—the courage of their own abilities and knowledge, because no young man, or young men, need be without a boat if they liked to go forward. Most probably there would be a " means test." He was keen on helping young men coming out of the Services. There would, he thought, be a possibility of chartering some of the vessels built by the Admiralty to tide the men over while they were having their own boats built. Substantial loans would probably be available ; for instance, on a vessel costing £3000 a grant of up to £1000 could be arranged. They would probably be asked to lay down 10 per cent. of the cost of a boat—£300—and the other £1700 would be loaned on the annuity principle of so much per annum to include capital and interest, spread over 20 years. Very big helps would also be available in procuring nets and gear. Nets were an extremely " perishable " form of capital, and a fisherman could not be expected to take on his hands capital which was so easily " perishable."

So far as selling and handling the herring was concerned, science would have to come into the picture. The trouble was that science had not been brought sufficiently into the fishing industry before. Before the war Russia took practically three-quarters of this country's catch of herring, but now they don't want them. In the White Sea they shut in live herring with electrified netting and took them out as they wanted them. There were shoals of herring swimming round our coast, representing one of the best forms of food that could be got so far as protein efficiency was concerned. What was needed was more scientific handling. The Provost thought that if the Herring Board used its powers some of the difficulties would quickly disappear.

Continuing, Provost Carstairs stated that facilities offered in all three ports in the district were excellent, especially in Anstruther, being the bigger port. There was no reason why East Fife should not be made one of the big centres, because Anstruther district represented the biggest winter herring fishing in Great Britain and that was their chance.

Speaking on the holiday industry, Provost Carstairs remarked that this was wholly dependent on housing, but as Mr. Carlow had pointed out at the last meeting, the Advisory Committee had nothing whatever to do with housing problems, but certainly housing would be at the bottom of the improvement of the locality and Burgh. Referring to the letter which he had read to the meeting, Provost Carstairs remarked that there was an example of two men who could not come to Anstruther unless they could be provided with a house.

Mr. Christie asked if meal and oil required processing.

Provost Carstairs replied that there were factories in Scotland, mostly in Aberdeen, where whitefish offal was converted into meal and oil, but he did not know of any where herring were dealt with.

The former Fishery Board was a Government Department and therefore could not buy and sell, but the new Herring Board had power to be buyer and seller. For several years they were greatly troubled with what was called " one man buying " by the Germans ; twenty or thirty firms in Germany buying Anstruther, Pittenweem and St. Monance herring, but often only one firm bought for the whole lot. They had had no counter to that, but Provost Carstairs was pleased to say that in the Bill the Herring Industry Board can be the one selling party and so counter the " one buying " idea with the " one selling " idea.

Mr. Carlow said it was always a pleasure to listen to an expert and he wished to ask one or two questions. He wanted to know whether young fishermen to-day understood that these grants were available for them and if there were any means of young fishermen being told how to go about obtaining those grants. He also wanted to know what had to be done to get a processing factory established in Anstruther for dealing with herring. Another question put by Mr. Carlow was whether meal and oil were made from offal or whether they were made from whole fish.

Provost Carstairs replying, assured Mr. Carlow that very wide steps would be taken to advertise in all the fishing and other papers setting out the conditions which would be available to fishermen for both boats and gear.

With regard to dehydration, Provost Carstairs informed the meeting that only very fresh herring could be dehydrated. Dehydrating could not be undertaken with herring two days old, but so far as meal and oil were concerned the whole fish was used without being gutted at all. The proposal was, of course, to enable prices to be levelled out, and that could be done very successfully so far as refrigeration of herring was concerned.

A member of the audience said, as a non-expert, he had been listening very carefully to explanations and gathered that the necessity for offal arises from gluts. He wished to know if gluts arose in different ports would a factory be required for each of these ports, to which the Provost replied that a plant would be set up at a central point suitable to the area in which the gluts occurred. The alternative was a floating plant, but that had grave disadvantages.

Mr. Carlow remarked that it was a new point to the Committee that prices for the natural herring would always be more profitable than possibility of dehydrating the fish.

Provost Carstairs explained that dehydration was not suggested as a matter for surplus herring. Dehydration could be added to the list already given by him as a sixth way of dealing with herring. Dehydration might easily be a means of increasing the sales of herring in our own home market.

Bailie Gardner inquired whether the Herring Industry Board had any powers to introduce distribution. It appeared to him that gluts were largely due to some difficulty in transportation and distribution, and he thought something on the lines of the Milk Marketing Board might help.

Provost Carstairs explained that gluts often occurred in a single night. The glut might be at Wick or Castle Bay, and it would be a difficult matter to hold transport and labour sufficient to handle a glut which might never occur. The Fishery Board lost a considerable sum of money one year in holding labour and transport at a port where gluts had often occurred, but it so happened that no glut occurred that year.

Bailie *Gardner* asked if that was not likely to occur with dehydration and refrigeration and Provost Carstairs answered " No." Dehydration and refrigeration would be within reasonable distance of landing ports, whereas in the past the only places to send surplus herring to were London, Manchester, Glasgow, and other more distant markets.

Rev. *J. A. Inglis* remarked that it seemed to him the Planning Committee's point was, was there any possibility of a dehydrating plant in this area or any possibility of a need for it and ought they to press for one.

Provost *Carstairs*—That would need to be gone into very carefully. For instance, if a glut had occurred only once in 10 years in this area then the possibility was that their chance would be less than other ports such as Fraserburgh, where gluts occur much more frequently, and all the facts would have to be taken into account by the Herring Board. The Committee could put forward the suggestion in view of the fact that dehydration was likely to be a future form of food and Anstruther was catching herring in the winter-time when no other ports were, to anything like the same extent.

Mr. *H. H. Edie* asked if the same dehydrating plant could be used for potatoes when there was a surplus. He had had to give away good potatoes at 10/- a ton when there was a surplus. Next year's potatoes went up to £4 or £5 per ton and if there was any surplus at all the prices slumped down. At present the Government have been buying best quality potatoes for dehydration. These potatoes were being dehydrated at a factory at Montrose.

Provost *Carstairs* said he could not answer that question but hoped it would be possible, as the usual thing to go with herring was potatoes!

Mr. *Taylor*, County Planning Officer, was then asked to say a few words to the meeting on dehydration. Dehydrating of fish was a comparatively new process, he said, as would be seen from the fact that when he had inquiries made in London his letter was passed from the Royal Institute of British Architects to the Ministry of Agriculture and Fisheries Library, London, on to Ministry of Agriculture and Fisheries, Edinburgh, from there to Department of Scientific and Industrial Research, Edinburgh, and on to Herring Industry Board. He said he was endeavouring to obtain as much information as possible on the matter.

Mr. *Carlow* expressed his appreciation of all the information supplied by Provost Carstairs on all matters dealing with the fishing industry.

With regard to housing, Mr. Carlow remarked that that question was not tied up with the Committee's remit and in his opinion the matter of housing would still be a problem 20 years hence.

Provost *Lawson* thought that Anstruther area lent itself to fishing and agriculture, but that apart from that there was coal in the area which, if it could be worked and yield a profit, would be a great asset. The next best thing, he thought, would be to develop the area into a sort of Brighton of the North to encourage summer visitors.

Provost Lawson asked if there was any grant available for restoring golf-courses, to which Mr. Dow, Town Clerk, stated that compensation from the Government was available for restoring any golf-courses which had been damaged by military operations, etc.

Mr. *Carlow* did not think that the coal seams in this area would attract exploitation because there were more certain places where a person could put down a pit with confidence. He had examined the coal at Grangemuir about 30 years ago but was not impressed by the prospects.

The question of visitors was entirely tied up with accommodation for visitors. If they could provide suitable housing then he felt sure the tourists would be attracted.

A *member of the audience* remarked that he gathered that the Committee's plans contemplated the position of 50 or 60 years hence when a huge population from the West would be expected to require holiday accommodation in this area. He wondered if it would not be possible to create a satellite town further along the coast, perhaps at Shell Bay, and have it developed by a development company or railway company.

Mr. *Carlow* said the Committee were trying to look ahead 50 or 60 years and plan now so that nothing would be done to prevent the natural development which might take place in 50 or 60 years' time. They didn't want to put down a housing scheme where there should have been an arterial road. What they were trying to do was to forecast the needs and requirements, drift of industry and development, in Fife so that nothing should be done to stand in the way of the development of the County to the best advantage of everybody.

Mr. *Christie* referred to the initial survey of the area when there was a suggestion that since the harbour at Pittenweem had been altered some time ago it was no longer safe anchorage in certain weather, and it was further stated that the people of Pittenweem were convinced that the expenditure of something like £7000 would cover the cost of making the harbour safe. Mr. Christie wondered if it would help in any way if the Advisory Committee took the matter up.

Mr. *Mackintosh, Town Clerk*, said that about 1904 the middle pier at Pittenweem was demolished and a new middle pier built further east to make the harbour easier for the type of craft then used. The unfortunate effect of the alteration, however, was to make the inner mouth of the harbour straight open to the sea, and now the greatest difficulty was being experienced in tying up small boats in safety. The proposal which was being discussed was to fill up the existing entrance and make a new entrance somewhat nearer the shore which would be quite easy anchorage for modern motor boats, and at the same time to put up a breakwater at the outside.

Mr. *Eadie, Cornceres*, speaking on the question of housing of the agricultural workers in community centres, said he was not quite sure that the ploughman would be pleased at that. That was taking the men away from their work to amenities and he wondered if it would not be more practicable to take the amenities to the workers. The men would have to go home for their meals and in order to be in time for their work in the mornings would have to leave the house at 5 o'clock. It was far better to have houses for the workers near their work and the men would have a greater interest in their work.

Mr. *Christie* replying, said that the Advisory Committee hoped to have a meeting with a number of outstanding agriculturists in Fife, at which the question would be thrashed out and the various points of view obtained. He referred to the report which had been received from the Gateside area. In this area there were 17 farms, and it was strongly represented to the Committee that as many workers as possible should live in community centres and travel from there to their work. It was admitted that workers such as shepherds, cattlemen and horsemen would have to be housed on the farms, but there were certain of the farm workers who could be housed in centres.

Mr. *Edie* wondered if a small industry in making fish-boxes could not be started. He felt that a lot of valuable space was being taken up in goods trains with these boxes.

Provost *Carstairs* said the proper method would be to have one-journey boxes. At the present time some of the boxes went 12 times to London and back and the bacteria in the boxes was really terrible. The difficulty of having boxes manufactured in the district was the lack of timber.

On the motion of Provost Carstairs the meeting accorded a vote of thanks to the Committee.

Letter received from Gilbert R. McGarva, Esq., Balcarres Estate Office, Colinsburgh, is given as an appendix to these notes.

APPENDIX REFERRED TO

The Chairman,
Fife Town and Country Planning
   Advisory Committee, Anstruther.

Balcarres Estate Office,
   Colinsburgh.
   30th April, 1945.

Rural Depopulation—Rural Housing

Dear Sir,

At the meetings of your Committee recently held at St. Andrews and Cupar, the County Planning Officer stated there is a steady depopulation in East Fife. He did not indicate whether it was rural, urban or both.

Generally, in the past, the private local residenter provided the housing of the village and hamlet. In the agricultural area it was provided by the landowner. Now, with the high costs, severe County byelaws and oppressive Rent Restriction Acts, the supply and maintenance of housing by the former has ceased as he declined to take the risk. The latter is financially unable to meet his obligations. The days of indulgent and prosperous house and land owners have gone. The day of trouble for the farm owner-occupier dawns when incomes based upon farming subsidies suffer serious reduction. In fact, evidence of this was recently disclosed in an agenda for an N.F.U. (Anstruther Branch) Meeting.

The recently issued Report of the Scottish Land and Properties Federation from a questionnaire circulated to 163 members in thirty Scottish counties on Landed Estate Maintenance gives piquant reading. Facts and figures stated therein are frequently not appreciated by those conversant with agriculture, whilst they are almost unknown to the public at large. The Report discloses that farm rents are practically the same as forty years ago, whilst in that period taxes, costs and wages have risen to as high as 300 per cent. The estimated capital value of the farm lands under review on a twenty years' purchase basis is almost 6½ millions. After maintenance expenditure and owner's local burdens have been met the percentage return on capital invested works out at 1¾ per cent. Government Departments for death-duty purposes demand a higher year's purchase ; therefore, the return is actually less than stated. This small return on capital very seldom allows of any sums being put to reserve to meet improvements of a capital nature of death-duties. Land ownership is a branch of a productive industry, and it is therefore not unreasonable to expect a return on capital in parity with other industries as it is desirable that money should continue to be brought back into the industry if agriculture as a whole is to be put on a high productive level. Farm buildings and equipment can only be kept up-to-date with substantial outlay. The lack of confidence in the future is definitely reflecting now on expenditure urgently needed, because there are strong suspicions that agriculture will be sacrificed in the interests of other industries after 1948, when the guaranteed prices cease. The evil effects of death-duties are another of the main contributing factors for the dilapidations in the past. Unless steps are now taken to assist rural housing, etc., another decade will witness small farms gradually being absorbed by their larger neighbours. This undoubtedly will lead to more economic production but disastrous to the industry and rural life.

It may be said that the foregoing report indicates that the time is ripe for land nationalisation. That obviously would be a far from profitable venture for the State. If the land were acquired by confiscation even without compensation the return to the State would be very small, because it would lose the revenue at present derived from it in the form of taxes, to meet which payment out of revenue from other sources is very frequently used. From the above it is evident that to provide the standard of housing now required for rural areas is quite outwith the ability of the average landowner. To modernise cottages under the various Housing Acts cannot be done for less than £850 per cottage. New cottages cost about £1000 each. The terms upon which grants have been administered in the past by the County Council are responsible for many cases of unsatisfactory reconditioning. The day has arrived when such work carried out fifteen to twenty years ago under subsidised schemes is out of date and new housing is necessary. Had terms been more favourable then, many more new cottages would have been erected and many fewer slums reconditioned in these parts. Local authority building regulations should be standardised, less reconditioning of existing cottages allowed and a general standard of enforcement of modern buildings instituted. Considering that local authorities supply housing *ad lib* for the occupation of miners, linoleum workers, co-operative, soap and oil workers, engineers, etc., etc., why should they not also provide the requisite housing for the agricultural worker ? Another unfortunate point is that reference to the agricultural wages fixed under the recent Acts discloses that a modern farm cottage of three rooms with hot and cold water circulation, w.c., hand-basin, bath, wash-tubs, etc., and garden is valued as a worker's perquisite at 4/6 per week=£11, 14/- per annum.

The agricultural worker is possessed of high technical skill but generally is paid at a less rate than the urban artisan, and, unfortunately, his housing accommodation is gradually comparing less favourably with the latter. If the rural depopulation, particularly in East Fife, is to be checked, the programme of housing must be accelerated, otherwise the prosperous agriculture anticipated in the Prime Minister's Declaration at the recent Conservative Party Conference cannot be obtained. Rural housing will affect the future of agriculture because, when the present generation of workers dies out, their successors will not be found if conditions are not to their liking and not comparable with other workers. With the exception of housing required on the larger farms for key workers, such as grieves, cattlemen and shepherds, the rural housing should be found by local authorities, placing it in or near existing villages or hamlets or in small groups at cross-roads. It is better that the worker shall have to travel some distance to his work than that he and his family shall reside remote from schools, 'buses, shops, church, and all other amenities of village life. These conditions cannot be obtained in scattered cottages about the countryside provided primarily to give accommodation to workers within easy reach of the farms where employed. Alternatively, to provide housing for rural workers by private enterprise, generous facilities and encouragement on terms at least equal to local authorities for their housing schemes must be forthcoming. Then, key and other workers may be housed on the farms on which they are employed. Further, the procedure for the release of rural houses which have been let to other than farm workers and are necessary for the periodic accommodation of them should be simplified and speeded up. Meantime, numerous houses stand empty on farms on account of this difficulty. Transport facilities should also be extended. Experience shows that farm workers select occupations where there is a 'bus service to the neighbouring town or village. Undoubtedly the linking-up of remote rural areas with communities and shops is, in the minds of the workers, an attraction and a valid convenience. Nowadays the farm worker has considerable leisure. He and his family are not content to spend their Saturday afternoons and holidays roaming round the house and garden situated on the edge of a farm road or field.

The provision of rural housing by the local authorities gives the worker security of tenure against his employer. He is entitled to it. His employer has it against his landowner. Further, he will render equal service under these conditions and will feel much more independent.

It is estimated that in Britain in 1951 the number of people over 65 years of age will exceed 5,600,000. Accommodation in rural areas in small houses for a portion of these should be provided by local authorities and, in like manner, for a considerable number of single people of middle age. Through this lack, these categories often occupy rural houses much in excess of their requirements simply because they cannot obtain suitable smaller accommodation. This causes an unnecessary waste of housing which could be utilised for larger families.

Yours faithfully,
   (Sgd.)   GILBERT R. McGARVA.

NOTES TAKEN AT INITIAL SURVEY OF THE LOCHGELLY AND DUNFERMLINE AREAS

7th May, 1945

LOCHGELLY

The Committee were met by the Town Clerk and the Burgh Surveyor, the Provost being unable to attend.

Mr. Carlow explained briefly to these gentlemen the purpose of the meeting and also the task undertaken by the Editorial Sub-Committee of the Planning Advisory Committee, which Committee consisted of Sir James Irvine representing the cultural side, Mr. Christie representing agriculture, and himself who could be looked upon as representing in part the industries of the County. The Committee were anxious to help the people of Lochgelly and district as much as they possibly could, and hoped that at the public meetings which were to take place later on the people would come forward with their views on what should be done to improve their district.

Mr. Lumsden, Burgh Surveyor, submitted a plan of the Burgh of Lochgelly. He explained that there was no room for development within the Burgh boundaries and that these would require to be extended. He mentioned two pieces of ground which the Town Council were anxious to have brought within the Burgh—a strip in Cartmore Road and piece lying to the south of the burgh bounding Old Newton Road. He went on to say that the Melgund Place area was full of coal and not suitable for building purposes.

In answer to Mr. Carlow's question regarding industries in Lochgelly the Burgh Surveyor said that coal was the mainstay in Lochgelly. The unfortunate thing was that in Lochgelly they had no employment for female labour except a laundry, employing about 20 girls.

Mr. Carlow raised the question as to whether the proposed Tay Road Bridge should be located at Newburgh or Newport. The Burgh Surveyor was of the opinion that a bridge at Newburgh would serve the needs of Lochgelly much better than a bridge at Newport. All metal and whinstone came from the Newburgh quarries.

Speaking on the question of water supply the Burgh Surveyor said that Lochgelly could not supply a much-extended Burgh without help, but he expressed the view that there should not be four or five water mains lying alongside each other. There should be one big main. The same thing applied to sewage. It should all come under one scheme. He maintained that piping should have been laid and the sewage carried to the sea instead of into the River Ore.

COWDENBEATH

The Committee proceeded to Cowdenbeath, where they were met by the Provost and members of the Town Council.

The Provost extended a hearty welcome to the Committee and Mr. Carlow thanked the Provost and members of the Town Council for being so kind as to meet them.

Mr. Carlow then briefly explained the purpose of the meeting and called upon Mr. Taylor to put forward any questions which he might have.

Mr. Taylor said he did not know Cowdenbeath as well as he would like, but there were one or two points which would crop up. One was that the present industry was mainly coal and Cowdenbeath might be termed a one-industry town, and therefore he assumed that the people of Cowdenbeath would like additional industries. The Provost stated that Cowdenbeath's linen industry had stopped and they visualised something such as Mr. Taylor mentioned. They realised that the coal, especially in the Burgh of Cowdenbeath, was being worked out. He remembered the time when there were 22 pits round about Cowdenbeath, but now there were only three or four. Visualising these things they contacted their M.P.s regarding the possibility of bringing some light industries into the Burgh. They were still trying to contact Mr. Dalton on the matter. Realising that they had all the necessary amenities, it was just possible that they might get a light industry for making shovels and picks, etc., which were very essential to the working of the pits. They had also had a discussion regarding the getting of material out of coal. Everybody knew that a great many of the by-products of coal were being lost. The Provost went on to say that Cowdenbeath had two railways and quite a number of sites could be suggested for light industries. It might be true to say that if the Government contemplated going in for that side of the business in connection with coal they could not do better than start in the neighbourhood of Cowdenbeath.

A member of the Town Council said he thought the Provost had pretty well outlined the discussions which had taken place inside the Town Council and also with the M.P.s. He supported the Provost's view that Cowdenbeath was a very suitable place in which to manufacture shovels, picks, etc., and he also thought that many of the safety appliances required in the pits could be made in Cowdenbeath. In the Burgh there were sites available for these industries, and they also prided themselves in the fact that they had a water supply which could serve a population three times the size of the present one. They had visualised as a Town Council that the trend of events was all to the West and they had marked out their programme. The two railways mentioned by the Provost could be utilised in so far as development was concerned.

Mr. Taylor wondered if he was right in assuming that the Cowdenbeath area might become a depressed one owing to the fact that the pits were moving away from there, but the Provost did not think that was likely to occur. The Burgh Surveyor said that the Town Council's idea was that Cowdenbeath so far as coal was concerned would be finished, and they were going to set about replanning the Burgh as a residential locality, knowing that to the east and west there would be big new mining developments. They felt that with modern transport there would be no difficulty in housing people in Cowdenbeath and transporting them to their work outside. The Provost remarked that Cowdenbeath had always been the centre for West Fife coal-mining area and would continue to be so for a long period of years.

Mr. Taylor then asked if tools for use in pits varied with the area, to which the Provost replied that in this area they were all very much the same.

The question of roads was then dealt with, and Mr. Carlow said the most important point was whether the proposed Tay Road Bridge should be in the Newburgh district or near Newport. The Provost stated that the Town Council had not reached a decision on the matter, but it seemed to him that the best place would be at Newburgh. The Burgh Surveyor thought the site of the bridge was more or less defined. The aim was to have a great arterial road right through Scotland, and he didn't see the purpose in going to Dundee. Mr. Mitchell stated it was right to say there was a school of thought that linked the new Forth Road Bridge with the proposed new Tay Bridge and that would be a trunk road, with an alternative to this road which would go via Kelty and Kinross to Perth. With the former you would have a road running right through Fife to Dundee. The main objection was that you would land yourself right in the centre of Dundee.

Mr. Carlow thought the trunk road might come east of Loch Leven and cross the Tay at Mugdrum Island and so serve the purpose of getting to Perth and the North, and also serve the purpose of connecting the coalfields with Dundee and the industrial belt south of Newburgh. Mr. Mitchell remarked that the County Road Board had backed the Forth Road Bridge with crossing at the Mackintosh Rock site. A member of the Town Council thought that agriculturists might have some arguments to set against the building of great new roads and bridges. Mr. Christie remarked that they were not quite sure on that as they hadn't met agriculturists to discuss the question. A huge road to Dundee would use up much agricultural land, and destroy farms which had been built up for years. Probably from the long-range view agriculturists would not be against the idea of the ultimate development at Dundee, but for immediate development Newburgh did seem to be the more sensible position for a bridge. One thing which had not been brought out was that if the bridge was built near Dundee there would be a tremendous outflow of people into Fife.

With regard to housing the Burgh Surveyor stated that Cowdenbeath was in need of approximately 2000 houses. They did not anticipate that Cowdenbeath would be any bigger in population than it was to-day, but accommodation would have to be found for people who were living in bad houses, overcrowded houses and for those who had no house at all. There was no ground available inside the Burgh for building purposes. After a long series of Mining Engineers' Reports they had been informed that the area to the west of the Burgh boundary near Hill of Beath was the only ground suitable and steps were almost completed for the feuing of that ground.

In local planning the Burgh Surveyor hoped the County Council would keep in mind the main street of Cowdenbeath. It was the only street they had for carrying through traffic, and at different times during the day it was almost impossible for anything to move. There was a definite need for a by-pass road to ease the main street.

In answer to Mr. Taylor's question regarding open spaces the Burgh Surveyor said they had a public park of about 15 acres along with three or four other open spaces which would be developed as playing fields. There was also a golf-course just outside the Burgh which, with a little money and attention, could be made one of the nicest golf-courses in Fife.

Raising the question of light industries Mr. Christie was anxious to know if there was any indication of approach by private enterprise to create such an industry or if it was just hoped that such a thing might develop. The Provost replied that there was nothing definite so far.

In answer to Mr. Carlow's question as to how many women were employed in the Fife Coal Company's Works, the Provost replied that there were 450 people working there who would not have been gathered together in Cowdenbeath had it not been for the fact that the Fife Coal Company had centralised their workshops and stores.

Mr. Christie asked if the Burgh's Milk Supply was brought in from a distance, to which the Provost replied that 90 per cent. of the milk distributed came from the Co-operative Society.

INVERKEITHING

Mr. Carlow thanked the representatives of the Town Council for meeting the Committee and gave a general outline of the task undertaken by the Advisory Committee. The Committee did not want roads to be put down where they would interfere with any proposed development. They wanted everything to be done for the general good of the County. Mr. Carlow intimated that a public meeting would be held in Dunfermline on 22nd May, at which meeting the Committee hoped that the Provost and others interested would be able to furnish the Committee with their views and ideas so that when they did make their plans they would endeavour not to interfere with the public's desires.

Mr. Carlow raised the question of existing industries and industries which might be brought into the district. He mentioned Caldwell's Paper Works and Ward's Shipbreaking Company. (At this point the Provost joined the meeting.) The Provost stated that the potentialities of this district were more or less limited, but that so far as the geographical position of the Burgh was concerned they were well situated by rail, sea and road. They had to depend on labour in the Dockyard at Rosyth in conjunction with the paper mill and some quarries.

Mr. Carlow said he assumed Inverkeithing would be in favour of the bridge over the Forth, to which the Provost replied that they wanted to see it as soon as possible.

Inverkeithing Town Council were anxious to introduce new industries into their district, but the difficulty was what inducement were they going to hold out to firms which might wish to come into their area. Mr. Carlow said the Committee had come against that difficulty often in the past and he had suggested that it would be a good thing if the inducements, such as gas, electricity, water supply, old factories, etc., could be set out in a schedule which might be kept in the County Offices, Cupar, or in Burgh Offices, and occasional advertisements put in the *Scotsman*. Mr. Carlow thought that the manufacture of wearing apparel attractive to the naval personnel at the dockyard or to workers in the dockyard would be a very suitable thing for Inverkeithing to develop.

Mr. Christie asked what quarrying work was going on as he felt that with development of all the proposed new roads and bridges there was going to be a great demand for material with which to build these roads. The Town Clerk replied that there were two quarries which could be worked and another one which might be opened up. The Provost stated that the quarries functioning in Inverkeithing district sent the bulk of their material to the South. They were greatly hindered by the tides. If a certain amount of dredging was done in the vicinity of these quarries they would employ three times the number of men. That would be one way to create employment in the district.

Inverkeithing harbour could take boats of 400-500 tons but would like to increase that to 1200 tons. On Mr. Christie asking what was preventing dredging the Provost replied that the firms concerned were not endowed with sufficient capital. Councillor Pattison remarked that Inverkeithing had one of the best harbours in the country. Full development of the harbour was necessary. The Town Clerk expressed the view that if additional harbour accommodation was available they might be able to bring boats right in. The harbour used to take vessels of 1700 tons, and if vessels of that size could not get in now the reason was silting up and it looked as if it would be possible to remove that by dredging. Mr. Christie inquired who was responsible for harbours and was informed that the Forth Conservancy Board dealt with all ports. Councillor Pattison remarked that Ward's Shipbreaking Company had built themselves a quay to take the largest vessel afloat.

The Town Clerk thought that the one difficulty in way of extension of existing industry was housing shortage. The position was, he said, that the paper mill could not obtain accommodation within the Burgh for their existing employees and therefore the existing employment level was about 200 below peace-time, and they anticipated still further extension in post-war period. With regard to the two quarries the position was much the same. Present employment level was about one-quarter that of peace-time.

In answer to Mr. Christie's question as to whether there were any good garages in Inverkeithing, Councillor Pattison said the garage they had was big enough for the size of the place. Mr. Christie expressed the view that with the building of the proposed new roads would come a great increase in traffic and that there would be room for development of garages.

Again raising the question of the harbour, Mr. Christie asked if any representation had been made to the Conservancy Board, to which the answer was in the negative. Councillor Pattison said the idea was to reclaim a great part of the bay which was shallow. Mr. Pattison thought there was one thing which ought to be kept in mind, and that was that even although the new roads came they did not want to lose their trade to the South.

The Provost thought it would be a very good investment if the County of Fife had a dredger to keep all the local harbours in good condition from year to year. Everybody would be surprised, he said, at the employment which could be developed if there were good ports.

The Town Clerk raised the question of the women employed at present in the Admiralty establishment. If the recent census was reliable these women wanted to remain in employment. He did not know if that was the case in this area, but if so he was anxious to know if anything could be done to provide them with employment.

After discussing the question of the proposed Tay Road Bridge the Provost expressed himself in favour of a bridge at Newburgh.

The Provost expressed the view that Inverkeithing was well placed to develop oyster-fishing.

CULROSS

Mr. Carlow apologised to the Provost and representatives of the Town Council for the Committee's late arrival and hoped that they had not been put to any inconvenience as a result. He then explained the purpose of the Committee's meeting and asked if there was anything they could do to help the people of Culross. He intimated that a public meeting would be held in Dunfermline and that the public would be invited to bring their suggestions to that meeting.

The Provost remarked that he could not say very much on the matter of planning. He had always looked upon Culross as an old-world burgh.

Mr. Ferguson, Depute Town Clerk, stated that their principal difficulty was that they didn't have any real information as to what was to happen as regards the much-talked-about pits. They had heard that one was to be opened west of Culross, and if that was true a large number of houses would be required. Mr. Carlow said he would not advise them to rely upon a pit being put down there within the period covered by the Committee's report. He did not think that any of them would see a pit sunk in the next 20 or 30 years. There was the one at Thornton first, then Dysart, and the third at Seafield. These were the most important pits. Then unproved ones which were doubtful were, one on foreshore two miles west of Valleyfield, one further north and another still further north. The three big ones would take seven or eight years each to sink, and unless the Coal Company were pressed by the Government or some other authority they would not want to start next pit until one was finished.

Culross was a residential burgh and had no industries whatsoever. The population were mostly miners who worked at Valleyfield or Dunfermline, and the travelling facilities were quite good.

In July and August quite a number of visitors stay at the hotel, but the majority were daily visitors.

A member of the Town Council stated that they wanted houses for the working-class people, and the Burgh of Culross was ideally suited with its southern exposure. Mr. Carlow asked if they would be in favour of miners staying at Culross and travelling to Comrie Pit, to which a member replied that by getting houses in their Burgh they would be able to bring down their rates. If they had sufficient houses the men could travel to Valleyfield, Comrie or Blairhall Pits. They required between 40 and 50 houses.

So far as could be seen Culross wanted to be a residential Burgh with attractions for tourists.

Mr. Christie thought that when the Forth Road Bridge came they could look forward to a great many more visitors.

The Town Clerk stated that they had had it minuted that they were in favour of the bridge. Mr. Mitchell said that the position meantime was that the Lord Provost of Edinburgh, the Town Clerk, General Crosbie and himself had been appointed to visit London to meet Lord Leathers on the subject of promoting a Provisional Order. That meeting had been held last Monday, and the Minister had indicated that he had given his approval to the Mackintosh Rock site, engineers had approved the design of the bridge and width of the roadway, and he rather encouraged local authorities to proceed with the drawing-up of a Provisional Order with a view to being in a position to move when the time came.

Raising the question of employment a member of the Town Council said that the female population mostly worked in Alloa.

NOTES TAKEN AT THE INITIAL SURVEY OF THE KIRKCALDY EAST AND WEMYSS AREAS
14th May, 1945

LESLIE

Mr. Carlow explained to the Provost and the representatives of the Town Council the purpose of the Editorial Sub-Committee's visit and the course of action in which they wanted the help of the people of Leslie and district. He explained that the County Council had appointed an Advisory Committee and the Advisory Committee had appointed a Sub-Committee to carry out the work. The Sub-Committee, he said, would be willing to meet the bigger industrial concerns if they so desired. He intimated that the public meeting would be held in the Town Hall, Markinch, on 4th June and expressed the hope that the public would come forward to that meeting with suggestions for the development and improvement of that part of Fife.

Provost Anderson thought that Mr. Carlow had made the purpose of the meeting very clear and remarked that by looking 50 years ahead they were setting a big problem to local authorities.

In Leslie they had a paper mill, flax factory, plastics and pen factory. Whether these factories would expand greatly or not Provost Anderson could not say, but assuming they kept at their present level the main thing was to obtain houses for the workers. Housing was hindering them in every way and was the keynote of all their problems. It was very difficult for industry to carry on without houses. The Provost remarked that one could get good workers if one had good houses in which to house them. Bailie Adam said they hoped to get started on their housing scheme whenever the Government said " go." They had received sanction to proceed whenever labour was available.

Leslie had problems of drainage and water which they were going into themselves.

Mr. Carlow then raised the question of the proposed Tay and Forth Road Bridges. Provost Anderson stated that Leslie was in favour of both bridges. Speaking as a business man, he said, they wanted to get as quickly as possible to Dundee and also to Aberdeen. Before the war they brought in materials for the paper mill to Dundee Dock. They also wanted to get to Edinburgh as quickly as possible. Before the war goods were transported via the Kincardine Bridge to Edinburgh. Here Mrs. Anderson remarked that the flax mill had a great interest in Dundee. Mr. Carlow then said—" Whether the bridge were at Dundee or Newburgh would not matter so long as there was a good road and good bridge," to which the Provost answered that they wanted a bridge which would serve both Aberdeen and Dundee.

There was a rumour that De La Rue wished to extend their factory, and the Town Clerk thought that if the Committee knew of any empty factories they might be interested. Mr. Christie thought that perhaps the Location of Industry Bill would prevent them from extending. Provost Anderson referred to the Conference which he had attended in Edinburgh as a representative of the Small Burghs' Association. They wanted Fife to be included in the development areas, he said, and considered that while Fife had two major industries in coal and agriculture it would have been an advantage to have had some subsidiary industries developed in the agricultural districts. His view was that where a factory existed one could go on extending but would not be allowed to set up a new factory. Mr. Carlow said that now they knew De La Rue was looking for floor-space the Committee might be able to do something as they went around. Provost Anderson remarked that his firm already had begun a big extension to their factory and it would be absurd if they were not allowed to continue. They were building a new bag factory, he said. Mr. Taylor explained that in the development areas the Government themselves were building factories.

Mr. Pollock asked if any problem was likely to arise between the Burgh and the surrounding landward area, to which he received the reply that the question of the River Leven might arise. All the industries used the river for power. Provost Anderson said his firm could get 1000 h.p. from the river with the use of turbines. In answer to Mr. Christie's question as to whether all the sewage drained into the river, the Provost replied that it did, but the Town Council were planning a new sewage scheme.

Mrs. Anderson remarked that the road transport charges in Fife had up to now been a deterrent to the setting-up of industries. Paper could be sent cheaper to Glasgow than to Edinburgh or Dundee.

MARKINCH

Mr. Carlow thanked the Provost for making arrangements to meet the Committee and explained very briefly what the Committee wished. He wanted to know in what way the Committee could assist the people of this neighbourhood to prosper. The public meeting would be held on 4th June in the Town Hall, Markinch, and this would be an opportunity for representatives of industry and all bodies interested to put forward their ideas before the Committee prepared a Report for the whole of the County.

Mr. Pollock asked the Provost if he would care to tell the Committee what he thought about the proposed large developments to the south of Markinch. The Provost was of the opinion that these would be all to the good. Mr. Carlow explained that there was to be a large colliery near Thornton Junction and the possibility of one at Wemyss. The County, he said, had the idea of making a subsidiary town near Coaltown of Balgonie. Mr. Pollock stated that they proposed to develop south of the ridge above Woodside, which was about 1½ miles from Markinch. Mr. Carlow went on to say there was a big community at Kirkcaldy and one of considerable size at Markinch. At each of these places there were schools, churches, picture-houses, and all that people wanted. Markinch, he said, was a very nice place, and it might be that if a new population was to come into the area it would be better to take part of that new population into Kirkcaldy and part into Markinch where all the necessary services were already available, rather than start a satellite town at Coaltown of Balgonie. By going to a new place it was not only necessary to break into good farm land but it was also necessary to build centralised buildings such as has already been mentioned. The Burgh Surveyor was of the opinion that instead of making a satellite town at Coaltown of Balgonie, Markinch should get the preference. Markinch was about three miles from Thornton.

In answer to Mr. Pollock's question as to how many houses were needed in Markinch the Burgh Surveyor replied, "Three hundred."

BUCKHAVEN

Provost Gray welcomed the Committee on behalf of the Burgh of Buckhaven and called upon Mr. Carlow to speak.

Mr. Carlow thanked the representatives of the Town Council for meeting the Committee and explained that their duty was to ascertain what were the best lines for the development of the County of Fife. Mr. Carlow explained that Mr. Christie, Sir James Irvine, who was unable to be present, and himself formed a Sub-Committee appointed by the Advisory Committee to draft a Report for the development of the whole of the County. In taking on that work they knew they were taking on a very heavy task and would need the co-operation and help of all men of goodwill in the County if they were going to succeed in making a Report which was to be worth while. He went on to say that the Committee hoped that as many people as possible would come to the public meetings to put forward their ideas and views for the development of their Burgh. The Committee in no way wished to interfere in things which the Burgh would rather they left alone. They were rather offering their assistance to the Burgh. He went on to say that the Committee knew about the principal industries in the Burgh and also a little about the subsidiary industries. They knew in a general way about the development of the coal-mining industry, as to what might happen between Leven and Dysart and what was likely to happen round about Kirkcaldy, and all that would be set forth in the Report which they hoped to have ready by the end of the year.

Provost Gray remarked that they had not been entirely idle in their Burgh. Their stumbling-block was the new Distribution of Industries Bill. A Sub-Committee had been appointed to consider what could be done to improve the Burgh. At the back of their minds was the idea that if they could get Methil Dock modernised it would considerably improve the general trade of the Burgh. They had had a meeting with those directly interested in the docks. A suggestion was made that a new road should be put into the dock from the Leven end. At present there is no proper road into the dock. Many other good suggestions were made and a memo. was submitted to the Railway Directors with a request that they meet the Committee to discuss the whole matter. They had received a very courteous reply from the Railway Company assuring them that they would be pleased to meet the Committee in about three weeks' time. Provost Gray wished to suggest that if the Committee had any difficulty with the Railway Company, the Editorial Sub-Committee might put forward in a stronger manner than they could the claims Buckhaven had for modernising the dock.

Provost Gray went on to say that a new industry was coming to the Burgh. A firm had bought a disused factory and assured the Council that they would employ nearly 200 girls. This was to be an oilskin and silk factory.

Mr. Carlow then raised the question of the proposed new entrance into the dock from the Leven end, and asked if this would necessitate another bridge over the Leven, to which Provost Gray replied that it would unless they could find some other way of dealing with the matter. Mr. Brown, Burgh Surveyor, expressed the view that an overhead road could be brought down over the sidings, and he thought Mr. Taylor would agree that it would be better to come down from the main high road direct into the dock rather than to go through an already congested area.

Bailie Slater said they were up against the problem of attracting new industries to the Burgh. Without industries there would be no need for a new road. In 1939-40 the Railway Company was approached for an additional entrance to Methil Dock, and they resisted the suggestion. In his opinion there was only one possible entrance, and that was at the east end of the dock going right over two main lines, entering into the tongues at the new docks. That was where the point of discharge would be for any imports. The whole area would have to be recast. It would be necessary to cross two main lines which fed the docks no matter where the new entrance was made. Provost Gray said they hoped the dock would induce new imports, and the only way they could be induced was by road traffic, and the only way road traffic could be facilitated was by a new entrance to get round to the tongues which Bailie Slater had been speaking about. A bridge was essential and that was one of the points the Committee was putting before the Railway Company.

Mr. Brown, Burgh Surveyor, stated that the development of the Burgh could not be completed until the many railway level crossings were removed. These railway lines crossed classified roads at three points and ordinary roads at many other points.

With regard to inducing new industries Provost Gray said they would agree that Buckhaven was handicapped by the new Distribution of Industry Bill, but they would be glad of help in getting industry because in normal times they had a surplus of female labour. Mr. Christie remarked that one of the remits to the Advisory Committee was to explore the question of light industries, and the great question was how to induce light industries to come. There had been an answer given to Mr. Henderson Stewart in the House of Commons that in the event of no industries going to a place where a Planning Authority thought an industry should go, that Planning Authority had the power to create an industry. Mr. Pollock explained that that was the new Planning Bill which was not yet on the Statute Book.

The Town Clerk stated that they had had people looking for a factory for women's knitwear, but there was trouble with the new Industries Bill. The people were not sure whether they would be allowed to start.

Mr. Christie said he raised the question some time ago with Mr. Mears as to the possibility of the development of a dock in the deep-water bay to the west of Buckhaven, and the answer he received was that it was absolutely impracticable because of coal. Provost Gray said that was perfectly correct. Mr. Christie then remarked that any development of Methil must take place towards Leven.

Mr. Carlow expressed the view that the dock was of sufficient capacity. They would get more imports, he said, if they had more import facilities, but the water basin for the ships was sufficient for export trade. Any question of a new dock was needless. It would be possible to make the present dock more commodious by putting up more hoists if the import trade was there, but the question of a road into the east end of the present dock was an important matter.

A member of the Town Council remarked that there was once a harbour at the west end of Buckhaven, but now the harbour was washed down and had been silted up with redd from the pits. Provost Gray stated that the Town Council's idea was to make that part attractive by erecting a swimming-pool, etc.

Mr. Christie asked how far the Burgh boundaries extended at the moment, and was informed that the River Leven was the boundary up to Balfour's Hill, roughly past old road to the cemetery, up to the Church at Methil cross-roads.

Mr. Carlow expressed the hope that a large representation of those interested would attend the coming public meetings.

LEVEN

Mr. Carlow said his first pleasure and duty was to thank Leven Town Council for agreeing to meet the Editorial Sub-Committee and also to thank them for the great kindness with which they had been received. It made a great difference, he said, to have an atmosphere of harmony created in that manner. He then explained the purpose of the meeting and named the members of the Sub-Committee who had been appointed to make a report for submission to the County Council. Arterial roads and trunk roads could not be constructed for one Burgh or community. They were things, he said, which affected the whole County and indeed the whole traffic and trade of Scotland from north to south. They could not discuss bridges with one particular party in Fife. These were matters in which the whole County was equally interested. The Committee, he said, wanted to have Leven's views on these matters. Furthermore the Committee had no wish or desire to interfere in matters which were not their business. A great deal of what the Council had in their minds would be of local interest only, but it was where one authority interlocked with another authority that a locus would be found, and what the Committee wanted to do was to produce a plan for Fife no part of which would block the other part.

Mr. Carlow then intimated that public meetings would be held in Buckhaven to which members of the public would be asked to bring forward their ideas and views so that these might be considered by the Committee in the preparation of their Report. In order to survey the matter as well as possible the Committee had sent out questionnaires to firms of valuation of £100 and more to get their views in writing. Mr. Carlow further stated that the Committee would be willing to meet any interested party or parties, if they so desired, and get from them in conversation what they might not perhaps be disposed to put in writing. He then called upon Mr. Christie to say a few words.

Mr. Christie stated that one of the difficulties of this work was that they were asked to look forward 50 or 60 years and it was exceptionally difficult to look so far ahead. They knew that tremendous mining developments were going to take place, and according to Mr. Mears' report and his analysis of the future population trends, apparently they had got to look forward to an increase of 42,000 people within the next 20 or 30 years in Fife ; and it seemed very clear to him that from Leven eastward to Crail they would probably see a tremendous development of the holiday industry taking place. In the Report which the Committee had to produce they would have to try to weigh up tendencies which were becoming obvious and as far as possible make plans to meet these future developments. In agriculture they had been losing skilled men for the last 30 years due to the fact that wages were low and housing conditions bad. Now it was suggested that instead of having men housed on farms they should live in community centres and travel to their work. On that point the Committee hoped to meet leading agriculturists in the County. Mr. Christie expressed the view that there was no reason why it should not work if done with wisdom.

Provost Gerrett said they had met this afternoon without any definite knowledge as to what line the Sub-Committee of the Advisory Committee were going to take. They didn't know whether the Sub-Committee were going to put forward suggestions or proposals or whether they were going to ask the Council to air their views, and it appears that the Council were to air their views.

At the present stage Provost Gerrett did not think it was very easy for them to do so because they had not been going into this matter. They had been confining their activities to the development of their Burgh, which, as Mr. Carlow suggested, was not a matter which concerned the Advisory Committee, but there were one or two developments which might be considered by the Regional Planning Committee. Mr. Christie had referred to the development in the East of Fife, and Provost Gerrett's view was that Leven would develop best if it tried to retain the residential atmosphere which had grown up so much during the last few years while at the same time retaining an interest in the industrial development in the area round about. In the Burgh they had no sites for industrial development but they were always keeping in mind that the County Planning Committee had earmarked an industrial belt on a site immediately to the west of their proposed first housing development at Mountfleurie, that was an industrial belt running along the south of the Leven-Windygates Road. Leven would be able to assist with that development through their housing proposals. They had a scheme in hand for the erection of a first instalment of 500 houses and after that site was filled up they proposed to develop a further site on the Windygates Road. If that area was developed and housing completed it would provide accommodation for workers who would be drawn to that industrial development.

Leven also proposed to go forward to the County Council with a scheme for the extension of their Burgh boundaries. That would be absolutely essential for private development apart from burghal development on the part of the Town Council. These were proposals which they hoped the Advisory Committee would keep in mind and recommend as being suitable for the betterment of the County.

Provost Gerrett went on to say that there was the question of a by-pass road from cross roads through by the National Steel Foundry and across the Windygates road. That by-pass had been discussed by the Regional Planning Committee and to the minds of the Town Council would be a very useful road, because it would by-pass a lot of the heavy traffic going through the Burgh of Leven and enable them to develop in the Burgh without any of the congestion from which they had suffered so long.

Another thing which the Burgh would require and which Provost Gerrett thought was absolutely necessary, was a more or less direct access road from Leven to the Kirkcaldy road. At present there was a road running through Leven up Methilhaven road, through Methilhill, and having as many turns as it was possible to have. Leven therefore wanted a very much better access and that would require to be considered in conjunction with the development in the Buckhaven and Methil areas. Provost Gerrett said he had suggested this road at earlier meetings of the Planning Committee and Leven certainly would press for that direct access, because as motor traffic developed again it would be absolutely essential to have a better road through to Kirkcaldy and the west.

Provost Gerrett made reference to an area to the east of Largo where Dumbarnie Links and Kincraig were situated. In his opinion this was an ideal area for summer camps, and he thought it desirable that some form of access should be provided so that people from this area and the west of Fife could take advantage of that area in the summer-time. Supervision of the area would be essential if it was to be a success. If an access road was made available to that area it would be to the benefit of the Burgh and the County generally.

These were one or two of the developments which Provost Gerrett thought were worthy of consideration.

Provost Gerrett went on to say that there had been a suggestion of a by-pass road running north from Windygates road through to by-pass Leven, Lundin Links and Largo to the coast. He did not know when that would develop, but any road there would have to be considered in conjunction with Leven's Burgh extension and their present development which would be going on within the next few years.

Mr. Carlow, referring to Provost Gerrett's reference to a large housing scheme immediately to the west of the Burgh and north of the Windygates road, said the Committee had had occasion to go to Kirkcaldy, Burntisland and Kinghorn. At Burntisland Mr. Carlow said he particularly asked the Provost what about the housing of those people who worked in the linoleum works and shipbuilding works, and the Provost informed him that a lot of these people lived in Kinghorn while quite a number travelled from Kirkcaldy to the shipyard. When the Committee visited Kinghorn they found to their surprise that there were practically no industries in Kinghorn, so Mr. Carlow had suggested that instead of building a large number of houses in Burntisland where the people would be near their work, and instead of building a large number of houses in Kirkcaldy where the odour of linoleum was constantly in the air, would it not be a good thing to concentrate future development in Kinghorn and take the people in 'buses to their work, preserving a green belt of two miles perhaps between Kinghorn and Burntisland and between Kinghorn and Kirkcaldy? Take the case of Leven, said Mr. Carlow, somebody has suggested that Kennoway is the place where development should be. He went on to say that he was not so much in favour of starting a new town altogether as there were certain amenities that people needed which would have to be developed. He rather favoured developing round a centre where certain of these amenities and necessaries were already existing and make better use of them. Another thing which had to be considered was agricultural land. There might, however, be something in the idea of concentrating workers in places where work was not.

Provost Gerrett thought what Mr. Carlow had said was a very good argument in favour of the development of the Burgh of Leven because Leven had the amenities which everybody wanted—ideal beach, ideal links—and it seemed to the Provost that Leven ought to be developed as a residential Burgh. Their development in Leven was going to be away from the industrial area which they already had; there was no room for industrial development on a big scale and the housing sites which the Burgh proposed to develop were ideal sites for housing workers away from their work.

Bailie Nairn said that if the idea was that housing of the people should be transferred up to Kennoway he disagreed with the suggestion. If Leven Town Council got what they wanted—extension of the Burgh boundaries—the people would be housed well away from any industrial area. He certainly disagreed with any idea of Kennoway expansion. Provost Gerrett remarked that he could agree that Kennoway should be developed, but not at the expense of Leven.

Bailie Nairn raised the question of the proposed new industrial belt to the west and hoped the Editorial Sub-Committee would take note to get the regional sewer in and so enable the River Leven to be purified.

Provost Gerrett expressed the view that the area suggested by Mr. Mears was an ideal one for light industries. It was more on the idea of Trading Estates which would be able to develop factories which would not be an " eyesore."

Bailie Lawrie upheld all that had been said by the Provost and Bailie Nairn because they wanted to maintain Leven as a partly industrial, but mainly residential area. For generations they had town-planned their Burgh. They had acquired the foreshore and an expanse towards Silverburn with a view to retaining them for the people of the surrounding district, and they felt that instead of building a satellite town the Burgh should be developed. So far as workers were concerned he thought they were living the right distance from their work. He thought the Council were agreed that the Burgh must extend north and west.

Mr. Carlow then asked what were their views about attracting light industries to Leven. A member of the Town Council replied that they could attract light industries to Leven because they had fairly low rates and they had also some of the finest working people in the country, who had applied themselves with zeal to any industry which had come along. Such industries as weaving and plastics, etc., could be centred in Leven. Provost Gerrett remarked, was it not the case that it was not in their province to suggest the type of industry which should be introduced ? What they could say was they could provide houses for the workers ; they were going to build 1000. It was up to the Advisory Committee to say " There is a site where there will be houses, railway facilities, etc. ; what do you want to put down there ? " Mr. Carlow stated that all any Committee could do was to keep a list of available sites which could be seen by any prospective industrialist. He had raised the question because he wondered if anyone present had any ideas as to how light industries could be attracted to come to the place. All he could suggest was that a list should be compiled showing rates, water supply, electricity, gas, etc., available sites, which could be kept in the County Offices, Cupar, and an occasional advertisement placed in the *Scotsman*. Provost Gerrett thought that was the lines they ought to adopt, but there had been many suggestions for the introduction of light industries simply because these industries had been dumped down during the war. Some people seemed to think that because they had plastics in one place they ought to be all over the country.

A member of the Town Council said they did not have the first essential, which was housing. What about the young people coming from the war ? he said. How could they talk about industry coming to Leven when they had no facilities to offer ? Provost Gerrett remarked that they were planning ahead.

Mr. Taylor, County Planning Officer, said he had received an inquiry for a site for a light industry in Leven which would employ female labour in the manufacture of woollen goods. The site in question was near Scoonie and he had been asked to pass observations on it. Provost Gerrett said they knew about it and wanted the industry. There was another site suggested but the man who had control of the feu wanted such an exorbitant price for it that it could not be considered. The type of building proposed was to be of a very attractive design. Mr. Carstairs was very keen on another site on the north-west corner of the present municipal golf-course, but the difficulty there was that when the feu charters were given to the proprietors a guarantee was given that the ground would not be built on.

A member of the Town Council raised another point in connection with the development of Leven as a holiday resort. He was anxious to see a promenade right round the Bay to Dumbarnie Links. Such a promenade would be a great asset to the Burgh, he said. Industry was so placed in Leven that it did not interfere with the pleasure side of the town.

Mr. Carlow again expressed thanks on behalf of the Committee for the kind reception they had received.

NOTES TAKEN AT PUBLIC MEETING HELD IN J.P. COURT ROOM, DUNFERMLINE
22nd May, 1945

Mr. Carlow (Chairman).

Mr. Carlow remarked that he supposed it was impossible to select a date without clashing with some other meetings, and he understood that they were poorly represented here because of some unfortunate clashing of dates.

He said he would like to explain very briefly and as clearly as he could what the Editorial Sub-Committee was, what it sought to do and how it sought to do it. The County Council had a Planning Committee entrusted with the planning of the whole of the County. Outside of the County Council there were three Planning Authorities, namely, St. Andrews, Kirkcaldy and Dunfermline Town Councils. These Planning Authorities had equal rights and powers with the County Planning Authority, and Mr. Carlow wished to make it clear that the Planning Advisory Committee did not wish to interfere in matters of local interest with which they had nothing whatever to do, but where one authority interlocked with another authority there should be general co-operation. The Planning Committee of the County Council was naturally composed entirely of County Councillors, and to assist them in their work they decided to appoint an Advisory Committee in order that the wishes, aspirations, hopes and fears of the people might be set before the County Council. They therefore appointed an Advisory Committee of some size, including the gentlemen before them to-day, namely, Mr. Christie and Mr. McArthur, and a number of others. This Committee was considered to be too big and a Sub-Committee consisting of Mr. Christie, Sir James Irvine, and himself were appointed to carry out the necessary work. This Sub-Committee had undertaken to visit every Provost in the County, and in this way the Committee had gathered quite a lot of information. They were also holding these public meetings in order that any individual persons who did not happen to be a member of a Town Council would have an opportunity of going forward with his views. Mr. Carlow hoped that any person who had views about the development of this part of Fife was represented at the meeting, and if not he begged of him or her to write a letter to the County Clerk giving his or her views. Mr. Carlow went on to say that if any industry wished to meet the Committee personally in regard to the planning or future development of their industry the Committee would be very pleased to wait upon any representation of that industry. For instance they were in the home of the textile industry, and if the Committee could help the textile industry in any way they begged of that industry to communicate with the County Clerk on any point which they wished to make and have a meeting arranged. In order that everybody might be given an opportunity of putting forward their views a questionnaire had been issued to firms whose valuation exceeded £100, and by the time the ground had been surveyed along these lines Mr. Carlow hoped that everybody would have had every opportunity of giving their views. His purpose was not only to collect information but to forestall anybody coming forward at a later date and saying that what had been done was all wrong. Now was their chance to speak, otherwise keep silent for ever.

Mr. Carlow then outlined the area covered by this meeting.

The question of transport Mr. Carlow said he would leave to other speakers. The question of the Forth and Tay Road Bridges and how the arterial roads should go through the County were all matters which obviously required to be planned out before-hand. It would never do if an authority built a village where an arterial road should go. Mr. Carlow thought everyone knew Dunfermline's views about the Forth Road Bridge, but he was not sure whether they had any mature views about the Tay Road Bridge. The question of housing shortage they knew quite a lot about, but he was not sure that it came within the Committee's purview. The Committee were there, said Mr. Carlow, if he had made himself clear, to know in what way they could serve the people of Dunfermline, and what they could put in their Report which would be of advantage to the trade of Dunfermline. He then called upon Mr. Christie to say a few words.

Mr. Christie said he would not talk for very long as they were there to get the public's views. One of the things the Committee had been asked to do was to look into the future up to 50 or 60 years to try and balance up the trends in development in industry, mining, imports, exports, increase of population, housing, new satellite towns, roads, and this was a very large piece of work and a very difficult one. Therefore they didn't wish to miss anything in the way of a good concrete suggestion dealing with the future.

Mr. Christie referred to the report prepared by Mr. Mears in which he brought out the fact that by 1970 there should be an increase of population in Fife of between 90,000 and 100,000. That was the number who would live in Fife and did not take into account the vast numbers who would be attracted in the future to utilise the new road bridge when it came. That bridge was to be very close to the Dunfermline area and would inevitably affect the area. So far as could yet be seen, the almost inevitable tendency was for the trunk road over the Forth to go almost straight up to Perth, but in addition to that it was almost certain that the County would have to develop a great new arterial road running through the centre of Fife and starting between Lochgelly and Cowdenbeath, with Kirkcaldy to the south, and the problem was whether to go straight to Dundee or to go to Newburgh. The Committee wished to collect as many views as possible on the question of routes for these arterial roads. Mr. Christie went on to say that some people thought it was not advisable to look too far ahead, but personally he felt that 50 years was very short from the planning point of view. He expressed the view that in the long-run there would be two bridges over the Tay.

With regard to agriculture Mr. Christie felt that one thing which was very badly needed was a Training College. The site had not been decided upon, but there was one very attractive one near Cupar. Mr. Christie said he was asking everybody to support the idea of having a Training College so that the young people might learn about the soils, etc., of their own county.

Mr. McArthur said how very pleased he was to be asked to come along and address the meeting. These things were very necessary in a district like Dunfermline which embraced Valleyfield, Blairhall and out to Crossgates, because as miners they had had to be satisfied for too long with their planning being done for them instead of having a share in planning the district in which they lived, so that when he was nominated as a member of the Advisory Committee he was only too pleased to accept. Mr. McArthur went on to say that he had met his colleagues, and the public could rest assured that their place in industry and their amenities were being well cared for. He made reference to a conference held in January at which ideas were put forward which were going to bring something to the County of Fife, with the help of Mr. Taylor, which had never been realised before. When a new mine or pit was sunk the village in which the people had to live was just set up round about the pit, but to-day, with the rapid increase of transport facilities, they would find that the miner was going to take his place in city life instead of being part of that village alone.

Mr. McArthur went on to speak of the foreshore at Torryburn and Low Torrie. The foreshore there was very much in need of clearing up, and he expressed the view that the reclaiming of that land from the sea would add very considerably to the amenities of that district.

Mr. McArthur said he had been very interested to read a very fine document prepared by Mr. Taylor on the Preservation of Trees, and expressed the view that it would be a very good thing if copies of the document could be circulated to libraries in the different districts of the County.

Like Mr. Christie, Mr. McArthur said he knew they were not there to lecture, but to get the audience's views on what they would like and what industries they felt would be an advantage to the County of Fife. He thought that most of them would have read the Distribution of Industry Bill, but nothing was going to stop the Committee from trying to get new industries for this part of Fife.

Mr. Taylor, *County Planning Officer*, said that as Planning Officer he would have to prepare a plan as far as possible to fit in with the wishes of the people and therefore he was there to hear what they had to say. It would be no use his drawing up a scheme unless it took into consideration the wishes of the people for whom that scheme was drawn up. The object of a Planning Scheme was to lay out the land in question so that it was put to its best use. A lot of people had run away with the idea that a Planning Scheme had something to do with housing, or with what an elevation was going to look like, or again perhaps that it had to do with roads. That was not so. A Planning Scheme took into consideration every phase of the country's life. The Dunfermline area, he said, looked forward to being one of the most interesting for future development. There was the proposed road bridge over the Forth with all the arterial roads, and then there was coal, particularly to the west of Dunfermline. Mr. Taylor then explained several maps to the meeting showing houses required for mining population, etc. Dunfermline area, he said, had a big future before it and he hoped that as Planning Authority they would do the best they could for the people in that area to see that their interests were looked after. No doubt many thousands of houses would be required.

Mr. Carlow then appealed for suggestions or questions from the audience.

A *member of the audience* stated that a lot had been said about coal but he wanted to know if there was any plan in mind for the shipment of that coal, especially in the west of Fife, instead of taking it to Methil or Burntisland. He thought that somewhere like Torryburn should be developed for the shipment of the coal.

Another *member of the audience* wished to know why in the geographical survey west of Fife had been drawn as finishing at Culross and no mention made of Kincardine.

Rev. J. M. Webster asked if it was the intention of the Planning Authority to build houses for miners in close proximity to the pit or that they should be built some distance from these places.

Mr. Carlow hoped that they had not by any misadventure failed to recognise the importance of Kincardine, but it was not possible for him to enumerate the villages in the area, but Kincardine certainly was included. Any suggestions from Kincardine would be considered.

With regard to the shipment of coal from elsewhere than Methil and Burntisland Mr. Carlow stated that these ports belonged to the Railway Company and they had spent a great deal of money in developing them. Further, in 1913 more coal had been shipped from these ports than was likely to be available for export in the near future, and he thought that it would be rather unfair, whether it were practicable or not, to start another shipping port which would take traffic away from the existing ports which the Railway Company had developed and spent money upon after a great deal of persuasion from traders. Mr. Carlow went on to say that a good many years ago he had been instrumental in drawing up plans for shipping coals near Valleyfield Pit. Preston Island stands there, and Mr. Carlow had had a perfectly good plan prepared by mining engineers for running out a gangway to Preston Island and carrying coal on rubber belts to deep water where ships could be tied up while the coal was run out from the land.

With regard to the question of filling up Torrie Bay Mr. Carlow remarked that that was a very serious problem as anyone who studied currents of water, especially in the Forth, would find. If Torrie Bay could be filled up as far out as Preston Island he ventured to say that a colliery might be sunk in the neighbourhood of the island.

Next there was the question as to how far away workers should be from their place of employment. Mr. Carlow wished to say that he did not think there would be a miner's house within two miles of the Fife Coal Company's new pit, and he was quite willing that this should be the case. Similarly, was it necessary for every farm worker to live on the farm? Was it not practicable to say that people who looked after the animals needed to be near the farm, but those who ploughed the land could be housed in community centres and conveyed to and from their work?

A *member of the audience* asked if he could have the assurance of the support of the Committee regarding Cairneyhill.

Mr. Carlow said he had received a very good suggestion from Cairneyhill. The purport of the letter was that Cairneyhill should be developed as a residential centre and that there should be suitable drainage and other facilities given for building a considerable number of houses at Cairneyhill.

Mr. Christie asked to be allowed to say one word with regard to the question of having the guarantee of the Committee. He wished to point out that the Committee was an advisory body whose duty was to put forward advice to the County Council.

Rev. J. M. Webster asked if the Presbytery of Dunfermline had been asked to be represented at the meeting in connection with setting up of churches in the new areas and whether they were expected as members of the Presbytery to send in their views, to which Mr. Carlow replied " yes."

Mrs. Harley Marshall referred to a meeting she had attended in Kirkcaldy in connection with the W.R.I. when Mr. Taylor, County Planning Officer, gave an address and referred to the decreasing population. Now, she said, there was talk of building a lot of houses and she wanted to know if it was intended to import population.

Mr. Taylor replying said there had been some little misunderstanding. It was the population of the East of Fife which was decreasing. Population in certain parts of West Fife was likely to increase.

Mr. McArthur said there was another point. In Lanarkshire they had a declining mining area and the people of Lanarkshire were bound to find their way into this area.

Mr. Alexander (*Clerk to Dunfermline Local Council*) said he had certain suggestions from the Youth Organisation which he would submit in writing. There was a great need for premises and recreational grounds and the young people were anxious to see slipper and spray baths as well as dance hall, crafts room, etc., incorporated in their Youth Centre. Mr. Alexander said the question of recreation grounds applied to all districts in the Dunfermline area. The membership of Youth Organisations was now in the region of 3000. He went on to say that he had asked a builder what the cost of a building would be and had been informed that it would probably be in the region of £20,000.

Rev. J. M. Webster asked what provision they would propose for open spaces in satellite towns.

Mr. *Carlow* replied that the Planning Authority would have to plan their new villages or extensions of villages in a workmanlike manner, making provision for churches, village halls, sports grounds, etc., in suitable places for these activities. It was not the Committee's duty to find a church or a village hall, but it would be the duty of the Planning Authority to see that places were available for churches, etc.

Rev. *J. M. Webster* asked if they had reasonable assurance that their wishes would be taken into consideration when building did take place.

Mr. *Carlow* replied that the Committee applied only to the landward area and could only promise consideration within the scope of their jurisdiction.

Mr. *Taylor*, referring to open spaces, stated that the amount of ground suggested used to be five acres per 1000 people, then seven acres was suggested, and now the aim was ten acres per 1000.

Mr. *Christie* remarked that there was no question that there was not enough recreation ground, but how that was to be overcome was another matter. He was going to stress very strongly that certain paragraphs dealing with the matter should be incorporated in the Committee's Report. Beyond that he felt there was a great need for bigger recreational areas for older boys and girls and hoped that it would be possible to have a meeting with Dr. McIntosh, Director of Education, on the subject. Mr. Christie had in mind places like Norman's Law and Tentsmuir where older boys might build their own huts.

Mr. Carlow then called upon Mr. Potter, Local County Councillor, to say a few words.

Mr. *Potter* said he had listened with great care to what had been said and knew that the answer came back every time to finance, and that was where the difficulty was going to be.

There were three problems, industry, housing and roads. Mr. Potter said he knew the position with regard to roads, and the County Road Board had agreed to the lines laid down by the Planning Committee. He was not so sure that he was in agreement with the housing side of the question so far as the planning people looked at it. In his opinion not one house should be built to bring incomers into Fife until everyone in the mining areas had a good comfortable house, and sub-letting was cleared out. It was no use asking the Planning Committee because all they could do was plan, but it would cause a great deal of unrest if new people were brought into Fife before those living in condemned houses, overcrowded houses and sub-lets had been put into new houses. He hoped the County Council would face the housing problem first. The Planning Committee, he said, would have to be very careful in planning satellite towns taking into consideration that coal doesn't grow again.

With regard to industries, Mr. Potter thought it was going to be a very difficult problem to get new industries. He was afraid that in the meantime it was going to be left to private enterprise to start industry where it would be of most value, and the County's job was to plan roads and housing to carry on. The County Council would help as much as they could so far as industry was concerned.

Mr. *Carlow*, speaking on housing, said there was one thing which must not be forgotten, that when houses were being spread over 30 persons to the acre, etc., and everyone was being given a garden and lots of space, agricultural land was being used up which could never be restored to agriculture. One thing was quite clear, that if they used up all the agricultural land they would be short of food although there were plenty of houses.

A *member of the audience* then raised the question of open spaces and asked if the planning expert indicated that for a population of 2000 the Committee would approve of 20 acres being set apart irrespective of sites for churches and schools, etc.

Mr. *Taylor* replied that each village would have to be considered on its merits. No hard and fast rule could be laid down.

Another *member of the audience* asked if it was the Planning Authorities' intention to distribute the houses round the rural district as much as possible. Places like Cairneyhill, Carnock and Saline, all small places, would be greatly helped if they were extended.

Mr *Carlow* said he was not a County Councillor but he could see some of the difficulties which would face the County Council in regard to the location of these houses. He recalled the difficulty encountered by the County Council at Lassodie where the people didn't want to leave. The question was whether it was desirable to build a few houses at Cairneyhill, Torryburn, etc., enlarging every village by a certain amount. Mr. Carlow was very keen that where there were existing facilities such as drainage, water supply, recreational places, etc., a few more houses should be built round about rather than going to a completely new place where all these services would have to be introduced, but that was really beyond the scope of the Advisory Committee.

Mr. *Potter* informed the meeting that the District Council had asked for estimates for drainage for Carnock, Cairneyhill and Hillend and were busy on these plans at the present moment. He couldn't see the County Council building a house there until drainage was in.

On the motion of Mr. Potter, Mr. Carlow and the Committee were accorded a vote of thanks.

Suggestions which are given as an appendix to these notes have been received from the following :—

(1) A.C.2 Blatchley, R.A.F. Station, Castle Kennedy.
(2) Jas. Fairley, District Councillor, Cairneyhill.
(3) James Morris, Morven Carnock Road, Dunfermline.
(4) Dunfermline Local Youth Council.

APPENDIX REFERRED TO

1829747 A.C.2 Blatchley, A.T.,
P.O. Staff,
R.A.F. Station,
Castle Kennedy,
Stranraer.

May 26th, 1945.

J. M. Mitchell, *County Clerk.*

County of Fife Planning Advisory Committee

Dear Sir,

Referring to notice in *Dunfermline Press* dated 19th May and your invitation to members of Forces regarding suggestions for the above.

My home address is Scottsbrae, North Queensferry, and naturally I am interested in developments in that area, and in connection with that I would like to put forward the following suggestion.

Having regard to the difficult geographical situation at North Queensferry for any further development of its housing scheme (Brock Street and Whinny Knowe), would it not be possible for the County authorities to acquire from the War Office the land and buildings situated at Carlingnose Barracks and Port Laing? These lands and buildings have not been occupied for three years or more by any large body of troops and with the total defeat of Germany should not be required any more by the War Office for warlike activities. The existing buildings such as married quarters and the two villas and possibly other premises could be adapted and made available almost immediately for occupation by returning Service personnel, and roads, drainage, water and electricity are available for further new houses. There is a playing field and ground available for proposed village hall or community centre, and possibly the building at Port Laing could be adapted as tenement flats and the vicinity laid out for recreation centre adjacent to the sands.

It is likely that there would be some delay and opposition for such a scheme from the War Office, but it would be better for these lands and buildings to be developed into something useful to the community than allowed to be derelict as they have allowed them to be in recent years. Funds have been expended on installing baths and renewing electrical installations. These, never used, have been damaged and destroyed by neglect and trespass, therefore wasting public funds.

The matter could be taken in hand by our Parliamentary representatives immediately, especially as we have quite a number of men of North Queensferry serving with the Forces who have married and will require some kind of accommodation for their wives and families when they return to civilian employment.

Yours faithfully,

(Sgd.) ALFRED T. BLATCHTEY.

THE ROSE GARDENS,
CAIRNEYHILL.
22nd May, 1945.

GENTLEMEN,

As a petition has been lodged with the Fife County Council praying for a drainage system for the village of Cairneyhill, permit me as District Councillor for the said village to request you to consider a housing development of this area, say to start with at least 100 houses, with the view of raising the assessable value in support of the suggested drainage scheme.

The village is situated close to Comrie where workers are conveyed from outlying districts in 12 or more 'buses each shift. Many of these workers would be pleased to obtain housing in this area. Further, the village is central between Culross and Dunfermline and on a main 'bus route, and would be very convenient in view of the prospective mining developments at Culross.

As a health area Cairneyhill is outstanding and is in a favourable position regarding any medical report.

I offer this suggestion, Gentlemen, for your favourable consideration.

Yours faithfully,

(Sgd.) J. FAIRLEY,
District Councillor.

MORVEN,
CARNOCK ROAD,
DUNFERMLINE.

DEAR MR. POLLOCK,

Sorry I shall be unable to attend this conference in Dunfermline. However, I should like to draw attention to the northern part of my district where a suitable site could be developed and a number of houses built—the stretch of road from the railway bridge at Lochend to the turn of the road to Kelty and Bowershall.

Also what steps can be taken by the Planning Committee in order to get drainage to enable further house-building in the Carnock Road area?

I am sincerely sorry this meeting is clashing with my other engagement as I am keenly interested in this matter.

Yours faithfully,

(Sgd.) JAMES MORRIS.

DUNFERMLINE LOCAL YOUTH COUNCIL.

The area administered by this Local Youth Council extends from Hill of Beath in the east to Kincardine in the west, and from Saline in the north to North Queensferry in the south. Small Burghs included are Inverkeithing and Culross.

It has not been possible to arrange a meeting of leaders of Youth Organisations whereby the specific needs of youth might have been discussed. The suggestions appended are partly the outcome of previous discussion on the subject of playing-field facilities, but those referring to Youth Centres are now submitted for consideration of the Fife Planning Advisory Committee.

Generally speaking, the requirements of Youth Organisations in this district are similar—recreation grounds and suitable premises.

RECREATION GROUNDS

These should be large enough to permit of more than one outdoor sport being engaged in at one and the same time. It sometimes happens that a game of football or cricket occupies the whole of the available ground.

YOUTH CENTRES

It is desirable that in each community there should be a Youth Centre situated either within the recreation ground or adjacent thereto. The suggestion is made that if, by reason of the size of the community, only one centre is visualised for all members of that community at least one wing should be definitely for the service of Youth.

A strong recommendation is made for slipper and spray baths to be included in the equipping of a Youth Centre. For those who have been participating in any active outdoor game the amenity provided by spray baths makes considerable appeal.

In this district there is an active Young People's Committee which is comprised of young people from every Youth Organisation. At a meeting of this Committee which was held on Thursday last opportunity was taken to find out, very informally, the features which they would wish to be incorporated in a Youth Centre. These are included with other suggestions.

GENERAL

In some instances ground is in use for outdoor games, but considerable improvement could be made in the layout. Stripping accommodation is rarely convenient.

Some Youth Organisations, e.g. Boy Scouts and Girl Guides, may wish to have their own meeting-place but would participate in the facilities afforded by a well-equipped centre.

(Sgd.) W. ALEXANDER,
Clerk.

Suggestions to Fife Planning Advisory Committee

Hill of Beath :—Boys' Club meets in Miners' Welfare Institute. No particulars regarding recreation ground.

Crossgates :—A number of Youth Organisations here. A Youth Centre is required. An extensive stretch of ground is available for recreation but would require levelling.

Inverkeithing Burgh :—It may be that the Town Council of Inverkeithing will submit suggestions for Youth Organisations. There is considerable youth activity in the burgh. Premises and recreation grounds essential.

North Queensferry :—Well-equipped premises are required. No particulars of recreation ground.

Crosbie :—One club started recently and meets in school.

Cairneyhill :—Extract from letter of Rev. Roy McVicar, The Manse, Cairneyhill, attached. Young people from Crossford attend Cairneyhill Clubs.

Torryburn, Newmills and Valleyfield :—Owing to the difficulty of providing a centre conveniently situated this area requires further consideration. Recreation grounds are necessary.

Culross :—It is understood that, owing to leaders being on Service, Youth Organisations are not functioning meantime.

Kincardine :—A Youth Centre would be of advantage. No particulars of recreation grounds available.

Saline and Steelend :—Youth Organisations meet in a mission hut in Lower Steelend. A community centre with a Youth wing might serve here. Ground is available for outdoor games but improvements are necessary.

Charlestown :—Recreation grounds are required.

The following are the suggestions of the Young People's Committee regarding equipment of a Youth Centre :—
1. Hall suitable for dancing, physical training, indoor games. Should be fitted with stage for presentation of plays and films. Necessary dressing-rooms.
2. Reading-room and Library.
3. Kitchen. Canteen.
4. Handcrafts Room.
5. Committee Room.
6. Cloak-rooms.
7. Slipper and Spray Baths.
8. Central Heating.
9. Storage.

Blairhall :—Premises are required. It is suggested that the present football pitch on the playing field might be moved ten yards east and so permit of a running track (cinders) being made round it. There is room for the construction of a jumping pit.

Oakley :—Club recently started.

Cairneyhill (extract from letter of Rev. R. McVicar) :—

A playing field which would give the boys football in winter, cricket in summer ; the girls, hockey and netball ; and for both, outdoor sports, racing, jumping, etc. I most cordially agree that there should at least be spray baths for them when they come off the field, to be open for them also at any time in order to encourage cleanly habits. As for indoor facilities, I should like to see these adequate for club activities, with a gymnasium for physical training for both sexes. This should, if possible, be adjacent to the playing field, so that the baths could be in the same building and be at hand for a spray bath after being in the gymnasium. Such a playing field and gymnasium could also be at the disposal of school children, as their use of it would be earlier than Youth Clubs.

I think such facilities, with proper equipment and qualified instructors, should be the accepted rights of youth in the new world. I lay stress on the Instructors, because nothing is more discouraging to youth than to have the opportunity of all these things and not to be able to make full use of them and learn to do them with a proficiency that enables them to compete with other clubs.

I don't know if this is just what you want, but these are some of the things I should like to see carried out in all planning for our communities.

NOTES TAKEN AT PUBLIC MEETING HELD IN THE TOWN HALL, LOCHGELLY
28th May, 1945

Mr. Carlow (Chairman).

Mr. Carlow said that they might have had an opportunity of reading reports in the newspapers of meetings which the Committee had held in other centres giving some idea of the purposes of the Committee and how it proposed to carry out the purpose which it had in view. He wished to make it clear that the Committee were out to assist the community. Some form of planning was necessary and it would never do to allow one set of works to interfere with the coming into operation of others. The example he always took in that matter was the proposed new collieries. They knew precisely where the new collieries were going to be situated, each requiring 150 or 200 acres of flat ground, because the situation had been fixed by the position of coal seams underground. The position on the surface had been fixed in regard to transport and many other things, and it would never do if a housing scheme were allowed to be situated on ground which obviously was the only place for a large colliery. Similarly, large trunk roads would have to be built through the County and bridges would have to be built over the Forth and Tay, and the County Council didn't want to do anything which would interfere with the development of the County on most economic lines. More than that, they knew that there were separate Planning Authorities in the County and didn't want to interfere with other people's business. It was only where the interests of the various Planning Authorities interlaced that the Committee wished to assist. Otherwise the Committee's attention was confined to the landward area of the County.

Mr. Carlow then explained the method adopted to learn the views and wishes of the people.

A week or two ago the Sub-Committee had the pleasure of meeting representatives of Lochgelly Town Council, and they knew that Lochgelly was strictly a coal-mining place. They had also learned that Lochgelly had problems in connection with water supply, sewage schemes and roads. The Burgh also had views as to where the main roads of the future should go. They might have views as to whether the bridge over the Tay should be near Abernethy or near Newport ; whether a really good arterial road between the coalfields and the industrial centres—Kirkcaldy, Ladybank, Auchtermuchty, Newburgh Falkland, Freuchie—suitable for heavy motor traffic would or would not be worth the time, labour, and money spent on its construction. It might be that both for transporting of personnel, of coal and of manufactured goods, such roads would more than pay themselves. These things were all within the scope of the Planning Committee. These were the things upon which the Committee would like to have local opinion. Mr. Carlow thought they would all agree, whether they were capitalists or workers, that some gain had to be got—wages or profits or something of the kind were necessary for industry to survive. Having settled these things the question of amenities could then be approached.

Mr. *Christie* said he would illustrate part of the problem by giving one or two small statistics. He had heard from someone who had been at Rothamsted that the land on both sides of the Firth of Forth was the most valuable in Europe. Mr. Christie said he found great difficulty in crediting that altogether, but the Department had the habit of knowing what it was talking about. Between 1903 and 1938, 25,000 acres of that land had been lost permanently to agriculture, and it was beginning to appear quite obvious that if our towns were going to extend in the way they have been extended in the past then they were simply destroying one of the finest things which had been handed down. Instead of these vast growths of small bungalows spread all over the country they might be forced in the future to think of some of the Continental methods of building large modern types of tenements which would be of enormous value to those who didn't want gardens.

Mr. Christie went on to say that in Mr. Mears' interim report on population trends, etc., they were told that within the next 30 years the population in the central part of Fife was expected to increase by at least 70,000 and the question was whether it would be advisable to create new towns or allow existing towns to grow.

Coming down to points dealing with Lochgelly and Cowdenbeath, Mr. Christie said it had been whispered to the Committee that the coal in this area was coming to an end and possibly the great increase in population might find that this area might be one of the dormitories where people might be housed and taken to their work in other centres. These were just suggestions which were being put forward for the public's views.

Mr. *Carlow* remarked that it was very useful to have the views of agriculturists regarding the using-up of agricultural land for housing purposes. The report referred to by Mr. Christie talked about using up good farming land for housing purposes, and one had got to consider whether it was not better to see if something in the nature of large blocks of flats couldn't be developed rather than utilise so much of our food-producing land for building upon. No doubt that was a matter on which most people would have something to say.

Mr. *McArthur* spoke of the very unsightly burning bings on which the people of Glencraig, Lochore, Dundonald, Bowhill, and many other mining villages had to look out day in and day out. They could rest assured, he said, that he would do everything in his power to see that these bings were removed for ever from the landscape.

In years gone past the miners had had their industrial life planned for them without consideration being given to the social side of life. Now they were going to try to house the miners so that they could enter into the life of the larger centres instead of being just a part of the particular village in which they lived.

Mr. McArthur then gave a few statistics as to the number of houses required in Lochgelly. There were 353 overcrowded houses ; 24 unfit for habitation ; the requirements of the area for general needs were 132 and for wastage 85, making a total of 594. Therefore it could be seen that there was much need for consideration to be given to the redevelopment of housing in Lochgelly district.

According to Mr. Mears' report the aim in the future was to establish mixed communities, and the ratio of 1 miner to 8 persons was considered a minimum basis for assessing the size of new communities in mining districts. Mr. McArthur thought this ratio could be considerably reduced if they planned to bring new industries to the County. As a Planning Advisory Committee, he said, they would do everything in their power to bring new industries to Fife and in this respect they had the sympathy of the Planning Committee. Iron and steel industries, and even textile industry, might be brought to Lochgelly. In Lochgelly they found that a large proportion of the female labour available had no means of finding employment in Lochgelly and had to be transported to Dunfermline.

Referring to the Forth Road Bridge Mr. McArthur said he was rather interested in the wording used by Mr. Mears in his report. Some people were prepared to criticise the new Forth Bridge, and Mr. McArthur thought they would do well to think of it in the terms used by Mr. Mears, viz. nobody should think in terms of the Forth Road Bridge as a luxury but should think of it as a natural development of the essential corridor for the industrial and social structure of this County of Fife.

Mr. *Taylor* said they had tried to put up one or two maps which they thought might interest the people in Lochgelly area. They mostly dealt with a thing about which he hardly dared to speak with the Chairman and Mr. McArthur present, and that was coal. He pointed out the situation of the new pits east of Lochgelly and stated that the main housing for mining communities would be round the Comrie area and the Kirkcaldy area. So far as he understood, the coal in the Lochgelly-Cowdenbeath area was pretty well worked out.

Mr. *Carlow* said that, as the people of Lochgelly knew, the coal in the Cowdenbeath-Lochgelly area was pretty well all sunk and there was no likelihood of any new pits, but the old pits might last for a long time. The three big new pits, he said, would be in the Kirkcaldy area : one near Thornton, one at Dysart and the third at Seafield. It was necessary to go to the Comrie district for deep pits. If one was looking ahead 50 or 60 years the population might find it difficult to get employment in the Lochgelly area, but there would be employment in Thornton, Dysart and Kirkcaldy, and it might be that in course of time the population might have to go, to some extent at least, eastwards for their work. Mr. Carlow thought the transport facilities would be such as to render that no very great difficulty.

Mr. *Taylor* then explained a map showing the contours of Fife. The information contained in that map, he said, would assist them to find suitable routes for the various roads.

The next map showed the amount of traffic passing over various roads, the width of the road indicating the density of traffic.

Mr. *Taylor* then exhibited a map showing the potential coal reserves in the various areas of the County. They would see, he said, that 1350 million tons were expected to be produced in the Kirkcaldy area, therefore they could imagine the number who would have to be housed in order to produce that quantity of coal. In the Lochgelly area there were some 225 million tons of coal.

Mr. *Carlow* explained that the coals in the Kirkcaldy area stretched underneath the sea for a good distance, one of the Fife Coal Company's leaseholds stretching to Inchkeith. Using underground locomotives, some day coal might be brought from near Inchkeith to be brought up the pit near Kirkcaldy. That was one of the reasons East Fife would be working and producing coal after most other coalfields were exhausted.

Mr. *Taylor* stated that maps were in course of preparation showing how the County Council and the Burghs were trying to meet the housing needs.

Mr. *Carlow* then appealed for suggestions as to how the Committee could best serve the needs of the community. There was one suggestion he wished to make—that Burghs which were so near together as Cowdenbeath and Lochgelly, together with villages like Glencraig and Lochore and neighbourhood, might be more closely interwoven by something in the nature of a Joint Committee or Joint Authority. He had received a very useful suggestion from Bailie Westwater on the same subject. (The suggestion is shown in the Appendix to these notes.) The same thing seemed to Mr. Carlow to arise in connection with other Burghs in Fife. He had in mind Kirkcaldy, Burntisland, and Kinghorn, Kinghorn being a residential Burgh without any industries, while Kirkcaldy and Burntisland were places of considerable magnitude. If people were taken to Kinghorn in 'buses they would spend their nights, week-ends, and spare time away from the atmosphere of their work. He had found in these three places, however, that none of the Provosts wanted the people to go out of their own Burghs.

Mr. *Sneddon* began by saying he was present not as Convener of the Planning Committee but as a ratepayer interested in the planning and development of the County.

Mr. Carlow in his remarks, he said, mentioned, probably quite rightly, that so long as we are under a particular system we might plan for the owners and plan another standard of living for those that produce. Mr. Sneddon said that speaking as a ratepayer he simply thought that if they planned that way the possibility was they were planning wrongly. For instance his colleague had mentioned the road over the Forth. They were beginning to ask themselves, when the whole community was in complete agreement that such a thing was necessary, why was it not materialising? Was it because of the cost? was it because some other persons with influence were interested in the non-development of that road across the Forth—because it might stultify something they were interested in? Mr. Sneddon went on to say that he was rather interested in what Mr. Christie had said about the loss of that valuable land. Mr. Christie had suggested that possibly it might be necessary to build tenement buildings, but he was anxious to know whether it was suggested that the tenement buildings required to be built just to house the people who worked to produce the very goods and material that were necessary for correct planning and for the prosperity of the whole of the country. Would he be wrong in suggesting that there was the possibility that correct planning had been stultified because of large estates where landowners had simply refused to allow that land to be developed notwithstanding that we thought it very necessary for correct planning of the County? Would Mr. Christie suggest that it was absolutely necessary, in order to preserve that very valuable land, which Mr. Sneddon agreed ought to be preserved, to house part of the community in large tenement buildings while another section of the community was allowed to have large estates? Mr. Sneddon said he was not singling out anybody. Then, would he say it was correct planning for Mr. Carlow to allow those very unsightly things to be added to every day because the possibility of the economic method of coal-cutting did not allow the coal-owners to put them down below? Mr. Sneddon referred to his visit to Comrie under the direction of Dr. Reid, when as a miner he was very interested to see the development so far as development was concerned, but was amazed to see the same unsightly bings there which he as a practical miner thought ought to have been left down below. As a planner interested in the planning of the County those things to him, whether they were a commercial success or not, ought not to be allowed.

Mr. Carlow had mentioned that it would be fine if the workers could be transported to their work so that they could enjoy relaxation away from the smoke and grime, but why should there be smoke and grime when they knew that this could be quite easily avoided? In the planning of the coal industry, which was Mr. Carlow's business, if they were going to plan correctly then they had to plan not only the surrounding community, but to get the best out of the products the workers produced, and Mr. Sneddon held that it was wrong to burn it in its raw state. These were just one or two of the questions which Mr. Sneddon wished to be answered. He was out to see that the County was planned correctly. He was out to say that if a bridge over the Tay was necessary then it ought to be put there irrespective of the opinion of anybody that it was stultifying development elsewhere.

Mr. Sneddon concluded by saying that he thought the Planning Advisory Committee in submitting their Report would be doing a great service to the community. The best thing one could give a community was service, service which would result in a better community for the coming generations.

Mr. *Carlow* said he had forgotten to mention that it was not necessary to give suggestions to-night as another opportunity was being given in Cowdenbeath on 22nd June, but meantime they wanted to explore the position and he would be glad to have another speech, critical or otherwise.

Mr. *J. C. Robertson (Local County Councillor)* said, looking at the question from the long point of view there was something in his mind which ought to come before building problems or industrial problems, and that was water. He felt very strongly on this point, that in the County of Fife there were far too many water authorities. The County Council, he said, had started a huge scheme which would cost a lot of money, but even with all their enthusiasm they found that Small Burghs were reluctant to collaborate. Why should all water resources not be utilised to their best purpose, he asked. What he could see was that some of the smaller water schemes were going to be left derelict, but if the whole thing was put under one water authority then the water could be utilised and a large amount of money saved in the cost of pipes and everything else.

Mr. Robertson's next point was drainage. The County Council, again due to their Provisional Order, laid down a scheme which had never been started, but it fell very much short of what was required; it only went the length of Thornton. If drainage was dealt with in the same manner as he had suggested for water, then there would be one scheme which would help considerably in the planning of the County. One point Mr. Robertson saw in small water authorities and small drainage schemes was that they were not able to pay a qualified man.

Mr. Robertson then referred to the question of unsightly bings. He thought the Chairman should know better than he did about this area, but there was in Scotland to-day a colliery at Whitehill which was 90 years of age where there were no bings. If it was possible to have a colliery as old as that with no unsightly bings, then he didn't see why it couldn't be carried out to-day.

Mr. *Moffat* said he had been very interested to receive the information he had from this Committee. He wished to raise a warning against our resources. There was much talk about waste, but that was not all; raw material was being exported for this war which we could ill afford. The nation came first at all times, and while the coal-owner might be willing to produce coal at a terrific rate if we wasted it we would certainly suffer.

Mr. Moffat was very glad Mr. McArthur had raised the question of the bing. He did not know what research had been made on this particular substance, but was it not possible to utilise this in prefabrication of buildings and so on? Was it not possible that we in this County could bring such an industry into the coalfield areas which were likely to become redundant in 50 years or so? He thought these points required consideration and was sure the community would be thankful for such service.

Bailie *Westwater* was very pleased the Chairman had raised the question of the combination of larger areas. This was a question he had propounded in the Lochgelly Council for some time, and he was sure that if there was closer co-operation between Burghs and the outlying districts it would be to the advantage of the area as a whole. They could all realise that if there wasn't some other industry introduced here the area was going to become derelict because coal was running out. From the point of view recreational point of view and then the industrial point of view. They could all realise that if there wasn't some other industry Bailie Westwater felt that a great deal more could be done jointly by Lochgelly, Cowdenbeath, Lochore, etc., than if Lochgelly asked for one thing and Cowdenbeath for something else. If the area was speaking as a whole he was quite sure very much could be accomplished. He suggested that the Planning Advisory Committee should explore the matter as much as they could.

Mr. J. C. Robertson speaking on the question of modern tenement buildings said he was not against these, but would only accept them so long as people with money were not going to have the liberty of occupying a cottage while the workers were to live in tenements.

Mr. Carlow said the impression seemed to be that the privileged would live in bungalows and the unprivileged in flats. The modern flats which he had personally had an opportunity of seeing in different countries seemed to possess numerous advantages rather than difficulties. The privilege was to get into these flats, but he would leave Mr. Christie to deal with the matter.

Mr. Carlow considered that in planning anything it had to stand on its own foundation. Mr. Sneddon, he said, had used the word " prosperity " time after time ; that meant that industry should stand on its own feet. A prosperous industry at least gave interest on the capital and a wage to the worker because capital could not function without interest and labour could not function without wages, and to build a beautiful place whether in the form of flats or bungalows, if everybody was going to be unemployed in a short period because the thing was uneconomic, would certainly be a blot on our planning. For instance, taking redd bings down the pit again, Mr. Carlow said, had been inquired into, but if that was going to get industry no trade and if they were going to compete with England and Wales apart from anything in the way of foreign countries, it was necessary to produce coal at a cost which would command a market. If they were going to put 1/- on the cost of coal by putting redd down the pit again, even if it was a possibility, which he didn't admit it was, it was the other phase of the picture which had to be considered, and he took the liberty of standing on the suggestion that things must stand upon their own feet if planning was to be fundamentally successful.

Mr. Robertson, he said, had fully explained his views about water and drainage and Mr. Carlow thought that one central authority seemed to be desirable. On the question of whether this could be done or not Mr. Carlow said he would have to get the views of the County Clerk, but if it was going to call for legislation it certainly couldn't be done in the near future.

With regard to the burning of raw coal Mr. Carlow agreed there was a great deal of waste, but again if it was going to cost 25/- to make £1 worth of coal then it would not be an economic proposition. The mining industry, he said, were spending hundreds of pounds to-day on research into the making of better use of coal. The best brains they could get and as much money as was necessary were being poured out in research work. Until they found the best method and until they found an economic method he didn't see how they could do much. One of the things which had made the problem much worse than it was was mechanisation. Mechanisation separated every individual man from his own bit of coal and nobody knew who put the stones among it. Unwashed coal used to be sold with considerable freedom, now everybody insisted that it was the proper thing to have washed coal, and every washer made dirt. Of 100 tons put in sometimes 25 tons came out as stones. These had to be put somewhere and couldn't be put down the pit again so they had to be added to the bing. As to its going on fire, they would be most grateful if anyone could put them in touch with better scientists than they were employing at present.

Speaking on the question of plastics Mr. Carlow said this was not a simple science. All the mining industry could do was to prepare a plastic powder. The question of plastic powder was at least held up by the war.

In America, he said, prefabrication was being carried out with material corresponding to a certain extent with our blaes and fireclay. This material was being used for prefabrication of not only cottages and small houses but of theatres and hotels. The process was very elaborate. American machinery had overcome some of the difficulties but it was necessary to have a very large number of houses being built in one place before it was worth while. They were not asleep in Fife, he said, and the County Clerk's Office had full particulars, supplied by him, for the use of their Housing Committees.

Mr. Christie said there were two points which he wished to deal with, the first raised by Mr. Sneddon. He remarked that if they wished to fill landowners' pockets they should continue as they were doing at present spreading houses over the countryside. Building in this manner was killing dairy farms, and they might find that in time to come they would have big sprawling villages but no milk. He wanted to see dairies continuing in the vicinity of our villages and towns so that they could get the pure clear article. Mr. Christie thought that some other method of building houses should be developed. There was a deep prejudice against tenements, but the modern type of tenement which he had visited in London was a very fine and beautifully worked building. It was people with money who were living in these flats. Mr. Christie held that so far as possible the choice should be left to the people to say whether they wished to live in a modern flat or in a bungalow. He wanted to see this Committee put forward the proposition that two or three centres should be left open in Fife for the erection of such flats, and that architects all over Scotland should be given the opportunity of submitting plans of modern flatted houses.

There would be difficulties and there would be differences of opinion, but Mr. Christie did hope in presenting their Report the Committee would produce something of value. The problem was so large and time so short that when their actual recommendations came it might look as if the " hen had laid a very small egg."

Mr. McArthur said there were one or two things which he would like to say. He thought that as workers they could all agree with everything Mr. Sneddon had said. He was also very much struck with Mr. Moffat's contribution because he thought that Mr. Moffat felt very much the same as they did.

Mr. McArthur then referred to an important feature in Mr. Mears' report dealing with the restoration of land. This meant, he said, that burning bings could be sent to places which had been suffering from subsidence caused by the extraction of coal and they could be covered with soil and planted for afforestation.

With regard to the question of prefabrication Mr. McArthur expressed the view that the machines which were in operation in America for this work could easily be brought to this country and used in this county, so providing a new industry for the people in Fife.

Provost Wilson called for a hearty vote of thanks to the Chairman. He thought they would agree that they had listened to something which had been more or less an education to them all. Mr. Carlow, he said, was a very busy man and it was up to every one of them to see what little hints they could give to the Committee which might prove a benefit to the district to which they belonged.

APPENDIX REFERRED TO

In response to invitation as advertised for suggestions for planning in the area, I respectfully submit the following :—
New Administrative Unit.—Before detailed Planning is finally decided on, I suggest consideration of a new Local Government

unit to comprise the parishes of Auchterderran, Beath and Ballingry (with adjustment on the eastern corner of the former parish, and including the Police Burghs of Lochgelly and Cowdenbeath).

My reasons for the suggestion are :—

1.   The area is exceptionally well adapted for such a scheme from every point of view.   Its topographical characteristics are eminently suited for planning a modern layout such as would furnish selective housing sites and attractive amenities.

New houses erected in any part of the area could be conveniently placed for people employed in any part of it.   Such parts of land unsuitable for cultivation could be utilised, at little cost, for recreational and pleasurable purposes.   Included in its boundaries are two lochs (Loch Gelly and Loch Ore) and part of a third (Loch Fitty) and a number of broad streams and burns.   Open-air bathing-pools could be constructed at comparatively small expense.   The whole could be usefully utilised in a layout.

2.   The area indicated has already, and indeed for a long period, been recognised as a homogeneous and well-adapted district for united public services.   Over sixty years ago consideration was given by public representatives for combined action between Lochgelly and Cowdenbeath to establish the utility services of water supply and lighting, but at that time parochial sentiment negatived these efforts.

The area was chosen under the Education Act, 1918, as one of Fife's Education Areas and confirmed by the Act of 1929 in the formation of one School Management Committee for the district outlined.   A similar arrangement was made by the County Council in 1930 in fixing it as a " Local Area " for administering Public Assistance and other delegated duties.

Higher education is centralised for the whole area in Beath High and St. Columba's Schools in Cowdenbeath, as well as a Technical School.

When war broke out in 1939 the area was chosen as a unit for Civil Defence purposes under the County Scheme, and as an area it provided a battalion of the Home Guard.

3.   The arrangement for constituting such a Local Government unit might have as basis :—

(a) Autonomy in local administration such as pertains at present in the case of the Smaller Burghs.

(b) The villages (at present administered by the County Council) have no boundaries and practically no executive power and consequently no inducement to develop enterprise in any direction.

(c) In the matter of the vital public services such as water supply, drainage, public health and welfare, education and main roads (such services are acknowledged to be regional or national concerns), the unit suggested would have direct proportionate representation on such Joint Boards as may be set up by the County Council or new regional authority.

(d) It would be a rating authority on similar lines to the Small Burghs, i.e. it would assess for its local responsibilities and, by a block payment, for other services.

4.   The area would be sufficiently large and rateable to take independent action in seeking to secure new industries.   Under the present restrictions on industrial development imposed on Fife (unjust and illogical), only smaller industrial concerns could meantime be possible ; but even so a number of light or minor industries would be of great value to the district.   The acquiring of land would be greatly simplified in allocating space for industrial development on a basis such as the Hillington Estate where individuals with ideas and application and a comparatively small capital could start small workshops or factories.   Such a scheme would give opportunities to ex-Service men in particular.

Potentialities should be considered because :—

(a) The area has positively only one industry, coal-mining, subject to the economic implications associated with it.   There is the further potentiality that in this particular district coal-mining will gradually decline.   According to the recent national report the axis of the coal industry in Fife will move from here to the east and west, to Thornton district and to the west of Dunfermline.   Accepting that as authoritative, a decline in population is inevitable.

(b) At present there is no industrial employment for women and girls.   It has always been their lot to travel by rail or 'bus to industrial centres to find employment.   This is not economic from any point of view.   It involves longer hours and extra physical strain.

(c) The male population has no opportunity or choice of industrial employment.   There is no alternative to the pits.

(d) The district is specially circumstanced in common interests, social, economic, scholastic, etc., a compact community eminently suited to be administered as a unit.

It may be adduced that under existing statutes there is no provision for setting up a new administrative unit. It should, however, not be overlooked that new co-operation ideas such as regional systems are expected to be a policy of the future.   These regional areas may be large or small, to be adapted presumably to secure the best possible communal and economic conditions for the people.   This particular area is a special case in point and, if the present local authorities were to present a case based on and amplified by our public representatives, it is not unlikely to be arbitrarily turned down by the higher authorities.

I have not presumed to enter into planning details. That is a matter for the specialist. It is certain, however, that such a unit as suggested would give great scope for planning on modern lines and in the well-being and general interests of the community.

(Sgd.)   A. G. WESTWATER.

Lochgelly, 25/5/45.

NOTES TAKEN AT PUBLIC MEETING HELD IN THE TOWN HALL, MARKINCH
4th June, 1945

Mr. Carlow (Chairman).
Provost Craik of Markinch called upon Mr. Carlow to address the meeting.

Mr. *Carlow* said he would like to explain as quickly as he could precisely who they were and what they wanted.   The County Council, he said, had a Planning Committee of members of the County Council but they wished to have advice in regard to industry and to the development of the County from people who were not members of the County Council.   Therefore they appointed a Planning Advisory Committee which consisted of a considerable number of people.   There were on this Committee, for instance, Sir James Irvine, Principal and Vice-Chancellor of St. Andrews University ; two from the coal-mining industry, one of whom was Mr. Carlow himself, and Mr. McArthur representing the miners ; two from the paper industry representing employers and employees, and so on.   They were therefore a body of employers and employed who had been deputed and requested to report to the County Planning Committee on what they considered to be the proper course for the development of the County and how that should be done in the opinion of industrialists.   Now, that

Committee was naturally too big and they therefore appointed three—Sir James Irvine, Mr. Christie, and himself. Sir James, he said, was not too strong at the moment and he was not able to come to all the meetings.

Mr. Carlow went on to explain that they had visited nearly all the Burghs in the County and had had the opportunity and advantage of discussing problems with nearly all the Provosts and representatives of the Town Councils, beginning at St. Andrews, Newport, Tayport, Crail on the east along to Dunfermline and Culross, the furthest on the west, and from one end to the other had been trying to get the views of the Provosts and Town Councils as to the planning of their respective areas. Over and above that, he said, they had also issued a questionnaire to all firms with a valuation of £100 or more. There were certain outstanding industrialists whom they were willing to wait upon personally to get any further information which these industrialists might desire to put forward. So it could be seen they had " ploughed the land " and indeed had sought for the " needle in the haystack " in the way of information and ideas. If, after all was said and done, people did not agree with what had been done, now was the time to speak, otherwise they should hold their peace for ever. Now was the time for every idea to be put in the pool. This afternoon, having had an opportunity of meeting with the Provosts and Town Councils of Leslie and Markinch, the Committee were now present to discuss finally any points which the public might wish to raise in regard to the future development of the area covered by this meeting. They hoped that the paper industry, Railway Co., etc., would send in their written notes—or speak of them now. Mr. Carlow said there were many things upon which the Committee wanted their views and he would only enumerate a few of them— roads, main arterial roads which would ultimately go through this County ; bridges, Forth Road Bridge and the Tay Road Bridge, and with regard to the latter they wanted to know if the people of Markinch and Leslie districts had any views as to whether it should be at Newport or Newburgh. Apart from the question of bridges and roads Mr. Carlow said there was another matter upon which he was sure they would wish to express their views, and that was whether there should be satellite towns in new places or whether existing towns should be developed and increased. Nobody, he said, could set down a general rule about these things. Mr. Carlow had in mind when the Committee went to Kirkcaldy and Burntisland that it would be a good thing to plan new housing schemes in the neighbourhood of Kinghorn where people would be taken away from the atmosphere of their work to a place where there was no industry. A similar problem, he said, was going to arise in this neighbourhood. This was a matter of decision which was not in the hands of the Committee at all. The new pits were to be in the neighbourhood of Kirkcaldy—the first at Thornton, the second in the neighbourhood of Dysart, and the third south of Kirkcaldy at Seafield. Evidence of all these Mr. Carlow had given before the Scottish Coalfields Committee set up by the Secretary of State for Scotland. The point was that the people who would work in these pits would have to be housed somewhere. One idea was they should be housed in the neighbourhood of Thornton ; another that the increase in housing should be at the east end of Kirkcaldy ; the third idea was that Milton of Balgonie might be enlarged into a satellite town, and another possibility was that the increase in population might be housed in the neighbourhood of Markinch. Markinch to Thornton was not far to take men to their work, and whether the increase in population should be housed at one of those four places was a matter which the Planning Committee might give advice upon and was a matter upon which the people of the district would have very definite and clear opinions.

In conclusion Mr. Carlow said that the Committee wanted to do everything possible to see that nothing would come in the way of future development and so that people would not come along in 50 years' time and say how stupid the people were in 1945. The Committee wanted to look ahead, and Mr. Carlow hoped they would be able to avoid major errors in the next 50 years. It was not, however, for him to give opinions. It was for him to indicate the scope of the Committee's inquiry and wait for the public views on any point affecting the development of this part of the County.

Mr. Christie thought from what Mr. Carlow had said it would be obvious that this work was exploratory in the hope of obtaining help for the production of this Report which had to be presented to the Planning Committee of the County Council. He thought he need hardly say it was an exceptionally difficult thing, dealing with the whole of Fife and the vast number of questions which were involved over 50 or 60 years, to produce anything but very general conclusions.

It was a very interesting point, he said, that between 1903 and 1938 25,000 acres in Fife, most of which was the best agricultural land in Europe, had been finally lost to agriculture. This was due partly, no doubt, to unwise spreading of towns in such a way that ground was simply absorbed and dairy farms overrun. It seemed to Mr. Christie that there was a possibility before them just now to make a suggestion to the County Council that an effort be made to see if there was another method of developing our towns so that this vast acreage would not be lost in future. There were examples of modern flats which were extraordinarily attractive to the people who lived in them. Mr. Christie went on to say that there was a prejudice in the country for tenement buildings, but he thought that if one could develop certain blocks of flats there might be development of very much more attractive towns, and those who did not want gardens would be freed from the necessity of keeping them up.

When they came to what Mr. Carlow had told them about the development of the new pits and added to that the information which Mr. Mears had brought out, that before 1970 they would have an increase of between 70,000 and 80,000 people for mining industry alone, the question had to be faced as to whether existing villages should be used for concentration areas or whether new satellite towns should be built up. Markinch was one of those places where a decision had to be taken. Was Markinch to be a centre round which a new town would develop, or should there be a completely new satellite town at Coaltown of Balgonie ? It seemed to Mr. Christie that in the event of Coaltown of Balgonie being used new churches, new halls, new everything would have to be built. The County, he said, had decided that Kennoway was to be one of those places which was going to be used for developing, and it is in regard to that point as to whether Markinch should be developed or a satellite town built that Mr. Christie was anxious to have opinions.

This increase in population of 70,000 people would probably mean that the area of Fife lying between Leven and Crail would become more or less a Riviera. They could see that it would develop along these lines. He thought that people in industrial areas would flock to that district and they would see the East Neuk of Fife develop as one of the most attractive Riviera areas there were in Scotland.

There were very many other lines upon which to explore. One was the question of recreation grounds and playing fields. Mr. Christie didn't know whether it was too visionary to hope or not that the County Council might in the future consider acquiring certain large areas where boys and girls might be taken to help with the planting of trees and where they would be able to go for week-ends to build their own huts.

Another point raised by Mr. Christie was that nearly every county in England had an experimental farm where boys could go to get certain insight into agricultural work and keep in touch with the very rapid progress in agriculture, while in Scotland it was necessary to send boys to Aberdeen or Auchincruive. Mr. Christie said he brought this matter up so that if anybody had any chance of supporting the scheme of a residential training farm they would please do so. The advances in scientific agriculture were very rapid at the moment and many of our good dairymen could not keep pace. If agriculture was to be the basic industry of the country they must see that their own agriculturists had the chance they ought to have.

Provost Anderson, Leslie, said there was the question of new developments in the coal pits. In the Burgh of Leslie they had

Scottish Plastics, De La Rue, Smith Anderson, and Ferguson & Co. All these firms wanted a considerable amount of female labour, and it would seem an advantage if they had a certain amount of mining population living in Leslie so that their daughters could have the opportunity of employment in these factories. The present great difficulty was lack of housing, but Leslie was very well situated and was relatively well off for parks and cinemas, and they were proud of their little Burgh.

Mr. Carlow then asked for discussion about satellite towns.

A member of the audience remarked that they had heard about 70,000 additional miners were likely to come to the County and asked what proportion of that number they might expect in this district of Markinch and Coaltown.

Mr. Carlow replied that he was not quite sure if he could give the correct figure. Mr. Mears had gone upon the basis of population in Cowdenbeath, which was eight non-miners to one miner. Mr. Carlow expressed the view that as the old pits ran out miners would be brought from those pits down to Thornton by train, and so avoid the necessity of finding houses for all the new miners. He visualised a train running from Dunfermline taking up passengers at Halbeath, Crossgates, etc., and bringing them to Thornton and taking them back again at the end of the shift. The apparent increase, he said, was not quite necessary if deductions were made for these factors, which were perfectly certain to take place. Between here and Kirkcaldy houses would be necessary and would be built perhaps in the next 10 years. The question was whether they wanted the concentration at Markinch, Coaltown of Balgonie, Thornton or Gallatown. In regard to the underground damage question Markinch was clear, Coaltown of Balgonie was not quite so safe, Thornton was not too good and Gallatown was very nearly safe.

Col. Balfour said that the question of dwellings had come before the Planning Committee about a year ago and the suggestion was that Markinch should be the centre of building for the Thornton mines. At that time Mr. Cameron, Thornton representative, said he was speaking for the railwaymen, and Markinch to Thornton was too far for railway workers to travel and that was the reason the area between Coaltown and Woodside was selected. Col. Balfour was anxious to have this question cleared up first and to know what distance miners could be away from their work.

Mr. Carlow said that the point was that living near the works had the great advantage that if any particular man was required for a break-down or emergency of any kind people didn't have to send miles to his house for him. However, what people wanted now was to get away from the pit. In the case of railways it might quite well be that the urgency of the calls upon railway servants made it more desirable that the railway servants should live near their junction than it was in the case of collieries. Mr. Carlow said he remembered one works where they didn't want any of their men to be far away because the works ran three shifts. In the collieries, however, the proportion of persons likely to be called away for emergency purposes was not so great. At Comrie they had a considerable number of houses within less than a mile of the pit, but all the miners lived at a much greater distance from the pit.

Miss Jobson said she had seen tentative plans for a new town at Coaltown of Balgonie and it did seem to her a bad scheme. She thought that once more miners were going to be segregated into a community. It seemed to Miss Jobson they wanted a mixture in a community and not a collection of people doing the same thing. There were no amenities in that part. All sorts of things would have to be built as there was nothing except a small hall ; whereas if they added to one of the present Burghs they had a good deal of accommodation there for the social side of the life of the people of the community. There didn't seem to be any point in having a satellite town when they had small towns already. Miss Jobson expressed the view that Kirkcaldy was big enough already and that it would not be good to add to its population. Markinch, she thought, would be a good place to put the housing.

Mr. White agreed with all that Miss Jobson had said. The workers might be some distance from their work but there were the added advantages of churches, parks, etc., also existing main line, and if a satellite town was built at Coaltown of Balgonie children proceeding to any of the Higher Grade Schools would have to travel to Markinch or perhaps to Cupar. From every angle the advantages were in favour of building at Markinch.

A member of the audience said he had listened to Miss Jobson and thought she had touched on the right solution. As they were aware, he said, the coal seam below Markinch was very thin as could be proved by the fact that in his time three pits had been opened up on Balbirnie but had had to be closed down. That was one thing he wanted to be kept in mind—it wouldn't be like Cowdenbeath, as coal wouldn't be drawn out below the houses. With regard to social services he thought Markinch was pretty well up to date. So far as drainage was concerned they knew that the drainage scheme which was proposed to come through Coaltown of Balgonie had been held up during the war ; water supply—they had a supply of their own, but drew from the County when water was short. So far as Coaltown of Balgonie was concerned it would not be right to build so near a burning bing, but on the west side of Markinch there was land owned by Colonel Balfour and this would be a very suitable place to build. Another point was that they had ample demand for female labour in Markinch.

Mr. Watson, Burgh Surveyor, said he would like to support previous speakers as regards concentration of houses round Markinch. In his opinion Markinch was the most modern, neatest and cleanest Burgh in Fife. It had also very good roads for transport and was on the main line. He thought it would be a mistake to make any more satellite towns as he thought Fife was a very bad example at the present time of town and country planning. It would be a mistake, he said, to make a satellite town at Coaltown of Balgonie. Markinch would not be very far from the new pit at Thornton, and provided roads were suitable there would be no transport difficulties. Perhaps a new road would be required to link up the new housing area with existing roads.

Another point was recreation ground. It was not good enough for Burghs and local authorities to find a park and say that was the recreation ground for the community, because he had yet to see a proper recreation ground in Fife. Most public parks were hilly and not suitable for sports and were used for grazing.

The only drawback Mr. Watson saw if housing was concentrated round Markinch was the drainage and water schemes. The existing sewage works was taxed to capacity at the present time but there was a scheme for the whole of the River Leven leading down from the paper mills to the estuary of the river, and it was proposed that Markinch should be linked up with that sewer. Then with regard to water supply this was not just too suitable or the quality too good for a big town, but when the regional water scheme came along they would be all right for a good and adequate water supply.

A member of the audience remarked that nobody seemed to have taken into account agricultural land. There was a lot of good agricultural land being ruined by the digging of coal on the surface. He mentioned a strip on the south side of Thornton running down to Gallatown.

Dean of Guild Guthrie inquired what number of houses they proposed to build at Markinch and what authority would be building them, and Mr. Carlow replied that he could not give particulars. Mr. Christie said that the long-range view on Kennoway was that there should be about 2000 houses, and he could imagine if Markinch was on the same scale it would be about 2000 or 3000, but that was just guess-work.

Col. Balfour remarked that if they were going to have a park at Milton of Balgonie and build churches and shops, that was going to take up far more land than enlarging Markinch, and from the financial point of view it must be much better to develop Markinch than build a completely new community.

A lady in the audience said Mr. Watson had referred to recreation grounds for youth, and she wished to stress that these were very necessary. She hoped that they would remember that it rained occasionally and that accommodation for indoor recreation was absolutely essential.

Mr. Carlow, speaking on the subject of female labour, said they were just as anxious that miners' daughters should find employment as the people of Markinch and Leslie were to have them. He did think that by the time their plans were drawn out, it might be found that the main arterial road would skirt the coalfields on the south side and come up round the Lomond Hills to a point between Abernethy and Newburgh to cross the Tay in that position. That would bring the arterial road very near Markinch giving direct access to Cowdenbeath, Lochgelly, Bowhill, and Kinglassie, and he thought that if workers were going to travel a few miles to their work it might be found that the main arterial road would come reasonably near the present mining centres and come reasonably near Leslie and Markinch, so that girls could get employment in Markinch and Leslie and go back to Cowdenbeath and Bowhill in the evenings. It would really be a coupling up of coalfields with the important manufacturing centres, which seemed to be a desirable thing.

With regard to the opencast workings, Mr. Carlow did not think that opencast workings had been so badly conducted as it might appear. He had been told that in Yorkshire coal seams had been worked and the land put back to its normal state and used for grazing purposes. At Woodbank it had taken a considerable time to take the soil out, but Mr. Carlow didn't think it would take so long to put it back. Mr. Carlow didn't think it would be desirable to move or alter a permanent housing scheme by a consideration such as the fact that the land had been damaged for 2 or 3 years by opencast coal operations. He was told that Markinch to Thornton was 2 or 3 miles, and didn't think that was too far for the general bulk of miners to live from the pit in which they worked. Apart from officials, engineers, etc., he agreed entirely with those people who didn't want to see the mining population isolated.

Mr. Carlow went on to say that there was another matter which had not been mentioned here, and although he knew he was treading on dangerous ground he felt it ought to be raised. At some of the places where they had had public meetings the idea had come to the surface that instead of having separate Burghs near together there should be some centralised authority to unify the control of water supply, drainage and many other things. It came to the surface at Lochgelly, where it was thought by people in the area that there ought to be some sort of unification of the Burghs of Cowdenbeath and Lochgelly and the rural areas of Glencraig, Lochore, Bowhill, Auchterderran and so forth, all of which could be grouped together in one area. They had learned when visiting Lochgelly that there were something like 5 water-pipes in one road, whereas if there had been a little planning one pipe would have done.

A member of the audience made reference to the condition of houses in the mining areas. If they went through any of these areas, he said, they would see new houses with battens and blocks of wood supporting them and cracks being kept together by various means. Of the three areas Mr. Carlow had mentioned, Gallatown, Thornton and Coaltown, none were safe from that sort of thing, but he had mentioned one area which was quite free from the danger of subsidence, and this the gentleman thought was a factor in favour of Markinch.

Mr. Carlow remarked that he had already said Markinch was free from any danger of subsidence. The last speaker, he thought, had grossly exaggerated the situation in the West of Fife.

Another member of the audience inquired if the question of the future power scheme had ever been thought of. One power scheme for the whole of the County of Fife, he thought, might be developed at one of the new pits and so save the transport of a tremendous amount of coal over the County.

Mr. Carlow replied that such a question was out of the hands of the Committee entirely.

Another member of the audience, referring to female labour, said that girls came from Methil, Methilhill, and Windygates to work at the distillery and they also came to the mills, and he felt that if houses were built in Markinch it would be in favour of the female labour.

Mr. Taylor, County Planning Officer, said that one question had not been brought up and that was the question of the green belt round Kirkcaldy. Somebody had mentioned a figure of 40,000 for population of Kirkcaldy, but Mr. Taylor believed that Kirkcaldy had in mind developing to 50,000 or 60,000 and the County Council was considering the question of a green belt round Kirkcaldy. He said the Committee were anxious to have observations and suggestions on that point.

Mr. Taylor went on to say that some people seemed to have got the idea that the County Council was proposing to build new satellite towns up and down the County. He didn't think the County Council was going to build an entirely new town unless it was round a nucleus of development. He thought that if possible existing amenities should be used and built round. The question of subsidence, he said, was being carefully considered by the County Council and wherever possible new houses would be built in perfectly safe areas.

Another question had been raised—why hadn't we brought along plans showing exactly what we were going to do ? As the Chairman had emphasised, they would have been very silly to bring plans without first obtaining the observations and views of the people of the district concerned, because any plans without their observations would be of little avail.

Miss Jobson referred to the question of the possibility of building tenements, and thought it would be of value if they had the views of some of those present as to the desirability of such buildings as against the present housing schemes.

Mr. Christie remarked that it was striking somewhat new ground, and what he would like to see would be the County Council throwing open to architects all over Scotland a competitive scheme for the production of plans for some form of new community dwelling suitable for erection in the future in connection with the big growth of population that might come in certain areas. One County in England had produced plans of 25 types of houses, and it seemed to Mr. Christie to be an opportunity to throw it open to architects to produce some of these plans so that they might be studied.

Lady Ruth Balfour remarked that the Department of Health had produced a booklet of approved designs so that if one of these designs was used there would be no delay in Government approval. Lady Ruth asked if Mr. Christie's idea of a tenement would include a lift and possibly continuous hot water, as these would be a marked improvement for any housewife.

Mr. Christie said he personally could not see anything against a type of building which did have a lift and continuous hot water and even a communal restaurant. If they had one of these buildings centred in a playing area they could develop an extraordinarily attractive town by having flats for those who didn't want gardens.

Lady Balfour remarked that the question of land would have to be considered.

Mr. Watson, Burgh Surveyor, said he would like to raise a point in connection with woodlands. Round about Markinch a great many beautiful trees were being cut down and Mr. Watson wished the County Planning Committee to keep in mind that trees blend into housing schemes of to-day.

Mr. Watson went on to say that he would like to support what Mr. Christie had said about blocks of flats. Before he came to Markinch, the local authority he was with put up blocks of flats, each with a sun balcony. One boiler also supplied hot water for the whole of the block and at the rear there was a playground for children. To Mr. Watson these blocks of flats were ideal. He was also of the opinion that in every town it was necessary to have a certain percentage of bungalows and semi-detached houses.

Mr. *Taylor* stated that no plan ever came before the County Council without the request being made that trees, if possible, should be worked into the layout.

A *member of the audience* thought it would be a very retrograde step to erect flats or tenements. He could not imagine people here, who had been used to bungalows, taking kindly to flats. They were detrimental to the health of the people and to the morale of the people.

Mr. *Carlow* hoped they would look at this question dispassionately. Don't let us think, he said, that flats are something to be ashamed of merely because they are flats. If people preferred bungalows, then it was because they had never seen the modern flat, otherwise they wouldn't be so tied to the bungalow type as the people he had met recently. Flats had many advantages over bungalows. In modern flats if you wanted your laundry done you had just to put it in a bag and it came back laundered. If you wanted to post a letter you didn't have to go out in the rain. There was a communal restaurant in nearly all blocks of flats, he said, and if people didn't want to be bothered cooking they could just go down to the restaurant for their meals.

A *member of the audience* inquired if these would be economic to the class of people for whom they were wanted. Our Burgh Surveyor, he said, spoke about putting down playgrounds for the children. That was going to use up land again. A certain number of flats with central heating had been put up in Dundee, but the rent of these was £52 per annum.

A *lady in the audience* thought it was time some progress was made and something done to relieve the housewives and let them get out with their children. As things were at present it was continual drudgery, and she felt that these modern flatted types of houses were just what the mothers of this country needed.

Mr. *Carlow* thoroughly agreed with the views of the previous speaker. The question would be, he said, how many could be accommodated in one block. It might be that 4 storeys would make them cheaper than having 3, and he didn't think they should close their minds to the possibility. For flats only the one foundation and one roof were required. Mr. Carlow was very pleased to note that in Markinch they didn't close their minds to the two possibilities, modern flats or modern bungalows.

A *member of the audience* remarked that he expected modern flats would be very different from the present flatted types of houses. The biggest difficulty there was noise.

A *lady in the audience* said there had been a lot of talk about improvements for the miners and mill workers but so far she hadn't heard anything about improvements for the agricultural workers. She was a farmer's wife and didn't think farm workers wanted to be isolated on the farms all the time. She thought that if they could have a few houses built in villages where there were a good number of surrounding farms it would take the agricultural workers away from the farms and let them mix with the community.

Mr. *Christie* had noticed that they had not touched on that question. He said the Committee had received a most excellent report from one or two of the main agriculturists in the Auchtermuchty area, who had, after examining in detail 17 farms, produced statistics that out of 99 workers 64 must be on the farms, but the other 35 could be accommodated in a community centre, and they strongly urged that this should be done. No doubt they were aware that the County Council had been experimenting with putting up untied houses for agricultural workers, and Mr. Christie thought it was inevitable that this should take place. Mr. Christie went on to say that he had been getting an insight into modern developments since becoming a member of the Advisory Committee. He had found that coal companies no longer housed their workers; Scottish Co-operative Society no longer housed their workers, and he remarked that landowners had been very slow to learn. Landowners, he said, had been in many ways exceptionally badly hit. During the last 40 years rents had remained the same, but costs had risen by between 300 and 400%, and he did think they were coming to the stage where some of them would have to go to the County and say " please house our workers."

A *member of the audience* remarked that there was plenty of ground which was not too good for agriculture and a few houses could be built there.

Provost Anderson, speaking on the question of female labour, said bringing in female labour from outside made a very long day, and he thought it would be better if the girls could be accommodated in the town.

Mr. *J. B. Rae* supported Provost Anderson and said they did feel it would be better if the girls were situated in Markinch area.

Mr. *Carlow*, in closing the meeting, wished to thank the people for coming to the meeting and giving the Committee their opinions, and called for a vote of thanks to Provost Craik for making things go so smoothly.

NOTES TAKEN AT PUBLIC MEETING HELD IN THE DENBEATH MINERS' INSTITUTE, WEMYSS AREA
11th June, 1945

Mr. *Carlow* (Chairman).

Mr. Carlow welcomed those present and hoped they would have a useful meeting. His purpose, he said, was not to occupy any more time than was necessary in explaining the situation in which they found themselves to-day in their planning campaign.

One of the purposes of this meeting was that those interested in the district would have an opportunity now of stating as fully as they could what they had in view, and a further opportunity would be given at a later date.

What the Committee set out to do was to survey the County of Fife with a view to planning for a period of perhaps 40 or 50 years, particularly having in mind not only the amenity and cultural side, but the commercial and industrial side. The Committee did wish to prevent themselves from doing something to-day they might be sorry for later on. For instance, Mr. Carlow took the example of the new collieries. The Fife Coal Company, he said, knew quite well where these new pits would be and they had informed the County Council accordingly. It was the duty of those interested in the County to see that that ground was not occupied by a housing scheme or anything else and so render it useless as a colliery. Similarly, they wanted to know developments which industry wished to make. For instance, the Editorial Sub-Committee were going to have meetings with people interested in paper, textiles, agriculture, etc. with a view to coming to arrangements so that these industries could develop to the best advantage. Mr. Carlow said he was always accused of being too economically minded and always looking to the pounds, shillings and pence, but he always said that bread and butter were very desirable before you put on the jam. Culture and beauty would lose a great deal of their charm and desirability if there were no wages coming in and unemployment was rife. Sir James Irvine, Mr. Carlow said, had come all the way from St. Andrews to attend this meeting and he hoped he might look upon Sir James as one of those particularly interested in the culture and elevation of the community, while he might be looked upon as a hard-hearted industrialist.

Here Mr. Carlow remarked that the second public meeting for the Wemyss area would be held in the Co-operative Hall, Leven, on 25th June.

Mr. Carlow pointed out on maps prepared by the County Planning Officer the area covered by the meeting. One of the features of the Wemyss area, he said, was that it was one of the richest, if not the richest, coalfield in Great Britain.

Mr. Carlow went on to say that, apart from visiting all the Provosts in the Small Burghs, they had also issued a questionnaire to all industrial firms in the County having a valuation entry in excess of £100 per annum. If they did not get all the information by public meetings and by the questionnaire, the Committee were prepared to meet any industrialists who wished to meet them, with the sole purpose of getting all the opinions and points of view possible so that their report might be worth while. Mr. Carlow begged any person who thought he could contribute to this big question to do so to-night or on 25th June, or to send his points to the County Clerk who would be glad to receive them on behalf of the Committee.

The Committee were anxious to have the ideas of the public as to whether workers should be housed near their work or whether they should be housed away from the smoke and smell of industry. Another point, which Mr. Christie was very keen about, was how many houses should be built to the acre as so much good agricultural land was being taken up for housing purposes. Arising out of this, Mr. Carlow said there had been quite a lot of discussion regarding flatted houses. With regard to the question of housing people away from their work Mr. Carlow related how, when visiting Burntisland, the Committee had found that most of the people lived outside Burntisland. He had therefore suggested that it would be a good thing to develop Kinghorn, which had water supply, churches, etc, and take the people away from the atmosphere of their work. Mr. Carlow said he was merely mentioning some of the points which had cropped up at previous meetings.

Mr. Carlow then dealt with the question of great arterial roads through the County and of road bridges over the Tay and Forth. In that connection, he said, the Committee were trying to get the location of industry in Fife, and assuming that they got the facts he felt that the compilation of these facts should indicate where the roads should be.

Mr. Carlow welcomed Sir James Irvine and called upon him to say a few words. He also apologised for the absence of Mr. Christie who was on holiday.

Sir James Irvine said he would like to pay tribute to the Fife County Council for the way in which it had approached this extremely complex problem. Taking it by and large he wondered if there was any County which presented problems so difficult as Fife. The way the County had gone about it was to get expert advice as to where there had been drifts of population ; why people left one area to go to another and, as far as possible, where drifts would come in the next 50 or 60 years. That had meant an enormous amount of work and he thought that most County Councils would have proceeded then to make their plans. In place of that the County Council had acted in a purely democratic way, and that was why the Sub-Committee were there to-night. Although there were certain things of a broad general nature which the County Council could decide there must be many problems of the individual—what did they want? What was going to add to the happiness of their life ? These were local problems, and that was why Mr. Carlow and his Committee had been going round the County for the last two months. The County Council, he said, deserved great praise for the way they had conducted the business. The Committee, he said, were there to hear what they wanted and to have their views.

Mr. Taylor said they were there to get the public's suggestions or observations for the general improvement of future planning of this area. The County Council could have prepared a Planning Scheme for this area, but if it did not take into account the general wishes of the population, it would have been of little use. If they could help in any way or suggest anything for the betterment of the County, the Committee would be very pleased to hear from them.

Mr. Taylor said the Planning Department had been able to draw up a series of pictures which might be termed the background from which they were working. You must take into consideration, he said, your natural features when drawing up a scheme. Mr. Taylor then explained maps showing the contours of the County ; another showing uneconomic coalfields and more productive areas ; one showing the best agricultural land in the County ; and another showing the various densities of traffic over the various roads in the County, the density being shown by the width of the roads.

Mr. Taylor explained that the object of a Planning Scheme was not to make the best use of every piece of land, but he would not like them to run away with the idea that once this Report was published a " New Jerusalem " would appear overnight. The Planning Committee's job was to control planning to the best advantage. It was there to see that a town was in the right place and to see that town land was allocated in the proper places for shops, schools, churches, etc.

Mr. Carlow then appealed for suggestions.

A member of the audience asked if the Advisory Committee, once they drew up their scheme, intended to try as far as possible to get it carried out in spite of the fact that Fife was not a development area. As they possibly knew, the Burgh had invited all organisations and interested bodies to form a Development Committee to come forward with proposals so far as the Burgh of Buckhaven and Methil was concerned. This Committee had arrived at certain suggestions which this gentleman thought could be considered. As was well known, the Burgh of Buckhaven and Methil was largely interested in the mining industry, and he thought the period between the two wars showed that any area which was dependent on one industry only was liable to get into a sort of a mess. The result had been that this Development Committee, with the approval of the Town Council, drew up a number of suggestions to invite new industries into this area so that they would not be entirely dependent on the mining industry. Some points were that it would be desirable to try to get plastic industry introduced in or around the Burgh. There was practically no work inside the Burgh for female labour. Due to the war most of their women had become semi-skilled and skilled, and it would be a crime if these women were thrown over after the war. It was therefore considered that carpet-weaving should be induced to come to the Burgh or perhaps silk industry, woollen industry, pottery or laundry. It was also suggested that they might have small boat building at Buckhaven. They also hoped it would be possible to get the Fife Coal Company and the Wemyss Coal Company to consider the matter of establishing by-products from coal in or near the Burgh. They considered that the Burgh of Buckhaven and Methil had something which other Burghs in Fife had not got. They had rail and road transport and also docks. It was recognised that the docks were built primarily for the export of coal, but there was the possibility that there would not be the same volume of coal as there had been in the past, but with modernising of the docks other facilities could be introduced for import. These were some of the points which were agreed upon with the Town Council so far as industry was concerned.

Mr. Goodwillie thought they had got to be indebted to Sir James and Mr. Taylor and to the explanatory position which the Chairman had put before them. Mr. Goodwillie thought that in Buckhaven they were about at the end of their tether until they could get extension of the Burgh boundaries. They wanted decent houses and places where children could romp about. He thought the Chairman would agree with them that workers expect, not only in the mining industry but in every industry, a decent standard of living.

Mr. Goodwillie was struck with Mr. Taylor's point in connection with the planning of the County and how they did in the old days. He thought the time had come to plan ahead. He assumed that the contention of the Advisory Committee was that the days were now past when houses had to be built round a coal-pit. The houses could be built in Kennoway and Windygates where the people would get away from the smoke and dust.

A *member of the audience* said he came from East Wemyss and he thought at this time of day it was a disgrace that people should be living in or about coal-mining areas beside burning bings. When he was younger he used to blame the Laird for refusing to give them sites on which to build, but now he saw the Laird was doing them a good turn because the ground was just a shell. They were now living in the age of transport and people could quite easily be transported to and from their work.

Mr. *Hudson* said he would like to deal with the question of the docks. The proposals which he was submitting, he said, were placed before the Town Council of Buckhaven and Methil by an Advisory Committee and were to the effect that the time was considered ripe when Methil Docks should be modernised and electrified. He pointed out that some of the hoists were built as far back as 1888, 1897, and the most modern hoist in 1910. He understood that the usual life of such machinery was 30 years. Of course, certain repairs had been carried out but they found hoists out of use for months on end. Mr. Hudson considered electrification of Methil Docks would be an economic proposition. He thought they would all agree that Buckhaven and Methil was a growing Burgh which was likely to have a much larger population than it had at present. He understood there were some proposals made for the opening of new coalfields in the immediate vicinity, somewhere between Leven and Kennoway and also somewhere near Balgonie. He was of the opinion that while coal export from the whole of Scotland might decrease there was a possibility that the coal export for this part of the country might increase, and with that end in view he thought full consideration should be given to having more modern machinery introduced. Mr. Hudson went on to say that some of the hoists could only lift 19 tons 10 cwts. and with these hoists stuff could not be handled adequately. One crane was capable of lifting 22 tons 10 cwts. ; one 3 tons 10 cwts. and the remainder 30 cwts., which was not adequate for present needs. Mr. Hudson understood it had been agreed to spend a quarter of a million pounds on Leith Docks, but in his opinion Methil Docks were the first docks in the Firth of Forth, and once again he stated it would be an economic proposition to modernise them. He thought Methil Docks could be developed for exports and also for imports with the possibility of new industries springing up.

Mr. Hudson suggested that the London and North Eastern Railway Company should be approached for a waggon building and repair shop at Methil. At the present time, he said, waggons were removed to repair shops at Leith, Ladybank and elsewhere. In his opinion such a workshop would be a great advantage and would also cause a certain amount of work in the district. He thought they could also put forward the suggestion that an additional roadway should be made into the docks.

Another point worthy of consideration was the landing of fish at Methil. In the past, cargoes of fresh fish salted had been sent from Methil to Germany. Sir James Irvine thought that a certain amount of these cargoes was used for fertilising.

Reference had been made to the Forth and Tay bridges, and in Mr. Hudson's opinion these were very necessary for the prosperity of Fife. Another point was the bridge between Leven and Methil. He understood plans were on the way, but one thing was certain, something had to be done immediately.

Sir *James Irvine* said it was not a case of answering questions so much as expressing his own appreciation of the form which the discussion had taken. He had been trying to get a broad picture of it all. With the modernising of Methil Docks a great many things must follow in its train, he said. Electrification, proper road access, and if that scheme was to grow then of necessity the railway companies would have to put down their own repair shops instead of sending waggons elsewhere.

They had also had the plea made by the first speaker—'' Woe betide any area which lives on one industry.'' When the day of hardship came everybody suffered, and Sir James thought the general idea of trying to interweave other industries with the stable industry was all to the good and should be prosecuted. Sir James believed there was a great future for plastics, but the great difficulty was access of the raw materials. With the docks at their door, however, this area was largely independent of the heavy costs of rail transportation, and therefore there was a possibility, which was not so easily available in other parts of the County which had been examined, for this all-essential industry.

Granted, with these developments coming along, enabling people to live in a decent way, in a happy way, they came down to the question of housing. Sir James was glad to hear the general expression of opinion that in these days of transportation it was not a hardship but an advantage for a man to live away from his work. That led up to the general scheme which was, instead of allowing a hamlet to be set up here and another about half a mile away these should be grouped into little centres where you would have, if not exactly a self-contained community, a decent neighbourly life with some form of entertainment which would take the people away from their work. A great many people in facing that part of the problem said that if you lived in the agricultural part of Fife you could go to the neighbouring towns and there have your decent entertainment. That was quite true, said Sir James, but in doing that they were losing the neighbourly spirit, they were leaving the place where they naturally lived and going to other places. In place of this, Sir James said, the ideal neighbourly way was to gather together in their leisure time ; hence this idea of community centres. They didn't mean anything highly regimented ; it wasn't going to be an altogether planned idea but was intended to give people a chance of living in friendly relationships with one another, and Sir James added '' God help this country if our standard of family life vanishes.'' These, he said, were general ideas which had crowded through his mind. In conclusion, Sir James thanked the various speakers for the way in which they had put forward their opinions.

Captain Wemyss said he was speaking as a member of the Wemyss village. On the question of housing he felt there was a point which was important. We divided the building of houses into two groups, he said—the first group by local authorities and the second by private individuals. He thought we had got to be very careful that in the building by local authorities we did not neglect the opportunity for a private individual to build his own house, and he felt that that was made very difficult unless they were very careful to have sites prepared with gas, electricity, water, etc. which could easily be taken up by a private individual. Captain Wemyss thought there should be a place where a feuar could take up his site and get gas or electricity handy, and he was anxious to see in Wemyss village an area scheduled where that could happen, and he said if they didn't do that they were going to delay their housing.

Another question was reconstruction of houses. He didn't know what percentage of people lived in new houses, but everybody seemed to want to live in new houses. When you came to think about it, quite a large number of the population lived in houses more than 25 years old. He thought that reconstruction should be carried out more and more.

One other question was factory sites. It has always been rather a difficult question. Captain Wemyss remembered when the British Aluminium Company wanted to come to Methil, but at that time they couldn't feu them the ground because the Fife Coal Company were working Leven mineral. Now there was not much coal to be worked near the river, and he felt that they should schedule an area close to the docks where factories could be built if somebody came along to do it. Those who would come along would be people who imported raw material and an industry which would consume a large quantity of coal. These, in Captain Wemyss' opinion, were the two types of industry they were likely to get and he did think the banks of the River Leven should be scheduled for such purposes.

One other point was co-operation between local authorities. They had a very good example in the fringe of land between the River Leven and Buckhaven Burgh, which was a sort of "No Man's Land." The County Council rightly wanted to put a drain along the River Leven, and if that was done you could drain houses on the land between the Burgh, but that land had been sterilised because the drain went along the main road. If the drain along the river had been put in years ago, Captain Wemyss thought they would have had good sites for houses. The difficulty was getting co-operation at the boundary between two local authorities. In this area you had the Burgh of Leven, Fife County Council and the Burgh of Buckhaven, and it was very difficult to get any reasonable plan agreed to by all three parties.

A member of the audience wished to suggest that when they came to build houses these should not be of the flatted type as people had absolutely no privacy in these houses. He was in favour of the bungalow type where people could get privacy and rest.

Another member of the audience remarked that he had glanced at the Coalfields Report and agreed with a lot of the proposals in regard to the placing of houses. At one time it might have served a good purpose to have houses near the works, but now he felt they should be built away from the works. While Captain Wemyss' idea of renovating houses was all right, you would never make new houses out of old. This gentleman also thought the bungalow type was the proper type for workers.

The next speaker said he was not going to deal with the type of house but thought they should discuss the practical aspect of how they were going to get the houses built as early as possible. So far they had been largely dependent in Fife on local authorities, and so far there had been no attempt made to introduce Housing Societies, who did not act as competitive authorities but acted along with the local authorities. He thought some consideration should be given in the Report to the formation of these Housing Societies. This speaker understood they could get 80% grant from the Government acting entirely on their own and where assisted by a local authority up to 90%.

Mr. *Taylor, County Planning Officer,* asked to say a few words before Mr. Carlow wound up the meeting. The first speaker, he said, mentioned that Buckhaven had a considerable number of detailed proposals. Whilst these might be too minute for the Advisory Committee, if they could send them along to the County Planning Committee they might be of value, or better still, if they would like to have a meeting to discuss them Mr. Taylor said he would be only too pleased to go down to Buckhaven.

The next point was the question of industries. Mr. Taylor said if they could find him an empty factory with 10,000 square feet he might be able to introduce them to a firm who wanted such a factory. Here a member of the audience suggested the old net factory, Randolph Street.

Mr. Taylor then mentioned the question of fish. He said they were hoping to make a short paper on fishing and would be very pleased to receive any information which the people of this area could supply.

Captain Wemyss, he said, mentioned the question of public services. The County Council, he said, was preparing a Planning Scheme, and one of the first considerations was to draw up a map showing all existing public services and try to limit development to areas, in the first place, where public services were available so that planning and development would be an economic proposition.

Mr. Taylor thought the Chairman would deal with the question of flats. He (Mr. Taylor) happened to live in a flat and did not experience the difficulties mentioned by some of the speakers. Flats, he said, need not be like that if properly constructed.

Mr. *Carlow* in winding up the meeting dealt with some of the more important points.

With regard to the Location of Industries Bill, Mr. Carlow said that this Bill had been withdrawn for the present. It might come on again, but they could be sure there were many districts as much opposed to it as they were. The whole object of it was to make an effort to influence manufacturers to put their works in places where there was the greatest risk of unemployment.

In connection with the question of plastics Mr. Carlow said all he could say on the matter was that they were in touch with the best scientists in the country. As soon as they saw a process which would contain more than an average chance of prosperity and success he would be very pleased to hear about it.

Mr. Carlow went on to say that he agreed with the desirability of finding work for the women population at carpet-weaving, wool, silk, pottery, linen. Again he suggested that if these things were a commercial possibility, if they contained a reasonable prospect of success, they would come naturally, and he thought their best chance was that somebody on behalf of the County Council should collect all information possible in regard to unused sites, vacant buildings, local rates and taxes, transport—road, rail and sea, and it might even be air—supply of water, labour supply and many other things, and occasionally these might be advertised in the *Scotsman* or other standard newspapers.

With regard to boat-building Mr. Carlow thought Buckhaven had old traditions in boat-building, but it was perhaps a matter of competition with Pittenweem, where boat-building was likewise a traditional industry among the people there, and he believed that possibly they retained boat-building because of the fishing-boats which were still being built. To try and uproot boat-building from Anstruther and Pittenweem and bring it up to Buckhaven would be unwise.

So far as modernisation of the docks was concerned, Mr. Carlow thought that in fairness to the Railway Company, until facilities at the docks threatened to be insufficient for our trade it didn't lie with us to make any concrete plan to the Railway Company. The moment the day came, however, when the export of coal was more than could be coped with by the docks, then he assured them he would be the first to start an attack on the Railway Company to extend the dock.

Mr. Carlow agreed that a new carriageway into the docks from the east end was desirable, but it meant a new bridge over the Leven which would land traffic on the crowded High Street or North Street and supplement the difficulties which already existed, but if the industry of this parish did call for that he would be the first to support it.

Somebody, Mr. Carlow remarked, wanted an extension of the Burgh. Well, he was very pleased that did not fall within his purview.

The question of housing workers away from the works, he said, had been debated. Take, for instance, farm workers. Every farm had a row of cottar houses, and they formed a community. He did not say that was ideal, but at every farm there were animals and those who looked after these animals had to live on the farm. Those who tilled the land could perhaps be housed away from the farm, but that would leave those who had to be on the farm more isolated than ever. In regard to people living near their work, certain kinds of industries, such as paper, required their workers to be near at hand because they ran 24 hours a day. If anything went wrong certain men particularly suited to the job were required to put it right, and it would be very detrimental to the success of their industry to have people living away from their work. Mr. Carlow remarked, "In principle, yes ; in practice, it is not so easy." Then people told him if you took men away the children had to travel to school. You either had to transport the children to school or transport the men to their work, and it appeared that each case called for special consideration. Mr. Carlow went on to say he did not think there would be a miner within a mile of the Fife Coal Company's new pits. They would have houses within three-quarters of a mile for key-men and junior officials, but the miners would be at least a mile away.

Reverting to the question of the capacity of the docks, Mr. Carlow remarked it mattered not whether the hoists were worked by electricity or hydraulically so long as the Railway Company shipped all the coal they could supply to them for the purpose. He did not think they could complain if the hoists might not be the most modern. As soon as they told him there was import business with which import cranes could not cope, if they wanted him to help them he would certainly do it.

With regard to waggon building and repairing, Mr. Carlow asked, " Why should one particularly seize upon waggon building and suggest it should be done at Methil Dock ? " Two-thirds of the coal shipped from Methil Docks, he said, was transported in traders' waggons. Why should the Railway Company set up repairing of waggons for one-third of the traffic ? The Fife Coal Company didn't want the Railway Company to repair their waggons. They repaired their own at Cowdenbeath and Lochgelly, and no doubt the Wemyss Coal Company would do their own in their own workshops.

The question of the Bawbee Bridge did not come within the scope of the Committee. As Mr. Carlow understood it they could look at the trade, business, amenities and culture of Fife and try to see that nothing was done which would stand in the way of the best development.

With regard to the deafening of flats, Mr. Carlow remarked that it was quite obvious the flats mentioned by various speakers had not been constructed in a decent manner. Mr. Carlow then told the meeting that Mr. Christie had informed him of a case where everybody had to have bungalow type houses. There were to be so many to the acre and 13 dairy farms were destroyed in the process, and when everything was finished they had plenty of houses but no milk.

In conclusion, Mr. Carlow thanked the audience for attending and for their expressions of opinion.

NOTES TAKEN AT PUBLIC MEETING HELD IN THE CO-OPERATIVE HALL, BROAD STREET, COWDENBEATH
22nd June, 1945

Mr. Carlow (Chairman).

Owing to the small attendance, the meeting took the form of an informal discussion.

Mr. Carlow asked how Cowdenbeath looked upon the suggestion made at the public meeting in Lochgelly that in places which were close together like Cowdenbeath and Lochgelly and villages in the neighbourhood there should be one governing body—something in the nature of a Joint Committee. Bailie Blamey said that Cowdenbeath had suggested that many years ago. They wanted amalgamation for water schemes, but Lochgelly said they had abundance of water although this had not been exactly borne out by the facts. Before the 1929 Act, he said, their minds were exercised about a drainage scheme. Many plans were discussed with the County authorities, Lochgelly and Cowdenbeath, but these came to nothing, and the result was that Lochgelly, Lumphinnans, Lochore and Glencraig all put their sewage into the River Ore in crude form.

The next point raised by Mr. Carlow was whether, in order to save good agricultural land, it would not be better to build at least some of the new houses in the form of flats. These had many advantages over the bungalow, provided, of course, they were well constructed.

Provost Drylie expressed the view that in cities flats might be all right, but so far as this area was concerned the people preferred to have bungalows with gardens.

Bailie Blamey remarked that census of public opinion was in favour of bungalows, but provided flats were modern and well constructed he was not against them.

Mr. Peter McArthur remarked that there was general criticism of the keeping up of workers' gardens, but it had to be kept in mind that the removal of railings did not help matters.

Mr. Carlow then asked Mr. Taylor, County Planning Officer, if he had any idea of the relative cost of building flats, to which Mr. Taylor replied that he did not have actual figures but it would be decidedly cheaper to house people in properly constructed flats than in bungalows.

Dr. Reid referred to a scheme in London, built in horse-shoe shape, and the density of movement in any one area was not great. They had a great many entrances and there was no prospect of footpaths being damaged by over-use.

Mr. Carlow then asked if it would be safe to say that the opinion of this little meeting was that provided flats were well built with good amenities there was not very much objection to the building of large blocks of flats where ground was valuable and space difficult.

A gentleman expressed the view that the question could only be answered by trial and experience. If they were going to embark on other forms of building, he thought they should experiment with flats. They did offer considerable facilities.

Mr. Carlow then raised the question of light industries. Cowdenbeath, he said, used to have a bleachfield and linen factory but both these had failed. Was there any other kind of industry, he asked, which anybody thought might do better in Cowdenbeath? Someone had mentioned the making of miners' tools instead of having them imported. The difficulty was mass production. A person making 100,000 shovels could sell them at a cheaper price than a man making, say, 100 and trying at the same time to switch over to something else. Mr. Carlow said the Committee were anxious to know what they could do about getting light industries established in a place like Cowdenbeath. He had told everybody that they were not industrialists in the sense that they could bring industries to the town ; all they could do was to advertise the place. He had said repeatedly that the County Clerk might have a list in his office compiled from information supplied to him by the Provosts and Town Councils, of vacant factories, vacant ground, and information such as low rating, good transport—road and railway—supply of female labour, etc., and an advertisement put in the *Scotsman* perhaps once a week. Mr. Taylor stated that a list of vacant factories in Fife was issued yesterday. Bailie Blamey thought the way to keep vacant factories in reasonable condition was to de-rate them.

Mr. Peter McArthur asked what the possibilities of light casting industry were in a town like Cowdenbeath.

Mr. Carlow explained that that industry was now concentrated near Falkirk, and the people there had persevered and were thoroughly engrained in the trade. It would be difficult to get that taken away from Falkirk, he said, unless somebody could invent a process which had not been thought of by the Falkirk experts. What Mr. McArthur visualised, however, was that with the great building operations to come the demand was going to outgrow the supply, and he felt there were glorious opportunities in a town like Cowdenbeath for the casting industry. Mr. Carlow expressed the view that fabricated steel was going to take the place of cast-iron, and Dr. Reid explained that the Fife Coal Company's new bay was for fabricated steel, and if this was successful, he said, they would build another one. He hoped they were going to make something new of this question of miners' tools and was hopeful that they would be able to turn out picks and shovels on very new lines. Mr. McArthur said they would have to consider the amount of female labour transported away from the town. Dr. Reid was of the opinion that female labour could be employed in the finishing of the shovels. The great snag was that the Fife Coal Company did not have a place to go to and had to experiment in a corner of the workshop.

Dr. Reid made reference to the James Street area in Cowdenbeath which he thought would make a very fine site for factories. It was free from subsidence, and rail connection would not be a serious difficulty. He wondered if the Town Council could not do something about it. The structural work, he said, could be done in Cowdenbeath and the bricks made at Kelty. There was another advantage in that the County Council had built a communal kitchen in the vicinity where the workers would be able to get their meals.

A member of the audience raised the question of plastic industry and wondered if the coal companies were doing anything in the matter. Dr. Reid replied that a great deal of research work was going on at the moment. Mr. Carlow then explained that the best advice he could obtain was that it was certainly possible to make a plastic powder of which nearly 80% was coal, but that was only the raw material of the plastic and such a small quantity was likely to be used that it was not worth while. In the years to come, he said, plastics would be more largely used and this coal plastic powder might come into its own ultimately. He had no hope that people were going to get plastic factories set up all over the County.

Mr. Frank Gibb then asked if the Planning Advisory Committee had ever considered the possibility of a larger industry with a view to export trade, and Mr. Carlow inquired what kind of large industry he had in mind. Mr. Gibb thought they would have to go further afield to find markets for their goods. Mr. Carlow explained that the British Council was exploring every possible market for their goods. Mr. Gibb then raised the question of the possibility of trade with Russia, and Dr. Reid stated that Russia had Commissars in London who were at the moment placing orders, but in the main for well-known makes of tools and machines, not consumer goods. It was mainly capital goods which were being sold to them, he said. They were prepared to put up their own industries.

Mr. Taylor thought their biggest hope would be agricultural industry because at present their main supply of implements came from Leeds. That was where one of the big casting industries would come in, he said.

Mr. McArthur remarked that in Cowdenbeath alone they were very badly off for blacksmiths' repair depots for relieving farmers of the responsibility of repairing their own machines.

Mr. Carlow remarked that farms were going to be mechanised more and more and the number of horses used would become less, and he thought the time would come when there would be a contractor within a radius of 10 or 20 miles who would have a motor waggon with a forge upon it and go round the farms mending machinery and shoeing horses, so saving the farmers' time.

The next point raised by Mr. Carlow was whether it was desirable in general interests that large towns should become larger and larger simply because they had factories, etc., in them or whether it would be better to take the people away from their industrial town at nights. This question arose, he said, in connection with Kinghorn. When the Committee visited the Provost of Kinghorn they found that Kinghorn was a residential burgh with practically no industries and that the people travelled to Burntisland for work. He had therefore suggested to the Provost that it would be a good thing to develop Kinghorn as a purely residential town instead of erecting more houses at Burntisland. This had met with the approval of the Provost of Kinghorn but was not so acceptable to the Provost of Burntisland. Of course, he said, they understood that there were certain key-men who could not be housed away from their work.

Mr. Alexander, Burgh Surveyor, thought that Cowdenbeath Town Council's idea was that although the coal in this area was being worked out and new pits going east and west, Cowdenbeath was not to be allowed to die out. It had to be replanned and become a residential area from which workers could go out to their work and return in the evening.

The question of what was considered to be an ideal size for a community was then considered, and Mr. Taylor gave the figure of approximately 50,000. A gentleman felt that to increase the size of Kinghorn, for instance, was going to ask Kinghorn to shoulder burdens which might become unbearable.

On the question of industries being set up in areas which were not development areas Mr. Taylor said the Board of Trade were sympathetic towards a factory being set up at Leven because it was going to employ female labour, and a member of the audience stated that they had the same difficulty in Cowdenbeath—employment of female labour. Mr. McArthur expressed the view that in transfer from war to peace there would be a tremendous amount of unemployment in this area. At present, he said, 930 workers were transported from this area to Comrie and Rosyth.

Bailie Blamey called upon those present to thank Mr. Carlow and his Committee for holding this very interesting informal meeting.

NOTES TAKEN AT PUBLIC MEETING HELD IN THE CO-OPERATIVE HALL, HIGH STREET, LEVEN
25th June, 1945

Mr. Carlow (Chairman).

Mr. *Carlow* opened by saying he was afraid the political situation had repercussions on our planning problems. He went on to say that he had introduced these matters to audiences throughout the whole of Fife so often that he was sure people were tired of hearing it from him. To-night, as they had in their midst the proprietor of Durie Estate, he proposed without more ado to ask Mr. Christie to explain the purpose of the Committee being here ; the constitution under which they were working ; some of the problems which they had to face and to invite the audience to assist in problems particularly arising in their own parish.

Mr. *Christie* said that the County Council of Fife had a Planning Committee composed of members of the County Council, and they were anxious to produce a plan for Fife which would be the basis for the development of all the planning in the main for the next 60 years. They were busily engaged in up-to-date problems ; they were busily engaged in long-range problems, but they took a good democratic way of approaching these by appointing 12 or 14 members of an Advisory Committee who were not members of the County Council. The only member of the Advisory Committee who was a County Councillor was General Crosbie and he was there as Chairman. It was thought that by appointing fewer members it might be possible to get a more unbiased view of the problem. This Advisory Committee had a number of meetings and approached the problem in a wide way, finding their way to see how they could deal with what really amounted to a colossal task, and in the end appointed a Sub-Committee of three to act as Editorial Sub-Committee—Mr. Carlow, Chairman ; Sir James Irvine, representing education and wider cultural aspects of the future ; and himself, as representative of the landowners. Mr. Christie remarked that he always refused to be limited by that representation. He came to the Committee as a citizen, not as a landowner. It was thought that this Committee should visit all the Burghs and areas in Fife, meeting Provosts and as many Councillors as could attend to explain to them the Committee's purpose ; ask them to attend a second meeting where the Committee could explain to the public who were interested what was in the wind ; and then to have a third meeting at which the public would be invited to give any suggestions they might have regarding not only their own area but in Fife generally. They had received some very valuable ones relative to Fife as a whole.

Mr. Christie then read the terms of the remit to the Advisory Committee. The County Council, as they would see, he said, had thrown its net very wide. The problems before them were not only education, transport, housing, satellite towns, purification of rivers, coal-mining, mining developments, future trends of population, bings, but every conceivable thing which was true to a town planner's heart, and as they could see it was a very wide remit and had entailed a great deal of work. They had just produced their interim report of all that had gone on at the meetings, and this afternoon had a long meeting with the parent Committee and this was going to form the basis of the Report which would be produced. Why they were particularly anxious to approach the public and the local authorities in the different areas was this—there were certain ideas forming in the minds of the planners for the future with regard, for instance, to the growth of a town. Mr. Christie said he was giving this as an example of the kind of thing on which they wanted guidance. Let us not take Leven, he said, but take, for instance, Burntisland. What is the size to which Burntisland should grow ? Should the various towns in the country be allowed to grow as they like in the future, spreading, developing, sprawling, utilising agricultural land round them, or should they be restricted to a certain optimum size for the development of a large town ? Should Leven, developing in the future, expand north, east and west until it joined with the development of Windygates and Lundin Links, so that Leven would be another example of a " Lang Toon " like Kirkcaldy, or should the Planning Committee of the County, consulting with the citizens of Leven, decide that so many fields, and so many fields only, should in future be absorbed by developing Leven ? That was one problem, he said, on which it would be very interesting to hear some of those present talking.

Mr. Christie then dealt with the question of roads. The Forth Road Bridge, he said, would ultimately go up, there was no question of that. He understood the Government had a plan of driving a great national road from the Forth Road Bridge to Perth directly to the North. That seemed to be more or less what would happen. The County of Fife would then have to develop a new arterial road going through the County, taking in existing factories and industries, and lead it—the question was where : direct to Dundee or to Newburgh ? If they went to Newport and built it across there it would probably cost £3,000,000 ; if at Newburgh it might cost between £300,000 and £600,000. Personally Mr. Christie said he felt there was need for both bridges and they might see both within the next 60 years. There was one advantage of the Newburgh Bridge as against the Dundee one. It would enable the County to bring their arterial road past all existing industries— Lochgelly, Cowdenbeath to the north of Kirkcaldy, up by Falkland, Auchtermuchty through the Lindores Gap, linking up with big quarrying developments which were going to be of enormous importance, and there slipping across the Tay just east of Mugdrum Island, depositing all traffic just midway between Perth and Dundee, and they would have a distance between Dundee and the Forth Road Bridge which would be very little longer than if the bridge went up at Dundee. So a case seemed to be clearly forming for the creation of a bridge at Newburgh as against Dundee, with a proviso that a bridge at Dundee was necessary but might be held up to be built at a time when a slump was coming.

With regard to educational matters, Mr. Christie said there was an idea very dear to his heart that some time in the future the County Council might gain control over three or four areas in Fife which could be recreational centres of the growing population of this County where they could get out of the urbanised districts and spend their week-ends. Mr. Christie referred to areas like Harper's Lea between the Lomonds, and Tentsmuir, and didn't see that it would be impossible to gain control of areas such as that. He pointed out that he had no knowledge whatsoever as to whom that ground belonged. As far as Mr. Christie could make out, the County did want to get children at school out into the country for some part of their training. What could be more beneficial, he said, than to take boys of 12, 13 and 14 up to areas like that and get them to plant trees, etc., and they would know they would have control of them in the future. Certain control would be necessary and a nice cottage for an ex-Service man would be ideal for giving a little employment and control. He hoped there was a seed in that which would bear fruit.

Mr. Christie said he had only touched on a very few points and would like to say they had discovered some points which were very interesting. One was that from Leven to the East Neuk of Fife should be marked down as the future Riviera of Fife. Mining population was going to increase by something like 72,000. The huge new pits were going to bring a tremendous inflow of workers and of all the trades that followed, and they would find an area there from which the people would be only too pleased to escape into an unspoilt area. Mr. Christie felt that from the river to the east should be kept as an unspoilt area, and that Elie, Anstruther, Pittenweem, Crail would in the future become great holiday resorts. It had also to be remembered that Pittenweem, Crail and Anstruther were fishing-towns and had boat-building industry which might increase in the future.

Mr. Christie went on to say that he had not dealt with any problems round about Leven because he had too many vested interests to talk quite impartially and would rather leave local problems to be brought up by members of the audience, with the exception of one which he was going to put forward as strongly as he could. Round the Jubilee Theatre, he said, there were a lot of 99-year leaseholds falling into his hands year by year. Most of these houses were falling in, and he was holding his hand in the hope that the County Council or Town Council would acquire those as they fell in and that in the long-term policy they would be left by them as an open space where they could build anything. This, he said, would be a magnificent centre for the future of the town. All Mr. Christie could say from the vested interest point of view was that he was open to give every help he could should they wish to acquire that property.

Sir James Irvine remarked that after Mr. Carlow's introduction and Mr. Christie's very able presentation there was not a great deal he ought to say, because the sooner they got down to the views of the citizens the better. He just wished to assure his fellow Fifers that he had this whole matter very much at heart.

Of the educational possibilities Sir James said not to think education was confined entirely to the University. His interests extended into all phases of education, and he did agree with what Mr. Christie had said, namely, that they had come to a time when in addition to their former orthodox schooling they recognised that these young boys and girls had other interests and a love of nature. A knowledge of nature, he said, was one of the most enduring of all interests. The thing was to give them their chance. You could not give them their chance if you just had the school and its surrounding playground. You had to give them something more. Sir James said he had seen how beautifully that worked in his travels in the United States. There they had a bit of forest land and a bit of mountain land to which, in relays, youths were taken for a complete day in the country. They had a definite job of work to do. It might be hedging, draining, planting, but they were doing something which was going to bring results, and they moved about and acquired all the most interesting knowledge of the field and ditch. This was a thing very well worthy of cultivation ; it was health-giving recreation as well, and that was why he hoped in their scheme something would be made to come of it.

Naturally enough, he said, they had found suggestions for the addition of extra industries. Everybody understood the hazards of an area dependent on a single industry. If hard times developed there was unspeakable hardship. Economically and for many other reasons it was an extremely good thing to mix up your industries. Now, in Fife the major industry was coal—that and agriculture. There was room to interweave the so-called light industries, but not in every place. That was his special point. There had been a natural desire, he said, that every place should have its share of light industries, but it wasn't every place that was well adapted to the kind of industries which were coming in our time. Most of these were highly specialised ; they required raw materials of a highly sensitive nature and you had to look at the point of origin. They could only be developed economically in the neighbourhood of the sea, where you had cheap transportation. That, said Sir James, was more or less his opinion. Sir James said he was not a planner, but he could at least act as adviser as far as his knowledge went, and any advice he could give would be very freely at the disposal of this beautiful County of ours.

Mr. *Carlow* said the purpose of the meeting was, having introduced the subject in a general manner, to see if they could get any enlightenment about development of their neighbourhood. The Committee visited the Provost and Town Council on 14th May and Mr. Carlow said he had made a few excerpts from the notes of that meeting. It was pointed out that Leven was a more or less residential area hoping to house some of the personnel occupied in industry in other parishes, notably the neighbouring parish of Wemyss and the Burgh of Buckhaven and Methil. It was pointed out that Leven had a considerable holiday industry which they must do all they could to cultivate. It was also pointed out that housing could go towards north and west and along the Windygates road. Mr. Carlow remarked he was also concerned in that and therefore would pass no criticism. It was pointed out that a better road was wanted to Kirkcaldy from the middle of Leven. It was also pointed out, he said, that a by-pass road to the North was wanted by-passing Leven, Lundin Links and Largo. Another thing which was thought worthy of consideration was a promenade going from Leven to Lundin Links, Largo and joining on to Dumbarnie Links and on to Kincraig, that being referred to as a centre for boys and girls for week-end camps, etc. That, he said, was part of the development outlined to the Committee.

Then there was the question of light industries which everybody wanted, but which were so difficult to attract. There were some of the points discussed last time, and Mr. Carlow said he would like members of the audience to amplify or contradict them or give some ideas of their own.

Mr. *Pollock, County Clerk Depute,* said he was not a local representative, of course, but his thoughts ran back to an occasion only a few months ago when he had spoken in connection with the ill-fated British Restaurant. One of the difficulties connected with that had been purely and simply related to the non-availability of a site. He could also remember looking with Mr. Christie and the then Planning Officer for a site for a kitchen, which had now found a home somewhere else not in Leven. He could also remember having been there with the County Road Board looking at a particularly serious example of ribbon development on the road between the cemetery and Lundin Links. All of these items could have been rendered much more simple of consideration by the County Council had there been adequate and well-considered planning in advance, and these were reasons which had influenced the County Council in so strongly going forward inviting the views of local people in regard to the planning of the area. He said he needn't mention items such as Scoonie roundabout or site from which 'buses should start in Leven, and Mr. Forrester could speak on some of the difficulties he had encountered because of drainage from Siller Hole. Mr. Pollock went on to say that he would like to mention a *cause célèbre* here, the Bawbee Bridge, and it would be of the utmost value to the County Council, having reached a decision in relation to the bridge itself, to have the views of the people of Leven in relation to the means by which this bridge should carry traffic eastwards. It might prompt suggestions at this meeting, he said, if he was to say he had seen a plan which would cut out one-way traffic which operated at present in a westerly direction along High Street and in an easterly direction along North Street. This plan obliterated the whole of the building area between the two streets and showed a vast demolition of buildings and the creation of an open space infinitely greater than that envisaged by Mr. Christie. One might say, how was a plan like this ever possible ? The answer to that, Mr. Pollock said, was given in the terms of the Planning Acts in which provision was made for payment of betterment from adjoining proprietors. This scheme might be far too great to be contemplated, but it was the sort of thing on which the Committee would like to have the views of the people.

Mr. *Forrester* began by saying that Mr. Pollock had referred to a matter which had been in his mind, namely, planning in advance. It would have been a splendid thing, he said, had they had some planning. They had had some form of planning between the County and the Burghs, but it hadn't materialised, and although plans were certainly made they weren't put into operation. One had just to stand in Den Walk either at the east end of Denbeath or at the west end to see a blot on the landscape, namely, Wemyss Brick Works.

With regard to the development of Leven the greatest development, in Mr. Forrester's opinion, would probably be with housing, because they were fortunate in having a variety of industries which could be considerably expanded. Leven also had a considerable influx of population in the summer-time.

Mr. Forrester went on to say he was interested in Mr. Christie's closing remarks with regard to a place for youth. Mr. Forrester said he had attended a meeting in connection with Youth work and the problem was discussed there about Youth Centre week-end camps. They visualised a place in Lanarkshire with about 50 acres of land and a mansion-house and that was receiving consideration by an organisation which was greatly interested in Youth work. There Mr. Forrester thought the Planning Committee were on the right lines.

Mr. Forrester then made reference to a site where houses built at the outbreak of war were still without proper drainage. That, he said, should not be allowed to exist. It did seem that what was lacking was good-will. He thought a little co-operation between the County Council and local authorities would go a long way and add greatly to amenities and other things.

Little had been said with regard to housing in general, but he supposed these things would already be prepared for the next 10 years.

Then there was still the question of the roundabout at Scoonie. Even the erection of a " Halt " sign, he said, was worthy of reconsideration.

Mr. *Carlow* then asked what Mr. Forrester had in mind about industries which could be expanded, to which Mr. Forrester replied the paper industry, also Boase's Works and Spinning Mills, Durie Foundry. They had been expanding and would no doubt continue to expand. There was also the Cleek Factory which had a world-wide market and employed quite a considerable number of people at the outbreak of war. Mr. Carlow then asked Mr. Forrester if he could think of any new industry which might be attracted to Leven. Could he tell them why the roperies had failed ? The paper mills had closed down. Could he give them any reasons for these things, and could he suggest any means by which industries of the town could be improved ? Mr. Forrester thought the closing down of these factories was probably largely due to transport.

The paper mills had had their ups and downs but war conditions had made them concentrate more on Markinch than Leven. He felt that once they returned to peace-time conditions the paper industry would come into its own.

Sir James Irvine thought Mr. Forrester was right in regard to the paper industry. He thought once war conditions were released there would be a great future for the paper industry because, paper was likely to be used for a great many other purposes than what it was being used for to-day.

A *member of the audience* said he had no doubt at all but that so far as Leven was concerned the paper industry would be opened up after the war. It had closed owing to shortage of material.

In regard to light industries, he said, every town wanted light industries, but everybody could not get them. Unfortunately in Leven they were devoid of sites for industry. They had one industry making inquiries just now, and they were starting in a small way. Apart from that there was only one site left in the Burgh for any light industry. So far as heavy industry was concerned they were pretty well served in the Burgh.

In regard to housing, as they knew, the Town Council were developing first the Mountfleurie site, and they proposed once that was finished to go further up. With regard to the extension of the Burgh, before the war they had a Burgh extension which was just blocked owing to the coming of the war, but it was practically agreed so far as the County was concerned and he had no doubt the County would carry it through. They proposed to have a further extension, however, in order to build roughly 1000 houses between Mountfleurie and the other side, and at the same time they were leaving plenty of ground for private enterprise. So far as housing was concerned he thought Leven was all right. To the disappointment of some of them the Education Authority had taken away some of their Mountfleurie site for a school.

Another point mentioned by this speaker was pollution of the River Leven. He did not know if the Committee could make any suggestion in regard to that, but it was a matter which had been talked about as long as he could remember and was a matter which should be tackled by the County Council. He understood, of course, it was a very big problem especially with so many other areas asking for light industries, because no matter what industry they got it would lead to more pollution and make the problem worse.

This speaker was very much interested in Mr. Christie's reference to open spaces. He had always visualised Dumbarnie Links as an ideal centre for young people, especially those employed in the mines.

Sir James Irvine then asked, as a matter of interest, what kind of houses they contemplated building, to which the gentleman replied that some of the houses would be prefabricated. The majority of the houses were to be of four apartments ; a very few three apartments, and some five apartments. Some were to be of the bungalow type and some of the flatted type. Sir James then asked what type they found favoured most, to which he received the reply that bungalows were most popular. When building flatted type they never put any more than four together. Mr. Carlow said there had been an argument about the relative advantages of bungalow and flatted houses, and a good number favoured flatted houses because of the amenities which, apart from the want of a garden, balanced a good many of the other drawbacks of bungalows, for instance centralised hot water. If they had a big enough block they might have a restaurant in the basement, a communal laundry and many other advantages. Then one could have a certain number of allotments in the vicinity where people who did want a garden would have the opportunity of taking an allotment. Mr. Carlow said he knew quite well how land had been wasted by spreading buildings over too big an area with too few houses to the acre and how much better it would have been if there had been a certain amount of flats giving more population per acre and using less land. Land occupied by houses, he said, never could be restored. It was lost for ever, and the time was going to come when the amount of foodstuffs grown would become less and less by so many acres being used for building development.

A *member of the audience* remarked that that plan was all right for congested areas, but he didn't think it was necessary in an area like this. So far as Leven was concerned far too much space had been given for gardens and not all of them were cultivated, but if they were given less land to cultivate they would all be looked after.

Mr. Carlow remarked that Mr. Mears gave the figure as 500 houses to three-quarters of a mile, but the previous speaker stated that the Scottish Board of Health laid down a certain percentage which had to be adhered to. Mr. Forrester said he thought the policy had been 12 to 20 houses per acre.

Mr. Forrester said this was the second meeting he had attended and had heard nothing about ugly lamp standards, posting boxes —were these still to go on or were there to be some improved methods?

Sir James Irvine said that was a point which had been very often in his mind, coming from the very beautiful corner of Fife where they ranked amenity high. He felt his higher self very much disturbed when he saw tawdry hoardings blocking a view. He disliked electric standards of a poor design. There were many things they could do, he said, to make the day-by-day task easier, the things they looked upon more beautiful. He did think that was just as important as big arterial roads and industries light and heavy. The surroundings wherein people lived, he said, had a big effect on their lives, and he felt great attention should be paid to these things.

Mr. Taylor, County Planning Officer, began by saying one or two points which had been mentioned to-night were worthy of consideration. Mr. Pollock, he said, brought up a very good point which he had never heard in this County—it sounded at first like too colossal a task—and that was the clearing away of property between two streets. This had been done on two occasions—in Hull and in Leeds. Mr. Taylor went on to explain how it was financed in Leeds. There the authority bought the property on each side as well as in the centre, and by doing that they obtained the building rights on either side and they found that property had so increased in value by the improvements made that they recouped their money time and again. In North Street, he said, there was some very poor ratepaying property, and there they would increase rateable value considerably by laying out the place, which would no doubt pay in a period of years for the amount of money spent in so doing.

Mr. Taylor made reference to the result of a ballot poll on holidays in Scotland. It was not, he said, any area in Fife which headed the list, but with such a large population in Edinburgh and Glasgow he did not see why this area could not top such a poll. All that was needed was a little bit of thought in the layout of the amenities.

Speaking on the question of housing, Mr. Taylor said unfortunately tenements had got a very bad name in Scotland. He thought Mr. Christie or Mr. Carlow might speak on the flats which had been erected on the Continent. These were an amenity to the area and to the people who lived in them.

A *member of the audience*, speaking on the question of amenities, asked if he could have any idea of what the recommendation was going to be in connection with bings. Bings, he said, were very prevalent throughout the County, and everybody knew they were an eyesore.

Mr. Carlow replied there was no doubt blaes bings were an eyesore and always had been. They were getting worse as time went on because seams were being worked with more stones in them than used to be the case. Formerly miners were more careful than they are to-day. Also customers were more scrupulous and the coal had to be cleaned much better than it was previously. It might be, he said, that machine mining had made that worse than if every man had been working as a craftsman. The possibility of putting the material down the pit again could be ruled out, he said. If the material had been half or quarter the quantity it might have been possible at some expense, but he considered it impossible to put blaes down the pit again. To keep them from going on fire was a scientific problem and a question which had been looked into for many years.

With regard to utilising material for brick-making and such like, that had been done in the past where material was suitable. In recent years there had been devised light-weight aggregates made from bings. There was no doubt that in America this light-weight aggregate was used for a great number of the big-scale housing developments. If tens of thousands of pieces of one particular pattern were being made it would be profitable to set up machinery for the purpose, but if it were not it would not be possible. This light-weight aggregate had been used not only for workmen's dwellings, but for hotels and many other buildings. Mr. Carlow remarked that he had sent a book about the whole story to the County Council, and it was in possession of all the information he had on the subject.

Lastly, if nothing else would serve the purpose they could put a little earth on the bings at the end of the day and plant trees. Although they were a curious shape they were less unsightly than when burning.

Sir James Irvine said to-night's meeting had opened his eyes on a number of things. Here they had a community which was pretty well contented. It had been active, had gone on with its housing scheme, and its industries had been thriving. He did not think they had been possessed with an undue desire to expand numerically. He thought it was an ideal policy to make the very best of what was there, and one could see that it made for happiness.

Mr. Carlow, in conclusion, thanked those present for the way in which they had put forward their views.

APPENDIX III

SUMMARY OF SUGGESTIONS AND POINTS
ARISING OUT OF THE MEETINGS HELD THROUGHOUT THE COUNTY BY THE EDITORIAL SUB-COMMITTEE

INDUSTRIES

ANSTRUTHER AREA

(1) *Dehydration and Refrigeration.*—The establishment of a dehydrating factory and refrigeration plant was suggested.

(2) *Drain Tiles.*—Mr. Edie, Cornceres, expressed the view that if brick works in the County were opened up there would be ample trade for them.

(3) *Coal.*—Provost Lawson, Pittenweem, felt it would be a great advantage if the coal in the district could be worked to yield a profit.

(4) Mr. Edie wondered if an industry for the manufacture of fish-boxes could not be started in the district.

(5) The Provost of St. Monance felt that to see their Burgh advancing it would be necessary to encourage some form of light industry to come to St. Monance.

(6) *Building Yard.*—The Provost of Pittenweem felt that if fishing conditions were more prosperous they could have a building yard at Pittenweem.

(7) *Cannery.*—It was suggested that a cannery would be a suitable industry for Pittenweem.

(8) The Provost of Crail expressed the view that a light industry connected with fishing, farming or golf would be welcomed.

(9) *Travelling Forge.*—Mr. Carlow suggested that travelling forges might come into being, so saving the time of the farmer.

CUPAR AREA

(10) *Light Industries.*—Captain Michael Black of Edenwood was of the opinion that rather than introduce new industries, existing industries in the area should be modernised, such as the blacksmith's shop. He visualised that in every rural village there should be a combined garage, blacksmith's shop, agricultural repair shed and joinery establishment. This was supported by J. K. Hutchison of Kinloch. Mr. W. G. Leburn also thought that before introducing new industries those in existence should be helped.

(11) Mr. Taylor made reference to the great need for the reservation of a site for light industry in agriculture in Cupar.

(12) Dr. Fyfe wished consideration to be given to the centralisation of cattle sales in Cupar so as to make Cupar the market town for the whole area.

DUNFERMLINE AREA

(13) *Quarries.*—Provost of Inverkeithing stated that if a certain amount of dredging could be done in vicinity of the quarries they would employ three times the number of men.

(14) *Harbour.*—Full development of Inverkeithing Harbour was said to be necessary.

(15) *Garages.*—Mr. Christie expressed view that with building of proposed new roads there would come a great increase in traffic and there would be room for development of garages.

(16) Provost of Inverkeithing put forward suggestion that County Council should have a dredger to keep all local harbours in good condition.

(17) *Inverkeithing* were anxious to introduce light industries to their Burgh. Mr. Carlow suggested manufacture of knitted wear for personnel at the dockyard.

(18) *Shipment of Coal.*—A suggestion was put forward that somewhere like Torryburn should be developed for shipping of coal from the new collieries.

KIRKCALDY AREA

(19) *Burntisland.*—Provost Meldrum suggested that a lot could be done at the docks by the Railway Company to improve facilities both with regard to loading and discharging of cargoes. Burntisland wished to be kept in mind in the event of extra export trade. They would welcome some form of light industry.

(20) *Kinghorn.*—Kinghorn would welcome some form of light industry.

(21) *New Collieries.*—Mr. Carlow emphasised that the Fife Coal Company desired the County authorities to reserve sufficient land for the three pits to be sunk in this area—(1) west of Thornton ; (2) Dysart ; and (3) Seafield.

LOCHGELLY AND COWDENBEATH AREAS

(22) Mr. McArthur thought iron and steel industries and even textile industry might be brought to Lochgelly.

(23) *Cowdenbeath* were anxious to have some light industries, possibly for the making of picks and shovels, etc. Mr. McArthur felt there were glorious opportunities in a place like Cowdenbeath for the casting industry. Mr. McArthur also mentioned that Cowdenbeath was very badly off for blacksmiths' repair depots.

ST. ANDREWS AREA

(24) *Light Industries.*—The Women Citizens' Association expressed the view that light industries which might be established near St. Andrews should be directed to the Guardbridge road beyond the golf-course, and that buildings erected should be pleasing to the eye.

(25) St. Andrews Co-operative Women's Guild wished encouragement to be given to the establishment of factories for glove-making ; lace-making ; cigarette-lighters ; jam-making, etc.

(26) *Newport* did not wish industries to be brought into their Burgh, but rather to remain as a residential area.

(27) *Agricultural Machinery*—Mr. J. C. Henderson suggested that assistance might be given in the creation of light engineering works , probably in connection with agricultural machinery, in Tayport district.

(28) *Boat-building*—There was also considered to be scope for the building of small boats at Tayport.

(29) *Sand at Tentsmuir*—Mr. Henderson also suggested that the vast resources of sand at Tentsmuir might be useful in solving housing difficulties in the future if solvent or binding properties could be found. It might also be suitable for glass-making.

(30) *Civil Airport*—Possible scope for civil airport in vicinity of Tayport.

(31) *Railway Station*—The need for a second railway station to the south-east of Tayport was expressed by Mr. Robert N. Robertson, Spearshill, Tayport. (Letter received after report of meeting completed.)

WEMYSS AREA

(32) *Industrial Development*—Referring to proposed industrial development to west of Leven, Bailie Nairn hoped the Committee would take note to get the regional sewer in and so enable River Leven to be purified.

(33) *Methil Dock*—Improvement of the docks and a new road leading in from the east end of the docks were suggested.

(34) *Buckhaven and Methil* would be glad of help in obtaining light industries for female labour, perhaps carpet-weaving, silk factory, woollen factory, pottery or laundry.

(35) *Small Boat Building*—Small boat building at Buckhaven was also suggested.

(36) *By-Products of Coal*—It was hoped Fife Coal Company and Wemyss Coal Company would consider establishing industry in by-products of coal in or near Buckhaven.

(37) Captain Wemyss favoured the scheduling of an area near Methil Docks for the building of factories. He also felt the banks of the River Leven should be scheduled for industry.

(38) *Waggon-building and Repair Shop*—Mr. Hudson thought the L.N.E.R. should be approached for a waggon-building and repair shop at Methil.

AMENITIES
ANSTRUTHER AREA

(1) *Parking of Caravans, etc.*—The County Planning Officer put forward a suggestion that parking of caravans and shacks should be controlled and proper sites located for the purpose.

(2) *Coastal Road*—The County Planning Officer was of the opinion that no buildings should be allowed to spring up between the coastal road and the sea.

(3) *Lighting*—Col. Baxter also hoped to see lighting introduced in all the country villages.

(4) " *Brighton* " *of North*—Provost Lawson, Pittenweem, thought Anstruther area might be developed into a " Brighton " of the North.

(5) *Community Centres*—Mr. Edie, Cornceres, was not in favour of these centres. He felt it was better to have the men housed near their work.

(6) *Train Service*—The Provost of Elie thought a good train service from Glasgow, Edinburgh, and other centres would be a great help to Elie.

(7) *Golf-course*—Town Clerk of Elie expressed the desire to have land to the east of Elie earmarked as a golf-course. (180 acres approx.)

(8) *Golf-course*—Need for an 18-hole golf-course at Anstruther was expressed by Provost Carstairs.

(9) *Entertainment*—Crail was very much in need of a cinema.

CUPAR AREA

(10) *Community Centres*—Miss Haig of Clayton remarked that community centres would be an advantage in districts where the farm roads were in a very bad condition. Captain Michael Black was in favour of such centres being developed.

(11) *Transport*—The need for adequate transport services to country districts was emphasised by Capt. Michael Black. This was supported by Mrs. Black and Mrs. Lindsay, Craigsanquhar, who made special reference to the 'bus service to and from Logie village. Bailie Scotland, Newburgh, referred to the fact that there was no 'bus service in the Balmerino district.

(12) *Telephone Kiosks*—Need for a telephone kiosk in Dura Den and also in many other country villages was stressed by Miss Low of Blebo.

(13) *Recreational Facilities*—Mr. J. K. Hutchison, Kinloch, thought all schools having not less than 15 pupils would benefit by having a gymnasium.

(14) Miss Moon, Springfield, expressed the view that the first essential for the health of Springfield was the cleaning out of Crawley Burn.

(15) *Freuchie*—A suggestion put forward by Mrs. E. G. Adamson, Freuchie, was that that part of the stream entering the village should be piped or a decent road bridge erected so that Lomond Road could be continued to Dykeside. A further suggestion put forward by Mrs. Adamson was that public conveniences should be erected in Freuchie.

(16) Dr. Arthur, Dunbog, stressed the need for having cheaper electricity so that country places might share in its benefits.

(17) *Playing Field*—Need for a playing field for adults was expressed by Falkland Town Council.

(18) *'Bus Service*—Reference was made to the lack of an adequate direct 'bus service between Cupar and Falkland.

(19) *Community Centre*—The Provost also mentioned the need for a community centre in Falkland area.

DUNFERMLINE AREA

(20) *Reclamation*—Mr. McArthur expressed view that the reclaiming of the foreshore at Torryburn and Low Valleyfield would add very considerably to amenities of district.

(21) *Drainage*—Mr. J. M. Morris, Morven, Carnock Road, Dunfermline, wished to know what steps the Advisory Committee could take in order to get drainage to enable further house-building in Carnock Road area.

KIRKCALDY AREA

(22) *Recreational Facilities*—Need for recreational grounds and indoor accommodation for youth was stressed.

(23) *Playing Fields*—Great need for playing fields for youth in Burntisland was emphasised by Rev. Michael Dabb.

Z

(24) Councillor Waddell, Burntisland, thought everything possible should be done to preserve " The Binn " and Grange Hill, Burntisland.

(25) Mr. Howie, Grange, Aberdour, expressed view that the A1 land round Kingdon ought to be preserved. He also hoped the amenities of Kinghorn would not be spoiled by washings and screenings from the proposed new pit at Seafield.

(26) *Green Belt*—Kinghorn favoured a green belt between Burntisland and Kinghorn and between Kirkcaldy and Kinghorn. Kirkcaldy also favoured green belt round their town.

(27) It was suggested that every effort should be made to preserve the very fine amenities of Kirkcaldy area and to encourage holiday makers.

(28) Mr. Cameron, Thornton, hoped that with regard to the new pit near Thornton it would be possible to stow the refuse underground.

(29) *Recreational Centres*—Mr. Christie (Advisory Committee) suggested that areas such as The Lomonds, Norman's Law, Tentsmuir, etc., might be acquired as sites to which young people could go for week-end camps, holidays, etc.

LOCHGELLY AND COWDENBEATH AREAS

(30) *Bings*—The need for some method of disposing of these very unsightly bings was stressed by Mr. Sneddon. Mr. Moffat wondered if it would not be possible to utilise this material in the making of prefabricated houses. Mr. McArthur suggested that the necessary machinery for carrying out this work might be obtained from America.

(31) *Water*—In the opinion of Mr. J. C. Robertson, water was the most important problem. He felt there were far too many water authorities at present. The Burgh Surveyor of Lochgelly was also of the opinion that there should be one large water main instead of 4 or 5 as at present.

ST. ANDREWS AREA

(32) *Green Belt*—The plea that the green belt round St. Andrews should be preserved was put forward by St. Andrews Preservation Trust.

(33) *Historic Views*—Citizens' Advisory Council were anxious that the historic views on the approach roads to St. Andrews should not be impaired by any future development.

(34) *Distinctive and Attractive Rural Architecture*—A plea was made by St. Andrews Preservation Trust that Fife's rural architecture should be maintained in any future development.

(35) *Coast Line*—The Preservation Trust also expressed the view that the adjacent coast-line should be preserved in its natural state.

(36) It was suggested that Newport might be developed as a seaside resort.

(37) It was also suggested that the pier at Newport should be improved.

(38) *Reclamation*—A suggestion that a large area of mud flats in the Tayport area—approx. 600 acres—might be reclaimed was put forward by Mr. J. C. Henderson.

WEMYSS AREA

(39) *Summer Camps*—Provost Gerrett felt that the area from Dumbarnie Links round to Kincraig was ideal for summer camps and expressed the view that some form of access should be provided to this area from the West of Fife and from the Leven area.

(40) *Promenade*—Desire for a promenade from Leven right round to Dumbarnie Links was expressed.

(41) *Future Riviera of Fife*—A suggestion was made that from Leven round to the East Neuk of Fife should be marked down as future Riviera of Fife.

(42) Mr. Christie made reference to property round the Jubilee Theatre, Leven, which was in poor condition, and expressed the hope that the County Council or Town Council would acquire this and that in the long-term policy this area would be left as an open space to be used for any purpose for which it might be required.

(43) Mr. Forrester hoped something would be done to improve appearance of lamp standards, posting boxes, etc.

(44) *Level Crossings*—Burgh Surveyor of Buckhaven complained of the number of level crossings within the Burgh.

HOUSING

ANSTRUTHER AREA

(1) Col. Baxter expressed the hope that the Advisory Committee would press for a more equal distribution of houses. This was supported by Rev. J. A. Inglis of Carnbee.

(2) *Satellite Town*—A suggestion was put forward that a satellite town might be created at Shell Bay to cope with the contemplated holiday traffic of the future.

CUPAR AREA

(3) *Living Conditions*—Captain Michael Black of Edenwood suggested that first of all the living conditions of the people in the country should be given priority and that little else should be done until such time as reasonable water, drainage and lighting facilities were provided. This was supported by Mrs. Black of Edenwood on behalf of Springfield W.V.S.; Miss Low of Blebo ; Rev. D. Laird ; Mr. J. K. Hutchison of Kinloch ; Miss Haig of Clayton ; and Mrs. Hutchison-Bradburne.

(4) Cupar W.V.S. were of the opinion that the most important question was housing.

(5) The need for housing in Freuchie was stressed by General Le Fanu.

(6) Falkland's greatest need was housing.

DUNFERMLINE AREA

(7) *Inverkeithing*—Lack of housing accommodation was the one difficulty in way of extension of existing industries. (Page 197).

(8) *Culross*—Housing for workers was of first importance. Some 40 or 50 required immediately.

(9) Mr. Potter, Crossgates, hoped County Council would face housing problem first.

(10) *North Queensferry*—A.C.2 Blatchley, R.A.F., put forward suggestion that County Council might acquire the land and buildings situated at Carlingnose Barracks and Port Laing and make these available for housing of returned Servicemen. The building at Port Laing, he suggested, might be adapted as flats and the vicinity laid out as a recreational centre adjacent to the sands.

(11) *Cairneyhill*—Councillor Fairley on behalf of District Council asked that consideration be given to housing development in Cairneyhill.

(12) Mr. J. M. Morris, Carnock Road, Dunfermline, brought up question of erecting houses on the stretch of road from the railway bridge at Lochend to the turn of the road to Kelty and Bowershall.

KIRKCALDY AREA

(13) *Satellite Town, Coaltown of Balgonie*—General view of people of Markinch appeared to be that instead of building a satellite town at Coaltown of Balgonie, Markinch should get preference of additional housing accommodation.

(14) *Types of Houses*—Markinch appeared to be quite in favour of modern flats, provided there was also a percentage of bungalows.

(15) A farmer's wife from the Markinch area was in favour of housing farm-workers in villages.

(16) Provost Anderson said Leslie's main requirements was houses. Lack of housing accommodation was hindering industry.

(17) Provost Anderson also stated industries in Leslie were in need of female labour, and it seemed to him it would be an advantage if they had a certain percentage of mining population living in Leslie.

(18) *Burntisland*—Provost Meldrum was not in favour of houses being erected in Kinghorn and Aberdour to accommodate people who worked in Burntisland. This was also the view of Burntisland industry. Immediate housing requirements are 500.

(19) *Types of Houses*—Mr. Sutherland, British Aluminium Co., Burntisland, suggested that to save good agricultural land modern flats might be built instead of bungalows. This was supported by Rev. J. Michael Dabb.

(20) *Kinghorn*—Present housing requirements 80.

(21) The view was expressed that it would be a mistake to house miners alongside agricultural population.

(22) Kinghorn would prefer to be developed as a residential Burgh.

(23) *Development of Kirkcaldy*—Councillor Dall said Kirkcaldy did not wish to lose its identity by being linked up with Burntisland and Leven.

(24) *Size of a Town*—Mr. Clark, Kirkcaldy, thought from juvenile delinquency point of view large towns were to be avoided. In his opinion a town should not have a population in excess of 10,000 approx. (Letter received after Notes completed.)

(25) *Anticipated Increase in Population*—To meet the expected increase in population (42,000) due to the proposed new collieries, Councillor Dall felt the best way was to create a completely new town to house something like 25,000 inhabitants ; Kirkcaldy had sufficient ground to provide for 16,000 and the remainder could be housed in the surrounding villages.

LOCHGELLY AND COWDENBEATH AREAS

(26) Mr. McArthur stressed the need for consideration of redevelopment of housing in Lochgelly district.

(27) *Flats*—Mr. Christie made the suggestion that two or three centres should be left open for the erection of modern flats and that architects all over Scotland should be given the opportunity of submitting plans.

(28) *Cowdenbeath*—Cowdenbeath favoured bungalows, but provided flats were well constructed they were not against them.

ST. ANDREWS AREA

(29) *Newport*—About 30 acres of best building land in Burgh cannot be supplied with water. This ground is between 200 and 230 ft. above sea-level.

WEMYSS AREA

(30) *Development of Kennoway*—Leven did not approve of the development of Kennoway if at the expense of Leven.

(31) *Housing Sites*—Captain Wemyss was anxious to see, in certain areas, sites reserved with services suitable for private feuars.

(32) *Reconstruction of Houses*—More widespread reconstruction of houses was favoured by Captain Wemyss.

(33) *Leven*—Provost Gerrett was of opinion Leven would develop best if it tried to retain its residential atmosphere while at the same time retaining an interest in the industrial area round about.

(34) Leven claimed to be able to supply houses for workers in any light industries which might come to Leven.

(35) Further extension of Leven Burgh boundaries was said to be necessary in order to build roughly 1,000 houses between Mountfleurie and the Council's other housing site.

(36) *Type of Houses*—Bungalows were favoured in this area.

(37) Extension of Burgh boundaries of Buckhaven and Methil was stated to be essential to enable Burgh to provide decent houses and places where children could play.

(38) The general view appeared to be that it was not a hardship, but an advantage for a man to live away from his work.

(39) *Housing Associations*—The introduction of housing associations was suggested as a means of speeding up the housing programme.

ROADS
CUPAR AREA

(1) *By-pass Road*—Need for a by-pass road round Cupar was emphasised by Mr. Christie.

DUNFERMLINE AREA

(2) *Forth Road Bridge*—Favoured by this area.

(3) *Tay Road Bridge*—Provost of Inverkeithing expressed himself in favour of a bridge at Newburgh.

KIRKCALDY AREA

(4) *Tay Road Bridge*—Leslie favoured a bridge which would serve both Dundee and Aberdeen.

(5) *Forth Road Bridge*—Burntisland favoured this bridge.

(6) Need for a trunk road from Kincardine Bridge to the north, perhaps 3 miles inland, was stressed.

LOCHGELLY AND COWDENBEATH AREAS

(7) *Tay Road Bridge*—Lochgelly Town Council were in favour of bridge at Newburgh.

(8) *By-pass Road*—The Burgh Surveyor, Cowdenbeath, stated there was a definite need for a by-pass road to ease the main street.

(9) *By-pass Road*—The need for a by-pass round St. Andrews was emphasised by the following :—St. Andrews Preservation Trust ; St. Andrews Advising Council; St. Andrews Women's Citizen Association ; St. Andrews Boys' Club. Col. Alford was in favour of a by-passs only in so far as it would pass by the oldest and easternmost part of St. Andrews.

(10) *Tay Road Bridge*—Newport favoured a bridge nearer Abernethy than Newport. Tayport would prefer the proposed new bridge further up river than the present railway bridge and thereby have transport facilities which would encourage development round that area.

Wemyss Area

(11) *By-pass of Leven*—Need for a by-pass from cross-roads through by National Steel Foundry and across Windygates road was stressed by Provost Gerrett.

(12) Another necessity was said to be a more or less direct access from Leven to the Kirkcaldy road.

(13) *"Halt" Sign*—Mr. Forrester thought the erection of a " Halt " sign at Scoonie roundabout was worthy of consideration.

(14) *Tay and Forth Road Bridges*—Both considered very necessary for the prosperity of Fife.

EDUCATION

Anstruther Area

(1) *Schools*—Opening of country schools as a means of stemming the drift from the country was advocated by Bailie Fleming.

Cupar Area

(2) Miss Haig of Clayton felt that if village schools were developed and children allowed to stay there longer that would be one of the things to keep people in the country districts.

(3) Monimail was in favour of having more educational facilities for agricultural workers.

(4) *Primary School, Cupar*—Need for a new Primary School in Cupar was emphasised by Mrs. M. S. Proctor, Cairnie, Cupar.

FISHING

Anstruther Area

(1) Bailie Gardner, Anstruther, thought something on the line of the Milk Marketing Board might help the difficulty of fish distribution.

(2) Pittenweem Harbour was said to be very dangerous and in need of some form of improvement.

GENERAL

(1) *Gateside*—See Report commencing on page 182.
(2) *Auchtermuchty*—See Memo appearing on page 188.
(3) *Ladybank*—See Memo appearing on page 189.
(4) *Cupar*—See Memo from Town Clerk, page 190.
(5) *Newburgh*—See Memo appearing on page 190.
(6) *Rural Depopulation—Rural Housing*—See letter from G. R. McGarva, Esq., Balcarres Estate Office, page 195.
(7) *Dunfermline Youth Council*—See suggestions appearing on page 206.
(8) *New Administrative Unit*—See suggestion from Bailie Westwater, Lochgelly, page 209.

MEMORANDUM by Mr. J. Gordon Dow, Joint Town Clerk, Crail, for the Editorial Sub-Committee of the Advisory Planning Committee of the County Council of Fife.

1. Crail is a Royal Burgh and a town of great antiquity. It was granted a charter from King Robert the Bruce and was a favourite residence of the Scottish kings. It has many old and interesting buildings, including Old St. Mary's Parish Church, which dates from the eleventh century and was a Collegiate Church prior to the Reformation. Its main streets are exceptionally wide, Marketgate in particular having wide " forelands " on either side of the carriageway and affording evidence of wise town planning two or three hundred years ago, when the practice prevailing at that time was to have narrow streets with the houses all huddled together, cheek by jowl. The general layout of the town, the many old and artistic buildings, the Town House with its seventeenth-century Dutch tower, the quaint old harbour, the fragments of the ancient castle of Crail and of pre-Reformation priories and nunneries, all combine to give it a pleasing architectural character and charm, which account for its being a favourite resort for artists as well as for discriminating visitors in search of mental and physical recreation. It has been the constant aim of successive town councils to ensure, when planning and developing the town, that nothing of architectural interest is destroyed.

2. The Town Council has adopted a progressive policy in regard to housing, a sphere of municipal activity which is closely linked up with planning. Housing schemes were promoted under the Housing Acts, 1924, 1930 and 1935. Many notices were served under Sections 14 and 16 of the Housing Act of 1930 calling upon owners to repair or reconstruct their properties. The Council's attitude has always been that everything possible should be done to encourage owners to reconstruct their houses in a way which fits in with the general character and appearance of the town in place of compelling them to carry out demolitions which invariably leave ugly scars. As a result a remarkably large number of interesting and well-planned re-constructions have been carried out.

3. The Council also made a scheme for assisting the building of houses by private enterprise under the Housing Act, 1923, and made grants of from £100 to £120 for this purpose. No less than 20 houses were built under this scheme, which is a large number for a small town and compares very favourably with towns of similar size. A scheme was also made under the Housing (Rural Workers) Act, 1926, and the maximum grant of £100 offered to owners of houses who were prepared to reconstruct them and introduce modern sanitary conveniences. Several houses which were reported on as unfit for human habitation have been reconstructed under this scheme to the entire satisfaction of the Medical Officer of Health and the Town Council.

4. Crail has an exceptionally large number of buildings of architectural, historic or artistic interest and worthy of preservation. In June 1937 the Department of Health for Scotland submitted a list of these buildings drawn up by the National Trust for Scotland, there being over 52 properties in all. In summarising this list the National Trust add to their Report the ollowing important statement, viz.:—" For the size of the town there are more old houses left in Crail than in most towns. A large number of these are extremely simple types but their grouping is interesting." Following upon receipt of this list the Council unanimously passed the following resolution :—

" That in connection with the list of buildings in Crail considered by the National Trust for Scotland to be of architectural, historic or artistic interest and worthy of preservation (52 properties in all) we decide to do everything in our power to help proprietors of these properties to retain the old characteristic simple style of building, and at the same time we will give every encouragement to the modernisation of the inside."

It was also unanimously resolved that the Dean of Guild be requested to pay particular attention to the carrying out of the Council's resolution.

As a result of these resolutions all plans for altering the properties referred to in the list are specially considered by the Dean of Guild Court from the point of view of preserving the features referred to by the National Trust, and some notable reconstructions have been carried out. As an example the reconstruction of " The Auld Hoose," 9 Marketgate, may be referred to. This is a very old house, over the door of which is a lintel dated 1686, and the house is referred to in the Royal Commission's Inventory of Ancient Buildings 1933, No. 131 (10), page 66. In this case harling has been removed from the outside walls of the house and the stone recess pointed, giving a very pleasing appearance, while there has also been a complete internal reconstruction.

5. A full report of the action taken by the Council in regard to the houses mentioned in the National Trust's list was submitted to the Department of Health for Scotland, and the following is an extract from the reply received from the Secretary of the National Trust dated 7th February 1938 :—

" I write on behalf of my Chairman and Council in connection with the above. They wish me first to thank your Council for their very thorough examination of the Survey of Old Houses in Crail which was forwarded on behalf of the National Trust for Scotland by the Department of Health. The Survey relating to Crail was the most comprehensive to be submitted up to date, and my Chairman and Council wish to express their appreciation to your Council for their co-operation.

The results of your Council's examination have now been forwarded to the National Trust. It is most gratifying to note that of the old houses at present under consideration by the Council, many have already been reconstructed, or are in course of reconstruction by their owners, and that their artistic features are being preserved.

My Council are fully aware that when action is taken under Section 16 of the Housing Act 1930 very much depends upon the attitude of the local authorities as to whether plans for reconstruction will be submitted, or whether demolition will take place as an easier solution. In the case of Crail, however, my Council feel assured that your Council are fully alive to the historic and architectural interest of many of its buildings, and that, in consequence, they will give every encouragement to the owners of houses requiring to be reconstructed in accordance with the modern standards."

6. As an example of the Town Council's anxiety for the amenity of the town, it may be mentioned that when the Fife Electric Power Company proposed to introduce electric power into Crail a few years before the war and suggested the erection of overhead wires the Council definitely declined to permit their erection in any part of the Burgh. They had fully realised their unsightliness where they had been erected in neighbouring villages, e.g. Colinsburgh and Kingsbarns, and they were determined that the amenity of Crail should not be destroyed in a similar way. After prolonged negotiations it was arranged that the Power Company would lay all their cables underground, and there is not a single electric pole or overhead wire in Crail.

7. The prosperity of Crail is dependent on its attraction as a summer resort, and for this purpose the Town Council have incurred large expenditure in purchasing and developing the municipal 18-hole golf-course at Balcomie, and they have also laid out a 9-hole beginners' course at Sauchope Links on lands which they bought. They have also given every encouragement to other recreative facilities, e.g. bowling, tennis, bathing.

APPENDIX IV
LIST OF PERSONS WHO CONTRIBUTED

1. St. Andrews Preservation Trust, Ltd.
2. St. Andrews Citizens' Advisory Council.
3. St. Andrews Women Citizens' Association.
4. St. Andrews Boys' Club.
5. St. Andrews Co-operative Women's Guild.
6. Falkland Town Council.
7. Auchtermuchty Town Council.
8. Ladybank Town Council.
9. Cupar W.V.S.
10. Newburgh Town Council.
11. Cupar Town Council.
12. Dunfermline Local Youth Council.
13. Mr. Andrew Methven, Fern Place, Leuchars.
14. Mr. Robert N. Robertson, Spearshill, Tayport.
15. Lieut.-Col. Henry Alford, Seaton Court, St. Andrews.
16. Philip M. Boase, Esq., Law Park, St. Andrews.
17. H. Chalmers, Esq., St. Andrews Burgh School.
18. W. Clark, Esq., County Offices, Kirkcaldy.
19. The late Michael Black, Esq., Edenwood, Cupar.
20. Messrs. G. T. Clark & W. G. Leburn, Gateside.
21. Mrs. Black of Edenwood (W.V.S.).
22. Miss Low of Blebo.
23. The late Miss Annie Moon, Edenfield, Springfield.
24. Rev. David Laird, The Manse, Springfield.
25. J. K. Hutchison, Esq., Kinloch, Collessie.
26. Mrs. E. G. Adamson, Home Cottage, Freuchie (W.V.S.).
27. Mrs. M. S. Proctor, Cairnie, Cupar (W.V.S.).
28. Mrs. Hutchison-Bradburne, Cunnoquhie, by Ladybank.
29. Rev. W. McCraw, The Manse, Bow of Fife.
30. Major-General R. Le Fanu, Eden Valley House, Freuchie.
31. Gilbert E. McGarva, Esq., Balcarres Estate Office, Colinsburgh.
32. A.C.2 Blatchley, R.A.F. Station, Castle Kennedy.
33. District Councillor J. Fairley, The Rose Gardens, Cairneyhill.
34. James M. Morris, Esq., Morven, Carnock Road, Dunfermline.
35. Bailie Westwater, Lochgelly.
36. Thomas Gray, Esq., 22 Denfield Gardens, Cardenden.
37. A. J. Cuthil, Esq., Easter Kincaple, St. Andrews.

APPENDIX V

ACKNOWLEDGMENTS

For the photographs which appear in the Report, the Editorial Committee wishes to thank the following :—

Aberdeen Journals, Ltd., Aberdeen.
Architect and Building News, London.
Alexander Bonthrone & Sons, Ltd., Freuchie.
The Burntisland Shipbuilding Co., Ltd.
Caithness Brothers, Kirkcaldy.
W. W. Carstairs, Esq., Anstruther.
C. J. Cousland & Sons Ltd., Edinburgh.
G. H. Cowie, St. Andrews.
The Fife Coal Company, Leven.
John Haig & Co., Ltd., Markinch.

Hay & Robertson, Ltd., Dunfermline.
F. Hill, Esq., Lancaster.
H. Jenkins, Ltd., Lowestoft.
The London News Agency Photos, Ltd.
Miners' Welfare Commission.
R. Lidell, Esq., London.
Sugar Beet Corporation.
Tullis, Russell & Co., Ltd., Markinch
Valentine & Sons, Ltd., Dundee.
Messrs. Marshall & Tweedy, Architects, Newcastle-on-Tyne.

INDEX